You're in Business
The Complete Textbook for Junior Certificate

Print an etest and give it for homework or a class test.

Gill & Macmillan

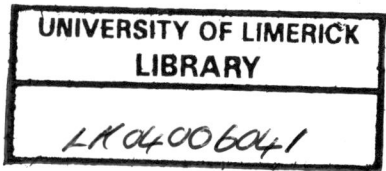

Gill & Macmillan Ltd
Hume Avenue
Park West
Dublin 12
with associated companies throughout the world
www.gillmacmillan.ie

© Dermot F. Reynolds 2004
© Artwork Kate Shannon 2004
0 7171 3706 6
Design, colour reproduction and print origination in Ireland by Ultragraphics Ltd

The paper used in this book is made from the wood pulp of managed forests. For every tree felled, at least one tree is planted, thereby renewing natural resources.

Contents

Preface

You're in Business is a new approach to teaching Junior Certificate Business Studies to Ordinary and Higher level students. This teacher-friendly and student-friendly edition is full of interesting and innovative teaching methods. It focuses on real life scenarios that students encounter in their day-to-day lives. Content is conveyed in the form of text messages, emails, diary entries and other communication devices familiar to students today.

The chapters are set out in a manner that will aid and assist the business studies teacher. Key concepts are highlighted in each chapter. There are practice questions to help with assimilating the new material. Bookkeeping sample questions and solutions can be seen at a glance on double-page spreads.

If you're in the business of teaching business or trying to learn business, then *You're in Business* will transform the way you approach the subject. To teachers and students alike, good luck and enjoy.

Dermot F. Reynolds
February 2004

Acknowledgments

To teachers and students in Ireland who have contacted me over the years and helped me by their insights to formulate this new edition.

1 Income

INTRODUCTION

1. How far do you agree with the following
    statements?
    (a) You must have a job to have an income.
    (b) I'm a young student and so I don't pay
         tax on anything.

2. What do you think the following terms mean?
    (a) Commission.
    (b) Overtime.
    (c) Perks.
    (d) Tax.
    (e) Unemployment benefit.

LESSON 1: TYPES OF INCOME

REGULAR INCOME

This is income that a
person receives every
week or month.
- Pocket money.
- Wages and salaries.
- Commission.
- Unemployment
  benefit or
  assistance.
- Pension.

ADDITIONAL INCOME

This is extra income
that a person receives
occasionally.
- Overtime.
- Interest on savings.
- Christmas or
  summer bonus.

OFFICIAL PERKS

These are additional
benefits given by the
employer and are
often called **benefits in
kind** or **fringe benefits**.
- Travelling expenses.
- Luncheon vouchers.
- Company car.
- Medical insurance.
- Social facilities.

UNOFFICIAL PERKS

These are practices
that have developed
that the employer is
either unaware of or is
prepared to ignore.
- Paper and
  pens taken by
  staff for personal,
  unofficial use.
- Phones used for
  private calls.

UNDERSTANDING YOUR PAYSLIP

GROSS PAY

Your gross income is the total income you have earned before any deductions have been made. It is usually made up of basic pay plus overtime, but it can also include a bonus or commission earned.

DEDUCTIONS

These are the statutory and nonstatutory items that are taken away from your gross pay.

NET PAY

The difference between your gross pay and your total deductions is your net pay. This is your take-home pay.

NAME	GROSS PAY			DEDUCTIONS					NET PAY
	Basic	O/Time	Total	PAYE	PRSI	Union	VHI	Pension	
David Kelly	600	100	700	146	42	8	20	35	449

PAYE

The main deduction from a person's income is tax. This is called the Pay As You Earn (PAYE) system. Under this arrangement, tax deductions are made by your employer before you get any money. Your employer passes this money on to the Revenue Commissioners – a government department. The money is used by the government to run the country, e.g. to build hospitals and schools and to pay the wages of doctors and teachers.

PRSI

Every employed person aged sixteen and over must contribute to Pay Related Social Insurance (PRSI). The amount you earn determines the amount of PRSI you pay. People who pay PRSI for thirty-nine weeks in a year are eligible for the benefits operated by the Department of Social, Community and Family Affairs, e.g. unemployment benefit, maternity benefit and old-age pension.

NONSTATUTORY DEDUCTIONS

PAYE and PRSI are statutory deductions and every employee must pay them. Most employees have other deductions from their wages, e.g. union dues, VHI or BUPA or pension contributions.

TAX CREDITS

Every person who pays tax is given tax credits. These reduce the amount of tax you have to pay.
- Single/widowed person – €1,520 per annum.
- Married couple – €3,040 per annum.

LESSON 2: THE CASH ACCOUNT

The cash account may be used to record a household's income and expenditure. Any money coming into the house is listed on the left (**debit**) of the account, e.g. wages. Any money going out of the house is listed on the right (**credit**), e.g. spending on food, telephone and electricity.

You can use Record Book 3 to help you lay out your cash account. Alternatively, draw a large 'T' on a page of your copybook. This divides the page

in three. Above the line is written the account name: Cash Account. On the left you list the income and on the right you list the expenditure.

To balance the account, add up the cash that came in (the items on the debit) and subtract the money spent (the items on the credit). This balance becomes the opening balance for the following week and is available for spending then.

Question

Mr and Mrs O'Neill keep the following record of their money for the first week of September.

Sep

1	Cash in house	90
2	Mr O'Neill received his wages	420
2	Paid supermarket	120
3	Mrs O'Neill received her wages	430
3	Paid butcher	18
4	Paid for petrol	35
5	Paid mortgage	500
6	Paid supermarket	23
7	Mrs O'Neill bought a new coat	99

Solution

RB 3

Cash Account						
Date	Particulars	Cash	Date	Particulars	Cash
Sep			Sep		
1	Balance	90	2	Supermarket	120
2	Wages	420	3	Butcher	18
3	Wages	430	4	Petrol	35
			5	Mortgage	500
			6	Supermarket	23
			7	Coat	99
			7	Balance	145
		940			940
8	Balance	145			

LESSON I: PRACTICE

1.   Match each word on the left with a word (or term) on the right, using each word once only.

travelling	in kind
unemployment	bonus
Christmas	vouchers
luncheon	expenses
benefits	assistance

2.   Find the different types of income hidden in this grid.

| wages | commission | salaries | pension |
| overtime | bonus | interest | benefit |

S	E	M	W	S	N	T	U	N	O	B
I	M	P	O	E	T	R	E	S	V	O
S	I	E	L	V	R	S	E	A	M	M
B	O	N	U	S	E	G	W	L	A	G
E	P	S	E	N	A	R	S	A	O	N
N	T	I	R	W	E	S	T	R	M	T
E	C	O	M	M	I	S	S	I	O	N
F	A	N	O	I	S	N	E	E	M	C
I	C	I	N	T	E	R	E	S	T	E
T	S	E	G	W	A	R	E	V	O	B

ARE WE PAYING TOO MUCH PAYE/PRSI?

Too many deductions – too few benefits

By Carol Dillon

Audrey is married to Liam with two children. They both work. Audrey works in the office of a printing company in town. 'I am paid €650 wages each week,' she says, 'and when I work overtime I earn another €150.' Her employer also gives her €20 in luncheon vouchers each week that she can use in local cafés. As she works in the office she can use the Internet or phone home when she is not busy.

Her husband, Liam, is a sales rep for a medical company. He has a company car and drives about 30,000 miles each year visiting hospitals. 'I get paid twenty per cent commission on all my sales,' he says. When he visits a hospital he gives staff free company pens and no one seems to mind when he keeps a few for himself. If the business is doing well he gets a €500 bonus at Christmas.

A few years ago Liam's father died and his mother, Mary, came to live with them. Every Friday she walks to the post office to collect her €120 old-age pension and then she uses her bus pass to go to town. Once a year at Christmas she withdraws the interest on her savings in the post office.

Audrey and Liam don't get to keep all the money they earn. Their employers must first deduct PAYE and PRSI from their wages. In addition Audrey pays €4 union dues each week and Liam pays VHI. Sometimes they complain about the deductions. 'Why do they take so much?' Audrey says. 'I don't mind paying union dues because I know the union will help me if I need them, but what benefit do I get from paying PAYE and PRSI?'

3. Scan the information in the article about the three people. The following figures are mentioned. What do they relate to?
(a) €650
(b) €150
(c) €20
(d) 30,000
(e) Twenty per cent
(f) €500
(g) €120
(h) €4

4. Read the article and answer these questions.
(a) Which of them can earn overtime?
(b) Which of them earns commission?
(c) Which of them gets a pension?
(d) Why don't they get to keep all the money they earn?
(e) What does the government do with the PAYE it collects?
(f) What is the PRSI money used for?

		Audrey	Liam	Mary
INCOME	Regular			
	Additional			
PERKS	Official			
	Unofficial			
DEDUCTIONS	Statutory			
	Nonstatutory			

5. Complete this table based on the information in the article.

NAME	GROSS PAY			DEDUCTIONS					NET PAY
	Basic	O/Time	Total	PAYE	PRSI	Union	VHI	Pension	
Siobhán Smith	165	25	190	9	5	3	12	15	146

6. Study the payslip above and match the questions below with the appropriate figure.

1. How much overtime did Siobhán earn?   (a) €146
2. What is Siobhán's total earnings this week?   (b) €9
3. How much tax did she pay?   (c) €12
4. How much does she pay for health insurance?   (d) €25
5. How much is her take-home pay?   (e) €190

7. Complete payslips for each of the following using the blank payslips in the Documents Book.
(a) Shane Tracy: basic pay €160, overtime €20, PAYE €8, PRSI €3, union dues €3, VHI €10, pension €15.
(b) Linda Tierney: basic pay €330, overtime €50, PAYE €47, PRSI €16, union dues €5, BUPA €20, pension €30.
(c) Kevin O'Neill: basic pay €570, overtime €60, PAYE €97, PRSI €30, union dues €6, VHI €30, pension €50.
(d) Sinead Ryan: basic pay €700, overtime €100, PAYE €131, PRSI €35, union dues €5, BUPA €35, pension €60.
(e) Brendan Doyle: basic pay €200, overtime €80, PAYE €27, PRSI €15, union dues €4, VHI €20, pension €25.

8. Questions on income and perks.
(a) List five types of income.
(b) Name the fringe benefits for:
   (i) an Aer Lingus employee.
   (ii) an Easons employee.
   (iii) a bank official.
(c) Write a brief note about unofficial perks.
(d) Explain the difference between gross and net income.
(e) Name two statutory and two nonstatutory deductions from a person's income.
(f) How does a person benefit from paying PRSI?

LESSON 2: PRACTICE

1. Study the cash account on the right for Philip and Marion and complete Marion's diary below for the first week of October.

RB 3

	Cash Account				
Date	Particulars	Cash	Date	Particulars	Cash
Oct			Oct		
2	Balance	80	2	Supermarket	130
2	Wages	500	3	Telephone	110
3	Wages	750	4	Mortgage	600
			5	Petrol	24
			6	Dress	99
			7	Dinner and cinema	74

October

2 Monday
Still have €80 left from last week. Philip got his wages today €500. We went to the supermarket and spent €130.

3 Tuesday

4 Wednesday

5 Thursday

October

Friday **6**

Saturday **7**

Sunday **8**
Still have _____ left for next week.

2. Study the cash account and answer the following questions.

RB 3

	Cash Account				
Date	Particulars	Cash	Date	Particulars	Cash
Nov			Nov		
2	Balance	70	2	Telephone	90
3	Wages	650	3	Supermarket	110
4	Wages	820	4	Mortgage	700
			5	Petrol	34
			6	Suit	199

True False

(a) They had €70 from last week to spend this week. ○ ○

(b) They earned €1,470 in total this week. ○ ○

(c) Total expenditure is €1,133 this week. ○ ○

(d) They have €407 left at the end of this week. ○ ○

3.   Practise preparing cash accounts.

(a) Michael keeps the following record of his money for the first week of July.

Jul

1   Cash on hand €0.50
2   Bought chocolate €0.60
3   Received pocket money €15
4   Went to the cinema €7
5   Bought magazine €5
6   Bus fares €2.80

(b) Brigid keeps the following record of her money for the first week of August.

Aug

1   Cash on hand €4.30
2   Bought magazine €4.70
3   Received pocket money €10
4   Went to the cinema €5.50
5   Bought chocolate €0.60
5   Bus fares €2.40
6   Received gift from aunt €50
7   Bought make-up €25
7   Bought CD music single €4.99

(c) Mrs Higgins keeps the following record of her money for the first week of September.

Sep

1   Cash on hand €90
2   Received wages €380
3   Bought a new coat €110
4   Paid for supermarket shopping €80
5   Paid butcher €15
5   Bought petrol €35
6   Paid supermarket €60
7   Paid butcher €12
7   Bought television licence €150

(d) Mr and Mrs Troy keep the following record of their money for the first week of October.

Oct

1   Cash on hand €60
2   Mr Troy received his wages €360
3   Paid supermarket €70
4   Paid butcher €10
5   Paid for cinema tickets €14
5   Paid supermarket €20
6   Paid butcher €14
7   Paid phone bill €110

(e) Mr and Mrs Nugent keep the following record of their money for the first week of November.

Nov

1   Cash on hand €80
2   Mr Nugent received his unemployment benefit €220
3   Paid supermarket €120
4   Paid butcher €12
5   Mrs Nugent received her wages €310
5   Paid gas bill €140
6   Paid chemist €60
7   Mr Nugent bought a new suit €230

2 Expenditure

TERMS COVERED IN THIS CHAPTER
Opportunity cost, accruals, false economies, fixed expenditure, irregular expenditure, discretionary expenditure, impulse buying, capital expenditure, current expenditure.

INTRODUCTION

Answer these questions, then discuss your answers with another pupil.

Congratulations, it's your birthday! Your uncle gives you €25 and your aunt gives you €35, so you go to town.

1. Make a list of four things to buy.
2. What is your total income?
3. What is your total expenditure?
4. What is your balance?

LESSON I: BILLS

Many family expenses are obvious, e.g. the trip to the supermarket, buying clothes and buying petrol for the car. Other expenses build up less noticeably, e.g. the phone bill, the electricity bill or household repairs.

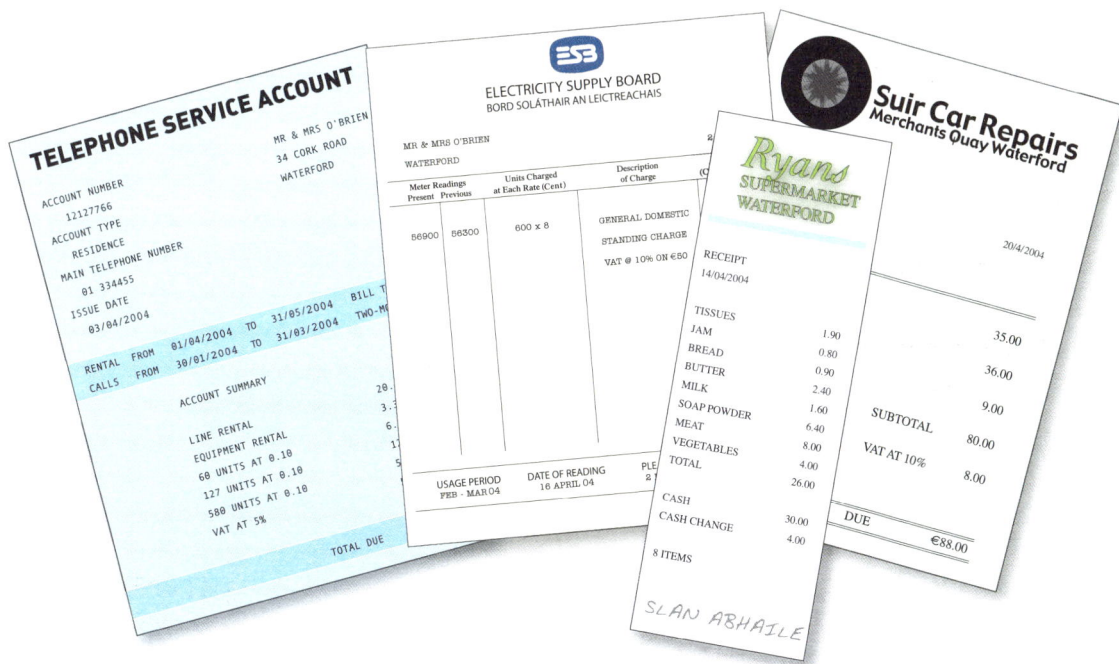

OPPORTUNITY COST

Most people don't have enough money and have to make choices about how they will spend it. For example, you might have enough money to go to the cinema or buy a book, but you don't have enough money to do both. If you decide to go to the cinema you must do without the book. This is known as the opportunity cost. The opportunity cost of going to the cinema is the book and the opportunity cost of the book is going to the cinema.

ACCRUALS

Accruals are items that are paid for after you use them. The use of electricity is an example of an accrual. When you watch television, listen to your stereo or use your computer you are using electricity but not paying for it. The household telephone is normally the same – you make a call but you don't pay for it at once. The bill arrives the following month and then must be paid.

FALSE ECONOMIES

A false economy is a purchase that has the appearance of saving you money but actually costs you more in the long run. It's all a matter of striking a balance between quality and value for money. Here are a few examples of the types of false economies consumers resort to.

- You buy a cheap school bag and it's broken by Christmas. You buy another cheap school bag and it's broken by Easter and so on. Would it have been better value to buy a more expensive, better quality bag that lasts the whole year? The original school bag could be considered a false economy because you ended up paying more in the long run than if you had bought the more expensive bag in the first place.
- You are thirsty and go into a shop to buy a cola. You could buy the 300 ml bottle for €1.50 or the 2 litre bottle for €2.50. You decide to buy the 2 litre bottle and have a good drink but there is still plenty left. By the time you get home you have shaken all the fizz out of it and end up throwing most of the cola out.
- You want a new printer for your computer. The Epson printer costs €200 and the Canon costs €120. You buy the Canon. A month later when your printer cartridge runs out you return to the shop to buy a replacement cartridge. You discover the Canon cartridge costs €80 and lasts a month while the Epson cartridge costs €90 and lasts six months.

TYPES OF SPENDING

FIXED EXPENDITURE

The mortgage repayment is normally the same amount each month and is an example of fixed expenditure. Other examples are the daily purchase of the newspaper, weekly milk bill and annual car insurance. It's possible to plan for these items, since it is known when they will occur and approximately how much they will cost.

IRREGULAR EXPENDITURE

The electricity bill is more difficult to work out as the amount varies each time. It doesn't follow a pattern and is said to be irregular. Other examples of irregular expenditure are phone bills, car and house repairs and emergency spending such as doctor's fees. With each of these either the amount or the timing of the bill varies, which makes planning for these bills more difficult.

DISCRETIONARY EXPENDITURE

This is the money you spend on luxuries like going to the cinema, taking a holiday or pursuing a sport or hobby. People spend most of their money on necessities, and any money spent after this is discretionary expenditure.

IMPULSE BUYING

Impulse buying is the purchase of unplanned items. For example, you go into a newsagent's to buy a magazine and you buy a bar of chocolate as well. Shop and supermarket displays are designed to make you buy on impulse with special offers and bargains positioned near the cash register to catch your attention. You can avoid impulse buying by using a shopping list.

CAPITAL EXPENDITURE

Spending on consumer durables, such as televisions, CD players and washing machines, is called capital expenditure. These goods will last a long time before they break or wear out.

CURRENT EXPENDITURE

Spending on day-to-day items like bread and milk is called current expenditure. For example, buying a car is an example of capital expenditure but buying petrol for the car is current expenditure, or buying a computer is capital expenditure but paying the electricity to run it is current expenditure.

LESSON 2: ANALYSED CASH ACCOUNT

The analysed cash account is used to group expenses together. This gives a household a clearer picture of where the money is being spent. Money coming into the household is listed on the left (debit) and money going out is listed on the right (credit). In the example below you can see that the Campbells took cash from an ATM to pay for some of their shopping. They paid other expenses by cheque and they paid the mortgage by standing order.

Question

Mr and Mrs Campbell keep the following record of their money.

Oct

11	Cash in bank	€60
14	Took cash from ATM to pay the supermarket	€110
16	Paid telephone bill by cheque (no. 81)	€130
17	Mr Campbell lodged his wages in the bank	€2,000
18	Mrs Campbell lodged her wages in the bank	€2,200
20	Paid for petrol by cheque (no. 82)	€40
22	Took cash from ATM to buy shoes	€80
25	Paid mortgage by standing order	€1,980
27	Paid for meat in butcher by cheque (no. 83)	€25
28	Paid for new suit by cheque (no. 84)	€220

Write up an analysed cash account using the following headings: Total, Food, Clothing, Other.

Solution

RB 1

Dr							Analysed Cash Account						Cr
Date	Particulars	Total				Date	Particulars	No.	Total	Food	Cloth.	Other	
Apr						Apr							
11	Balance	60				14	Supermarket	ATM	110	110			
17	Wages	2,000				16	Telephone bill	81	130			130	
18	Wages	2,200				20	Petrol	82	40			40	
						22	Shoes	ATM	80		80		
						2	Mortgage	S0	1,980			1,980	
						27	Butcher	83	25	25			
						28	Suit	84	220		220		
						28	Balance		1,645				
		4,260							4,260	135	300	2,150	
23	Balance	1,675											

LESSON 1: PRACTICE

1. Lara and a few friends hire an apartment in France for a week. She e-mails her brother the day before she is due to fly home.

   (a) How much did Lara spend in the market?

   (b) What is the opportunity cost of the shoes?

   (c) What accrual does she have?

   (d) How was the melon a false economy?

From:	Lara
To:	Kevin
Subject:	Greetings from Nice

Hi Kev,

Weather here is lovely and the apartment is small but clean.

I went to a local market this morning. Bought a leather belt for €10 for Dad and a straw hat for €15 for Mum. Got you a surprise that knocked me back €8. I also bought a huge melon for €3 that will last a week. It was a real bargain because they were selling one slice for €1. I don't think we'll get through it all by tomorrow and I discovered later that none of the others like melon! I had €35 left to buy either a pair of Italian shoes or a silk blouse. I treated myself to the shoes.

My money is nearly all gone and we still have to pay the landlord for the electricity we used during the week. He comes around tomorrow but we don't know exactly what we owe him yet.

Off to the beach for a final swim. *A bientot!*

Lara

ELECTRICITY SUPPLY BOARD
BORD SOLÁTHAIR AN LEICTREACHAIS

MR & MRS FAY

NAVAN   21 APR 2004

Meter Readings		Units Charged at Each Rate (c)	Description of Charge	Amount (Cr = Credit)
Present	Previous			
14762	12962	x 10	GENERAL DOMESTIC	?
			STANDING CHARGE	6

USAGE PERIOD	DATE OF READING	PLEASE PAY BY	TOTAL
FEB - MAR 2004	12 APRIL 2004	4 MAY 2004	?

2. (a) How many units of electricity did Mr and Mrs Fay use?
   (b) What is the general domestic charge for this bill?
   (c) What is the total owed for electricity?
   (d) How much of the total owed is fixed expenditure?
   (e) How often do Mr and Mrs Fay get an ESB bill?

	True	False
3. (a) They get a phone bill every three months.	◯	◯
(b) If they didn't make any phone calls, they wouldn't owe any money.	◯	◯
(c) The total fixed charge is €40.	◯	◯
(d) The total owed for this phone bill is €110.	◯	◯

TELEPHONE SERVICE ACCOUNT

ACCOUNT NUMBER   MR & MRS BRADY
   13457865   MONAGHAN
ACCOUNT TYPE
   RESIDENCE
MAIN TELEPHONE NUMBER
   467913
ISSUE DATE
   05/04/2004

RENTAL FROM 01/04/2004 TO 31/05/2004 BILL TYPE
CALLS FROM 30/01/2004 TO 31/03/2004 TWO-MONTHLY

ACCOUNT SUMMARY

LINE RENTAL	30
EQUIPMENT RENTAL	10
DIALLED CALLS	70

PAYMENT DUE BY 17/04/2004   TOTAL DUE €

December

2 Monday

Bought milk, bread, jam and butter €4.50. Hope to buy a new CD player on Thursday in town.

3 Tuesday

Bought milk, ham and eggs €7.80.

4 Wednesday

Bought milk, bread, steak and chips €8.70. Had a headache all day and went to the doctor €30.

5 Thursday

Bought milk, tissues and pizza €6.30. Bought the CD player €120.

December

Friday

Started my new diet today. Bought milk, water, fruit, lettuce and tomatoes €5.40.

Saturday **7**

Bought milk, fruit but could not resist cakes €5.90.

Sunday **8**

Bought milk but went out for dinner €23. So much for the diet!

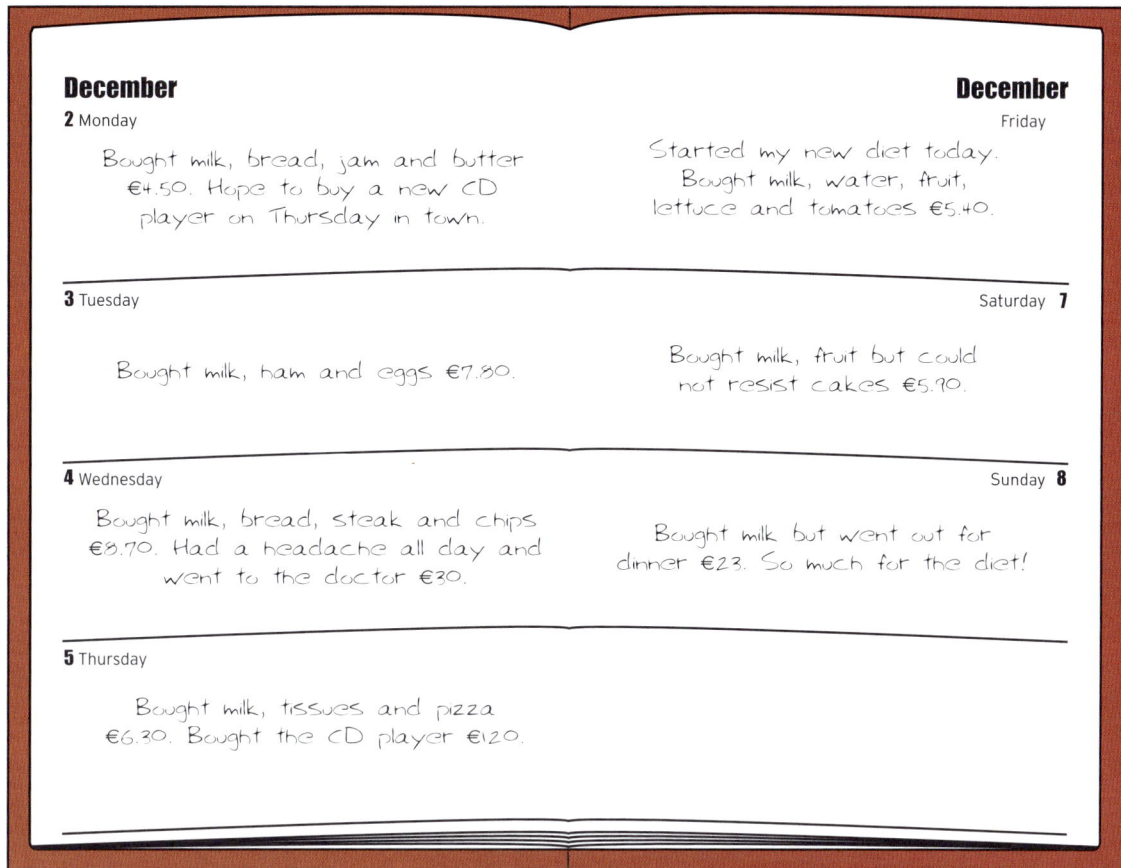

4. Study Sally's diary and identify the following (you may use the same item more than once if you like).

(a) One fixed expenditure item.

(b) One irregular expenditure item.

(c) One discretionary expenditure item.

(d) One impulse purchase.

(e) One item of capital expenditure.

(f) One item of current expenditure.

(g) What is her total expenditure for the week?

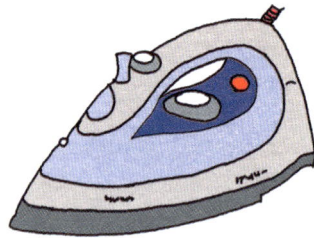

5.

	Capital Expenditure	Current Expenditure
(a) Purchase of new camera.	◯	◯
(b) Purchase of film for the camera.	◯	◯
(c) Purchase of burger and drink.	◯	◯
(d) Purchase of electric iron.	◯	◯
(e) Phone call to a friend.	◯	◯
(f) Paint the bedroom.	◯	◯
(g) Purchase of new computer.	◯	◯
(h) Get taxi home from town.	◯	◯

LESSON 2: PRACTICE

		RB 3

		Cash Account					
Date	Particulars	Cash	Date	Particulars	Cash
Nov			Nov		
2	Balance	80	2	Supermarket	120
2	Wages	600	3	Electricity	150
3	Wages	800	4	Mortgage	900
			5	Dentist	100
			6	Cakes	10

1. Study the cash account above for the Cunningham family and match the statements below with the appropriate figures.

1. Fixed expenditure.
2. Irregular expenditure.
3. Discretionary expenditure.
4. Cash they had at the start of the week.
5. Cash left over at the end of the week.

(a) 10
(b) 80
(c) 150
(d) 200
(e) 900

2. Philip has a current account in the local bank and had the following transactions with the bank during December.

Dec
1   Cash in bank, €70
2   He lodged his wages, €800
7   He paid for petrol by cheque (no. 50), €30
9   He took cash from the ATM to pay for supermarket shopping, €110
14   He paid for petrol by cheque (no. 51), €30
15   He took cash from the ATM to go to the cinema, €15
21   He paid for petrol by cheque (no. 52), €30
23   He paid for supermarket shopping by cheque (no. 53), €120
28   He paid for petrol by cheque (no. 54), €30
29   He paid for car service by cheque (no. 55), €120

(a) Write up an analysed cash account using the following headings.
    INCOME (debit side): Bank
    EXPENDITURE (credit side): Bank, Food, Car, Entertainment
(b) Name one fixed item of expenditure for Philip.

3.   Rachel has a current account in the local bank and had the following transactions with the bank during January.

Jan

1	Cash in bank, €80
3	She lodged her wages, €2,000
8	She paid for weekly train ticket by cheque (no. 59), €15
9	She paid for supermarket shopping by cheque (no. 60), €40
13	She paid for weekly train ticket by cheque (no. 61), €15
16	She took cash from the ATM to buy clothes, €80
22	She paid for weekly train ticket by cheque (no. 62), €15
26	She took cash from the ATM to pay for supermarket shopping, €55
29	She paid for weekly train ticket by cheque (no. 63), €15
30	She took cash from the ATM to pay for rent of flat, €800

(a) Write up an analysed cash account using the following headings.
   INCOME (debit side): Total
   EXPENDITURE (credit side): Total, Food, Travel, Other

(b) Name (i) one fixed and (ii) one discretionary item from Rachel's expenditure.

4.   Ms Caffrey keeps the following record of her bank transactions for the first week of February.

Feb

1	Cash in bank, €145
1	She paid for new dress by cheque (no. 90), €80
2	She lodged her wages, €1,300
3	She took cash from the ATM to pay the supermarket, €64
4	She bought cakes and sweets and paid by cheque (no. 91), €12
5	She paid the rent of her flat by cheque (no. 92), €300
6	She bought cakes and sweets and paid by cheque (no. 93), €12
7	She paid for a silk blouse by cheque (no. 94), €25

(a) Write up an analysed cash account using the following headings.
   RECEIPTS SIDE (debit side): Bank
   PAYMENTS SIDE (credit side): Bank, Food, Clothing, Housing

(b) Name (i) a luxury and (ii) a necessity from Ms Caffrey's expenditure.

5. Mr and Mrs Benson have a joint account in the bank. They keep the following record of their bank transactions for the first week of March.

Mar

1   Cash in bank, €70
2   Mr Benson lodged his wages, €402
3   Mrs Benson paid for a new skirt by cheque (no. 60), €49
3   Took cash from the ATM to pay doctor's fee, €30
4   Paid for petrol by cheque (no. 61), €25
4   Paid for medicine by cheque (no. 62), €30
5   Paid supermarket by cheque (no. 63), €43
5   Took cash from the ATM to buy bread, €3, and bought cakes as well, €11
5   Mrs Benson lodged her wages, €420
5   Mortgage payment by standing order, €220
6   Paid supermarket by cheque (no. 64), €32
7   Mr Benson bought shoes by cheque (no. 65), €35

(a) Write up an analysed cash account using the following headings.
    RECEIPTS SIDE (debit side): Bank
    PAYMENTS SIDE (credit side): Bank, Food, Clothing, Housing, Travel, Medical
(b) Name (i) one irregular and (ii) one impulse item from Mr and Mrs Benson's expenditure.

6. Mr and Mrs Moore have a joint account in the bank. They keep the following record of their bank transactions for the first week of April.

Apr

1   Cash in bank, €34
2   Mr Moore lodged his unemployment benefit, €210
2   Mr Moore bought a new jacket and paid by cheque (no. 40), €15
3   Mrs Moore lodged her wages, €290
3   Mortgage payment by standing order, €280
3   Mr Moore bought flowers for Mrs Moore by cheque (no. 41), €5
4   Mrs Moore took cash from the ATM to pay the supermarket, €23
4   Mr Moore paid doctor's fee by cheque (no. 42), €30
5   Mr Moore took cash from the ATM to pay for a prescription, €16
6   Mr Moore lodged children's allowance, €110
7   Mrs Moore paid butcher by cheque (no. 43), €14

(a) Write up an analysed cash account using the following headings.
    RECEIPTS SIDE (debit side): Bank
    PAYMENTS SIDE (credit side): Bank, Food, Clothing, Medical, Other
(b) Name one discretionary item from Mr and Mrs Moore's expenditure.

STATE EXAM PRACTICE

1. Mary Carter from Wexford opened a current account in her local AIB on 1 March. She was given the account number 47319426. She lodged €500 to the account the next day and received a blank cheque book and an ATM card in return. During the month of March she had the following dealings with the bank.

Mar

3   Groceries €120 from Foodmarket with cheque no. 1.

4   She paid for household expenses €50, which she got from the bank by using her ATM card.

7   She used her ATM card again to get €30, which she gave to her son for a birthday present.

9   She paid ESB bill €160 with cheque no. 2.

12   She paid Jordan's Garage €40 for car service by cheque no. 3.

14   She lodged wages cheque for €320 in the bank.

17   She paid instalment of car loan €150 to Auto Finance Ltd by cheque no. 4.

20   She purchased groceries €140 from Foodmarket with cheque no. 5.

24   She paid cheque no. 6 to Jordan's for petrol, €25.

30   She made a lodgment of €470, made up of wages cheque €330, child benefit cheque €60 and cash from sale of old furniture €80.

(a) Assuming you are Mary Carter, complete (i) the cheque for 12 March and (ii) the lodgment form of 30 March. (Use the blank documents in the Documents Book.)

(b) Enter all the above transactions in Mary Carter's analysed cash book under the following headings.

INCOME: Total

EXPENDITURE: Total, Household, Light and Heat, Car, Present

Total all the columns in your analysed cash book and show the balance on 31 March.

(JCOL, adapted)

2. Tom Roche, 14 Forest Drive, Galway opened a current account in the local branch of AIB on 1 May. His account number is 57364217. He was given a cheque book, cheque card and a Pass card. He made his first lodgment of €580 on the same date. It was made up as follows: salary cheque €500 and €80 in cash won in a local raffle. During the first two weeks of May he had the following bank transactions.

May

2   Paid for groceries by cheque (no. 901), €60

3   Paid telephone by cheque (no. 902), €133

5   Withdrew cash by Pass card for entertainment, €25

9   Paid ESB by cheque (no. 903), €64

10   Paid for groceries by cheque (no. 904), €59

11   Lodged cash from sale of old furniture, €150

13   Paid for home heating oil by cheque (no. 905), €104

14   Paid monthly mortgage payment by standing order, €150

(a) Assuming you are Tom Roche, complete the lodgment form fully for 1 May. (Use the blank document in the Documents Book.)

(b) Write up an analysed cash book using the following money column headings.
RECEIPTS SIDE: Bank
PAYMENTS SIDE: Bank, Groceries, Light and Heat, Entertainment, Other

(c) Based on the figures in Tom's analysed cash book, do you think he was living within his means in May? Explain your answer briefly.

(JCHL, adapted)

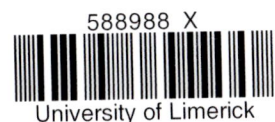

588988 X

University of Limerick

3 Household Budget

TERMS COVERED IN THIS CHAPTER
Estimates, surplus, deficit, budget, budgeting, comparisons.

INTRODUCTION

Make a list of the money you think you will spend from next Monday to Sunday. Compare your list with another pupil's list.

1. Which items are similar?
2. Which are different?
3. Which items are special purchases that you will only make next week?
4. Which purchases do you make every week?
5. Will you buy any luxuries?
6. Do you think you will have enough money to pay for everything?

LESSON 1: ESTIMATES

The best way to get control of your money is to make a plan. This plan should show estimates of future income, expenditure and savings. A plan like this is called a **budget**, and making plans into budgets is called **budgeting**.

Everyone who will be affected by the budget can be involved in its creation. In a household the estimates of income may rest with just one or two people, i.e. those earning a wage or salary. However, everyone can get involved in the estimates of expenditure.

The total income and total expenditure are subtracted to see how much is left at the end of the month. Usually there is some money left over – this is called a **surplus**. But sometimes the expenditure is greater than the income – this is called a **deficit**. To finance a deficit the family may:

● alter their spending habits.
● use some of their savings.
● take out a short-term loan (overdraft).

Estimate of income for January
Mum's salary €1,600
Dad's wages €1,600
Child benefit €240

Estimate of fixed expenditure for January
Car loan repayment €800
Mortgage €1,000

Estimate of irregular expenditure for January
Household costs €700
Car running costs €120

Estimate of discretionary expenditure for January
Family holiday €500
Entertainment €160

The O'Briens are having a family meeting to discuss money. So far the two children are keeping very quiet. Here is what the parents have to say.

Mrs O'Brien:	I didn't think that making out a family budget would lead to a row!
Mr O'Brien:	And I didn't think that so much of our hard-earned money was going to finance their telephone conversations and mobile phone credit.
Mrs O'Brien:	Don't exaggerate. Money is being spent on more than that.
Mr O'Brien:	Like what, for example?
Mrs O'Brien:	Well, our food bills are higher lately. But everyone is complaining about that so it's not just this family, and you did get the Internet connection so maybe you're to blame for the higher telephone charges.
Mr O'Brien:	I only use the Internet at night and it's cheaper then.
Mrs O'Brien:	And we got a top-up on our mortgage to do all the repairs around the house, so our mortgage repayments are higher.
Mr O'Brien:	Well, we're all going to have to take more responsibility for the money in this house.
Mrs O'Brien:	I don't know what we can cut down on. We need to eat, and we don't go out very often.
Mr O'Brien:	Well, that's the purpose of this meeting, to try to decide how we can save some money.
Mrs O'Brien:	So any ideas?

LESSON 2: LAYOUT FOR A HOUSEHOLD BUDGET

	A	B	C	D	E	F	G	H
1		Jan	Feb	Mar	Apr	May	Jun	Total
2	**INCOME**							
3	Mrs O'Brien's wages	1600	1600	1600	1600	1760	1760	9920
4	Mr O'Brien's wages	1600	1600	1600	1600	1600	1800	9800
5	Child benefit	240	240	240	240	240	240	1440
6	**A>TOTAL INCOME**	3440	3440	3440	3440	3600	3800	21160
7	**EXPENDITURE**							
8	**Fixed**							
9	Annual car tax	0	0	160	0	0	0	160
10	Car loan repayment	800	800	800	800	0	0	3200
11	Annual car insurance	0	0	500	0	0	0	500
12	House insurance	0	180	0	0	0	0	180
13	Mortgage	1000	1000	1000	1000	1000	1000	6000
14	**B>Subtotal**	1800	1980	2460	1800	1000	1000	10040
15	**Irregular**							
16	Household costs	900	900	900	900	900	900	5400
17	Car running costs	120	120	120	250	120	120	850
18	ESB	0	200	0	200	0	150	550
19	**C>Subtotal**	1020	1220	1020	1350	1020	1170	6800
20	**Discretionary**							
21	Family holiday	0	0	0	0	0	1900	1900
22	Entertainment	160	160	160	160	160	160	960
23	Birthdays	0	0	80	0	100	0	180
24	**D>Subtotal**	160	160	240	160	260	2060	3040
25	**E>TOTAL EXPENDITURE (B+C+D)**	2980	3360	3720	3310	2280	4230	19880
26	F>Net cash (A–E)	460	80	(280)	130	1320	(430)	1280
27	G>Opening cash	300	760	840	560	690	2010	300
28	Closing cash (F+G)	760	840	560	690	2010	1580	1580

The O'Briens draw up the household budget above. They use a spreadsheet since they are able to place formulas in some cells to help with the calculations. Each cell can be identified by a letter and a number. For example, A2 contains the word 'INCOME' and D9 contains the figure '160'. Here is an explanation of some of the figures.

- B6: The total income for January.
- B25: The total expenditure for January.
- B26: The amount of cash they don't spend in January.
- B27: The cash they have at the beginning of January.
- B28: The amount they do not spend plus the cash they have at the start of January. This becomes the opening cash for the following month (shown in C27).
- H27: You must be careful to show the opening cash here. This is the same figure as appears in B27.
- B6: Contains a formula for adding up the income. The formula is '=B3+B4+B5'. The formula must start with '=' and is followed by the names of the cells you wish to add up.

LESSON 3: COMPARISONS

By comparing the actual and the budgeted income and expenditure it is possible to spot trends and avoid mistakes in the next budget. Here is a comparison of the budgeted and actual spending for the O'Briens.

	A	B	C
1		Budget	Actual
2	**INCOME**		
3	Mrs O'Brien's wages	9920	9600
4	Mr O'Brien's wages	9800	9600
5	Child benefit	1440	1440
6	**A>TOTAL INCOME**	21160	20640
7	**EXPENDITURE**		
8	**Fixed**		
9	Annual car tax	160	200
10	Car loan repayment	3200	4000
11	Annual car insurance	500	480
12	House insurance	180	210
13	Mortgage	6000	6000
14	**B>Subtotal**	10040	10890
15	**Irregular**		
16	Household costs	5400	5000
17	Car running costs	850	1000
18	ESB	550	600
19	**C>Subtotal**	6800	6600
20	**Discretionary**		
21	Family holiday	1900	2300
22	Entertainment	960	850
23	Birthdays	180	250
24	**D>Subtotal**	3040	3400
25	**E>TOTAL EXPENDITURE (B+C+D)**	19880	20890
26	F>Net cash (A–E)	1280	(250)
27	G>Opening cash	300	300
28	Closing cash (F+G)	1580	50

1: They got the wages wrong. Mrs O'Brien did not get the increase she was expecting and Mr O'Brien did not get the bonus he was expecting.

2: They were correct about the child benefit. The car tax was higher than they expected.

3: They thought the car loan would finish in April but it did not finish until May.

4: The car insurance was cheaper than they expected but the house insurance was higher.

5: They got the mortgage right.

6: The household costs were lower than they expected but the car running costs and the ESB were higher.

7: They spent more on the family holiday than they budgeted for but their entertainment during the six months was lower. The money they spent on birthdays was higher.

8: They thought they would have €1,580 left but they only had €50 left at the end of the six months.

LESSON 1: PRACTICE

I.   Choose words from the box below to complete the sentences.

total	savings
estimate	surplus
discretionary	budget
income	salary
deficit	expenditure

A ^{1}_____ is a plan that estimates your ^{2}_____ and expenditure.

Those earning a wage or ^{3}_____ should provide an ^{4}_____ of their income.

Everyone can help to estimate the ^{5}_____ on fixed, irregular and ^{6} _____ items.

There is a ^{7}_____ if total income is greater than ^{8}_____ expenditure.

When expenses are greater than income there is a ^{9}_____ in the budget.

To finance this the family could spend less or use their ^{10}_____.

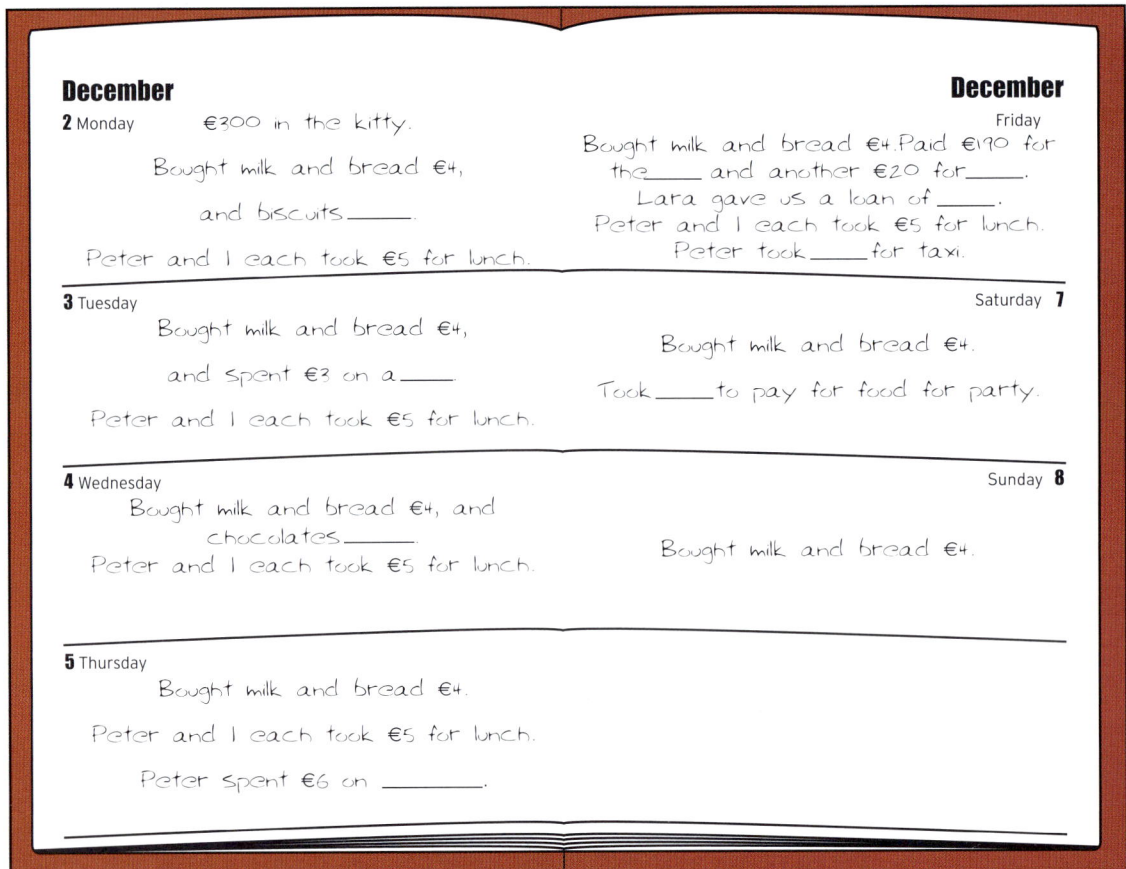

December

2 Monday   €300 in the kitty.

   Bought milk and bread €4,

   and biscuits_____.

Peter and I each took €5 for lunch.

3 Tuesday

   Bought milk and bread €4,

   and spent €3 on a_____

Peter and I each took €5 for lunch.

4 Wednesday

   Bought milk and bread €4, and

      chocolates_____.

Peter and I each took €5 for lunch.

5 Thursday

   Bought milk and bread €4.

Peter and I each took €5 for lunch.

   Peter spent €6 on _____.

December

                                    Friday

Bought milk and bread €4. Paid €190 for

   the_____ and another €20 for_____.

   Lara gave us a loan of_____.

Peter and I each took €5 for lunch.

      Peter took_____ for taxi.

                               Saturday **7**

   Bought milk and bread €4.

Took_____ to pay for food for party.

                                 Sunday **8**

   Bought milk and bread €4.

2. Peter and Larry are two students who share a flat. Complete Larry's diary for last week using information in the conversation.

Peter:	I have no idea where the money is going to.
Larry:	Yes, it's only Tuesday and the kitty is nearly empty.
Peter:	We put €150 each into that every week.
Larry:	I kept a diary of our expenditure last week and I think we need to start budgeting.

Peter:	Well, I know we buy bread and milk every day and that's about €4 a week.
Larry:	It's €4 a day, Peter! Did you know we spent €5 on biscuits, €3 on a cake and €2 on a box of chocolates last week?
Peter:	OK, but the rent is €190 a week. I know I'm correct about that.
Larry:	Yes, but we have to pay extra for electricity. Last week that was another €20.
Peter:	We also get lunch Monday to Friday in the college. That's €5 each for five days.
Larry:	We would have starved last week only Lara gave us a loan of €40. We've got to cut back.
Peter:	Well, I've been using the bicycle now to go to college. That's a saving.
Larry:	Sure, but you spent €15 on a taxi home last Friday. Did you forget the bike?
Peter:	I couldn't use the bike and get my suit creased.
Larry:	Oh yeah, dry cleaning the suit was another €6 last Thursday.
Peter:	And what about your birthday? That party cost us a fortune.
Larry:	€10 for the food is hardly a fortune. Everybody brought their own drink and I was the DJ for the night.
Peter:	Do you know, you're getting real fussy in your old age!

(a) Give an example of fixed expenditure for Peter and Larry.

(b) Identify an item of irregular expenditure for them.

(c) Name a discretionary expenditure item they have.

(d) What is their total income for the week?

(e) What was their deficit last week?

(f) How did they finance the deficit?

LESSON 2: PRACTICE

Use the budgets in the Documents Book.

1. Complete a budget for the Keely household for the first four months of the year, given the following information.
   Opening cash in hand was €60.

   Planned income:
   - T. Keely earns €1,900 net per month.
   - M. Keely earns €1,400 net per month.
   - Child benefit is €120 per month.

   Planned expenditure:
   - Annual car tax €150 due in January.
   - Repayments on car loan will cost €400 per month.
   - Annual car insurance €600 due for payment in February.
   - Car running costs are expected to be €120 per month.
   - Household expenses are expected to be €800 per month.
   - ESB bills for light and heat are expected to be €160 in February and €180 in April.
   - House mortgage is expected to be €900 per month.
   - House insurance premium amounts to €110 per year, payable in January.
   - Entertainment will cost €150 each month.
   - Birthdays will cost €90 in January and €80 in March.

2. Mr and Mrs Maguire from Naas have one child, John. Complete a budget for the Maguire family for the months of June, July, August and September, given the following information.
   Opening cash in hand was €280.

   Planned income:
   - Mr Maguire earns €1,200 net per month.
   - Mrs Maguire earns €1,200 net per month.
   - Child benefit is €120 per month.

   Planned expenditure:
   - Groceries are usually €700 per month.
   - The house insurance premium of €80 is to be paid in July.
   - The telephone bill is expected to be €100 in July and €110 in September.
   - ESB bills are expected to be €90 in June and €80 in August.
   - House mortgage will be €300 per month.
   - Annual car insurance €340 due for payment in July.
   - Car running costs are expected to be €150 per month.
   - Repayments on car loan €160 per month.
   - A school uniform and books for John will cost €500 in August.

- John turns fifteen in June and is getting a present costing €60.
- Pocket money each month for John €20.
- The family holiday in August is expected to cost €1,200.
- The Maguires spend €60 a month on entertainment.

3. Complete a budget for the Sweeney household for the first four months of the year, given the following information.
Opening cash in hand was €90.
Planned income:

- A. Sweeney earns €950 net per month.
- K. Sweeney earns €800 net per month.
- Child benefit is €120 per month.

Planned expenditure:

- Car running costs are expected to be €110 per month except in February, when the annual service to the car will cost an extra €80.
- Annual car tax €130 due in February.
- Repayments on car loan (to be fully paid by end of March) will cost €180 per month until then.
- Annual car insurance €380 due for payment in February.
- House mortgage will be €360 per month.
- House insurance premium amounts to €120 per year, payable monthly from January.
- Household expenses are usually €380 per month.
- Birthdays will cost €40 in March and €60 in April.
- Entertainment will cost €60 each month.
- ESB bills for light and heat are expected to be €90 in January and €100 in March.

4. Complete a budget for the Ryan family for the months of June, July, August and September, given the following information.
Opening cash in hand was €320.

Planned income:

- Mr Ryan earns €1,100 net per month and expects to get an extra €500 in August as a bonus.
- Mrs Ryan earns €1,100 net per month.
- Child benefit is €120 per month.

Planned expenditure:

- Groceries are usually €450 per month.
- Car running costs are expected to be €130 per month.
- ESB bills are expected to be €80 in July and €70 in September.
- House mortgage will be €350 per month.
- Repayments on car loan €140 per month.
- Annual car insurance €370 due for payment in July.
- House insurance premium is €60 per year, payable monthly.
- The telephone bill is expected to be €60 in June and €70 in August.

- School uniforms and books for all the children will cost €300 in August.
- Birthdays will cost €30 in July and €50 in August.
- Entertainment will cost €80 each month.

5. In the Documents Book there is a partially completed personal budget for the Ruane household for the first three months of the year. You are required to complete this form for April, May and June as well as all the total columns. The following information should be taken into account.
- S. Ruane expects to earn €200 a month in extra overtime in May and June.
- D. Ruane will be getting a holiday bonus of €200 in June.
- Child benefit is the same for each month.
- The house mortgage is expected to increase by five per cent beginning with the April payment.
- Annual car insurance of €400 is due in full in May.
- Car loan will be fully paid off by the end of May.
- Household costs are estimated as follows: April €600, May €650, June €700.
- ESB is estimated at €80 for April and €90 for June.
- Car running costs are estimated at €70 per month, plus a car service in May costing a further €90.
- Birthday presents are expected to cost €50 in April.
- Entertainment expenses are estimated at €60 a month for April and May and €70 for June.

6. In the Documents Book there is a partially completed personal budget form for the Burke family. You are required to complete this form by filling in the figures for the 'Estimate April to December' column and the 'Total January to December' column. The following information should be taken into account.
- M. Burke is due a salary increase of ten per cent from 1 April.
- G. Burke expects a special bonus of €200 in December.
- Child benefit will continue each month as for the first three months of the year.
- House mortgage is expected to increase by €50 a month from 1 April.
- Annual car insurance of €700 is due for payment in June.
- Household costs per month are expected to remain the same for each month until June and to increase by €50 a month beginning in July.
- Car running costs are expected to remain at €70 a month with an additional car service cost of €80 in June.
- ESB is expected to cost €80 in May, July, September and November.
- Christmas presents are expected to cost €300 in December.
- Entertainment will continue each month as for the first three months of the year.

7. In the Documents Book there is a partially completed personal budget form for the Rice family. You are required to complete this form by filling in the figures for the 'Estimate April to December' column and the 'Total January to December' column. The following information should be taken into account.

- V. Rice's salary will continue each month as for the first three months of the year.
- W. Rice is due a salary increase of ten per cent from 1 July.
- Interest on savings is expected to be €1,000 in July.
- Annual car tax of €200 is due for payment in June.
- Car insurance is paid monthly and will continue each month as for the first three months of the year.
- House mortgage is expected to increase by ten per cent a month from 1 July.
- Groceries per month are expected to remain the same for each month until June and to increase by €50 a month beginning in July.
- Car running costs are expected to remain €80 a month with an additional car service cost of €100 in June.
- Telephone charges for the year are expected to be €480.
- ESB for the year is expected to be €450.
- Christmas presents are expected to cost €400 in December.
- A holiday in June is expected to cost €2,000.

8. In the Documents Book there is a partially completed personal budget form for the McGuinness family. You are required to complete this form by filling in the figures for the 'Estimate April to December' column and the 'Total January to December' column. The following information should be taken into account.

- Mr McGuinness expects a bonus of €200 in December.
- Mrs McGuinness is due a salary increase of ten per cent from 1 October.
- Mrs McGuinness is expecting a baby in July and the child benefit will increase to €40 each month.
- House insurance payments will continue each month as for the first three months of the year.
- House mortgage is expected to decrease by €10 a month from 1 July.
- Car running costs are expected to remain at €120 a month with an additional car service cost of €100 in July.
- Household costs per month are expected to remain the same for each month except for December, when they expect to spend an additional €500.
- ESB for the year is expected to be €490.
- Christmas presents are expected to cost €300 in December.
- Entertainment costs will continue each month as for the first three months of the year.

LESSON 3: PRACTICE

	A	B	C	D
		Budget	Actual	Difference
1				
2	**INCOME**			
3	Mrs Hyland's wages	10,000	11,000	+1,000
4	Mr Hyland's wages	10,000	9,000	−1,000
5	**A>TOTAL INCOME**	**20,000**	**20,000**	**0**
6	**EXPENDITURE**			
7	**Fixed**			
8	Annual car tax	150	180	+30
9	Car loan repayment	1,800	1,800	0
10	Annual car insurance	300	400	+100
11	House insurance	90	100	+10
12	Mortgage	3,600	3,600	0
13	**B>Subtotal**	**5,940**	**6,080**	**+140**
14	**Irregular**			
15	Food	6,000	8,000	+2,000
16	Petrol	480	960	+480
17	ESB	420	500	+80
18	**C>Subtotal**	**6,900**	**9,460**	**+2,560**
19	**Discretionary**			
20	Entertainment	720	1,000	+280
21	Birthdays	100	200	+100
22	**D>Subtotal**	**820**	**1,200**	**+380**
23	**E>TOTAL EXPENDITURE**	**13,660**	**16,470**	**+3,080**
24	F>Net cash (A–E)	6,340	3,260	−3,080
25	G>Opening cash	300	300	0
26	Closing cash (F+G)	6,640	3,560	−3,080

The above is the budgeted and actual income and expenditure for the Hyland family.

(a) Name one item of capital expenditure for the Hyland family.

(b) How much did the Hyland family budget they would save over the year?

(c) How much did they actually save over the year?

(d) What is the monthly mortgage payment for the Hyland family?

(e) How does the budget show the Hylands have no young children?

STATE EXAM PRACTICE

l.   The following is a budget for the Hughes household for the first four months of the year.
Opening cash in hand was €150.

Planned income:
- Aidan Hughes earns €825 net per month.
- Fiona Hughes earns €650 net per month and expects to receive an increase of €40 per month in April.
- Child benefit is €120 per month.

Planned expenditure:
- House rental is €400 per month but will increase by €50 per month from the beginning of March.
- House contents insurance premium of €120 per year is payable monthly from January.
- The Hughes family pays health insurance of €55 per month to VHI. This will increase to €60 per month from the beginning of March.
- Groceries are usually €350 per month.
- Aidan pays €50 a month and Fiona pays €55 a month on bus and train fares to travel to work.
- The family expects to spend €600 on clothes in the January sales.
- ESB bills for light and heat are expected to amount to €95 in January and €80 in March.
- A fill of heating oil costing €220 will be needed in February.
- A birthday will cost €100 in February.
- Entertainment will cost €120 each month except March, when it will be €300 extra due to a wedding.
- The Hughes family hopes to buy a new television and video recorder costing €700 in April.

(a) Complete the blank household budget form in the Documents Book using all the above figures.

(b) Do Aidan and Fiona own the house in which they live?

(c) Will the Hughes family have enough money to pay for the television and video recorder in April? Give one reason for your answer.

(JCOL, adapted)

2. The following is a budget for the Mullins household for the four months May, June, July and August. Opening cash in hand was €240.

Planned income:

- John Mullins earns €1,225 net per month.
- Brenda Mullins earns €1,250 net per month and expects to receive an increase of €50 in August.
- Child benefit is €150 per month.

Planned expenditure:

- House mortgage will be €340 per month.
- House insurance premium of €480 per year is payable monthly from May.
- John's annual car insurance is €450. Brenda's annual car insurance is €375. Both are payable in June.
- Household expenses are usually €550 per month except in July, when they are €250 less.
- Car running costs are expected to be €100 per month for John and €125 a month for Brenda.
- Irish college for the children will cost €550 in June.
- ESB bills for light and heat are expected to amount to €110 in May and €80 in July.
- The Mullins family has a home telephone and a mobile phone. The home telephone bill is expected to be €165 in June and €150 in August. The mobile phone bill is expected to be €30 per month.
- A birthday party will cost €350 in August.
- The family expects to spend €2,500 on a holiday in July.
- Entertainment will cost €200 each month except July, when it will cost nothing as the family is on holiday.

(a) Complete the blank household budget form in the Documents Book using all the above figures.

(b) Work out the total cost of having two cars in the family for the four months.

(c) Apart from cash or cheque, name one other means by which the Mullins family could pay their ESB bill.

(JCOL, adapted)

3. (a) In the Documents Book there is a partially completed personal budget form for the O'Malley family for the year. You are required to complete this form by filling in the figures for the 'Estimate April to December' column and the 'Total January to December' column. The following information should be taken into account.

- Enda O'Malley is due a salary increase of five per cent from 1 July.
- Gráinne O'Malley expects to earn an extra €100 per month in November and December.
- Child benefit will increase by €10 per month from 1 October.
- House mortgage is expected to decrease by €50 per month from 1 November.
- House insurance, payable monthly, will continue as for the first three months of the year.
- Household costs per month are expected to remain the same for each month until September and to increase by €40 a month beginning in October.
- Car running costs are expected to remain at €60 a month with an additional car service cost of €70 each in June and December.

- ESB for the twelve months (January to December) is estimated at €460.
- The telephone bill is paid every second month and it is estimated that the cost will remain the same as at the beginning of the year.
- Christmas presents are expected to cost €230 in December.
- Entertainment is estimated at €750 for the twelve months (January to December).
- The family holiday in August is expected to cost €1,000.

(b) Answer the following questions.
   (i) Did the O'Malley family have a surplus, deficit or balanced budget in each of the months January, February and March?
   (ii) How much cash did they save in total from 1 January to 31 March?
   (iii) Give a reason why the house mortgage costs declined.

(JCHL, adapted)

4. (a) In the Documents Book there is an original budget and a revised budget form for the O'Hara family from July to September.

After preparing the budget for July to September Mr O'Hara, who had been drawing unemployment assistance, secured permanent employment. This would result in a substantial increase in the family's income starting in July. The O'Haras decided to revise their budget in view of the changed circumstances.

You are required to complete the revised budget form, taking the following into account.
- Mr O'Hara's annual salary will be €9,540 net, payable monthly.
- Mr and Mrs O'Hara decided to buy a second family car by getting a loan. The total cost of the loan including interest will be €7,920, repayable monthly over three years beginning in July.
- The insurance on the new car will cost €750 per annum, payable on 1 July.
- The road tax on this new car is €180 per annum, payable quarterly from 1 July.
- Car running costs will increase by eighty per cent.
- It is estimated that entertainment will increase to €100 per month.
- They intend to decorate the sitting room in September at a cost of €1,000.
- All other income and expenses are to remain the same.

(b) Answer the following questions.
   (i) Comment on the O'Haras' finances before July.
   (ii) If the O'Hara family hadn't received an increase in income would you consider the original budget a good one? Give reasons for your answer.
   (iii) Is their revised budget a good one for their new circumstances? Give reasons for your answer.
   (iv) What financial advice would you offer to the O'Haras?

(JCHL, adapted)

4 Being a Good Consumer

INTRODUCTION

'Fizzy' is a new soft drink that is under development. You have been asked to design the label that will go on the 1 litre bottle. Use the following information and make up anything else that you think you need.

- Price 99c.
- Made in Ireland.
- Serve chilled.
- Ingredients: carbonated water, sugar, natural flavourings, citric acid.

In the last chapter you learned the value of budgeting. In the next few chapters you will learn how to get better at buying goods. Good buying is good budgeting, as you make better use of your money and have greater personal satisfaction with a lot less pressure.

LESSON 1: SHOPPING WISELY

The wise consumer knows how to shop sensibly. This means you must avoid false economies and impulse buying, look for value for money and know your consumer rights. Before you buy anything you should consider the following.

- Can you afford it?
- Do you really need it?
- Is it safe?
- Do you have room for it?
- Are there any hidden extras?
- What does the description on the product tell you?
- What is the unit price of the product?

If you take the time to answer these questions, you'll be a more informed consumer and in a better position to make a sensible purchase.

DESCRIPTIONS ON PRODUCTS

By law product descriptions must not be false or misleading. They should be read carefully since they will help you decide if you are really making a good purchase.

- **Price:** This is useful to note so that you can compare the price of similar products or the same product in another shop.
- **Illustrations:** These are optional but must not be misleading.
- **Name and address** of producer, packager or seller.
- **Product name:** This is a name to describe whether it is cheese, bread, coffee, etc.
- **Origin:** Where the product is from, e.g. made in Ireland.
- **Ingredients:** The ingredients are given in descending order of weight.
- **Date:** This will take the form of a 'sell by', 'best before' or 'expiry' date.
- **Weight:** The net weight or quantity.
- **Storage** conditions and/or conditions of use.
- **Symbols:** These give assurances of quality and standards, e.g. Guaranteed Irish, Caighdean Éireannach (Irish Standard), Woolmark (Pure New Wool) and Approved Quality Symbol. Other symbols are used to encourage the consumer to recycle the packaging.

A consumer buys products and services. When you go to the cinema or catch a bus to town you are a consumer of a service. When you buy sweets or a magazine in a shop you are a consumer of a product. Another name for products is goods.

UNIT PRICE

The unit price is the cost of one unit of the product. It is useful to calculate this when comparison shopping. For example, which is better money value: a packet of Wipers tissues for €1.80 containing 180 tissues or a packet of Softies tissues for €1 containing fifty tissues? To find out, divide the price by the quantity and compare.

$$\text{Unit price} \quad = \quad \frac{\text{Price}}{\text{Quantity}}$$

(a)

$$\frac{180 \text{ cent}}{180 \text{ tissues}} \quad = \quad 1 \text{ cent per tissue}$$

(b)

$$\frac{100 \text{ cent}}{50 \text{ tissues}} \quad = \quad 2 \text{ cent per tissue}$$

In this case Wipers are better money value, but you may have to try both packets once to know which brand is better quality.

BAR CODE

The bar code is a series of vertical lines that represent the numbers shown below the lines. In supermarkets they are read by computer scanners to detect the product at the checkout.

The first two or three digits on the left identify the product's **country of origin**. Ireland and Britain have the code 50.

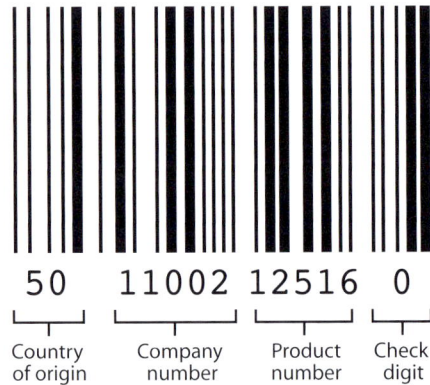

50	11002	12516	0
Country of origin	Company number	Product number	Check digit

LESSON 2: CONSUMER QUESTIONS

HOW AM I PROTECTED WHEN I ORDER BY POST, PHONE OR THE INTERNET?

You have the same rights when you order goods by post, phone or the Internet as when you buy goods in the shop.

However, you must take great care to ensure the goods you order are the ones you want. After all, you have not inspected them yet. You are only judging them on what you have read or seen. This way of buying goods is becoming more popular and most of these firms offer a 'money back if not satisfied' guarantee. Before you pay for anything you should also:

- compare prices.
- check postage and delivery fees.
- order early to allow plenty of time for delivery.
- keep receipts and website printouts.

Goods ordered by post, phone or Internet will normally be paid by cheque or credit card. Here is some advice.

- Never send cash in the post.
- Cheques sent by letter should always be crossed.
- Make sure you are at a secure server when giving credit card details to pay for goods on the Internet.

CAN I INSIST ON SOMETHING BEING SOLD TO ME?

No. The shopkeeper offers goods for sale and invites you to buy the goods. However, the shopkeeper can still refuse to sell you the goods. A contract is only made when you agree to buy the goods and the shopkeeper agrees to sell them to you.

CAN I GET MY DEPOSIT BACK?

No, not usually. A **deposit** is an amount of money equal to a small part of the overall cost of the goods. This is to ensure that you will return to collect the goods and pay the balance of the money due. If in the meantime you change your mind about the goods, you normally lose your deposit. This compensates the trader for the inconvenience you have caused.

CAN I INSIST ON A RECEIPT?

No. It's a good idea to ask for one and most shops issue them, but the law does not insist on shops providing receipts.

However, a receipt may be your only proof of purchase in the event of a complaint at a later stage. Written on the receipt will be:

- the date.
- details of the items purchased.
- the prices.
- the name of the shop.

The receipt is often asked for by a shop when you have a problem covered under a guarantee. A **guarantee** may be for one year from the date of purchase, and the receipt shows this date.

Receipts should be kept carefully. In the case of durables, such as CD players, cameras or computers, keep the receipt for at least the duration of the guarantee. Other receipts should be kept until you have checked them carefully for accuracy, e.g. a hotel bill or a supermarket receipt.

DO I HAVE TO ACCEPT A CREDIT NOTE?

No, not usually. Shops prefer to issue credit notes because they can keep your money and your custom. However, if you have a strong case you may be able to insist on a cash refund.

A **credit note** entitles you to buy something else in the shop at the value stated on the note. The problem is that the shop may not have anything else you are interested in or the shop may be some distance from where you live. In these cases it is sensible to insist on a complete refund and use the cash elsewhere.

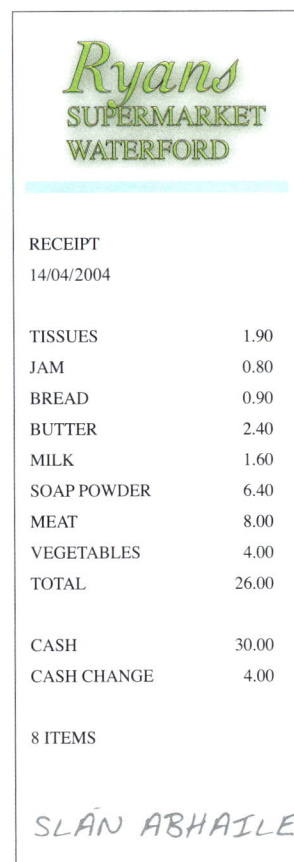

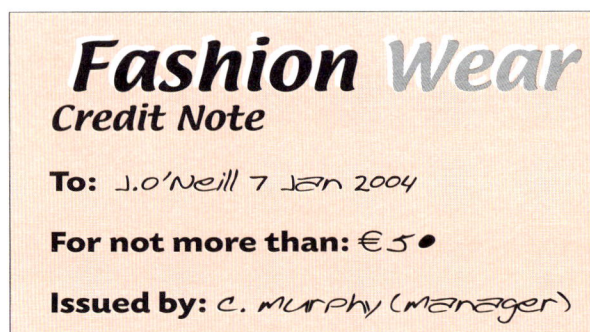

Ryans
SUPERMARKET
WATERFORD

RECEIPT
14/04/2004

TISSUES	1.90
JAM	0.80
BREAD	0.90
BUTTER	2.40
MILK	1.60
SOAP POWDER	6.40
MEAT	8.00
VEGETABLES	4.00
TOTAL	26.00
CASH	30.00
CASH CHANGE	4.00

8 ITEMS

SLÁN ABHAILE

Fashion *Wear*
Credit Note

To: J.O'Neill 7 Jan 2004

For not more than: €50

Issued by: C. Murphy (manager)

LESSON 1: PRACTICE

I.   Complete the word grid with the type of descriptions found on the products described below, as in the example.

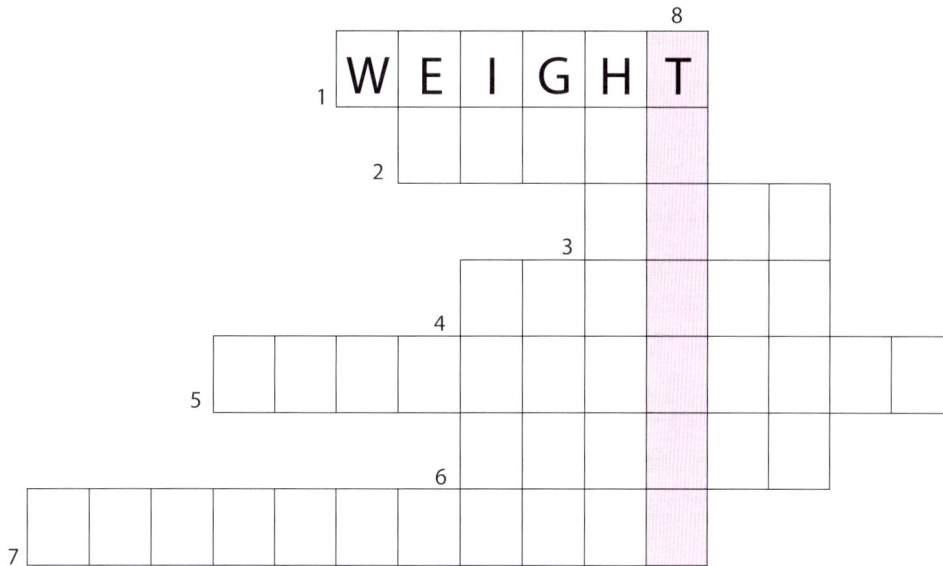

	1.	500 g net		5.	Cup and saucer
	2.	€2.50		6.	Blended in Ireland
	3.	SEP 04		7.	Tea
	4.			8.	The product name

2. Find the unit price in each of the following and indicate which is better money value.
   (a) Eighty tea bags for €2.40 or forty tea bags for €1.60.
   (b) 1.5 litres of 'big value' washing-up liquid for €1.20 or 500 ml for 70 cent.
   (c) 800 g sliced pan for €1.60 or a 300 g sliced pan for 60 cent.
   (d) Three dozen eggs for €5.40 or half a dozen for €1.20.
   (e) A box of forty matches for 20 cent or a box for €1 containing 250.
   (f) A copy book with fifty pages costing 20 cent or one with eighty pages costing 40 cent.
   (g) A box of ten computer disks for €12 or two disks for €3.
   (h) A 500 g box of breakfast cereal for €2.50 or a 750 g box for €3.
   (i) 1.5 kilos of washing powder for €4.50 or 2.5 kilos for €8.
   (j) Fifteen garden bulbs for €2.25 or six for 78 cent.

3. Collect bar codes (excluding those on books) from the following countries and file them on a page in your copy or folder.

First digits	Country of origin
00–09	USA and Canada
30–37	France
40–43	Germany
49	Japan
50	Britain and Ireland
520	Greece
54	Belgium/Luxembourg
560	Portugal
57	Denmark
80–83	Italy
84	Spain
87	Netherlands

LESSON 2: PRACTICE

		True	False

1. (a) A shop must return your deposit if you change your mind about wanting the product. ○ ○

(b) Never send cash in the post. ○ ○

(c) A receipt shows evidence of purchase. ○ ○

(d) A shop can insist that you accept a credit note. ○ ○

(e) A 100 g jar of coffee for €4.00 is better money value than a 200 g jar of coffee for €5.50. ○ ○

2. (a) Name two things a consumer should check on the item being bought.

(b) Explain what the unit price indicator is.

3. (a) List five descriptions that manufacturers must write on their products.

(b) The ingredients of a product are written as W, X, Y and Z. Which is the least of these ingredients?

(c) How does the consumer benefit from descriptions on products?

4. (a) What are bar codes?

(b) What are the advantages of using bar codes (i) for the supermarket and (ii) for the consumer?

5. (a) Explain these terms: 'deposit', 'guarantee', 'receipt' and 'credit note'.

(b) Why should some receipts be kept while others need not be?

(c) Name three items that should be written on a receipt.

5 Consumer Rights

TERMS COVERED IN THIS CHAPTER
Rights, merchantable quality, sample, complaining.

INTRODUCTION

Answer these questions, then discuss your answers with another pupil.

1. Did you ever have a problem with a product or service?
2. How did you deal with the problem?
3. How did the shop deal with it?

LESSON 1: WHAT ARE YOUR RIGHTS?

The Sale of Goods and Supply of Services Act, 1980 details your rights. Here is a guide to them.

1. Goods should be of merchantable quality. This means that the goods should be of reasonable quality, taking into account what was said about them, what they are supposed to do, the price paid and how long they should last, e.g. a pen should write.
2. Goods should be fit for their purpose, e.g. glue used for the purpose of fixing ornaments may not glue wood successfully.
3. Goods should be as described, e.g. a hotel that advertises itself as being 'beside the sea' should not require a 2 km car journey to reach the beach.
4. Goods should conform to the sample, e.g. the wallpaper you buy should be the same as the sample shown to you in the shop.

YOU BUY A DVD PLAYER AND IT BREAKS A FEW DAYS LATER. WHAT DO YOU DO?

Stop using the product. If you continue to use the faulty DVD player you may not be able to get a full remedy.

Inform the shop. Tell the shop you are having a problem with the DVD player. You could call into the shop, phone, e-mail or send them a letter.

Bring the product back. The person you buy the goods from (usually the shop) is the one you complain to. You must do this soon after you discover the fault. If you delay and continue to use the goods, you may lose your rights. Some faults are easy to prove and you will have no trouble getting your rights. However, if the fault doesn't appear until awhile after you buy the product, the retailer may say the fault is due to misuse.

Agreement. Try to reach a sensible agreement. This may be:

- a refund – where you get your money back.
- a replacement – the faulty DVD player is exchanged for a good one.
- a repair – the least you can expect.

You may be entitled to get a full refund of your money provided you complain promptly. You have no rights if you misuse the goods or if you change your mind about wanting the product. If you cannot come to an agreement with the shop, you will have to consult a **third party**. This is dealt with in the next chapter.

SHOULD I GO BACK TO THE SHOP OR MAKE A CLAIM UNDER THE GUARANTEE?
You have a choice to do either. The shop you buy the goods in is normally the place you complain to. However, if you decide to claim against the manufacturer under the guarantee you should inform the shop about this. Tell the shop that if you aren't happy then you reserve the right to get a full refund from the shop.

CAN I INSIST ON A REFUND OR MUST I ACCEPT A REPAIR?
You are entitled to a complete refund. You don't have to accept a repair, nor can you insist that the shop carries out a repair.

LESSON 2: COMPLAINING

If you have a problem with a product or service you will either make the complaint in person (a verbal complaint) or in writing. In either case you should follow these suggestions.

DO

- Adopt a calm approach.
- State the purchase date, the problem and the remedy you want.
- Keep to the point.
- If you aren't happy, leave and get a third party to help you.

DON'T

- Get angry or lose your temper.
- Apologise for complaining.

MAKING A VERBAL COMPLAINT

Shopkeeper:	How can I help you?
You:	I wish to make a complaint.
Shopkeeper:	What's the problem?
You:	I bought this DVD player last week and the cover broke yesterday.
Shopkeeper:	We can take it in and repair it.
You:	No, I want a complete refund.
Shopkeeper:	I'm sorry, we don't give refunds.
You:	You sold me a faulty DVD player and I am entitled to a refund.
Shopkeeper:	I'm sorry, we don't give refunds.
You:	You aren't listening to me, so I'll go now. But I'll get the help of a third party to make my case to you.

MAKING A WRITTEN COMPLAINT

Your address ——————————————————→

Harbour View
Howth
County Dublin

Today's date ——————————————————→

19 June 2004

The shop's address ——————————————→
(find it in the phone book)

Home Sound and Vision
Shop Street
Dublin

Greeting (use Sir or Madam when ——————→
you do not know the person to
complain to)

Dear Sir or Madam,

I wish to complain about a DVD player I bought in your shop
last Monday, 16 June 2004.

Problem ——————————————————————→

The cover broke the second time I used it.

Remedy you want ——————————————→

I would like a complete refund.

Do not send your evidence! ——————————→

I enclose a photocopy of my receipt.

Yours sincerely,

Frank Ryan

Sign your name here ——————————————→

Frank Ryan

LESSON I: PRACTICE

1. Complete each sentence below using words from the box.

sample	quality
refund	product
purpose	described
shop	back

(a) Goods should be of merchantable _____ .

(b) Goods should be fit for their _____ .

(c) Goods should be as _____ .

(d) Goods should conform to the _____ .

(e) Stop using the _____ .

(f) Inform the _____ .

(g) Bring the product _____ .

(h) Get a repair, replacement or _____ .

2. Are you entitled to a complete refund in each of these cases? Tick the correct circle.

	True	False
(a) The salesperson in a shop insists a new computer game will work on your machine. You buy the game but it doesn't work.	○	○
(b) You buy a pair of runners. They break within a week but you continue to wear them and you don't complain until six months later.	○	○
(c) You go to the cinema but halfway through the film you realise it is stupid and you should have gone to a different movie.	○	○
(d) You buy a bar of chocolate and when you unwrap it you see that it's bad.	○	○
(e) You buy a watch and the strap breaks within a week.	○	○

3. What happened on each of these dates mentioned in the e-mail on the next page?

(a) 29 February

(b) 7 March

(c) 4 April

(d) 9 May

(e) 6 June

(f) 11 July

(g) 8 August

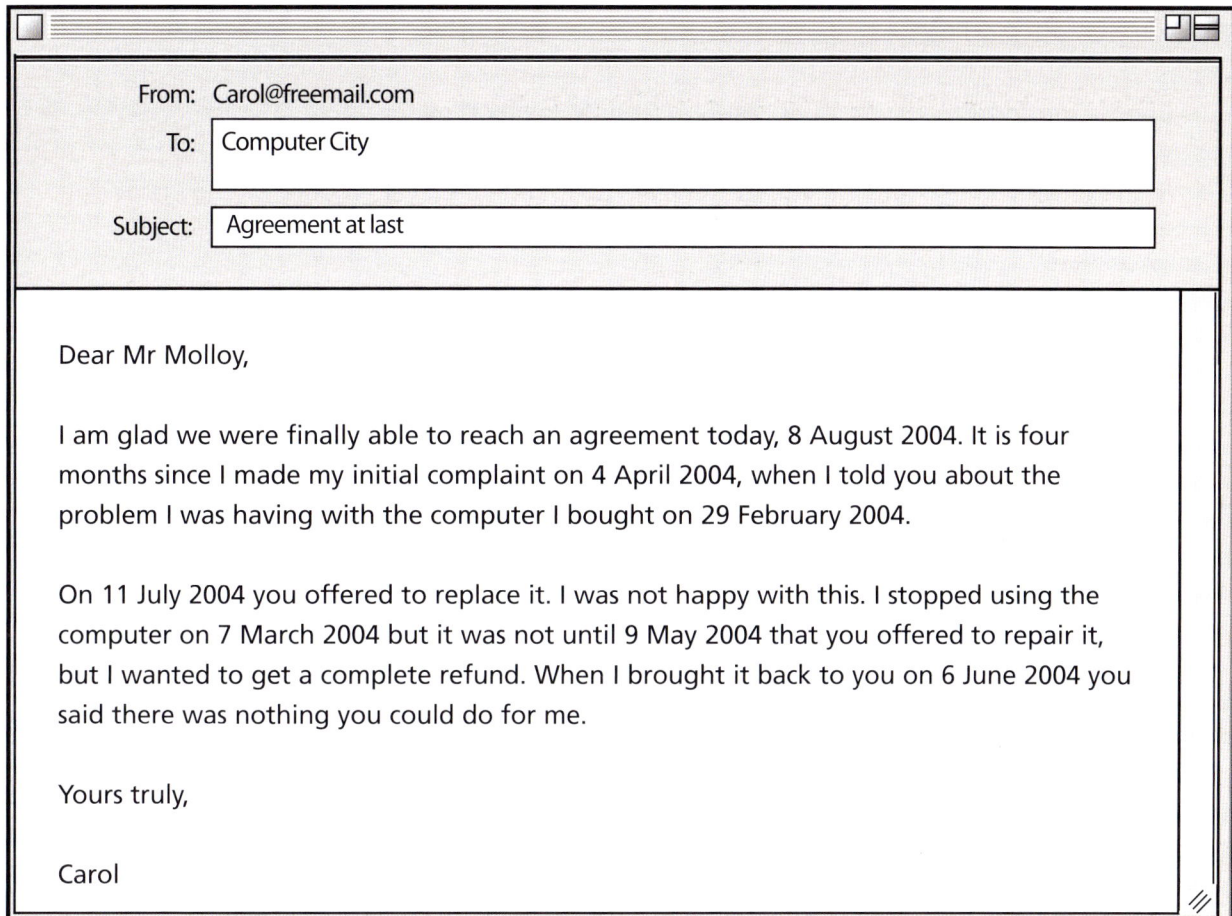

From: Carol@freemail.com

To: Computer City

Subject: Agreement at last

Dear Mr Molloy,

I am glad we were finally able to reach an agreement today, 8 August 2004. It is four months since I made my initial complaint on 4 April 2004, when I told you about the problem I was having with the computer I bought on 29 February 2004.

On 11 July 2004 you offered to replace it. I was not happy with this. I stopped using the computer on 7 March 2004 but it was not until 9 May 2004 that you offered to repair it, but I wanted to get a complete refund. When I brought it back to you on 6 June 2004 you said there was nothing you could do for me.

Yours truly,

Carol

LESSON 2: PRACTICE

1.   Choose the correct words to fill the gaps in this letter.

Dear [1] Mister / Sir or Madam / Director,

I wish to complain about a [2] CD player / mobile phone / television I bought in your shop on [3] 1 May / 1 June / 1 July of this year.

The [4] remote control / screen / cover was broken when I took it out of the box.

I enclose a photocopy of my [5] guarantee / receipt / credit note for your attention.

I would like a [6] repair / replacement / refund as soon as possible.

[7] Get in touch with me at once. / Yours sincerely, / Goodbye,

John Condon

2.   In each of these cases, clearly state the date, problem and the remedy you want.

(a) You go out for a meal on 12 January to The Steak Restaurant, Balbriggan, Co. Dublin and pay by cheque. When you get home you study the receipt and discover they have overcharged you: they have included three items that you didn't have to eat. Write a letter of complaint to the restaurant about this.

(b) On 15 February you inspect one roll of wallpaper in DIY Home Supplies, New Street, Wexford. You take home a sample of it and order ten rolls by phone. It is only after you have decorated your room that you notice that the colour in some parts of the rolls is different. Write a letter of complaint to DIY Home Supplies about this.

(c) You buy an expensive new stereo CD player on 17 March. A fault develops in the first few days after you take it home. Write a letter of complaint to The Discount Store, Cork where you bought the stereo.

(d) You bought a hairdryer four weeks ago from Power Electric, Sligo but didn't use it until tonight. When you switched it on, smoke started coming from the motor. You find the guarantee and it says that the dryer is guaranteed for one year. Write a letter of complaint to the shop about this.

(e) You buy a toy doll for your niece as a present for her birthday in two weeks' time. When she plays with it the button nose falls off. Write a letter of complaint to Toy World, Naas about this.

Q I bought a gold rope chain in a city jeweller in December and was always careful when wearing it. Eleven months later the chain snapped eight inches from the catch and when I brought it back I was told there was no guarantee on jewellery and I couldn't get an exchange or refund. I had to pay €6 for a shoddy repair and within two weeks the chain broke again in a different place. It seems outrageous that customers have to pay for repairs each time and constantly run the risk of losing the chain if it breaks while being worn. Am I entitled to a refund or exchange? — S.S., Co. Wicklow.

A We appreciate what you say and whether or not there is any guarantee, the jewellery must be of merchantable quality when sold. However, gold is a soft metal and the purer it is, the softer, and since you had the use of the chain for eleven months, it would be hard to show that it was not merchantable when you bought it. Unless you are prepared to take a gamble on possible District Court action, we feel there is little that can be done except to learn from the experience.

3. Broken chain.
   (a) What problem did S.S. have with the chain?
   (b) Where did S.S. complain?
   (c) What remedy did S.S. want?
   (d) Was there a guarantee with the chain? If so, how long was it?
   (e) Why can't the 'experts' help S.S.?

4. (a) Why must the buyer beware when purchasing goods and services?
   (b) What are the consumer's legal rights?
   (c) State the remedies a consumer may be entitled to if a fault develops in a product he or she bought.

5. (a) What steps should be taken in making a complaint?
   (b) Why is the consumer advised to complain in writing?

STATE EXAM PRACTICE

l. The following advertisement appeared in a Sunday newspaper.

Trá Bán Hotel
Ballybunion
Co. Kerry

AMAZING VALUE AT OUR LUXURY SEASIDE HOTEL, COMPLETE WITH
LEISURE CENTRE, SWIMMING POOL, GOLF, TENNIS AND MUCH MORE.

WEEKLY RATES:
€210 PER PERSON FROM 1 JUNE TO 30 JUNE.
€280 PER PERSON FROM 1 JULY TO 31 AUGUST.
€175 PER PERSON FROM 1 SEPTEMBER TO 30 SEPTEMBER.

FOR RESERVATIONS CONTACT RONAN MURPHY, MANAGER.

On 25 May, Mary Daly, Clogher Downs, Drogheda, Co. Louth wrote a letter to the hotel manager booking a reservation for herself and her husband for the week of 5–12 August. In the letter she stated that she was enclosing a cheque for €50 as a deposit. She also requested a receipt and confirmation of her reservation from the hotel.

(a) Write the letter sent by Mary Daly.

(b) Complete the receipt issued to Mary Daly on 1 June. (Use the blank receipt in the Documents Book.)

(c) Why is the hotel more expensive in July and August?

(d) Name two other methods that Mary could use to pay the deposit.

(e) In June, Mary won a family holiday to Spain in a raffle. She immediately contacted the Trá Bán Hotel cancelling the holiday in Ballybunion and requested a refund of her deposit. Is she legally entitled to a refund? Give a reason for your answer.

(JCHL, adapted)

6 Consumer Protection

TERMS COVERED IN THIS CHAPTER
Claims, Consumer Information Act, prices, third party, Ombudsman.

INTRODUCTION

Work with another pupil on this task.
Here are some claims made by famous products and services over the years. Can you identify them?
1. The best to you each morning.
2. Better value – beats them all.
3. Before you make up your mind, open it.

LESSON I: CLAIMS AND DESCRIPTIONS

Traders or manufacturers make claims to entice you to buy their goods and services. These claims about their goods and services must be true. If you buy something because of the claim made about it and that claim is false, then you may be entitled to compensation.

In 1978 the government passed the **Consumer Information Act**. This act is designed to protect consumers from false and misleading descriptions or advertisements about goods, services and prices. This means that advertisements in the media, catalogues and pictures on packets must not contain any claims or descriptions that might mislead the consumer.

TYPICAL CLAIMS

About goods
• Pure New Wool
• Irish made
• Waterproof
• No artificial additives

About services
• One hour cleaning
• Bord Fáilte approved
• Open all day
• Direct flights

PRICES

It is an offence to mislead the consumer about:

● the price.
● the previous price.
● the recommended price.

Suppose you saw this CD player in a shop. What exactly does the price label mean? The price you will have to pay is clearly €99 and €130 is the previous price. For this sign to be legal the CD player must have been on sale for €130 for at least four consecutive weeks in the previous three months.

You should also check if the price includes delivery and installation.

It would be wrong to quote €180 for a bike and then charge another €50 for the saddle. In this case the consumer expects the saddle to be included in the price quoted.

LESSON 2: GETTING MORE HELP

If you aren't happy with the way the shop has handled your complaint then you will have to consult a **third party**. This is someone who will act on your behalf to try to reach a settlement with the shop. In some cases your parents may act as a third party for you. In other cases you may have to use some of the third parties listed below.

THE OFFICE OF THE DIRECTOR OF CONSUMER AFFAIRS

This office publishes pamphlets to inform you about your rights as a consumer. The office is run by the Director of Consumer Affairs. They are concerned about the truth of advertisements and the descriptions of goods and services.

ADVERTISING STANDARDS AUTHORITY

The Advertising Standards Authority checks the standards of advertising in Ireland. You can write or phone them if you find an advertisement offensive, misleading or false. They will investigate your complaint and they have the power to get advertisements withdrawn or altered.

TRADE ASSOCIATIONS

There are many trade associations in Ireland that may be able to deal with your complaint in relation to one of their members. Many travel agencies, for example, are members of the Irish Travel Agents' Association. Local shops could be members of the Retail Grocery, Dairy and Allied Trades' Association (RGDATA). An electrician could be a member of the Association of Electrical Contractors. An insurance broker could be a member of the Irish Insurance Federation.

THE OMBUDSMAN

The Ombudsman is appointed by the government to investigate complaints by the public relating to state agencies. For example, if you have a problem with An Post, the health boards or a government department and you aren't happy with the way they deal with your complaint, you can ask the Ombudsman to investigate and see if you have been treated fairly.

SMALL CLAIMS PROCEDURE

If you're looking for a remedy of €1,200 or less from a trader then you can use the small claims procedure in the District Court. This doesn't involve the expense of a solicitor and is very informal. Claims can be made for bad workmanship and faulty goods. The fee for making a small claim is €8.

CONSUMERS' ASSOCIATION OF IRELAND

This association publishes the monthly information magazine *Consumer Choice*. The magazine is distributed to members of the association and is not available in shops. It has articles about consumer issues, e.g. toothpaste claims, insurance costs compared, etc. It will represent members who have a complaint against a government department or private company.

CONTACTING A SOLICITOR

Before you contact a solicitor, make sure you:
- complain quickly.
- be polite but firm.
- ask to see the manager if the shop assistant won't or can't help.
- put your complaint in writing as the time and trouble of taking legal action is immense, even if you win the case.

LESSON I: PRACTICE

I.   Rewrite the following list of products and claims so that the products match the correct claims.

Product	Claim
jam	burns to ashes
chair	will not shrink
radiator	childproof
builder	genuine silk
taxi service	television in all rooms
supermarket	stainless steel
disco	solid gold
coal	fireproof
jumper	solid oak
knife	luxury drive
hotel	home-made
car door	well stocked
tie	no job too small
wedding ring	dancing until 2 am
suite of furniture	will not leak

	True	False

2.   A sweater is priced at €19 in the shop window and €27 inside the shop.
You have the right to insist on the sweater for €19.   ◯ ◯

3.   You buy a pair of runners and one year later the sole breaks. You have
the right to insist on a complete refund from the shop.   ◯ ◯

4.   You buy a school bag that the shop assistant says is pure leather. Later you
discover a label inside the bag that states the bag is plastic. You have the right
to insist on a complete refund from the shop.   ◯ ◯

5.   You see a washing machine in a shop marked €480, with a label 'free
delivery to all areas'. The shop assistant asks you to pay an extra €40
delivery charge because you live too far away. You have the right to insist
on the free delivery.   ◯ ◯

6.   You go into the Galway branch of a nationwide chain of stores to buy a
coat advertised on television for €62. However, the coat is marked as €93.
The assistant says the €62 price applies to the Cork branch of the store.
You have the right to insist on the coat for €62.   ◯ ◯

LESSON 2: PRACTICE

1. You are just back from a holiday in Greece that you booked through Inter-Travel. The brochure described your hotel as 'quiet and beside the beach', when in fact it was beside a noisy building site and three miles from the beach! You have complained to Inter-Travel but they say they can't help you.
    (a) What principle of consumer law has been broken in this situation?
    (b) Do you feel you're entitled to a full or a partial refund? Give one reason to support your answer.
    (c) How could the Irish Travel Agents' Association help you?

2. Your VCR won't rewind tapes and you bring it to a local shop for repair. You choose this shop because a sign in the window says it guarantees all repairs and that it is a member of the Association of Electrical Contractors. The repair costs you €40. Two days later it won't rewind tapes again. When you return to the shop they insist that the repair will cost another €40.
    (a) What is the legal basis for your complaint? Explain it briefly.
    (b) Are you entitled to a complete refund? Give a reason for your answer.
    (c) What third party could you ask to help in this situation?

3. Your neighbour receives a bill for €1,000 from the ESB. She refuses to pay it, as her bill is normally under €100. The ESB are threatening to cut off her power supply. She feels the ESB's computer is at fault.
    (a) Do you think she should pay any of the bill and if so, how much?
    (b) How could the Ombudsman help in this situation?

4. Your family takes a short break in a Bord Fáilte-approved cottage in Kerry. The brochure stated that the price was €100 per night for a family, but your parents end up paying €150. When you get home, your parents decide to complain to the guesthouse.
    (a) What is the legal basis for the complaint? Explain it briefly.
    (b) Are your parents entitled to a complete refund? Give a reason for your answer.
    (c) What third party could your parents ask for help in this situation?

5. (a) Why do consumers need protection?
    (b) How might a consumer be misled (i) by the description of a product or (ii) by the price of a product?
    (c) What is impulse buying?

6. (a) Which act protects consumers, and how does it work?
    (b) Name (i) a government organisation and (ii) a private agency that protects consumers' rights.

7. Write a note about:
    (a) the Director of Consumer Affairs.
    (b) the Ombudsman.
    (c) the small claims procedure.

8. Write a note about the work of the Consumers' Association of Ireland.

STATE EXAM PRACTICE

1. (a) Peter Cooney of 16 Castle Street, Ennis bought a new Roller bicycle, Model RB 25, from Frank Clarke, manager of The Bike Shop Ltd of Nenagh Road, Limerick on 11 April. He paid €179 by cheque. After a few days' use, the bicycle started to give trouble. It made a lot of noise when he was cycling and the chain seemed to slip every time he went up a hill. After a week he had to get off and walk up every hill with it. He was very disappointed. You, as Peter Cooney, are asked to write a suitable letter of complaint to The Bike Shop Ltd.
    (b) If The Bike Shop Ltd does not satisfy him, suggest two steps that Peter Cooney could take.
    (JCOL, adapted)

2. Mary Noonan bought a new jacket in Angel's Boutique on a recent holiday. She paid €45 for it. On her return home she noticed that the stitching on one sleeve was ripped and also that one shoulder was larger than the other. She was very disappointed. As the boutique is over seventy miles from where she lives, she has decided to write to them about it and return the jacket. She isn't sure whether or not she should return the receipt. She is looking for a full cash refund.
    (a) Using your knowledge of consumer legislation, answer the following questions.
        (i)   What is the legal basis for Mary's complaint? Explain it briefly.
        (ii) Do you think Mary is entitled to a full refund? Give a reason for your answer.
        (iii) If the boutique owner offered Mary a credit note for the full amount should she accept it? Explain your answer.
        (iv) What advice would you give Mary on whether or not she should include the receipt with her letter?
    (b) Assume you are Mary Noonan. Write the letter of complaint to the manager of Angel's Boutique. (You may choose any address, date, etc. that are required for yourself.)
    (JCHL, adapted)

3. Your friends went shopping recently and asked you to advise them with their consumer problems.
    (a) David bought a tin of paint in a sale for half the normal price. When his mother saw the paint she said it was a very inferior brand and its purchase was a *false economy* and a typical example of David's *impulse buying*. David wishes to return the tin of paint to the shop with the receipt.
        (i) Is David entitled to a full refund of his money? Give a reason for your answer.
        (ii) Explain the above italicised terms.
    (b) Aisling bought a dress in a shop from a stand that displayed a sign stating that the goods were shop-soiled. When Aisling fitted on the dress at home she noticed that the collar was faded. Aisling decided to return the dress to the shop. The shop assistant refused to accept it back even though Aisling had proof of purchase.
        (i)   Was the shop assistant correct? Explain your answer.
        (ii) The manager of the shop knew that Aisling was a regular customer and offered her a credit note, which she accepted. Why did the manager do this?
        (iii) Give two reasons why it is important to get a receipt when you buy goods.
    (c) A consumer is considering the purchase of a new household electrical item. List three factors which he/she should take into account when choosing one brand or model over other brands or models.
    (JCHL)

TEST YOURSELF AT
my-etest.com

7 Money and Banking

TERMS COVERED IN THIS CHAPTER
Money, divisible, portable, durable, credit card, laser card, charge card, ATM, DIRT, saving, current account, standing order, direct debit, bank statement.

INTRODUCTION

Answer these questions, then discuss your answers with another pupil.

1. List all the places that you can think of where you can save money.
2. Do you save in any of these?
3. Why or why not?

LESSON 1: MONEY

Money is anything that people are prepared to accept as payment for goods and services. Cattle, gold and silver were all used as money at one time or another. A good form of money is:

- divisible (can be broken down into small values).
- portable (can be carried around easily).
- durable (will withstand normal wear and tear).

When people lose confidence in money they often revert to an old form of trade called **barter**. This simply involves swapping goods. It is likely that you have engaged in some form of bartering at one time or another.

FORMS OF MONEY

There are five main forms of money used in Ireland today: cash, cheques, laser cards, credit cards and charge cards.

Cash: The notes and coins in daily use. These are **legal tender**, i.e. they must be accepted as payment for goods and services.

Cheques: A person who has a current account is able to write cheques to pay for goods and services.

Laser card: You use a laser card to pay for shopping and also get cash while at the checkout. It is also known as a debit card and is cheaper than writing a cheque.

Credit card: A credit card allows a person to buy goods and services now and pay for them later, e.g. MasterCard, Visa. You get a statement each month and you can pay the full amount due or make a partial payment. However, you will pay high interest on the outstanding balance on your account.

Charge card: This is like a credit card except you must pay the amount due when you receive your statement each month, e.g. Diners Club, American Express.

Automated teller machine (ATM): ATMs or cash dispensers are a handy way to use many of the banks' services. Customers who wish to use ATMs are given a cash card and a personal identification number (PIN). After keying in the PIN at the ATM the customer may then lodge or withdraw money and pay a bill such as gas, electricity or telephone.

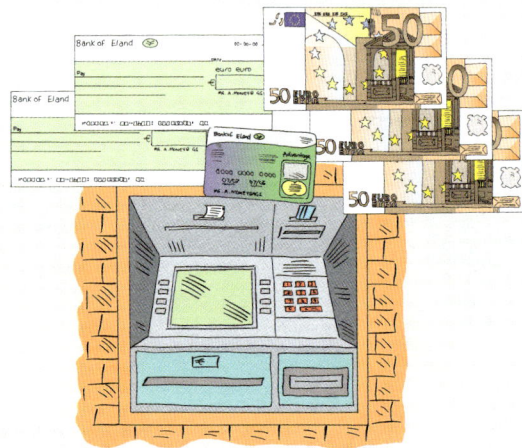

GOOD PLACES TO SAVE MONEY

Saving is a good habit and the earlier you begin, the better. You can start by setting aside a little of your pocket money each week. You could keep this in a box beside your bed, but it's safer if you deposit your money in a financial institution. There are several to choose from. Here are some questions to ask yourself before you decide on one.

Will my savings be safe? Keeping cash at home is not a safe place to save. It could be stolen and is too easy to 'dip into'. Soon your savings will be gone. It is much wiser to use a financial institution.

What am I saving for? Good savers have a target – something they want to buy that they can't afford yet. When you get older you may want to buy an apartment or house. At that time it would make sense to save in the institution you intend asking for a mortgage loan.

Is it easy to withdraw my savings? If you keep your money in a financial institution you will be able to withdraw your money easily. Large sums may require written notice.

Will my savings earn interest? You will get interest on your savings but you will have to shop around to get the best rates. An interest rate of three per cent means you get €3 on every €100 you save for a year.

Will I have to pay tax? In most cases you have to pay Deposit Interest Retention Tax (DIRT). You don't have to pay DIRT on some schemes operated by An Post.

AN POST

This is a good place to save as there may be a branch near you and you get a high rate of interest on your savings. All savings in the post office are state guaranteed so your money will be safe. Savings Certificates, Savings Bonds and Instalment Savings are worth considering, as they aren't subject to DIRT.

Savings Certificates	Invest from €50 to €80,000 and earn sixteen per cent after five years and six months on deposit.
Savings Bonds	Invest from €100 to €80,000 and earn eight per cent after three years on deposit.
Instalment Savings	Invest from €25 to €500 each month for a year and earn fifteen per cent after five years on deposit.

CREDIT UNION

Credit unions are located all over the country and it's likely there is one in your local area. You can save your money in a savings account and get interest in the form of a dividend each year. The dividend paid is related to the amount of cash available to the credit union and the amount you have saved. Or you can lodge your money in a deposit account and get interest on the amount saved at a higher rate than in the bank. It is well worth saving in the credit union as you will be entitled to get a personal loan at a low interest rate.

BUILDING SOCIETY

The main reason for saving in a building society is to get a mortgage loan to buy a house. Most people begin by opening a savings account. This is a deposit account in which you save money by buying shares in the society.

COMMERCIAL BANK

The main commercial banks are Bank of Ireland, Allied Irish Banks, National Irish Bank, Ulster Bank and Permanent TSB Bank. They offer two main accounts.

Deposit accounts	This is where you save money and earn interest on your deposits.
Current accounts	Holders of current accounts get a cheque book. This is not a good account to use to save money as there is no interest paid and it's too easy to take out money.

LESSON 2: CURRENT ACCOUNTS

Money lodged in a current account doesn't earn interest. However, this account is popular as there are several easy ways to take money out of it, e.g. cheques, standing order and direct debit.

CHEQUES

Writing a cheque for €150 is the same as going to the bank and taking €150 out of your account except that you don't have to go to the bank, fill in a form and wait in a queue. It is therefore a convenient way to pay bills while you are shopping.

STANDING ORDER

A standing order is an arrangement with the bank whereby they pay your bill (using your money) at a certain time each month. It is a convenient way to pay bills that occur regularly and where the amount doesn't vary, e.g. a mortgage or loan repayment.

DIRECT DEBIT

This is similar to a standing order but it is used where the amount of the bill is not known in advance, e.g. the electricity or phone bill. You give the bank permission to pay the amount requested by the ESB or phone company.

OPENING A CURRENT ACCOUNT

To open any bank account you will have to fill in a form giving details about your name, address, occupation, annual income and listing other bank accounts you may have. In addition, for a current account you must give a specimen signature. You will be issued with an account number, cheque book and cheque card. You may then lodge money into the account and write cheques.

Counterfoil: It is wise to complete the counterfoil (stub) in order to have a record of the cheques you write. As a minimum you should write the date, the amount and the payee's name.

Date: A cheque must have a date. Normally this is the same as the day of issue.

Payee: The name of the person or company receiving the cheque (the one who is being paid the money).

Drawee: The name of the bank that has issued the cheque book. The customer writing the cheque has a current account in this bank.

7 Sep 2004	7 Sep 2004
Pay EBS	Pay Educational Building Society
	Four hundred and fifty euro
Previous Balance 800	
This Cheque 450	
New Balance 350	

Bank of Ireland

or order

€450—

D. O'Brien

D. O'Brien

00049 93 4416 22440066

Cheque number   Current account number   Amount in words   Amount in figures

Stamp: Every cheque has a government stamp on it to show the stamp duty has been paid.

Bank sort code: This is used by the bank's computers to sort the cheques.

Drawer: This is the customer's signature and must be the same as the specimen signature given to the bank when opening the current account.

CROSSED CHEQUES

Crossing a cheque makes it safer, as it must be paid into another bank account and not simply cashed.

(a) This is the most commonly used crossing: two parallel lines are drawn on the face of the cheque.

(b) This cheque must be paid into the account of the payee named.

(c) This cheque must be presented at the Bank of Ireland, Galway.

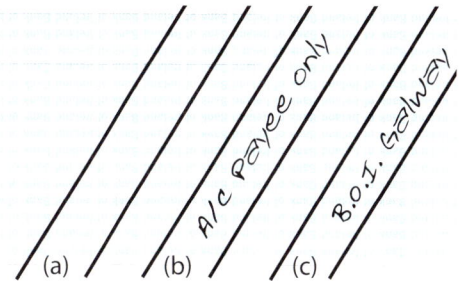

(a) (b) A/c Payee only (c) B.O.I. Galway

Bank of Ireland

12 Sep 2003

Pay   Educational Building Society   or order

Two hundred euro

€200

J. Kelly

REFER TO DRAWER

J. Kelly

00049 93 4416 22440066

DISHONOURED CHEQUES

A dishonoured cheque is a cheque that the bank will not pay – it is also known as a 'bounced cheque'. It is marked RD (refer to drawer). This can happen if:

● the cheque is more than six months old (stale).
● the amount in words doesn't match the figure.
● the cheque isn't signed.
● the signature doesn't match the sample signature.
● there isn't enough money in the drawer's account.

ENDORSED CHEQUES

A cheque may be passed on to someone else as payment of a debt. To do this the payee signs or endorses the back of the cheque. A general endorsement contains the payee's name only. A special endorsement contains the name of the person receiving the cheque and the payee's endorsement.

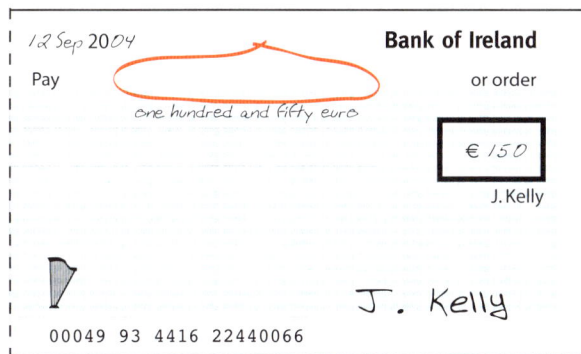

David Lawlor

Pay Elaine O'Toole or order
David Lawlor

Bank of Ireland

12 Sep 2004

Pay   or order

one hundred and fifty euro

€ 150

J. Kelly

J. Kelly

00049 93 4416 22440066

OTHER CHEQUES

A blank cheque lacks the date, the amount of money or the payee's name. An open cheque is a cheque with no crossing on it. A postdated cheque has some future date on it and may not be cashed before that date. An antedated cheque has a previous date as the date of issue.

CHEQUE CARD

Most people and firms will accept a cheque instead of cash, especially if the cheque is supported by a cheque card. This is a guarantee by the financial institution issuing it to pay cash to the person receiving the cheque. The shopkeeper compares the signature on the cheque card with the signature on the cheque and makes sure the card is not out of date. Then the card number is written on the back of the cheque.

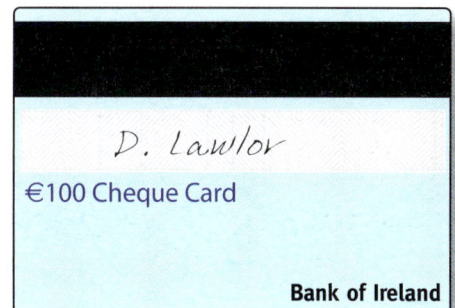

D. Lawlor

€100 Cheque Card

Bank of Ireland

LESSON 3: THE BANK ACCOUNT

If you write cheques for a value greater than the amount of money you have in your current account you will overdraw your account. Interest is charged on overdrafts and you may have the embarrassment of your cheques 'bouncing'. To avoid overdrawing your account you should keep a record of cheques paid out and lodgments made to your account. A simple bank account is the handiest way of recording these transactions. If it looks familiar it is because it is very similar to the cash account you learned about in Chapter 1.

Question

Mr and Mrs Healy keep the following record of their money for the first week of October.

Oct

1	Debit balance in bank account	€1,700
2	Mr Healy received his weekly wages and lodged it	€510
3	Mrs Healy received her weekly wages and lodged it	€520
4	Paid for petrol by cheque no. 125	€42
5	Paid for groceries by cheque no. 126	€120
6	Withdrew cash from ATM	€200
7	Paid EBS monthly mortgage	€2,000

Solution

RB 3

Bank Account							
Date	Particulars		Bank	Date	Particulars	No.	Bank
Sep				Sep			
1	Balance		1,700	4	Petrol	125	42
2	Wages		510	5	Groceries	126	120
7	Wages		520	6	ATM	ATM	200
				7	Mortgage	SO	2,000
				7	Balance		368
			2,730				2,730
8	Balance		368				

LESSON 4: BANK RECONCILIATION STATEMENT

A bank statement is a letter from the bank giving details about your current account. It lists the flow of money in and out of the account. The balance column of the statement shows a running balance. This decreases when payments are made (debit) and increases when there are lodgments (credit). The final figure (€233) is the amount of money the bank considers the Healy family has in their account.

On the other hand we have already seen the Healys' bank account record. They think they have €368 in the bank (the balance in the bank account). To find the correct figure a bank reconciliation statement is prepared. By comparing the statement with the account on the **previous** page you will notice some figures missing from the statement that the bank doesn't know about yet: the lodgment of €520 and the cheque for €120. When these are shown you get a new bank figure of €633.

Bank Statement				
Date	Particulars	Debit	Credit	Balance
June				
1	Balance forward			1,700
2	Lodgment		510	2,210
6	Cheque no. 125	42		2,168
6	ATM Mullingar	200		1,968
7	Credit transfer		280	2,248
7	Standing order	2,000		248
8	Bank charges	15		233

Money going into the account

Money going out of the Healys' account

Running balance

Bank Reconciliation Statement	
Balance per statement	233
Lodgment not yet credited	+520
	753
Cheque not yet presented	-120
Balance per bank account	633

Actual spending money

Finally, to bring the Healys' own bank account up to date the bank charges and the credit transfer are entered into the account. This gives a new balance of €633, which is the same as the final figure in the bank reconciliation statement and is the money the Healys have available to spend.

RB 3

	Bank Account						
Date	Particulars		Bank	Date	Particulars	No.	Bank
8	Balance		368		Bank charges		15
	Credit transfer		280		Balance	c/d	633
			648				648
	Balance	b/d	633				

LESSON 1: PRACTICE

1.   The different types of money are hidden in this grid. Find them and then use them to complete the five sentences below. The words can be read across or down.

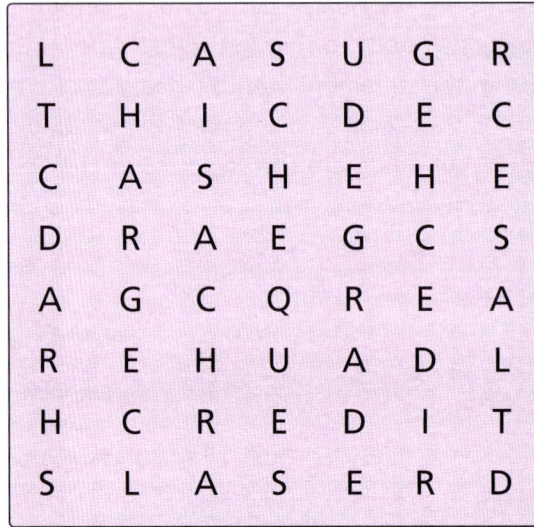

L	C	A	S	U	G	R
T	H	I	C	D	E	C
C	A	S	H	E	H	E
D	R	A	E	G	C	S
A	G	C	Q	R	E	A
R	E	H	U	A	D	L
H	C	R	E	D	I	T
S	L	A	S	E	R	D

(a) Barry paid €60 _____ for his shoes.

(b) Pamela wrote a _____ for €110 for car repairs.

(c) Mrs O'Dowd used her _____ card to pay for her shopping and get cash.

(d) Finbar used his Visa _____ card to pay his restaurant bill.

(e) Mr Nolan sent off a cheque for the full amount of his Diners Club _____ card bill.

2.   Refer to the pie chart, which shows John Power's savings.

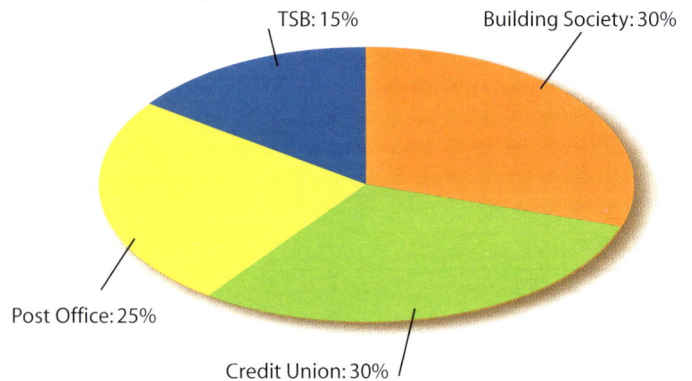

(a) Name the four institutions where he saves his money.

(b) In which institutions has he equal amounts of money saved?

(c) Where has he the least saved?

(d) If his total savings are €2,000, how much is in each institution?

John's Savings

TSB: 15%

Building Society: 30%

Post Office: 25%

Credit Union: 30%

3. Paula is looking for somewhere to save her money so she talked to the local bank manager. Make up the questions she asked for the answers she was given.

(a) _____ ?

It is much better to keep your money in a bank rather than leaving it somewhere it could easily be stolen.

(b) _____ ?

You just have to fill out a withdrawal form and go to one of the tellers over there.

(c) _____ ?

You will be given 0.5 per cent on your savings.

(d) _____ ?

You have to pay DIRT on any interest you earn.

4. (a) What is bartering?
    (b) What forms of money are used in Ireland?
    (c) Why wouldn't sand be a good form of money?

5. (a) Why do people save money?
    (b) What factors will influence where you save your money?
    (c) List four institutions where you could save your money and name the savings schemes offered by one of those you mention.

6. (a) Why are cash dispensers so popular?
    (b) What services are available at a cash dispenser?
    (c) Name two bank services not available at a cash dispenser.

7. (a) What do the letters ATM stand for?
    (b) What is a PIN used for at the ATM?
    (c) Why do people prefer to use the ATM rather than go into the bank?

LESSON 2: PRACTICE

1. Complete this word grid with the names of the different types of cheques.
    (a) A _____ cheque is safer.
    (b) An _____ cheque has no crossing on it.
    (c) A _____ cheque is missing the date.
    (d) A _____ dated cheque has a future date on it.
    (e) An _____ cheque can be passed on to someone else.
    (f) An _____ dated cheque has a previous date on it.
    (g) A _____ cheque is a cheque the bank won't pay.

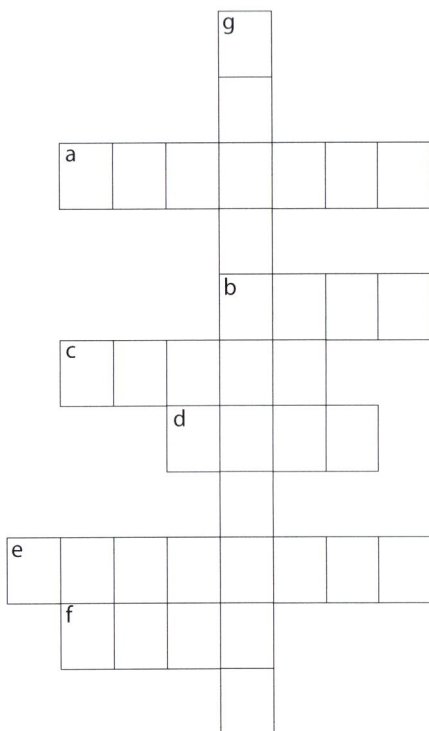

2. Write the following amounts in words.
    (a) €45   (f) €294.73
    (b) €51   (g) €615.25
    (c) €89   (h) €819.38
    (d) €37   (i) €1,070.54
    (e) €63   (j) €3,413.92

3. Write the following amounts in numerals.
    (a) Seventeen euro.
    (b) Eighty-five euro.
    (c) One thousand and four euro.
    (d) Two hundred and seventy-five euro.
    (e) Four hundred and sixteen euro.

4. Make out the cheques referred to in the following transactions. Use the cheques in the Documents Book.
    (a) On 12 November John Kelly issued a cheque for €400 payable to Seán Nolan.
    (b) On 14 November John Kelly received his wages by cheque from his employer, Mary Burke, for €456.
    (c) On 3 December James Peat bought a typewriter from O'Neill Office Supplies Ltd. It cost him €62.97 and he paid by cheque.

5. (a) What are the differences between a current and a deposit account?
    (b) Give two reasons why a current account is not a good place to save.

6. (a) Explain what the following terms mean:
        (i) stale cheque (ii) blank cheque.
    (b) What does each of the following do to a cheque?
        (i)   drawer
        (ii) drawee
        (iii) payee
    (c) Why would a bank refuse to cash a cheque?

LESSON 3: PRACTICE

1. (a) Make out the bank account for Christopher Ryan given the following information and balance the account. Use the cheque in the Documents Book.

    Jun
    1   He had €210 debit balance in his bank account.
    5   He lodged €317 in the bank.
    10   He sent a cheque for €56 by letter to Dermot Pitcher.
    18   He paid a telephone bill of €106.
    23   He received a cheque for €7 and lodged it in the bank.

    (b) Make out the cheque referred to on 10 June.

    (c) What is an overdraft?

2. (a) Make out the bank account for Denis Kissane given the following information and balance the account. Use the cheque in the Documents Book.

    Jul
    1   He had €345 debit balance in his bank account.
    7   He sent a cheque for €93 by letter to Brenda Close.
    13   He lodged €522 in the bank.
    19   He paid an electricity bill of €112.
    27   He received a cheque for €3 and lodged it in the bank.

    (b) Make out the cheque referred to on 7 July.

    (c) Why is a current account not a suitable place to save money?

3. (a) Make out the bank account for Áine Cowley given the following information and balance the account. Use the cheque in the Documents Book.

    Aug
    1   She had €153 debit balance in her bank account.
    3   She received a cheque for €679 from Helen O'Neill and lodged it in the bank.
    12   She bought a computer from Comsupp Ltd for €1,354 and paid by cheque.
    15   She paid a credit card bill of €254 by cheque.
    24   She paid for theatre tickets by cheque for €16.

    (b) Make out the cheque referred to on 12 August.

    (c) How much should she lodge to her current account to clear her overdraft?

4. (a) Make out the bank account for Liam Smith given the following information and balance the account. Use the cheque in the Documents Book.

Sep

1	He had €23 credit balance in his bank account (overdrawn).
9	He lodged €1,264 in the bank.
12	He paid the mortgage by cheque €250.
17	He paid car insurance of €317 by cheque.
29	He received a cheque for €7 and lodged it in the bank.

   (b) Make out the cheque referred to on 12 September.

   (c) What does '€23 credit balance' mean?

5. (a) Make out the bank account for Aisling Hayes given the following information and balance the account. Use the cheque in the Documents Book.

On 1 October she had a €235 debit balance in her bank account.

On 4 October she lodged €354 in the bank.

On 9 October she sent a cheque for €76 by letter to Margaret Hand.

On 17 October she bought chocolates for €7 and groceries for €15. She paid Handy Stores by cheque for the total amount.

On 27 October she received a statement from the bank and noticed bank charges of €7 that she didn't know about.

   (b) Make out the cheque referred to on 17 October.

   (c) What is the statement referred to on 27 October?

LESSON 4: PRACTICE

Prepare a bank reconciliation statement for each of the following questions and bring the bank account up to date.

RB 3

Dr					Bank Account			Cr
Feb				Feb				
1	Balance	b/d	451	3	Cash	ATM	231
11	Wages-lodgment		616	14	Telephone	986	174
21	Wages-lodgment		642	19	EBS	987	741
				27	Matty's Garage	988	168
				28	Balance	c/d	395
			1,709				1,709
28	Balance	b/d	395				

1. Here is Amy Smith's bank account and statement for February.

	Bank Statement			
Date	Particulars	Debit	Credit	Balance
FEB		€	€	€
1	BALANCE FORWARD			451
3	ATM	231		220
11	LODGMENT		616	836
15	BANK CHARGES	3		833
18	CAR LOAN DD	14		819
21	CHEQUE 987	741		78
25	CREDIT TRANSFER		73	151

RB 3

Dr					Bank Account			Cr
Mar				Mar				
1	Balance	b/d	340	2	Supermarket	916	114
12	Wages-lodgment		1,100	9	Telephone	917	80
29	Bonus-lodgment		100	16	Cash	ATM	120
				26	Dr Maguire	918	15
				30	Balance	c/d	1,211
			1,540				1,540
30	Balance	b/d	1,211				

2. Here is Joe Burke's bank account and statement for March.

	Bank Statement			
Date	Particulars	Debit	Credit	Balance
MAR		€	€	€
1	BALANCE FORWARD			340
4	CHEQUE 916	114		226
10	CHARGES	20		206
12	LODGMENT		1,100	1,306
18	INTEREST	10		1,296
21	CASH ATM	120		1,176

RB 3

Dr	Bank Account				Cr	
Apr				Apr		
1	Balance	b/d	60	3	ESB	317	90
5	Wages-lodgment		220	6	Cash	ATM	50
12	Wages-lodgment		220	8	Telephone	318	70
19	Wages-lodgment		220	13	Superquinn	319	85
26	Wages-lodgment		220	22	Irish Life	DD	60
				24	Roches Stores	320	80
				31	Balance	c/d	505
			940				940
30	Balance	b/d	505				

Bank Statement				
Date	Particulars	Debit	Credit	Balance
APR		€	€	€
1	BALANCE FORWARD			60
5	LODGMENT		220	280
6	CHEQUE 317	90		190
8	ATM	50		140
9	INTEREST	14		126
10	CHEQUE 318	70		56
12	LODGMENT		220	276
22	IRISH LIFE DD	60		216

3. Here is Mary Moroney's bank account and statement for April.

RB 3

Dr	Bank Account				Cr	
May				May		
1	Balance	b/d	280	3	Cash	ATM	70
2	Wages-lodgment		250	5	Dunnes	805	110
9	Wages-lodgment		250	17	EBS	SO	90
16	Wages-lodgment		250	21	Telephone	806	60
24	Bonus-lodgment		200	31	Balance	c/d	900
			1,230				1,230
30	Balance	b/d	900				

Bank Statement				
Date	Particulars	Debit	Credit	Balance
MAY		€	€	€
1	BALANCE FORWARD			280
2	LODGMENT		250	530
4	ATM	70		460
6	CHEQUE 805	110		350
9	LODGMENT		250	600
11	INTEREST	12		588
16	LODGMENT		250	838
20	EBS SO	90		748

4. Here is Jim Cahill's bank account and statement for May.

RB 3

Dr			Bank Account		June			Cr
June								
1	Balance	b/d	150		4	Jury's Hotel	408	200
12	Wages-lodgment		540		15	Telephone	409	90
30	Wages-lodgment		540		18	Superquinn	410	80
					28	Dunnes Stores	411	70
					30	Balance	c/d	790
			1,230					1,230
30	Balance	b/d	790					

Bank Statement				
Date	Particulars	Debit	Credit	Balance
JUN		€	€	€
1	BALANCE FORWARD			150
10	ESB DD	100		50
12	LODGMENT		540	590
15	INTEREST	5		585
18	FIRST DIRECT DD	60		525
21	CHEQUE 410	80		445
30	CREDIT TRANSFER		70	515

5. Here is Liz Curtis's bank account and statement for June.

RB 3

Dr			Bank Account		Jul			Cr
Jul								
1	Balance	b/d	300		2	Quinnsworth	505	100
13	Wages-lodgment		700		9	ESB	506	84
29	Wages-lodgment		700		21	Cash	ATM	100
					29	Chemist	507	34
					30	Balance	c/d	1,382
			1,700					1,700
31	Balance	b/d	1,382					

6. Here is Pete Conroy's bank account and statement for July.

Bank Statement				
Date	Particulars	Debit	Credit	Balance
JUL		€	€	€
1	BALANCE FORWARD			300
5	CHEQUE 505	100		200
10	CHARGES	15		185
13	LODGMENT		700	885
20	CHEQUE 506	84		801
21	CASH ATM	100		701

RB 3

Dr			Bank Account				Cr
Aug				Aug			
1	Balance	b/d	50	3	Dunnes Stores	210	70
7	Wages-lodgment		200	8	Cash	ATM	80
14	Wages-lodgment		200	10	Telephone	211	100
21	Wages-lodgment		200	21	Dunnes Stores	212	80
28	Wages-lodgment		200	23	Statoil	213	20
				24	Dunnes Stores	214	40
				31	Balance	c/d	460
			850				850
31	Balance	b/d	460				

7. Here is Deirdre Davy's bank account and statement for August.

	Bank Statement			
Date	Particulars	Debit	Credit	Balance
AUG		€	€	€
1	BALANCE FORWARD			50
7	LODGMENT		200	250
6	CHEQUE 210	70		180
8	ATM	80		100
9	ESB DD	85		15
13	CHEQUE 211	100		85 OD
14	LODGMENT		200	115
24	CHEQUE 213	20		95

RB 3

Dr			Bank Account				Cr
Sep				Sep			
1	Balance	b/d	100	4	Cash	ATM	100
2	Wages-lodgment		300	5	Superquinn	700	50
9	Wages-lodgment		300	20	First Active	SO	260
16	Wages-lodgment		300	28	ESB	701	80
24	Bonus-lodgment		100	30	Balance	c/d	610
			1,100				1,100
31	Balance	b/d	610				

8. Here is Terry Martin's bank account and statement for September.

	Bank Statement			
Date	Particulars	Debit	Credit	Balance
Sep		€	€	€
1	BALANCE FORWARD			100
2	LODGMENT		300	400
4	ATM	100		300
6	CHEQUE 700	50		250
10	LODGMENT		300	550
11	INTEREST	15		535
17	LODGMENT		300	835
9	FIRST ACTIVE	260		575

STATE EXAM PRACTICE

1. Linda Jones received the following bank statement through the post.

| \multicolumn{5}{c}{**AIB Bank, Ennis, Co. Clare**} |
| ACCOUNT: | Linda Jones 12 Shannon Street Ennis | ACCOUNT NO: DATE: | 71429533 31 May 2004 | |

DATE	PARTICULARS	DEBIT	CREDIT	BALANCE
		€	€	€
May 1	Balance b/d			125
4	Lodgment		250	375
10	ATM Limerick	60		315
15	Cheque no. 113	120		195
26	Bank charges	10		185

(a) In what bank and branch does Linda have her account?

(b) Is it a current account or a deposit account?

(c) Explain what happened on 10 May 2004.

Linda's own bank account in her record book looked like this on the same date.

Dr			\multicolumn{4}{c	}{**Bank Account**}	Cr
Date	Details	Amount	Date	Details	Cheque No.	Amount
		€				€
May 1	Balance	125	May 10	Cash (Limerick)	ATM	60
4	Lodgment	250	12	Rent	113	120
			29	Groceries	114	40
			31	Balance	c/d	155
		375				375
May 31	Balance b/d	155				

Linda noticed that one of the items on the bank statement had not yet been entered in her bank account.

(d) Bring Linda's bank account up to date and show her adjusted balance.

(e) Make out a bank reconciliation statement for Linda.

(JCOL, adapted)

2. Bríd O'Mara has a current account with Ulster Bank. She received this bank statement on 31 March.

	Statement of Account with **ULSTER BANK LIMITED** Celbridge Branch, Co. Kildare	Branch Code: 91-63-24 Account No.: 473815 Type of Account: Current Statement No.: 73		
Account Holder Bríd O'Mara, Oak Lawn, Celbridge.				
DATE	PARTICULARS	DEBIT	CREDIT	BALANCE
1 Mar	Balance forward			157 DR
9 Mar	Cheque 454	84		241 DR
10 Mar	Lodgment		879	638
11 Mar	ATM	59		579
13 Mar	Cheque 452	124		455
16 Mar	SO EBS	118		337
18 Mar	Credit transfer		93	430
22 Mar	DD Telecom	57		373
25 Mar	Cheque 455	88		285
30 Mar	Current A/C fees	8		277
31 Mar	Interest	6		271

Study this statement and answer the following questions.

(a) Explain what is meant by DR on 1 March.

(b) Explain the appearance of interest on the bank statement on 31 March.

(c) Name one use for an ATM card and a cheque card.

(d) Bríd O'Mara's employer has offered to pay her salary using Paypath. Explain what this means and state one advantage of it to her.

(e) The following is Bríd's own account of her bank transactions. Compare this bank account/cash book with the bank statement she received from the bank and answer (i) and (ii) below.

  (i)   Make whatever adjustments are necessary to Bríd's own records to update her bank account/cash book.

  (ii) Prepare a bank reconciliation statement as on 31 March.

(JCHL, adapted)

Bank Account/Cash Book								
		F	€			Chq. No.	F	€
Mar 7	Salary		879	Mar 1	Balance			157
Mar 31	Sale of bicycle		45	Mar 6	Foley's Hardware	453		87
				Mar 8	Car Repairs	454		84
				Mar 11	ATM Groceries			59
				Mar 16	SO EBS			118
				Mar 21	Insurance	455		88
				Mar 31	Balance		c/d	207
			924					924
Mar 31	Balance	b/d	207					

8 Borrowing Money

TERMS COVERED IN THIS CHAPTER
Credit, loans, collateral, guarantor, interest, APR, bankruptcy, credit card, overdraft, HP, moneylenders, pawnbrokers.

INTRODUCTION

What do you think? Work with another pupil on this task.
You have €5 and another pupil asks you for a loan of 50c for bus fare.
1. Why might you give the loan?
2. Why might you not give the loan?

LESSON I: SOURCES OF FINANCE

Credit involves buying something now and paying for it later. It may seem simple enough but there are many ways to borrow and the cost can vary greatly. The wise borrower will shop around and get the best deal.

SHORT TERM
Credit cards: Credit cards can be used for short-term borrowing to pay for holidays or to buy goods in many shops. The credit card company only requires you to pay a certain minimum amount each month, but they charge high interest on the outstanding balance.

Bank overdraft: This is a short-term loan available to people with a current account. Under this arrangement you can write cheques even though you don't have enough money in your account and the bank will honour these cheques up to your overdraft limit.

MEDIUM TERM
Medium-term loan: Medium-term loans are available from credit unions, banks and building societies. They have to be paid back over a period of one to five years.

Hire purchase (HP): HP is mainly used for the purchase of cars and expensive household goods. It is costly but popular because no security is necessary, the repayments are small and you get the goods at once. With HP you pay a deposit and then you make regular payments for a few years. The longer the period of time, the lower the repayments but the higher the total cost of the goods. You do not own the goods until the last repayment has been made.

LONG TERM
Mortgage: A mortgage is a long-term loan used to buy a house. You usually have to save with the bank or building society in order to get this loan and you have from five to twenty-five years to repay it.

BORROWERS' RIGHTS
Borrowing is so complicated that the rights of the borrower are protected by several laws, including the **Hire Purchase Acts 1946** and **1960** and the **Sale of Goods and Supply of Services Act 1980**. The main objective of these laws is to safeguard the hirer by making the lender disclose:
● the cash price of the goods.
● the interest being paid.

Credit Union

Credit unions offer loans at very low interest rates. The loans can be repaid as quickly as you like without penalty. Members take out loans for a variety of reasons, e.g. to buy a car, build a house extension or take a holiday. Every loan is insured by the credit union at no cost to the member. In the event of the member's death during the term of the loan, the loan is cleared by the insurance – this avoids any extra hardship on the family.

LESSON 2: HOW DO I GET A LOAN?

To begin with, it's necessary to fill out an **application form** giving your name, address, occupation, earnings, other loans you may have and the purpose of this loan. You may have to get a guarantor or provide some collateral. Of course, you also have to prove that you will be able to pay the interest on the loan.

GUARANTOR

If you have no regular income or are under eighteen years of age you may be required to get a guarantor. This is a friend or relative who signs a document agreeing to pay the interest and loan if you do not.

COLLATERAL

When borrowing large sums of money some form of collateral or security may be necessary. For example, in the case of a person borrowing money to buy a house, the deeds of the house are given as collateral to the building society or bank. This means that if the borrower fails to pay the money due, then the house can be sold and the debt cleared.

INTEREST

In most cases credit is expensive to buy. The price paid for credit is called interest.

Rates of interest: The level of interest charged is called the interest rate. For example, an interest rate of five per cent per annum means a person is charged €5 each year on every €100 borrowed. This is the cost of the loan, and different finance companies will charge different interest rates. Paying cash for a product is certainly cheaper than getting a loan. However, it takes time to save the necessary cash to buy what we want and so most people have to borrow to buy expensive goods.

Annual percentage rate (APR): The APR is the real cost of a loan when interest and additional charges related to the loan are taken into account. If you want to find the cheapest loan then compare the APR of the loans available to you. In the table below we can see the interest rate on a loan is the same in each of the banks. However, Bank A is the cheapest loan as the APR is 4.6 per cent. The percentage difference may appear small to you but on large sums borrowed this difference can amount to hundreds of euro each month.

BANKRUPTCY

If a person cannot pay part or all of debts owed, certain assets given as collateral may be sold or the guarantor may be required to pay the balance due. If this is not enough to pay the debt, the person may be declared **bankrupt** or **insolvent**.

A loan will normally be granted when:

- you can show you will be able to repay the loan and the interest.
- you can give suitable collateral.
- you have a good savings record.
- you were able to repay previous loans.

Loan	Interest Rate	APR
Bank A	4%	4.6%
Bank B	4%	5.1%
Bank C	4%	4.8%

If You Can't Get a Loan

Not all loans will be granted and that is why we often have to wait until we have saved enough money to buy many of the things we want, or sometimes we have to do without certain things altogether.

Moneylenders: There are about 150 licensed moneylenders in Ireland but there are also many more unofficial moneylenders. Moneylenders have a bad name because the unofficial ones charge huge interest rates, which makes it very difficult for their client to repay the loan. The reason people continue to borrow from them is that they find it difficult to borrow from the other institutions mentioned.

Pawnbrokers: Pawnbrokers give money on security of a valuable, such as jewellery. If the valuable isn't reclaimed within a certain period, then it becomes the property of the pawnbroker.

Renting: If you can't get a loan then you might be able to rent instead. Of course, if you rent then you will never own the goods. The rental company will usually repair the product free of charge and may replace it after a number of years with a newer model.

LESSON 3: WORKED EXAMPLES

1.   **Question**

On 1 February 2004 Pat Carey bought a mountain bike on hire purchase. He paid a deposit of €20 and agreed to pay twelve monthly instalments of €15 beginning on 1 March 2004.

(a) What is the total cost of the bike for Pat?

(b) When will Pat own the bike?

Solution

(a)

	€
DEPOSIT =	20
REPAYMENTS (12 x €15) =	180
TOTAL COST =	200

(b) There are twelve monthly repayments as follows.

12 MONTHLY REPAYMENTS

1	2	3	4	5	6	7	8	9	10	11	12
1 Mar	1 Apr	1 May	1 Jun	1 Jul	1 Aug	1 Sept	1 Oct	1 Nov	1 Dec	1 Jan	1 Feb

Pat will own the bike on 2 February 2005.

2.   **Question**

Jill Cleary got the following details about a €2,000 home cinema system.

Hire purchase: Deposit of €300 plus €160 per month for one year.

Rental: €50 per week.

(a) What is the total cost by hire purchase?

(b) What is the total rent for a year?

Solution

(a)

	€
DEPOSIT =	300
REPAYMENTS (12 x €160) =	1,920
TOTAL COST =	2,220

(b) TOTAL RENT = 52 x €50 =   2,600

HIRE PURCHASE AGREEMENT

For the purchase of home cinema system

Cash price	€2,000
Deposit	€300
12 monthly repayments of	€160
Starting on 1 April 2004	
Hire purchase price	€2,220

Jill Cleary

3. **Question**

John Kane got the following details about a €400 guitar.

Hire purchase: Deposit of €100 plus €14 per month for two years.

Personal loan: A €400 loan costs €5 each month per €100 borrowed for two years.

(a) What is the total cost by hire purchase?

(b) What is the total cost by personal loan?

Solution

(a)

		€
DEPOSIT	=	100
REPAYMENTS (24 x €14)	=	<u>336</u>
TOTAL COST	=	<u>436</u>

(b) MONTHLY REPAYMENT =   €5 per €100 borrowed

=   €5 x 4 = €20 per month

TOTAL COST =   24 x €20 = €480

LESSON I: PRACTICE

1. In each of the cases listed below, tick the circle for the most appropriate source of finance from the options given.

	Credit Union	Credit Card	Mortgage	HP
(a) A teenager wishes to buy a bicycle. She can pay €2 each week off a loan.	⦿	○	○	○
(b) An engaged couple wants to buy a house.	○	○	⦿	○
(c) A woman needs to purchase a car. She can afford to pay out €50 each month, and she doesn't live near any credit union.	○	○	○	⦿
(d) A family wishes to borrow €2,000 for a holiday.	⦿	○	○	○
(e) A man is temporarily short of money and is in a shop planning to buy a video.	○	⦿	○	○

2. Match the questions on the left with the responses on the right to create a conversation between a bank manager and a customer looking for a loan.

BANK MANAGER

1. How can I help you? d
2. Do you have a regular income? f
3. What age are you? e
4. Do you have someone who can act as a guarantor? c
5. How much do you need? b
6. How long do you want the loan for? a

CUSTOMER

(a) Two years.
(b) I have some savings so I only need to borrow €1,000.
(c) Yes, my father said he would pay the loan and interest if I don't.
(d) I'd like to get a loan to buy a motorbike.
(e) I'm seventeen.
(f) I have a part-time job earning €100 a week.

3. Find the six items that you must fill into a loan application form hidden in this grid (look down, across and diagonally).

Pg 79

Name & Address
Occupation & Earnings
Purpose
Other Loans

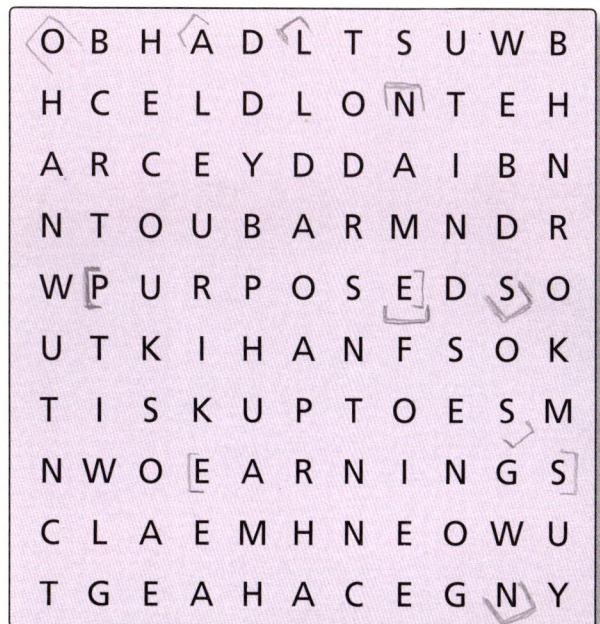

O	B	H	A	D	L	T	S	U	W	B
H	C	E	L	D	L	O	N	T	E	H
A	R	C	E	Y	D	D	A	I	B	N
N	T	O	U	B	A	R	M	N	D	R
W	P	U	R	P	O	S	E	D	S	O
U	T	K	I	H	A	N	F	S	O	K
T	I	S	K	U	P	T	O	E	S	M
N	W	O	E	A	R	N	I	N	G	S
C	L	A	E	M	H	N	E	O	W	U
T	G	E	A	H	A	C	E	G	N	Y

4. During the summer Monica is offered a great part-time job in a country hotel earning €150 a week, but the hotel is too far away to walk to and she can't get a lift or a bus. She desperately needs €200 to buy a bicycle. Her friends each agree to lend her the money if she gives them some collateral. She gathers all her possessions and this is what she gets.

- She borrows €15 from Shane and gives him a radio alarm clock as collateral.
- Margaret takes the CD player as collateral and gives Monica a loan of €95.
- Monica's mobile phone is given as collateral for a €75 loan from Robbie.
- Joe takes Monica's watch as collateral and gives her a loan of €20.
- She borrows €14 from Phyl and gives her styling brush as collateral.

(a) How much does she end up borrowing?
(b) Make up a similar story about a person who has to give collateral for a loan.

5. (a) What is credit?
(b) What is the difference between:
   (i)   a guarantor and a guarantee?
   (ii)   a personal loan and a home loan?
   (iii) a loan and a lease?
   (iv)   income and interest?
   (v)   a credit card and a cheque card?

6. (a) What services are offered by banks to facilitate short-term borrowing?
(b) Explain how any one of these services works.

7. (a) Which law protects the rights of the borrower?
(b) By law what information must the lender disclose?

LESSON 2: PRACTICE

1. (a) What is 'collateral'?
   (b) What collateral would be used on a mortgage loan?

2. (a) Why is HP so popular?
   (b) Under HP when do you own the goods?
   (c) Name two items that will be included in a HP agreement.

3. Calculate the cost of borrowing in each of these cases.
   (a) €700 borrowed for eighteen months if it costs €7 per €100 per month.
   (b) €1,500 borrowed for twelve months if it costs €10 per €100 per month.
   (c) €1,500 borrowed for eighteen months if it costs €6 per €100 per month.
   (d) €2,000 borrowed for twenty-four months if it costs €5 per €100 per month.
   (e) €3,000 borrowed for thirty-six months if it costs €4 per €100 per month.

4. A fridge-freezer costs €650 cash or €15 per week over one year with no deposit.
   (a) What is the HP price?
   (b) By how much is the HP price greater than the cash price?

5. A car may be bought for €14,000 cash or for a €2,000 deposit and €400 each month for three years.
   (a) What is the HP price?
   (b) By how much is the HP price greater than the cash price?

6. A washer-dryer costs €589 cash or €11 weekly for one year after paying a €75 deposit.
   (a) What is the HP price?
   (b) By how much is the HP price greater than the cash price?

7. A friend of your family is buying a cooker and has asked your advice about HP. Which of these is a better HP arrangement?
   (a) A cooker for €600 cash or €200 deposit and €10 weekly for one year.
   (b) Another cooker for €600 cash or €100 deposit and €50 monthly for one year.

8. Write the following percentages as fractions: 50%, 40%, 20%, 25%, 15%, 12.5%, 10%, 7.5%, 5%, 2.5%.

9. Find:
   (a) 25% of €240
   (b) 15% of €800
   (c) 12.5% of €750
   (d) 7.5% of €400
   (e) 5% of €520

LESSON 3: PRACTICE

Ross has no cash left after too many party nights and it will be another two days before he gets his wages. In the meantime he needs €80 to buy some groceries in the local supermarket.

Carol has plenty of expensive jewellery but no cash and she needs to borrow €700 to go on a holiday. She will repay the loan over the next twelve months.

George has a boat but he wants to buy a car. He has no money so he needs a loan of €11,000. He will take three years to repay this loan.

Rachel is making the biggest purchase of her life: she wants to buy a small apartment. She does not have enough money so she needs a loan of €180,000 for the next twenty years.

1.   Scan the information about the four people. The following figures are mentioned. What do they relate to?
     (a) €80
     (b) €700
     (c) €11,000
     (d) €180,000
     (e) Two days
     (f) Twelve months
     (g) Three years
     (h) Twenty years

2.   Read the information about Ross.
     (a) How long does he need a loan for?
     (b) Why would a credit card be a suitable source of finance for him?
     (c) Name another source of finance that he could use.
     (d) Why wouldn't it be a good idea for him to use a medium-term loan?

3.   Complete this table.

	Term of loan	Type of loan	Collateral
Ross			
Carol			
George			
Rachel			

STATE EXAM PRACTICE

1. On 1 December 2004 Gary McCarthy bought a Sonar CD Music System on hire purchase. He paid a deposit of €50 and agreed to pay twelve monthly instalments of €40 beginning on 1 January 2005. The hire purchase company's name is High Finance Ltd, 25 Main Street, Limerick.
    (a) What was the total cost of the music system for Gary?
    (b) When would Gary become the owner of the music system?

    Gary lost his job on 5 May 2005. He was made redundant because the firm for which he worked went bankrupt. On 10 May he wrote to the manager of the hire purchase company telling him about this. He also wrote that because of losing his job he was unable to keep paying the instalments on the Sonar CD Music System. He told the manager that he wished to end the hire purchase agreement and asked him to send someone to take away the music system.
    (c) Write the letter that Gary sent to the hire purchase company. Gary's address is 12 Strand Road, Tralee, Co. Kerry.
    (JCOL, adapted)

2. Kevin Dillon lives at 44 Shannon Street, Athlone in a house he purchased in 2000 with the help of a mortgage of €30,000 from the National Building Society. His telephone number is 0902-12488.

    Kevin is employed as a sales assistant with Skyline Ltd, Industrial Estate, Athlone where he started work in 1999. He earns a salary of €1,300 per month.

    Kevin would like a new car for his next birthday. He will be thirty years old on 15 July 2004. In order to buy the car he needs to borrow €9,000, which he hopes to repay in monthly instalments of €200 over the next four years. He gets a loan application form from his local Bank of Ireland branch.
    (a) Complete Kevin's loan application form (in the Documents Book) on today's date.
    (b) Explain three of the following terms: 'interest', 'hire purchase', 'collateral', 'mortgage', 'bankruptcy'.
    (JCOL, adapted)

TEST YOURSELF AT
my-etest.com

9 Personal Insurance

TERMS COVERED IN THIS CHAPTER
Risks, encash, proposal form, premiums, compensation, policy, actuary, broker, loss adjuster, assessor, assurance, insurance.

INTRODUCTION

What do you think? Work with another pupil on this task.
Life is often dangerous and risky. List ten risks that you might find:

- at home.
- at school.
- at a factory.

LESSON 1: BACKGROUND

The insurance business began 600 years ago. It came about largely because of the dangers of the sea, e.g. storms, pirates and scurvy. These dangers interfered with the lucrative business of trading European wool and cloth for Eastern silks and spices. Insurers or underwriters, as they are also called, agreed to compensate sailors and merchants who lost their cargoes and ships at sea, which encouraged trade.

How Insurance Works

1. Insurance companies create a pool of money from the premiums they collect from policyholders.

Premiums

Expenses

4. They have the usual expenses of running a business: wages and salaries, advertising, light, heat and so on.

INSURANCE PEOPLE
ACTUARY

The actuary is employed by the insurance company to determine the risk involved in something. Actuaries make extensive use of statistics to calculate risks and the premiums that should be charged.

INSURANCE BROKERS

If you require insurance you may go directly to an insurance company or to a broker. He or she is an agent for several insurance companies and will advise you on which policy will best suit your needs. A small commission, called brokerage, is charged for this service.

LOSS ADJUSTER

The loss adjuster is hired by the insurance company to determine if the amount of the claim is fair. The loss adjuster studies the claim and may inspect the damage. He or she then decides on a fair settlement.

ASSESSOR

The person making a claim may also hire a person to determine the amount of compensation. In this case the person is known as an assessor.

Compensation

Investments

Income

2. They use some of this money to pay compensation to policyholders who have suffered losses. They work on the basis that a tragedy will not happen to everybody.

3. Part of thè money is invested in property and shares. They get income from these investments and this is put back into the pool of money.

LESSON 2: RISKS

Insurance is concerned with risks, and most risks may be insured against. Examples of **insurable risks** are:

- insuring a house against fire or burglary.
- insuring your family while on holiday.
- insuring your car against accident.

Risks that inevitably will happen, such as death or retirement, are covered under life assurance policies. Other risks that may happen are covered under **general insurance**.

There are also **noninsurable risks**. For example, you can't insure against the risk of failing an exam as it would be very difficult to quantify the risk involved and therefore the premium can't be calculated. In general, risks of a gambling nature can't be insured against.

LIFE ASSURANCE

Life assurance covers death, retirement, school fees and investment schemes. It is concerned with risks that will occur. There are two types of policies offered.

- **Whole life assurance:** The earliest life assurance policies were taken out in the sixteenth century by sailors to provide ransom if they were captured by pirates. Nowadays these policies are taken out by people on their lives. On the death of the insured person a lump sum is paid to the person named on the policy, often a relative or close friend. A husband may insure the life of his wife and she may insure his life. Payment is made to the remaining spouse on the death of either.
- **Endowment assurance:** This is a type of savings scheme designed to give you a lump sum of money after a number of years. Most are taken out for ten years, and during that time the insured pays monthly contributions. The benefits are:
  - ➤ If the insured dies during this time, money is paid to a relative or close friend. Thus, it gives valuable life assurance cover.
  - ➤ Most schemes allow the insured to **encash** the policy. This means that the insured stops the policy and gets cash before the term is finished. The money received is the surrender value of the policy.
  - ➤ It is a useful way of saving and at the same time insuring your life.

CALCULATING LIFE ASSURANCE PREMIUMS

The price paid for insurance is called the **premium**. This will vary between companies and depends on the type of cover involved. In general, the greater the risk, the higher the premium.

In the case of life assurance there will definitely be a claim at some time, and the compensation is agreed when the policy is drawn up. Therefore, the premium is based on the sum agreed and the possible length of time between signing the policy and the death or retirement of the insured.

A €1 million policy on a person with a history of heart disease will cost more than a €100,000 policy on a young person certified to be fit. In calculating the premium you must also consider these special cases.

- **Loadings:** There is an increase in the premium charged – a loading – if the person has a dangerous occupation or engages in a risky sport, e.g. flying.
- **Discounts:** A discount is normally given if the person is a nonsmoker.

Question

A young lady is quoted a basic life assurance premium of €650. There is a loading of twenty per cent of the basic premium as she is an enthusiastic scuba diver. However, she gets a discount of ten per cent of the basic premium because she is a nonsmoker. Calculate her premium.

Solution

Basic premium	€650
Add loading for scuba diving	€130
	= €780
Less deduction for nonsmoker	€65
	= €715

HOUSE INSURANCE

Most householders insure their house and its contents. The house is the actual bricks and mortar of the building. The contents are the furniture, clothes, wallpaper, carpet and so on. The risks covered are fire, floor and burglary. Two special cases are worth mentioning.

- **All risks:** Certain valuables, such as jewellery, golf clubs or laptop computers, may be specified in the policy for a special cover called 'all risks'. These items are covered in the event of loss or accident and are even insured while they are outside the house.
- **Loadings:** There is a loading if the house is located in a risky area, e.g. somewhere prone to flooding.
- **Discounts:** There may be a discount if the house has an alarm.
- **Average:** If a house has a market value of €250,000 but is only insured for €125,000 then the insured can only claim €125,000 if the house is completely destroyed. In the case of partial damage the average clause takes effect. In our example on the next page the house is underinsured so the insured person will only get a fraction of the damages claimed. If, for example, the claim is for €800 then only €400 would be paid in compensation.

CALCULATING HOUSE INSURANCE PREMIUM

In the case of a house it isn't possible to predict whether an accident will occur at all. Similarly, it isn't possible to forecast the amount of the claim for compensation. Some of the factors an insurance company looks at to decide on a suitable premium for a house are location, type, alarm installation and age of building.

Question

A house is valued at €300,000 and the contents at €100,000. Insurance for the house costs €3 per €1,000 value and contents cost €5 per €1,000 value. The owners decide to get the contents insured for the full value but they only get the house insured for €200,000.

(a)   Calculate the total premium.

(b)   In the event of fire damage to the house of €30,000, how much compensation will be paid out?

Solution

(a)

$$\text{House} \quad \frac{€200,000}{€1,000} \quad X\ €3 \quad = €600$$

$$\text{Contents} \quad \frac{€100,000}{€1,000} \quad X\ €5 \quad = €500$$

(b)   The average clause applies because the house is underinsured.

$$\frac{€200,000}{€300,000} \quad X\ €30,000 \quad = €10,000$$

MOTOR INSURANCE

The first motor insurances were taken out in 1896 and originally were not compulsory. Today, however, motor insurance is compulsory. A few special cases are worth mentioning.

- **Third party, fire and theft:** This is the minimum insurance that a car must have. The policy doesn't cover the driver or any damage to his or her vehicle. It only covers damage to a third party, i.e. someone you crash into or injure in some way.

- **Fully comprehensive:** This policy covers third parties as well as the driver and his or her vehicle. Although this type of motor insurance is not compulsory and is more expensive, many vehicle owners prefer it.

- **No-claims bonus:** If the insured person doesn't make a claim during the year, the next premium paid will be reduced by a certain percentage. This is known as a no-claims bonus.

- **Loadings:** There is a loading if the driver is under twenty-five years of age, the car is over ten years old or if the driver lives in an urban area.

- **Discounts:** A nondrinker may be given a discount.

CALCULATING MOTOR INSURANCE PREMIUM

Just like with house insurance it isn't possible to predict whether an accident will occur or how compensation will be claimed. Some of the factors an insurance company looks at to decide on a suitable premium for a car are the driver's age, occupation, previous experience and type of vehicle.

Question

A family has two cars. The €14,000 car has third party, fire and theft insurance costing €40 per €1,000 insured. The €18,000 car has fully comprehensive insurance costing €60 per €1,000 insured.

(a)   Calculate the total premium for each car.

Solution

Car A $\dfrac{€14,000}{€1,000}$ X €40   = €560

Car B $\dfrac{€18,000}{€1,000}$ X €60   = €1,080

LESSON 3: DOCUMENTS

PROPOSAL FORM

You have heard of a marriage proposal – when you ask her the big question, she may or may not accept! It's a bit like this in insurance. To begin with you must first ask for insurance. You do this by filling in a proposal form. This is like an application letter where you must tell the truth and reveal all the facts. There is usually a delay of a few days while the insurance company decides whether to insure you or not.

In the meantime a temporary insurance, known as a cover note, may be issued. Two important principles of insurance are relevant when applying for insurance.

- **Utmost good faith:** All facts must be revealed. If some details are withheld then the insurance company may refuse to pay out a claim.
- **Insurable interest:** The insured must suffer a loss in the event of the item insured being damaged.

HIBERNIAN INSURANCE COMPANY LIMITED

HOMEPAK PROPOSAL

Name of proposer	*Seán and Sheila Murphy*
Occupation	*Journalist/secretary*
Address	*28 Carrickduff Road, Dublin 18*

Estimated value of house:	€70,000
Estimated value of contents:	€30,000
All risks cover on Jewellery:	€2,500
Computer:	€3,000

Have you any other insurance on the above property?	*No*
Have you made a claim in the last five years?	*No*

We declare that the above details are true.

Signature(s):　*Sheila Murphy*
　　　　　　　　Seán Murphy

HIBERNIAN INSURANCE COMPANY LIMITED

HOMEPAK POLICY

POLICY NUMBER: 10A005522
PERIOD OF INSURANCE
FROM 8 APRIL 2004 TO 7 APRIL 2005

INSURED	SEÁN AND SHEILA MURPHY
PROPERTY INSURED	28 Carrickduff Road
	Dublin 18

Estimated value of buildings:	€70,000
Estimated value of contents:	€30,000
All risks on Jewellery:	€2,500
Computer:	€3,000
Premium:	€240

POLICY

This is the contract between the insurance company and the insured. It gives details of the risks covered and any conditions attached to the policy. It is prepared by the insurance company.

HIBERNIAN INSURANCE COMPANY LIMITED

CLAIM FORM

Name of Insured	Seán and Sheila Murphy
Address	28 Carrickduff Road, Dublin 18
Policy Number	10A005522
Details of Loss	House burglary on 20 June 2004

Details of claim

Description	Date of purchase	Cost price	Wear and tear	Amount claimed
JBM computer	June 2002	€2,500		€2,500
Printer	June 2002	€500		€500
Desk lamp	May 2003	€30	€10	€20
				TOTAL: €3,020

We declare that the above details are true.

Signature(s):   Sheila Murphy
                 Seán Murphy

CLAIM FORM

In order to make a claim for compensation it's necessary to complete a claim form. You may be required to support this claim with estimates or quotations for the cost of repairing the damage or replacing the loss.

COMPENSATION

This is the money paid out by an insurance company as a result of a claim for damages or loss. The amount paid will depend on the damage caused. The insurance company will apply three insurance principles when a claim is made.

- **Contribution:** Suppose you have two insurance policies covering the same risk. In the event of a claim each company will only pay a portion towards the loss.
- **Indemnity:** When an accident occurs, the insured person is entitled to compensation. However, he or she cannot make a profit out of the loss.
- **Subrogation:** When an insurance company pays you compensation it can then take over your rights against the person causing the loss.

LESSON 1: PRACTICE

1.   Complete this e-mail that Tina sends to Michael.

From: Tina

To: Michael

Subject: My latest news

Hi Michael,

I'm thinking of starting my own driving school [1] b_____. I know I must get [2] i_____ so I have made out a list of [3] r_____ that I feel I must [4] c_____. The only problem is that I am sure the [5] p_____ will be very high. Anyway, I have to do it so that I can get [6] c_____ if there is an accident. I talked to an insurance [7] b_____ and he was able to suggest the type of [8] p_____ that would suit me.

Wish me luck!

Best wishes,

Tina

---

2.   Explain the role of the following in insurance:
    (a) broker.
    (b) underwriter.
    (c) actuary.
    (d) loss adjuster.

LESSON 2: PRACTICE

1. Imagine you're going on a school outing to Paris for five days. You will travel by coach to Rosslare, by boat to Le Havre and by train to Paris. You will stay three nights in Paris before returning.
(a) List fifteen risks that may occur while on such a holiday.
(b) What insurance is necessary to cover these risks?

2. You are going on a holiday to a sports centre that caters for every sport. You take out an insurance policy for €50,000 to cover sports accidents. The policy states that if you engage in certain sports the insurance company will not be liable for the full €50,000. For example, they will only pay seventy-five per cent of the sum insured for scuba diving, fifty per cent of the sum insured for skiing and for hang-gliding they will pay nothing at all, as they consider it too dangerous.
(a) How much will they pay if you are seriously injured while (i) scuba diving, (ii) skiing or (iii) hang-gliding?
(b) List ten other sports and estimate an insurance rating.

3. Refer to the graph.
(a) At what age is car insurance most expensive?
(b) When is car insurance cheapest?
(c) What premium is payable at twenty-five, thirty-five, forty-five, fifty-five and sixty-five years of age?
(d) Why does car insurance get more expensive as you get older?

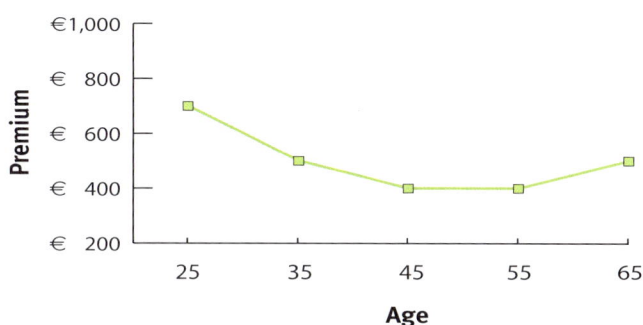

LESSON 3: PRACTICE

1. You take out insurance on your new house, valued at €260,000, and house contents, valued at €50,000. You also arrange all risks cover on new golf clubs, which cost €500, and jewellery, which cost €1,000. You have no other insurance on these and have made no previous insurance claims.
(a) Complete the proposal form in the Documents Books for the house insurance.
(b) Six months later there is a house fire. The jewellery and the golf clubs are destroyed and you make a claim for their full value. Furniture that cost €5,000 is also destroyed but you estimate there was €500 wear and tear. Complete the claim form in the Documents Book.

2. Give the meanings of the following principles of insurance:
(a) utmost good faith.
(b) contribution.
(c) indemnity.
(d) subrogation.
(e) insurable interest.

STATE EXAM PRACTICE

1.   The Hynes family wishes to insure their house for €100,000 and its contents for €20,000 (covering all risks). They receive quotations from three different insurance companies, which only offer those rates if buildings and contents are both insured with them.

	ABC Insurance Co.	DIY Insurance Co.	FAX Insurance Co.
Buildings	€2 per €1,000	€2.50 per €1,000	€3 per €1,000
Contents	€6.50 per €1,000	€5 per €1,000	€4 per €1,000

   (a) Which one of the three insurance companies' quotations would you advise the Hynes family to accept? Clearly show your workings.
   (b) When filling out the proposal form for insurance, the Hynes family must use utmost good faith. Explain what this means, giving one reason why it's important.
   (c) Name two risks that would usually be covered under the building's insurance.
   (d) Name three risks that would usually be covered under the contents' insurance.
   (JCHL, adapted)

2.   The Noonan family purchased their first house recently with the help of a building society mortgage. They paid €90,000 for their home and they have spent €15,000 on furniture and fittings. Tom and Mary are now wondering about insurance and ask for your advice. They want to know the following.
   (a) Are they required by law to insure the family property? (Give an explanation for your answer.)
   (b) Tom and Mary want you to calculate the total premium they would have to pay using the following information. It costs 20 cent for each €100 of buildings insured and 90 cent for each €100 of contents insured. (Show your workings.)
   (c) The Noonans think that the premium is very high, especially for the contents. They are now thinking of insuring the contents for just €10,000. They don't see the point in insuring the contents for the full value. Show what compensation they would get if they had the contents insured for just €10,000 and if, as a result of a small fire, €3,000 worth of contents were destroyed.
   (d) Tom and Mary are also considering taking out life assurance but they know very little about it. Briefly explain for them the following:
      (i)   the difference between insurance and assurance.
      (ii) the difference between a whole life assurance policy and an endowment policy.
   (JCHL, adapted)

3. (a) Explain the difference between insurable and noninsurable risks. (Give one example of each.)

(b) Before taking out insurance, a person must complete a proposal form. State three pieces of information that must be answered in the proposal form for house insurance.

(c) What do insurance companies mean by the term 'insurable interest'? Explain briefly.

(d) John and Mary O'Brien live in their own house, have a family car and are both employed in full-time jobs.

   (i)   What insurance cover, if any, are they required to have by law?

   (ii) State two other insurance/assurance policies that you would recommend to them.

(JCHL, adapted)

4. David Egan, 13 River Road, Athlone has his house and contents insured with Delta Insurance Co. Ltd for a premium of €200 per year.

On 24 April he received a letter from Delta Insurance Co. Ltd stating that his premium was being increased to €600 a year because he lives in an area that is often flooded.

The next day, 25 April, he wrote to the insurance company stating that he was upset and disappointed over this huge increase in his annual premium. He stated that although he lives near a river, his house is built on high ground and has never flooded. He would not mind paying a small increase but if Delta Ltd insisted on a premium of €600, he would have to transfer his business to another insurance company.

(a) Explain what a premium means.

(b) Name one type of insurance that is necessary by law for a person to take out.

(c) Assume you are David Egan. Write the letter that he wrote to Delta Insurance Co. Ltd on 25 April.

(JCOL, adapted)

5. (a) A female driver has fully comprehensive insurance on her car, which covers the contents being stolen. She also has her €3,000 computer covered under an all risks house insurance policy. She brings the computer in her car one day and it is stolen from the car.

   (i)   Can she claim €3,000 under each insurance policy?

   (ii) What is the maximum compensation she can receive?

   (iii) Which insurance company will compensate her?

(b) Under the average clause, how much compensation is likely to be paid out in the following cases?

   (i)   A motorbike is crashed and completely destroyed. It was insured for €1,800, but the insurance company estimates that its true value before the accident was €2,600.

   (ii) A house fire ruins a carpet valued at €750. The house contents were insured for €3,000. However, the insurance company estimates that the true value of the contents before the fire was €6,000.

   (iii) A car insured for €5,000 is stolen and €1,600 worth of damage is caused by the thieves. The insurance company claims that the car was underinsured and that its true value before the robbery was €8,000.

(c) Calculate the premium payable on each of these properties.

   (i)   A semidetached house valued at €350,000, rate of premium fifty cent per €1,000 insured.

   (ii)   A bungalow valued at €460,000, rate of premium forty cent per €1,000 insured.

   (iii) A terraced house valued at €230,000, rate of premium thirty cent per €1,000 insured.

   (iv) A detached house valued at €500,000, rate of premium forty cent per €1,000 insured.

   (v)   An apartment valued at €190,000, rate of premium thirty cent per €1,000 insured.

(d) (i)   A family car is valued at €14,500. The rate of premium is forty cent per €1,000. Calculate the premium payable if there is a forty per cent no-claims bonus allowed.

   (ii)   A nineteen-year-old is quoted a basic premium of €900 for car insurance, to which must be added €400 for underage loading. If a fifteen per cent beginner's discount is allowed, what premium is payable?

(JCHL, adapted)

TEST YOURSELF AT
my-etest.com

10 What is Economics?

TERMS COVERED IN THIS CHAPTER
Scarcity, choice, resources, economising, inflation, CPI, factors of production, entrepreneur, economic growth, GNP, enterprise.

INTRODUCTION

What do you think? Work with another pupil on this task.
You are going on a camping holiday for two nights in the mountains with the pupil beside you. You will not be near any shops, houses or other people for the two nights and three days. You and your friend each have a rucksack. List the items of food, clothing and shelter you will take and anything else you feel you will need.
1. How did you choose what to bring?
2. What items will you have with you that could become scarce?

LESSON 1: SCARCITY AND CHOICE

Economics looks at wealth – what it is and what causes it. By using the country's economic resources we are able to create wealth, but because these resources are scarce we have to make choices to determine how to use them.

SCARCITY

In economic terms, everything is scarce. This may seem reasonable when you look at underdeveloped countries but in Ireland the supermarkets and stores are packed with goods. So how can everything be scarce? Economic resources are said to be scarce because almost everyone, everywhere wants more and better goods and services. Scarcity exists because the economic resources available to satisfy people's wants are limited.

CHOICE

Ireland is a small country, accounting for about one per cent of the EU population and 0.07 per cent of the world population. It has an abundance of human and material resources and yet it still has to make choices in the way it uses these resources. For example, if the government decides to pour money into new roads, then less money will be available for housing, health and education. The process of making choices is known as **economising**. Economising ensures you make the best use of the resources available to you.

INFLATION

Inflation means rising prices. Rising wages sometimes follow rising prices but people aren't really any better off as the wages only go to buy goods which now cost more. Inflation makes it difficult for a family to budget because it's hard to guess what the prices of some goods will be. Inflation is also bad for savers since the money saved isn't worth as much. An inflation rate of ten per cent a year means that something which cost €200 last year will now cost €220.

The official measure of inflation in Ireland is called the **Consumer Price Index (CPI)**. The CPI gets the price of a basket of goods and services each month. These prices are then compared with the price of the same goods and services from the previous month. The change in prices is then combined to give a single index measuring the overall level of prices.

The main reason for inflation in Ireland is increases in wages, which pushes up prices. However, high inflation in Ireland has both positive and negative effects.

- People who borrow money from banks benefit because the real rate of interest is reduced as prices rise.
- Irish exporters suffer because their goods become less competitive as prices rise.
- People who keep their savings in cash suffer as the purchasing power of cash is reduced and as prices rise their money buys less.

	1986	2003
Average cost of buying a house	€47,000	€250,000
Daily newspaper	57c	€1.45

LESSON 2: FACTORS OF PRODUCTION

There are four factors of production. The purpose of our society is to decide how to use these in order to get the highest standard of living for the largest number of people.

LAND

Ireland has many natural resources, such as land, forests, rivers and the sea. From these we are able to get meat, cereals, wood, fish and other materials that can be used directly or processed in factories. People with land are paid **rent** for the use of the land.

LABOUR

These are the people available to do the work on the land, in factories and in other businesses. They are paid **wages** for the work they do.

CAPITAL

This is the money needed to run a business. This money is used to build factories and get the equipment needed to produce new products from raw materials. The money comes from people's savings and they are given **interest** for the use of their money.

ENTERPRISE

All resources need someone with a business idea and the courage to take a risk and start a business. This person is called an entrepreneur (a risk taker), and he or she gets **profit** as a reward for the risk involved in running a business.

ECONOMIC GROWTH

Economic growth occurs when during one year more goods and services are produced than in the previous year. For example, if a factory worker makes four chairs in one week and five in the next week, then his productivity has increased by twenty-five per cent. In other words, he is producing more in the same time by making better use of the resources available to him.

The official measure of economic growth in a country is called the **gross national product** (GNP). The economic consequences resulting from growth in the economy are:
- a rise in standard of living.
- a rise in the number of people employed.

Low Interest Rates
The advantages of low interest rates are:
- cheaper loans.
- more people are willing to invest in businesses.

The disadvantages are:
- there is no incentive to save.
- people may borrow more than they need and if interest rates rise again they may not be able to afford the repayments.

LESSON 1: PRACTICE

1.   Find the words in the list
in the word search.

scarcity	prices
inflation	needs
choices	wants
resources	CPI
economy	increase

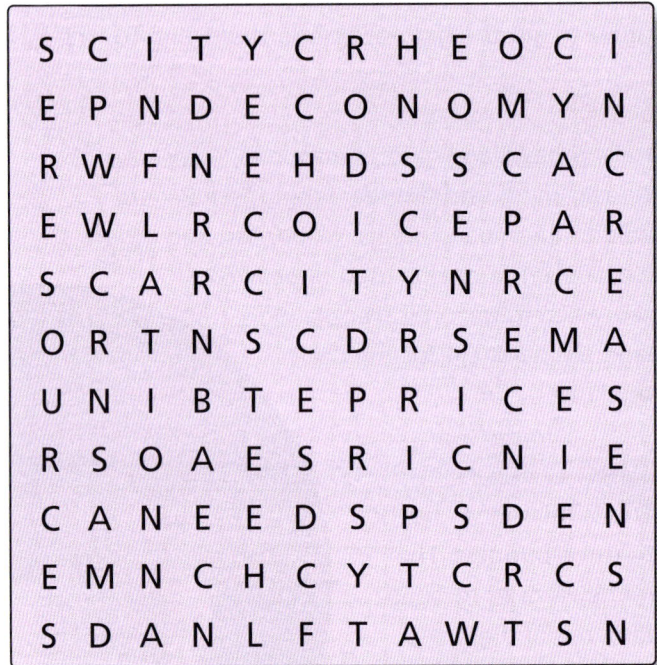

```
S C I T Y C R H E O C I
E P N D E C O N O M Y N
R W F N E H D S S C A C
E W L R C O I C E P A R
S C A R C I T Y N R C E
O R T N S C D R S E M A
U N I B T E P R I C E S
R S O A E S R I C N I E
C A N E E D S P S D E N
E M N C H C Y T C R C S
S D A N L F T A W T S N
```

2.   Here are some definitions of economics.

It is the study of the way people _____.

It looks at the nature and _____ of wealth.

It is the process by which _____ is produced and _____.

It is the study of the way people go about their _____ lives.

daily
distributed
wealth
causes
behave

(a) Rewrite and complete the above definitions using the words from the list.

(b) Compare these definitions with your own understanding of economics. Write down what you think economics is.

(c) State the reasons why everything is considered scarce.

(d) Give two examples of how a country makes a choice in the way it uses its resources.

3.

gold	scientists
bank deposits	tobacco
fertile land	cocoa
coffee	shipbuilding
rubber	wood
space shuttles	live animals
natural gas	wool
nuclear	fish

(a) Pick out Ireland's economic resources from the list of world resources on the left.

(b) List five other Irish resources not on your list.

(c) List five other non-Irish resources not listed here.

LESSON 2: PRACTICE

1. Match each factor of production with its relevant price.

land	profit
labour	wages
capital	interest
enterprise	rent

2. Andy's teacher asks him to summarise this chapter for his homework. Complete his homework using words from the list.

economy
consumers
negative
labour
enterprise
rates
inflation
land
services
business

An [1]_____ is a system which provides goods and [2]_____ for [3]_____. The performance of the economy has a positive or [4]_____ effect on [5]_____. Since an economy is dependent on land, [6]_____ , capital and [7]_____ , many things can affect its performance, such as unemployment, interest [8]_____ and [9]_____. The outbreak of foot and mouth disease in Ireland could have had disastrous consequences for our economy, which is heavily dependent on [10]_____.

3. (a) Name five of Ireland's economic resources.

(b) Why are all economic resources scarce?

(c) Explain how a country must make choices in the way it uses its resources.

4. (a) What is meant by 'inflation'?

(b) What is the price of these goods now?

Price last year	Annual inflation rate
€120	10%
€80	5%
€500	3%

(c) What is the inflation rate in each of these instances?

Price last year	Price this year
€100	€115
€50	€53
€20	€30

(d) What is the effect of inflation on (i) wages and (ii) savings?

5. (a) What causes economic growth?

(b) What is the effect of economic growth on the economy?

(c) If a carpenter makes fifty tables a month, what will the output be if she increases productivity by (i) five per cent (ii) ten per cent (iii) fifteen per cent (iv) twenty per cent and (v) twenty-five per cent?

STATE EXAM PRACTICE

1. (a) The bar graph below refers to the inflation rate of a country called SOMBIA.

Bar Graph of Inflation Rates (1989–1993)

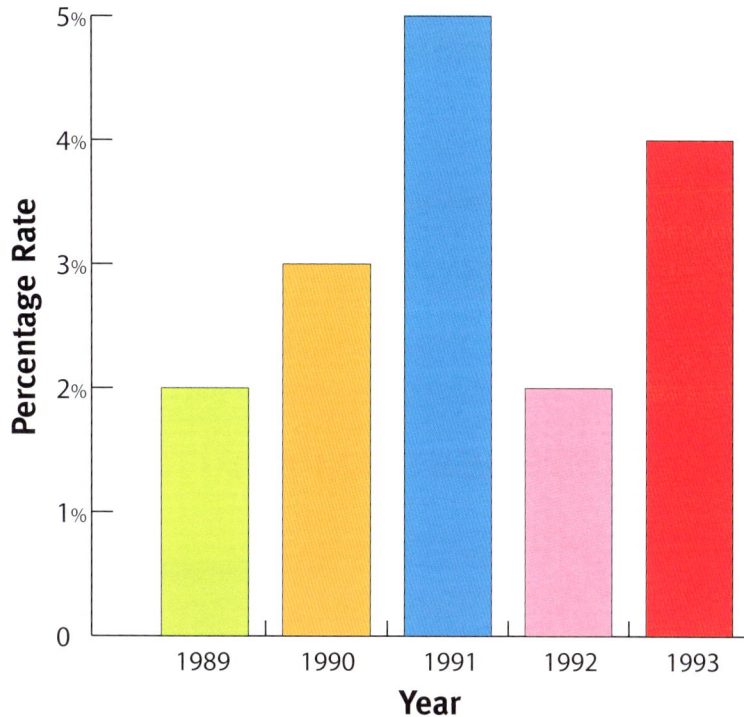

(i) Explain what is meant by the term 'inflation'.

(ii) Calculate the average rate of inflation for the five years shown in the graph.

(iii) What change occurred in the rate of inflation in 1992 compared to 1991?

(iv) Give one economic benefit to Ireland of having its inflation rate lower than that of its main trading competitors.

(b) (i) What is the official measure of inflation called?

(ii) Give one cause of inflation.

(iii) The present rate of inflation in Ireland is nearest to which one of the following figures?

(1) Two per cent

(2) Ten per cent

(3) Eighteen per cent

(4) Twenty-seven per cent

(c) Explain briefly how high inflation in Ireland would affect the following:

(i) people who have borrowed money from banks.

(ii) Irish manufacturers exporting their produce.

(iii) people who keep their savings in cash.

(d) A family's weekly grocery bill costs €111 in January 2003. If the inflation rate for the year was eleven per cent, what would the same groceries have cost in January 2004?

(JCHL, adapted)

11 The National Budget

TERMS COVERED IN THIS CHAPTER
Privatisation, customs duty, excise duty, nontax revenue.

INTRODUCTION

The government spends billions of euro each year on our towns and cities. They also allocate money to local authorities, county councils and health boards that then provide services such as refuse collection, fire service, ambulance service, library service and much more. On your way to school every morning you see many examples of government spending on roads, buses, parks and even street lighting. Describe your journey to school and list examples of the government spending you pass on the way.

LESSON 1: TYPES OF GOVERNMENT EXPENDITURE AND INCOME

The national budget is a forecast of government income and expenditure for the next calendar year (1 January to 31 December). It is prepared by the Department of Finance and is used to control what will happen to the economy in those months.

Budget Day is usually in December each year. For weeks before this the various government departments send in their estimates of expenditure to the Minister for Finance. In general the spending by the departments will either take the form of capital expenditure or current expenditure.

CAPITAL EXPENDITURE

This is the money the government plans to spend on long-term investments, such as:
- development of harbours and airports.
- farm improvement schemes.
- improving tourism facilities.
- roads, transport, refuse collection.
- electricity power stations, hospitals, school buildings.

CURRENT EXPENDITURE

This is money they plan to spend on day-to-day items, for example the wages of medical staff, soldiers and Gardai. This also includes social welfare expenditure, which is by far the biggest item in the budget. Building a new school is capital expenditure but paying the teachers' salaries is current expenditure.

The total of the capital and current expenditure usually comes to millions of euro. The Department of Finance must get money to pay for this level of expenditure. They do this in two ways. They use capital income to pay for capital expenditure and current income to pay for current expenditure.

CAPITAL INCOME

This is also known as **nontax revenue**, which takes the form of money the state gets from the sale of state companies (**privatisation**) or borrowing from banks and from the EU. This money is used on long-term capital expenditure projects such as new roads, schools and hospitals. The state also gets nontax revenue from the National Lottery and from state company profits.

CURRENT INCOME

The main source of current income for the government is tax. You pay tax when you buy clothes or a bar of chocolate (VAT), buy a banana (**customs duty**) or smoke a cigarette (**excise duty**). You also pay tax on your savings (DIRT). The current income is then used to pay for the current expenditure during the year, such as old-age pensions, teachers' salaries, nurses' salaries, unemployment benefit, Gardai salaries and children's allowance.

Privatisation

Privatisation is the sale of a state company to the public. In June 1999 the government received €3.8 billion from the sale of Telecom Éireann (now called Eircom). In 1991 the government received €483 million from the privatisation of Irish Life and the Irish Sugar Company (now called Greencore).

The advantages of privatisation are:

- more competition is introduced into the service, which can increase efficiency and reduce prices for the consumer.
- the government receives money from the sale of the state company.

The disadvantages of privatisation are:

- the privatised company often reduces the number of employees in order to be more efficient and maximise profits.
- the privatised company may not provide a service into an unprofitable area, e.g. if the postal service was privatised the new company may not deliver into remote areas.

LESSON 2: PREPARING A NATIONAL BUDGET

The national budget lists the expenditure and the income for the coming year. The difference between the total income and total expenditure is either a deficit or a surplus.

DEFICIT

When expenditure is greater than income there is a deficit. A government needs to borrow money in order to finance a budget deficit. This is called the **national debt**.

SURPLUS

When the income is greater than the expenditure there is a surplus. This money could be:

- invested.
- used to pay off loans.
- used the following year and thus taxes could be reduced in that year.

Effects on the National Budget

Different events will have different effects on the national budget. Consider the following.

What will be the effect on the national budget of more children being born in Ireland?

- There will be more expenditure on children's allowance.
- There will be more expenditure on maternity benefit.

What will be the effect on the national budget of an increase in employment in Ireland?

- There will be less expenditure on social welfare.
- There will be more tax revenue from income tax.

Question

(a) Draft a national budget from the following information.

- Income: VAT €2,000 million; customs and excise €1,500 million; income tax €3,000 million; corporation tax €400 million; other income €80 million.
- Expenditure: Education €1,200 million; health €1,500 million; security €700 million; social welfare €2,500 million; agriculture €300 million; debt service €2,000 million; other expenditure €50 million.

(b) What is (i) the amount of the difference between the income and the expenditure and (ii) what is the economic term used to describe this difference?

Solution

(a)

Current Expenditure	
	€ million
Education	1,200
Health	1,500
Security	700
Social welfare	2,500
Agriculture	300
Debt service	2,000
Other	50
Total Expenditure	**8,250**
Current Income	
	€ million
VAT	2,000
Customs and excise	1,500
Income tax	3,000
Corporation tax	400
Other	80
Total Income	**6,980**

(b) (i) €1,270 million.

(ii) Deficit. The expenditure is greater than the income so there is a deficit. The government needs to borrow €1,270 million to finance this deficit. About half of this will be borrowed in Ireland and the rest abroad.

LESSON I: PRACTICE

I.   Complete the word grid with the information described below.

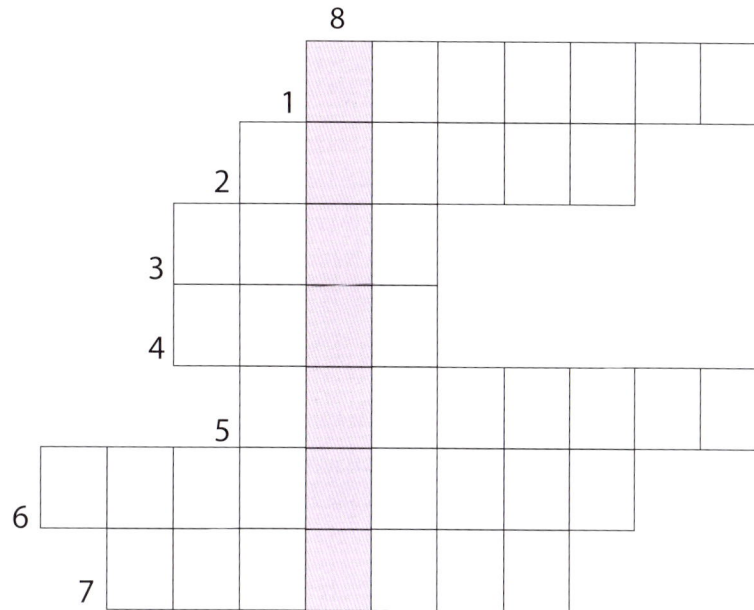

1. A new school is an example of _____ expenditure.
2. The national _____ is prepared every year.
3. Capital income is spent on long-_____ projects.
4. You pay _____ tax on your savings.
5. Budget Day is usually in _____ each year.
6. The Irish Sugar Company is now called _____.
7. Many goods imported into Ireland are charged _____ duty.
8. Paying teachers' salaries is _____ expenditure.

FAX

To: Roinn An Taoisigh
From: An Roinn Airgeadais
RE: Budget Day

Taoiseach, a Chara

I have received all the estimates from the various departments and interested bodies. In advance of Budget Day I would like to inform you that some difficult decisions will have to be made in regard to government spending over the coming year. I would like to put forward the following proposals.

1. Most grants for new school buildings and repairs will have to be cancelled for this year.
2. I propose to increase the pension age from sixty-five to seventy years of age.
3. Present work on monuments and parks will cease as and from April.
4. I propose to increase the excise duty on cigarettes by eighty cent and on alcohol by sixty cent.
5. I propose to put a forty cent tax on chewing gum. This should reduce the demand for chewing gum and help make our streets cleaner.
6. We could also consider selling off Aer Lingus.

I look forward to your support in these proposals on Budget Day.

Mise le Meas
Minister for Finance

2. Study the above fax from the Minister for Finance to the Taoiseach and answer these questions.
(a) What capital expenditure does the minister wish to cancel?
(b) Are repairs to school buildings an example of capital or current expenditure?
(c) What effect will increasing the pension age have on the budget?
(d) What effect will a forty cent tax on chewing gum have?
(e) Which state company does the minister wish to privatise?
(f) Which expressions in the fax mean the following?
   (i)   The time you can retire. _____
   (ii) The tax on tobacco. _____
   (iii) Privatising. _____
   (iv) Nonrepayable source of money. _____
   (v)   Lower the number buying. _____

3.   Tick the correct circle to show whether these are examples of capital or current expenditure.

	Capital Expenditure	Current Expenditure
(a) Paying nurses salaries.	◯	◯
(b) Social welfare payments.	◯	◯
(c) Development of new airport terminal.	◯	◯
(d) Purchase of new army rifles.	◯	◯
(e) Purchase of bullets for army rifles.	◯	◯
(f) Building a new tunnel under the River Lee.	◯	◯
(g) Building extension to community school.	◯	◯
(h) Paying teachers, salaries.	◯	◯
(i) Construction of new tourist interpretative centre.	◯	◯
(j) Construction of new prison.	◯	◯

LESSON 2: PRACTICE

1.   What will be the effect on the national budget of the following situations? Tick the correct box.

	More expenditure on pensions	Less expenditure on pensions	More expenditure on education	Less expenditure on education
(a) Government decides to reduce the number of students in each class.				
(b) Government decides to shorten the school day.				
(c) Government decides that children should not be allowed to begin school until they are seven years of age.				
(d) New medical advances cause people to live longer.				
(e) New unknown disease kills thousands of people over sixty years of age.				
(f) Government decides to allow people to retire at fifty-five rather than sixty-five.				

2. For each of the following questions (i) draft a simple budget to show the sources of income and expenditure and (ii) estimate and identify whether there is a deficit or a surplus.

(a) INCOME: Income tax €2,500 million; VAT €1,600 million; customs and excise €1,483 million.

EXPENDITURE: Security €700 million; social welfare €2,498 million; education €1,015 million; health €2,100 million; agriculture €400 million; interest payments €1,990 million.

(b) INCOME: Corporation tax €1,527 million; customs and excise €897 million; income tax €2,950 million; VAT €2,310 million.

EXPENDITURE: Health €2,300 million; security €600 million; education €980 million; interest payments €1,670 million; social welfare €2,127 million.

(c) INCOME: EU receipts €70 million; corporation tax €245 million; customs and excise €1,254 million; income tax €3,500 million; VAT €2,780 million.

EXPENDITURE: Health €2,090 million; defence €236 million; Gardai €265 million; primary education €402 million; postprimary education €426 million; interest payments €1,173 million; social welfare €2,186 million; agriculture €168 million; fishing €120 million; roads €124 million; housing grants €215 million.

(d) INCOME: Income tax €3,400 million; customs and excise €2,100 million; capital tax €200 million; EU receipts €1,500 million; corporation tax €400 million; VAT €2,300 million; other receipts €1,200 million.

EXPENDITURE: Security €700 million; agriculture €300 million; social welfare €2,900 million; health €1,500 million; debt service €2,500 million; education €1,200 million; miscellaneous €2,100 million.

(e) INCOME: Income tax €3,200 million; EU and other receipts €2,100 million; VAT €2,100 million; customs and excise €1,900 million; corporation tax €500 million; capital tax €100 million; other receipts €1,000 million.

EXPENDITURE: Security €800 million; social welfare €3,000 million; education €1,368 million; health €1,400 million; agriculture €400 million; debt service €2,432 million; miscellaneous €2,000 million.

3. (a) What is the national budget?
(b) Who prepares the national budget?
(c) What is the difference between capital and current expenditure?

4. (a) Where does the government spend its money?
(b) What are the government's sources of income?
(c) What is a budget deficit and what effects does it have on the economy?

5. (a) What is the national debt?
(b) Where does the government borrow money?
(c) What is the cost to the country of government borrowing?
(d) How does the country benefit by government borrowing?

6. (a) What are the various types of tax operated by the government?
    (b) Name a government department responsible for collecting tax.

7. (a) Some workers often criticise the PAYE system. Why might they think it is unfair?
    (b) Can you identify any new areas where the government could earn extra income by charging tax?
    (c) Sometimes the government cuts back on spending when it is short of money. Can you name some services in your area that have been reduced or abolished by government cutbacks?

STATE EXAM PRACTICE

1. (a) The Central Bank revealed the following figures for interest rates for the years 1994–1998. Show this information in a graph (bar or trend).

Year	1994	1995	1996	1997	1998
Rate of Interest	13%	10%	15%	9%	8%

    (b) (i)   Name two benefits of low interest rates to the economy/general public.
        (ii) If a record-breaking number of new cars were sold this year, state the economic effect it would have on the national budget and balance of payments.

2. (a) (i)   Which government department prepares the national budget?
        (ii) In what month is the Irish national budget presented in the Dáil?
        (iii) Did the national budget for the last three years plan for a surplus or deficit in current account?
    (b) List two options open to the government when they have a budget surplus in current account other than increasing current expenditure.
    (c) The government receives income from sources other than from taxation, which is known as nontax revenue/income.
        (i)   Give two examples of nontax revenue/income.
        (ii) What is meant by the term 'privatisation'?
        (iii) Name a state company that was privatised in recent years.
    (d) Ireland has achieved very high levels of economic growth in the past ten years.
        (i)   What is meant by the term 'economic growth'?
        (ii) What is the official measure of economic growth called?
        (iii) Name two economic consequences resulting from this growth in the economy.

3. The following figures were produced by a Minister for Finance on Budget Day as projections for the year 2002.

Main Items of Revenue and Expenditure	Estimated Figures in Millions (IR€)
Health and social welfare	275
PAYE	338
Education and science	166
Customs duty	18
DIRT	73
Excise duty	129
Defence	49
VAT	144
Debt servicing	198
Agriculture	76
Corporation tax	57

(a) From the above information, draft the national budget for 2002. Is this budget a surplus or deficit budget?

(b) Give one example of capital expenditure by:
   (i)   the Department of Health and Children.
   (ii) the Department of Education and Science.

(c) The Minister for Finance stated in the budget speech that all government departments would have to keep within their budget limits because of *scarce resources.* He said that there was an *opportunity cost* involved in every item of expenditure and in pursuing any particular project.

   Explain what the minister meant by each of the italicised terms above.

(d) Suggest two effects each of the following would have on a national budget:
   (i)   an increase in the birth rate
   (ii) a decrease in the unemployment rate.

12 Trade

TERMS COVERED IN THIS CHAPTER
Visible/invisible trade, balance of trade, balance of payments.

INTRODUCTION

When you were young you probably collected football cards and stickers. If your friend had one you wanted you were able to trade with your friend. Countries also trade. They trade goods and services in exchange for money. This is called importing and exporting.

Work with another pupil on these tasks.
1. List ten products made in Ireland.
2. List ten products imported into Ireland.
3. Name the countries of the EU.

LESSON 1: IMPORTS AND EXPORTS

Goods purchased from other countries and brought into Ireland are called **imports**. On the other hand, goods sold to foreign countries are **exports**. This exchange of goods is known as foreign trade. By trading with other countries Ireland is able to get additional consumer goods, raw materials and producer goods. This gives consumers extra choice in what they buy.

CONSUMER GOODS

About twenty-five per cent of imports are consumer goods, such as food, electrical goods and cars. Many of these goods are not made in Ireland and so these imports improve Irish people's standard of living.

RAW MATERIALS

Most of the goods we import are raw materials used in the manufacture of other products. For example, oil is imported from the Middle East and used in the production of plastics, paper is imported from Norway and used in the production of books and oranges are imported from Spain and used to produce marmalade. These raw materials have to be imported because they are not produced in Ireland. Cheaper manufacturing costs in foreign countries have led to increased competition from abroad. As a result some products that could be made in Ireland are now imported, e.g. shoes and clothes. These goods can be imported into Ireland and sold at cheaper prices. As a result many Irish shoe and clothing firms have been put out of business.

PRODUCER GOODS

These are used to make other products. For example, Cadbury Ireland imports chocolate-making machinery from the UK. These machines are then used to make sweets for the Irish and export markets. Cadbury cannot buy the equipment in Ireland because it is not made here.

Many other companies are in the same position, and so producer goods are an important import for Ireland.

EXPORTS

Exports help Ireland earn foreign currency. Most of our exports are industrial products such as clothes, computers and chemicals. We also export plenty of agricultural, forestry and fishing produce. These exports are essential so that we can pay for the goods we wish to import.

Our exports fall into three main areas:
- industrial produce, e.g. computers, clothes, medical equipment.
- agricultural produce, e.g. fruit, vegetables and dairy produce.
- forestry and fishing produce, e.g. salmon, oysters, wood.

BALANCE OF TRADE

The difference between visible imports and exports is called the **balance of trade**. This difference is either a surplus (exports are greater than imports) or a deficit (imports are greater than exports).

Visible and Invisible Trade

The import and export of goods such as cars, food and computers is called visible trade. Ireland usually exports more visible goods than she imports. On the other hand, invisible trade deals with the import and export of services, e.g. tourism, banking, insurance and transport. Ireland usually has more invisible imports than exports.

BALANCE OF PAYMENTS

When invisible trade is added to the balance of trade we get the **balance of payments**. If there is a deficit in the balance of payments then we must pay for it by borrowing foreign currency. When it is a surplus we can increase our foreign currency reserves or invest more money abroad.

Visible Trade	€ million	€ million
Exports	45,000	
Less Imports	30,000	
Balance of Trade (Surplus)		**15,000**
Invisible Trade		
Exports	13,000	
Less Imports	25,000	
Invisible Balance (Deficit)		**(12,000)**
Balance of Payments (Surplus)		**3,000**

LESSON 2: OUR TRADING PARTNERS

Ireland trades with over a hundred countries around the world. However, the bulk of our trade is with European Union (EU) countries, the United States and Japan. The chart below lists the principal countries to which we buy and sell.

Principal Source of Irish Imports (2002)	
	€ billion
Britain	19
United States	9
Germany	4
France	2
Japan	2

Principal Destination for Irish Exports (2002)	
	€ billion
Britain	21
United States	17
Belgium	14
Germany	7
France	5

THE EUROPEAN UNION (EU)

The EU is a market of 430 million consumers in twenty-five countries. There are no barriers to trade between the member states. Most of the members now use the euro currency and citizens in the member countries may move to and work in any EU state. With all this talk of business it's easy to forget that the real reason for the EU is to promote peace within Europe. Here are some of the main benefits to Ireland of EU membership.

- Ireland has received much grant aid from the EU to assist farmers and industry and to improve roads.
- We have also benefited by access to a wider market for Irish goods.
- Since Ireland joined the EU in 1973, hundreds of overseas companies have set up here. Today, more than 80,000 people are employed in over 850 of these foreign firms. Almost all of the production from these companies is exported and it goes mostly to other EU countries.

Initially, the EU consisted of just six countries: Belgium, Germany, France, Italy, Luxembourg and the Netherlands. Denmark, Ireland and the United Kingdom joined in 1973, Greece in 1981, Spain and Portugal in 1986 and Austria, Finland and Sweden in 1995. In 2004 the biggest-ever enlargement took place with ten new countries joining: Cyprus, the Czech Republic, Estonia, Hungry, Latvia, Lithuania, Malta, Poland, Slovakia and Slovenia.

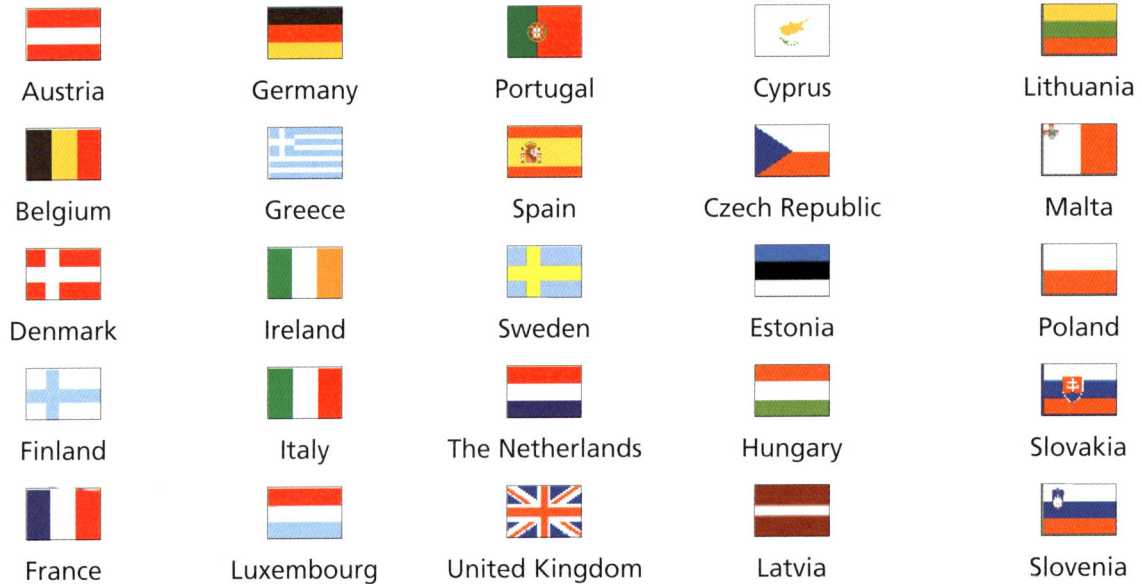

Austria	Germany	Portugal	Cyprus	Lithuania
Belgium	Greece	Spain	Czech Republic	Malta
Denmark	Ireland	Sweden	Estonia	Poland
Finland	Italy	The Netherlands	Hungary	Slovakia
France	Luxembourg	United Kingdom	Latvia	Slovenia

FOREIGN EXCHANGE

Foreign currency may be bought and sold at a bureau de change. Many banks, building societies and department stores offer this service. These institutions have two rates: the 'sell at' rate and the 'buy at' rate.

Bureau de Change

COUNTRY	CURRENCY	BANK SELLS	BANK BUYS
Britain	Pound (£)	0.68	0.72
Norway	Krone (Kr)	7.27	7.70
USA	Dollar ($)	1.11	1.16
Japan	Yen (¥)	132	141

When you are converting from the euro then the bank is selling you a foreign currency. In this case use the bank sells rate. When you have foreign currency that you wish to change into euro, use the bank buys rate.

Converting from euro – multiply by the bank sells rate

Question
Convert €200 to pounds sterling.

Solution
€200 x 0.68 = £136

Converting to euro – divide by the bank buys rate

Question
Convert $150 to euro.

Solution
$150 ÷ 1.16 = €129.31

The euro currency can be used in Austria, Belgium, Finland, France, Germany, Ireland, Italy, Luxembourg, Portugal, Spain and the Netherlands.

LESSON I: PRACTICE

I.   Complete these sentences using words from the list. (One of the words does not fit any sentence.)

choice	trades
industrial produce	currency
import	raw materials

Paper, oil and wood are examples of ¹_____ that we import. Our major exports are ²_____ from factories. Exporting earns us the foreign ³_____ that we need to pay for imports. Ireland ⁴_____ with over a hundred countries. Foreign trade gives Irish people a greater ⁵_____ in what we buy.

2.   The sentences below describe the objects in the table. Complete the table as in the example.

Television	Oil	Chocolate-Making Machinery	Dell Computer
i			
c			

(a) It's a consumer good exported from Ireland.

(b) It's used in the production of plastics.

(c) It's sold in electrical shops.

(d) It's a producer good.

(e) It's imported from Saudi Arabia.

(f) It's imported from an EU country.

(g) It's a consumer good imported into Ireland.

(h) It's a visible export from Ireland to Europe.

(i) It's imported from Japan.

(j) It's a raw material.

(k) It's manufactured in Ireland.

(l) It's used by Cadbury Ireland Ltd.

3.   Tick the category to which each good or service belongs.

		Visible Import	Visible Export	Invisible Import	Invisible Export
(a)	Irish horses winning prize money in England.	○	○	○	○
(b)	Italian shoes bought in Ireland.	○	○	○	○
(c)	Irish people holidaying in Spain.	○	○	○	○
(d)	American people hiring Irish aircraft.	○	○	○	○
(e)	Dell computer sold to a French customer.	○	○	○	○
(f)	Irish family buys subscription to Sky Sports channel.	○	○	○	○
(g)	Aer Lingus ticket bought by a German tourist.	○	○	○	○
(h)	Spanish oranges bought in Ireland.	○	○	○	○
(i)	Dutch family rents a holiday cottage in Ireland for two weeks.	○	○	○	○
(j)	Japanese cars bought in Ireland.	○	○	○	○

4.   Study the following statistics.

(a) Estimate the value of the missing figures (a) to (e).

(b) Draw a bar chart to represent the trade surplus column.

Year	Visible Imports € million	Visible Exports € million	Trade Surplus € million
1990	16	18	2
1991	(a)	19	3
1992	17	21	4
1993	19	(b)	6
1994	21	28	7
1995	26	35	9
1996	28	38	(c)
1997	32	44	12
1998	39	56	17
1999	44	(d)	22
2000	56	83	27
2001	57	92	35
2002	(e)	93	38

5. In relation to the statistics in the previous question, choose one of the following answers in each case.

(a) What is this data about?
  (i)   Internal trade.
  (ii)   Balance of payments.
  (iii) Balance of trade.

(b) How is the trade surplus column calculated?
  (i)   Add imports and exports.
  (ii)   Subtract imports and exports.
  (iii) Multiply imports and exports.

(c) What is the trend of this data?
  (i)   The balance is the same each year.
  (ii)   The balance is dropping each year.
  (iii) The balance is rising each year.

(d) What would be a good title for this chart?
  (i)   Balance of Payments.
  (ii)   Balance of Trade.
  (iii) Invisible Trade.

6. (a) From the following details prepare a balance of trade and indicate if there is a surplus or a deficit.
  (i)   Visible imports €16,000 million, visible exports €19,000 million.
  (ii)   Visible imports €12,000 million, visible exports €15,000 million.
  (iii) Visible imports €13,000 million, visible exports €11,000 million.

(b) From the following details prepare a balance of trade and a balance of payments and indicate if there is a surplus or a deficit.
  (i)   Visible imports €15,000 million, visible exports €17,000 million, invisible imports €6,000 million, invisible exports €9,000 million.
  (ii)   Visible imports €9,000 million, visible exports €12,000 million, invisible imports €5,000 million, invisible exports €4,000 million.
  (iii) Visible imports €14,000 million, visible exports €15,000 million, invisible imports €5,000 million, invisible exports €2,000 million.

7. Cadbury's Time Out bar is totally Irish made. It is manufactured at the Cadbury factory in Coolock, Dublin where an additional 220 jobs were created to meet the demand for the product. The main export market for Time Out is the UK.

(a) Why do 220 people consider Time Out an important Irish product?

(b) Is Time Out a visible or invisible export? Give one reason for your answer.

(c) Although they are not mentioned above, can you name two of the Irish raw materials used in the production of Time Out?

(d) What would be the effect on the Irish balance of trade if Cadbury decided to import these raw materials?

8. Fiacla toothpaste has been around for over fifteen years and is the only toothpaste made in Ireland. It is manufactured in Bray, Co. Wicklow, where thirty-five people are employed. One in ten tubes of toothpaste sold in Ireland is a Fiacla toothpaste. However, the Bray factory also exports toothpaste to the UK, Poland, Spain, France, Hong Kong and the Middle East.

    (a) Name the EU countries where Fiacla toothpaste is sold.

    (b) What is the language and currency of each of the countries you have listed in (a)?

    (c) Fiacla sells seventy per cent of their production abroad. Is this an invisible export, invisible import, visible export or visible import?

    (d) Name an imported toothpaste that Fiacla competes with.

    (e) How is Fiacla toothpaste an example of import substitution?

LESSON 2: PRACTICE

1. Chivers & Sons has been manufacturing jam in Ireland since 1935 and they now employ 120 staff. One of their most successful products is marmalade, which is made from the finest Spanish oranges and contains no artificial preservatives, colouring or flavouring.

    (a) Name an import used in the manufacture of Chivers marmalade.

    (b) If more Irish people bought Chivers marmalade rather than a foreign import, what would be the effect (i) on Chivers & Sons and (ii) on the Irish balance of trade?

2. If €1 = £0.68, convert these amounts into pounds.

    (a) €5

    (b) €10

    (c) €20

    (d) €99

    (e) €128

3. If $1 = €1.10, convert these amounts into euro.

    (a) $55

    (b) $11

    (c) $88

    (d) $99

    (e) $242

Bureau de Change			
COUNTRY	**CURRENCY**	**BANK SELLS**	**BANK BUYS**
Britain	Pound (£)	0.68	0.72
Norway	Krone (Kr)	7.27	7.70
USA	Dollar ($)	1.11	1.16
Japan	Yen (¥)	132	141

4. Using the above table, answer the following. Convert to two decimal places in each case.
  (a) Convert €26 to pounds sterling.
  (b) Convert €50 to Norwegian krone.
  (c) Convert €70 to US dollars.
  (d) Convert €90 to Japanese yen.
  (e) Convert €40 to pounds sterling.
  (f) Convert ¥30,000 to euro.
  (g) Convert US$5,000 to euro.
  (h) Convert Kr2,000 to euro.
  (i) Convert GB£60 to euro.
  (j) Convert US$300 to euro.

5. You have been appointed treasurer of the organising committee for next year's school tour to Norway. There are thirty students travelling and the cost per student is €220. Students have been saving €20 each per week for the five weeks up to 31 May. This money was kept in the school safe until 31 May. As treasurer, you are responsible for collecting this money and investing it wisely.
  (a) Suggest three possible places where this money could be invested, giving one advantage for each place mentioned.
  (b) Calculate how much money has been saved by 31 May.
  (c) A deposit of €600 is sent to the tour company on 31 May. The balance is invested on 1 June. Assuming a rate of interest of eight per cent per annum, how much money would be in the investment account on 1 September? (Ignore tax.) Show your workings.
  (d) All the students pay the balance due on their return to school on 1 September.
      (i)   Calculate how much money the students pay on 1 September.
      (ii) If this money is added to the same investment account on 1 September, calculate how much money would be in this account, in total, on 1 December. (Rate of interest eight per cent per annum; ignore tax.) Show your workings.
  (e) One of the students wants to know how many Norwegian krone he will get for €75. Your local bank has the following information on a display board in the bank. (Show your calculations.)

	Bank Sells	Bank Buys
Krone (Kr)	7.27	7.70

STATE EXAM PRACTICE

1. International trade is essential for the well-being and success of the Irish economy.

(a) (i) With which country does Ireland do most of its trade?

   (ii) Give one benefit of imports to the Irish consumer.

   (iii) State one reason why exporting is important for the success of the Irish consumer.

   (iv) State one reason why exporting is important for the success of the Irish economy.

   (v) State one difficulty which an Irish firm would experience when exporting goods.

(b) International trade is both visible and invisible. Give two examples of Ireland's invisible imports.

(c) The following data relates to the international trade of a country called Agohin for the year 2002.

Visible Exports	€9 billion
Invisible Exports	€18 billion
Visible Imports	€13 billion
Invisible Imports	€6 billion

Calculate the following trade figures in relation to Agohin and state whether they are a surplus or a deficit. Show your workings.

   (i) Balance of trade.

   (ii) Balance of payments.

(d) An Irish importer was quoted GB£18,600 for a new car by an English garage. Your local bank had the following information on a display board in the bank.

	Bank Sells	Bank Buys
Sterling	61.71	62.34

   (i) Calculate the cost of the car in euro.

   (ii) State one suitable way for the Irish importer to pay the English garage.

13 Forms of Business

TERMS COVERED IN THIS CHAPTER
Private sector, public sector, sole trader, franchise, co-operative, private limited company.

INTRODUCTION

There are two broad areas of business activity in Ireland: the **private sector** and the **public sector**. Companies in the private sector are owned by individuals or groups of individuals and aim to make a profit by getting as large a share of the market as possible. Companies in the public sector are owned by the state and aim to provide essential services, ensure national security and protect jobs.

What do you think? Work with another pupil on these tasks.
1. Why are some firms bigger than other firms?
2. Why does the state own ESB? Why isn't it owned by a private company?
3. What would it be like if there were many small postal companies delivering letters rather than one big company like An Post?

LESSON 1: PRIVATE SECTOR

SOLE TRADER

There are approximately 230,000 sole traders in Ireland, e.g. the local butcher, newsagent, hairdresser, farmer, builder and solicitor. They are the most common form of business ownership for the following reasons.

- **Set-up**: They are easy to set up as there are no legal requirements and the only procedure is to register for VAT.
- **Ownership and control**: The sole trader has complete control over the running of the business and is his or her own boss. All decisions, plans and ideas belong to and are implemented by the owner.
- **Profits**: There is a great incentive to work hard, since any profit the business makes belongs to the sole trader.

The main drawbacks of this type of business are:

- **Finance**: The owner provides the initial funding for capital and running expenses by using savings or getting a loan. As there is only one person supplying the funds there is usually not much money available and the business grows slowly.
- **Losses and risk**: The sole trader has unlimited liability. This means that the sole trader takes all the risk and is personally liable for any debts of the business, even to the extent that his or her own personal possessions may be sold to pay business debts, e.g. house, car, furniture.
- **Size**: In many cases the sole trader works alone in a small business. There is nobody to ask for help unless staff are hired.

FRANCHISE

A franchise is a licence to operate a particular type of business. There is a wide variety of products and services being sold under franchise at the moment. The best known of these is probably McDonald's, but there are others involved in food (Abrakebabra), cosmetics (The Body Shop) and clothes (Benetton). Franchises are popular because:

- **Set-up**: The franchiser owns the licence and the franchisee pays for the right to use the franchiser's business name and reputation. The franchisee pays an initial fee to start the franchise and thereafter pays a fee to the franchiser that is usually related to profits. In return, the franchisee receives training and documentation describing how to set up and run the new business. This is like a formula that strictly adhered to will generate profits for the new business.
- **Finance**: The new business is financed by savings and loans or by getting a number of investors to buy shares in the company. It's easier to get a loan for a franchise as the bank manager can see that similar businesses have been successful.

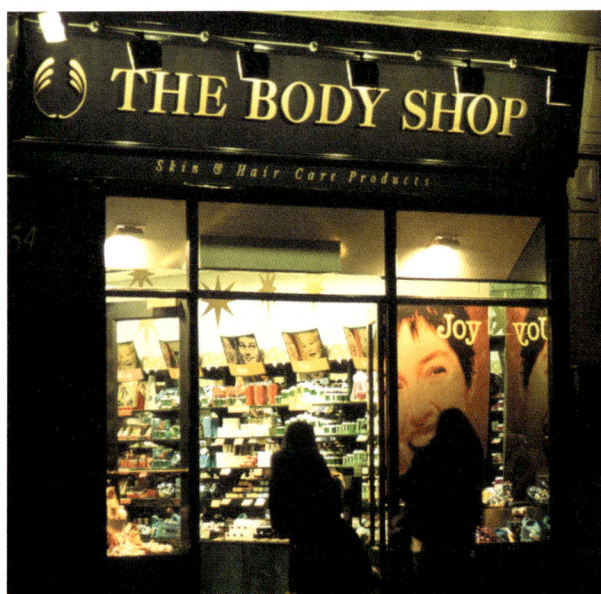

- **Losses and risk:** The business has limited liability. There is less risk associated with this type of business as the product has a proven success rate.
- **Profits:** Although a royalty is paid to the franchiser, the franchisee keeps most of the profit.

The main drawbacks are:

- **Ownership and control:** The franchiser owns the business. The franchisee pays rent to the franchiser. The franchiser controls the product lines, packaging and slogans used. The franchisee has a certain degree of control over the day-to-day operation of the business.
- **Size:** The franchisee is given exclusive rights to trade in a particular city or agreed area. This can place a limit on the size the business can grow to. To trade outside this area will require buying another franchise.

Abrakebabra

Abrakebabra is a leading fast food brand in Ireland with over fifty franchisees. The turnover for the group is €33 million each year, which means it has huge purchasing power that can be passed on to its franchisees. The start-up costs for an average Abrakebabra fast food restaurant are €50,000. The projected sales with this outlay are €300,000. Each franchisee must pay seven per cent of gross sales after VAT to the franchiser.

CO-OPERATIVES

A co-operative is a business that is run for the benefit of its members. In Ireland there is a long tradition of establishing co-operatives because:

- **Set-up:** The members are usually customers, workers or suppliers of the co-operative who come together to solve a common problem.
- **Finance:** Co-operatives are mainly financed by members buying shares in the business. Sometimes the members will give the co-operative a loan, which means the co-operative has access to a cheap source of funds.
- **Losses and risk:** The members have limited liability. By coming together and pooling their resources the members are able to reduce the risks normally associated with a new business.
- **Ownership and control:** The co-operative is owned by the members and as each member only has one vote there is a democratic control process.
- **Profits:** The profit in a co-operative is distributed in relation to the amount of work a member does.

The main drawback is:

- **Size:** No matter how successful a co-operative becomes it is still only able to grow to a certain size depending on the number of members. Credit union co-operatives are very large, with thousands of member-owners. Other co-operatives, like group water schemes, will only have a few local people as members. Some creamery co-operatives, however, found that they couldn't get enough funding for expansion and changed from being a co-operative to becoming a public limited company.

Credit Unions

Credit unions are co-operatives that provide a place for their members to save. Some of the money saved is given out as loans to other members. In Ireland there are 534 credit unions with 2.5 million members. These have saved over €8 billion between them. The average credit union loan to a member is €6,000 and the total of credit union loans to members is in excess of €5 billion.

PRIVATE LIMITED COMPANY

A private limited company usually has the letters Ltd (limited) or Tta (teoranta) after its name, e.g. Brookwood Motors Ltd. It can't sell shares to the public, whereas public limited companies (PLCs) are quoted on the stock exchange and can sell shares to the public. Private limited companies are set up because:

- **Finance:** Private limited companies are financed by people who buy shares in the business. There can be from two to fifty shareholders and they are often from the one family.
- **Losses and risk:** The shareholders have limited liability.
- **Ownership and control:** Shareholders own the company but the board of directors controls it. Each year the board is elected by the shareholders at the annual general meeting (AGM). Each share has one vote, so a shareholder with 1,000 shares has 1,000 votes.
- **Size:** Normally a private limited company can raise more money than a sole trader, and therefore it's usually much larger. Dunnes Stores is an example of a private limited company.

The main drawbacks with this type of business are:

- **Set-up:** These firms are complicated to set up. (The process is studied in more detail in the next chapter.)
- **Profits:** The profit gets divided at the end of the year between the shareholders. This is known as a dividend. The more shareholders there are, the lower the dividend that can be distributed.

Dunnes Stores

Dunnes Stores is a private limited company. It is one of the largest companies in Ireland and the number-two supermarket retailer (behind the Musgrave Group). It has 120 stores located in Ireland, the UK and Spain. It has 18,000 employees and a turnover of around €1.6 billion each year.

LESSON 2: PUBLIC SECTOR

The state has been involved in commercial enterprises for over seventy years. There are many reasons for this, namely:

- **Finance:** Businesses such as Aer Lingus, ESB and RTÉ require more money than private enterprises can provide. The government steps in and provides the capital to start these businesses and acts as a guarantor for loans taken out.
- To ensure national security and defence, e.g. the army, navy and An Garda Siochana.
- In order to protect natural resources and develop them for the good of the state, e.g. Bord Gáis, Coíllte and Bord na Móna.
- To provide essential services.
- To avoid wasteful duplication.

Here are some other characteristics of state companies.

- **Losses and risk:** Any losses sustained by the business are financed by getting additional loans or extra funding from the state.
- **Ownership and control:** Each state company is responsible to a government minister. The minister appoints a board of directors to run the company. This board decides the firm's policy and appoints executives to carry out their policies on a day-to-day basis.
- **Profits:** Any profit not retained is given to the government in the form of a dividend.
- **Size:** State companies are usually very large and often employ thousands of people.

ESB

The ESB was started in 1927. It is responsible to the Minister for Energy and employs over 9,000 people. It has sixteen power stations delivering electricity to 1.6 million customers. The power stations use either peat, coal, oil, gas or water to generate the electricity. It is also building windfarms. At the moment the ESB has a dominant position in the provision of electricity but we can expect to see other companies setting up power stations and competing with the ESB in the years to come.

LESSON 1: PRACTICE

1. All these businesses are mentioned in the lesson. Sort them into sole traders, franchises, co-operatives and private limited companies.
    - Benetton
    - The local butcher
    - The credit union
    - Dunnes Stores
    - A hairdresser
    - Abrakebabra
    - The local group water scheme
    - Brookwood Motors Ltd

2. The figures below are mentioned in the lesson. What do they relate to?
    (a) 6,000
    (b) 1
    (c) 9,000
    (d) 50
    (e) 33,000,000
    (f) 230,000
    (g) 534
    (h) 120
    (i) 2

3. Sort the following into two lists showing four advantages and four disadvantages of being a sole trader.
    (a) Unlimited liability.
    (b) Easy to set up as there are no legal requirements.
    (c) Keeps any profit the business makes.
    (d) Has to work long hours.
    (e) Has to provide all the initial funding.
    (f) Does not have to consult anyone when making decisions.
    (g) Lacks continuity as the business may have to be sold when the owner dies.
    (h) Gets to know all the customers personally.

4. The following words are frequently used in relation to franchises. Complete the e-mail below using the words in the list, then write a reply to your friend pointing out the main drawbacks.

successful   manager   royalty
rights   loan   businesses
profitable

From: John

To: Ashley

Subject: Good news about the loan

Hi Ash,

You were right. The bank [1]_____ said I will have no trouble getting a [2]_____. He had information on similar [3]_____ and they have all been [4]_____. I have exclusive [5]_____ to the east side of the city. It should be very [6]_____ even after I pay the [7]_____.

I'm just worried that I'm missing something. Can you think of any drawbacks?

Best wishes,

J

5.   Tom (a sole trader), Richard (who owns a private limited company) and Harriette (who is buying a franchise) meet for lunch one day. Put their conversation in the correct order, indicating who says what, as in the example.

_____   The bank manager has agreed to give me the loan. She knows other businesses like the one I want to start and they're all successful.

_____   You all share the profits too. At least I get to keep every cent I earn after I pay my VAT and income tax.

_____   Well I'll buy the wine because I'm celebrating too. We had our AGM yesterday and I've been elected onto the board of directors. How did you get on at the bank?

_____   I wish I could get a loan that easy. I've been trying to get money to buy new equipment but the bank says my business is too risky.

____1____   **Hariette:** Hello everyone. Let's order straightaway as I have to rush back to open up the shop.

_____   I told you years ago to sell up and put your money in my firm. We have ten investors in the business now and we all share the risk.

_____   OK, but lunch is on me. I'm celebrating because I managed to buy the licence for the new business.

6. Tick a circle to indicate the most suitable form of business for each of the following and give a reason for your choice.

	Sole Trader	Co-op	Ltd Co.
(a) A woman who has won the lottery plans to open a guest house in the country.	◯	◯	◯
(b) A factory is being closed down because the owners say it's no longer profitable. A group of workers in the factory are being given redundancy money and they feel they could make the firm profitable again.	◯	◯	◯
(c) A state company imports one of the raw materials it uses in the manufacture of fertilisers. A manager employed by the company decides to leave and form a business. He plans to manufacture the raw material.	◯	◯	◯
(d) A city garage has experienced a slump in business and is letting three mechanics go. The mechanics decide to open a small business repairing private vehicles. They are afraid their private homes and property will be sold if the business fails.	◯	◯	◯
(e) A group of women with a keen interest in horticulture decide to open a garden centre in a busy urban area.	◯	◯	◯
(f) A sole trader who has a thriving grocery business wants his son and daughter to become more involved in the firm. They have indicated that they will if he expands into other areas and gives them more say in running the firm.	◯	◯	◯

7. Alice attends a lecture on forms of business in Ireland. Complete her notes using words from the list.

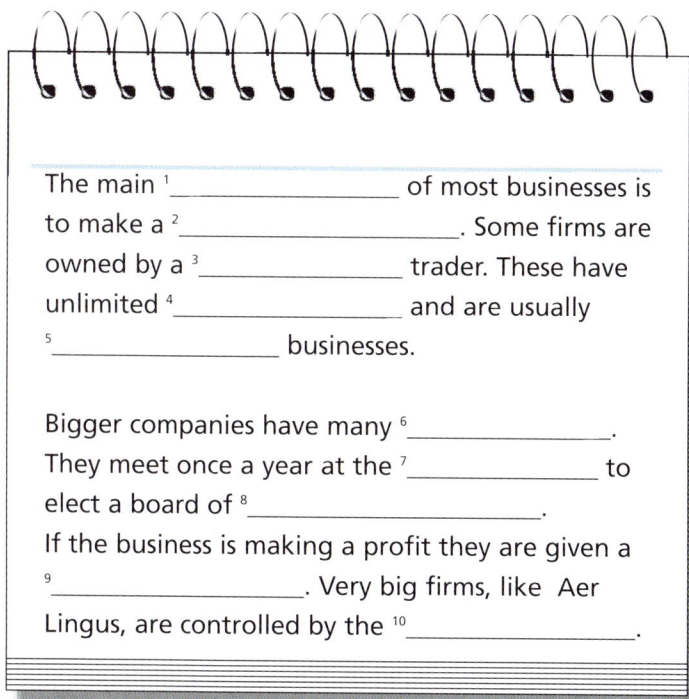

The main ¹_____ of most businesses is to make a ²_____. Some firms are owned by a ³_____ trader. These have unlimited ⁴_____ and are usually ⁵_____ businesses.

Bigger companies have many ⁶_____. They meet once a year at the ⁷_____ to elect a board of ⁸_____. If the business is making a profit they are given a ⁹_____. Very big firms, like Aer Lingus, are controlled by the ¹⁰_____.

sole
shareholders
directors
objective
profit
state
dividend
small
AGM
liability

LESSON 2: PRACTICE

1. Five of your friends text you to say where they'll meet you in town. Using the map, determine where they are.

(a)
I'll meet you at the state organisation opposite the co-op...Laura

(b)
Meet me at the premises between the two private limited companies...Joe

(c)
I'll wait for you at the franchise opposite the sole trader...Mel

| BUTCHER | ABRAKEBABRA | ESB OFFICE | BROOKWOOD MOTORS LTD | CREDIT UNION | KELLY ELECTRICAL LTD | SOLICITOR |

PATRICK STREET

| GROUP WATER SCHEME OFFICE | DUNNES STORES | THE BODY SHOP | NEWSAGENT | GARDA STATION | HAIRDRESSER | BENETTON |

(d)
I'll be at the shop between the private limited company and the sole trader...Pete

(e)
See you at two at the premises between the sole trader and the state organisation...Jake

2. The state companies below are involved in the different areas shown in the table. Complete the table as in the example.

Health	Producing a Product	Providing a Service	Training	Finance
b		c		

(a) An Foras Áiseanna Saothair (FÁS)

(b) National Blood Transfusion Service

(c) Bord Iascaigh Mhara

(d) Bord na Móna

(e) Central Bank of Ireland

(f) Council for Education, Recruitment and Training (CERT)

(g) Bus Éireann

(h) Electricity Supply Board (ESB)

(i) Coíllte

(j) Industrial Development Authority (IDA)

(k) Irish Trade Board

(l) Radio Telefís Éireann (RTÉ)

(m) Voluntary Health Insurance (VHI)

3. **A newsagent, RTÉ, Furniture Supplies Ltd**
   In the case of each of the above businesses:
   (a) state the form of the business.
   (b) name the main source of finance.
   (c) who makes the long-term decisions?
   (d) who runs the company on a day-to-day basis?

4. (a) Compare a sole trader and a private company from the point of view of (i) finance (ii) size (iii) control and (iv) distribution of profits.
   (b) Why might a businessperson prefer to remain a sole trader rather than form a private limited company?

5. (a) What is the maximum number of shareholders allowed in a private limited company?
   (b) 'In a private limited company, ownership and control are divorced.' What is meant by this statement?
   (c) Explain how limited liability protects the owners of a private limited company.

6. (a) Why do people form co-operatives?
   (b) How are co-operatives (i) controlled and (ii) financed?
   (c) Name a co-operative involved in (i) producing a product and (ii) providing a service.

7. Complete the table to show the differences between the forms of business discussed in this chapter. (This table is reproduced in the Documents Book.)

	Sole Trader	Private Limited Company	Co-operative	State Company
Size				
Examples				EBS, IDA
Liability		Limited		
Finance	Savings, loans			
Control			Management committee	
Ownership		2–50 shareholders		
Risk			Shared	
Profits	Owner gets all profit			

STATE EXAM PRACTICE

1. (a) The following figures show the changes in the forms of business ownership in a town over a number of years.

YEAR	1990	1991	1992	1993
Sole traders	24	21	18	15
Private limited companies	9	12	15	18

Illustrate the above information on a suitable chart or graph using graph paper.

(b) State ownership and co-operatives are two other forms of business ownership. In each case, state two reasons why these forms of business ownership have been used in Ireland.

(c) Compare sole traders and private limited companies under the following three headings:
   (i)   ownership.
   (ii) profits.
   (iii) liability.

2. Trudy isn't very good at Business Studies. When asked to write about the work that state companies do, she mixed up her answers. She had all the correct answers but she put them in the wrong sentences.

Here is what she wrote:
1. The VHI *delivers letters every morning.*
2. RTÉ *runs the railways in Ireland.*
3. Bord Fáilte *provides finance for farmers.*
4. An Post *provides a television service for the country.*
5. Aer Lingus *provides telephone and fax services.*
6. The ESB *produces turf and briquettes.*
7. The ACC Bank *provides insurance for people's health.*
8. Iarnród Éireann *provides power for light and heat.*
9. Bord na Móna *provides an air transport service.*
10. Eircom *promotes the tourist industry in Ireland.*

(a) Write out each corrected sentence fully.
(b) Name two other state-owned companies that aren't mentioned above, and write one sentence about the work that each one does.
(JCOL, adapted)

14 Private Limited Company

TERMS COVERED IN THIS CHAPTER
Authorised share capital, issued share capital, loan capital, nominal share capital, memorandum of association, articles of association, Companies Registration Office, Certificate of Incorporation, assets, liabilities, trial balance, balance sheet.

INTRODUCTION

Working in small groups, complete the following tasks to set up a company supplying paper, pens and other stationery to schools. (Refer to the sample documents on the next page.)

1. Decide on a company name.
2. Design the letterhead for notepaper and a sample blank invoice for your company.
3. Prepare the memorandum and articles of association for your company.
4. Decide on a bank you will use.

LESSON I: FORMING A PRIVATE LIMITED COMPANY

A private limited company is owned by shareholders. These shareholders contribute the capital by buying shares in the company. This is the money used by the firm, together with any loans the company can negotiate.

These are the steps to follow in setting up a private limited company.

1. Select a company name.
2. Design stationery, e.g. letterhead and invoices.
3. Draft the memorandum and articles of association.
4. Send the following documents to the Companies Registration Office.
   (a) Memorandum of association.
   (b) Articles of association.
   (c) Statement of nominal share capital.
   (d) Declaration of compliance with Companies Acts.
   (e) Statement of consent by the people who get together to form the company (the promoters) to show they have agreed to be directors of the company.
5. Decide on a bank to use for the business.
6. Await Certificate of Incorporation.
7. Order stationery.
8. First board meeting: appoint chairperson, secretary and open a bank account.

CERTIFICATE OF INCORPORATION

The Registrar in the **Companies Registration Office** gives a Certificate of Incorporation to companies that comply with the Companies Acts. The Certificate of Incorporation gives the company a separate legal identity and it gives the shareholders limited liability. This means they only stand to lose the amount they have invested in the company by way of shares. Their private resources cannot be sold to pay company debts.

THE MEMORANDUM OF ASSOCIATION

This shows the relationship between the company and the outside world, i.e. the external rules. It must be signed by at least two people and should contain:

- the name of the company.
- the company's address.
- the company's objectives (the type of business it is going to conduct, i.e. whether it will be a factory making computers, a shop selling clothes and so on).

Memorandum of Association

1.	Company name:	PJs Ltd
2.	Company address:	Castle Avenue
		Kilkenny
3.	The liability of the members is limited.	
4.	Company objectives:	To manufacture clothes
5.	Authorised share capital:	50,000
		€1 ordinary shares

Shareholder's name and address	**Number of shares taken**
Pat McCarthy	
Castle Ave, Kilkenny	15,000
Jill McCarthy	
Castle Ave, Kilkenny	15,000
Total	30,000

Date: 1 October 2004

Signed: Pat McCarthy   Jill McCarthy

Witness: P. O'Bryne, High Street, Kilkenny

Articles of Association

1. The AGM will be held on 15 January each year.

2. Each share will have one vote.

3. Directors will be elected at the AGM for three years.

Directors' names and addresses

Pat McCarthy: Castle Ave, Kilkenny

Jill McCarthy: Castle Ave, Kilkenny

Date: 1 October 2004

Signed: Pat McCarthy   Jill McCarthy

THE ARTICLES OF ASSOCIATION

This document shows the relationship between the members (shareholders) and the company, i.e. the internal rules. The articles will contain:

- The frequency of meetings for shareholders. A company must hold at least one meeting each year for the shareholders – the annual general meeting (AGM). They may hold an extraordinary general meeting (EGM) if there is an emergency.
- The election procedures and the voting rights of shares. Normally each share has one vote.

CAPITAL

This is the money used to finance the running of the company.

- **Authorised ordinary share capital** is the maximum amount of ordinary share capital a company may issue. This is also called the **nominal share capital**.
- **Issued ordinary share capital** is the actual amount of ordinary shares the company has sold. It is the money invested in the company by the shareholders (the owners).
- **Loan capital** is money given to the firm as a loan, i.e. it must be repaid. It may be from the shareholders or from financial institutions.

LESSON 2: FINANCIAL RECORDING OF A FIRM'S RESOURCES

A firm gets money from the owners and uses this money to buy resources. These resources are the firm's **assets**. The capital is a **liability** of the firm. In its simplest form, this can be recorded as assets = liabilities.

Question

On 1 October Alan, Barbara and Carol form a limited company called ABC Ltd. The company has an authorised share capital of 200,000 €1 ordinary shares. Alan, Barbara and Carol each buy 30,000 shares in the company. The money received from the sale of the shares is lodged to the company bank account. On 3 October the company buys a van by cheque costing €17,000.

(a) Show the entries in the bank account and the ordinary share capital account.

(b) Balance the bank account and extract a trial balance.

Solution

Bank Account

Date	Particulars		Cash	Date	Particulars		Cash
Oct			€	Oct			€
1	OSC		90,000	3	Van		17,000
				3	Balance	c/d	73,000
			90,000				90,000
4	Balance	b/d	73,000				

Ordinary Share Capital Account

Date	Particulars		Cash	Date	Particulars		Cash
				Oct			€
				1	Bank		90,000

Van Account

Date	Particulars		Cash	Date	Particulars		Cash
Oct			€				
3	Bank		17,000				

LEDGER ACCOUNTS

A ledger account is created for each asset and liability of the firm. Each transaction affects the ledger twice. This is known as double-entry bookkeeping.

In the bank account money coming in is recorded on the debit (left) and money going out is recorded on the credit (right). In our example €90,000 comes into the business and so it is entered on the debit. The double entry for this is in the capital account. The €17,000 spent on the van is shown on the credit as money goes out of the business. The double entry for this is in the van account. Notice that the double entry is always on the opposite side.

Trial Balance as at 3 October 2004	Debit	Credit
	€	€
OSC		90,000
Bank	73,000	
Van	17,000	
	90,000	90,000

Balance Sheet as at 3 October 2004	€	€	€
Assets			
Van			17,000
Bank			73,000
			90,000
Liabilities			
Capital			90,000
			90,000

TRIAL BALANCE

The trial balance is used to check that there is a debit for every credit. It does this by taking the balance from each ledger account. The balances are listed in two columns: one for the debits and one for the credits. The two lists are added up and should be equal.

THE BALANCE SHEET

The balance sheet is used to record the assets and liabilities of a firm. The assets are the things the company owns, i.e. what it spends its money on. The liabilities are the things it owes, i.e. the money the company owes. The total assets must equal the total liabilities.

LESSON 1: PRACTICE

1. In this word chain the last letter of one word is the first letter of the next word. Complete the chain using the definitions below.

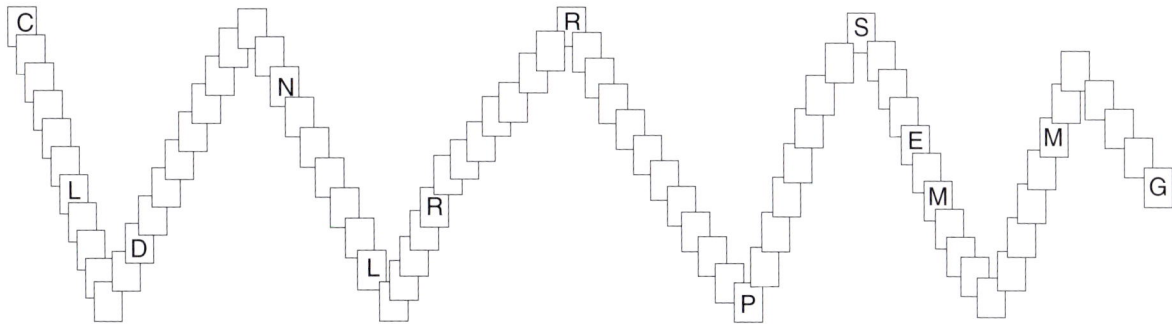

(a) The issued share _____ is the amount of ordinary shares the company has sold.

(b) The Certificate of Incorporation gives a company _____ liability.

(c) The _____ of compliance with the Companies Acts is sent to the Registrar.

(d) Another name for the authorised share capital is the _____ share capital.

(e) One of the first jobs in setting up a limited company is to design the _____ headings and invoices.

(f) The memorandum and articles are sent to the _____ in the Companies Registration Office.

(g) The articles of association show the _____ between the shareholders and the company.

(h) The _____ must sign a statement showing they have agreed to be directors of the company.

(i) The articles of association state the voting rights of each _____ and the election procedure.

(j) In an emergency a company may hold an _____.

(k) The _____ of association lists the external rules of the company.

(l) A company must hold an annual general _____ once a year.

Riverview
Consultancy Ltd
Your partner in business communication
Forest Crescent Business Centre
Directors: John Fitzgerald (Chairperson),
Marie Teeling, Pat Burke

Riverview
Training Ltd
Helping you make the change
Beach View Industrial Estate
Directors: Marie Teeling (Chairperson),
Pat Burke, John Fitzgerald

Riverview
Technology Ltd
The one-stop centre for your technology needs
East Point Business Park
Directors: Pat Burke (Chairperson),
John Fitzgerald, Marie Teeling

2. Three promoters meet to finalise the creation of their new company. They don't like any of the sample designs of stationery. Read their conversation and then prepare the new stationery based on what they agree.

John: We're more than just a training company so we can't use this stationery.

Pat: I agree, but we're going to help firms change the way they do business.

Marie: Yes, we should emphasise that we will help companies change but that we also provide staff training.

John: So we don't want to focus on being a partner for our clients.

Pat: No, and we don't want to be a one-stop centre either.

Marie: That's agreed. I had another look at the business park yesterday and I would much prefer it to the industrial estate.

Pat: John and I agree with you. Location is very important and East Point is certainly the most central.

John: So we locate to the business park. That suits me fine as I will only have a short walk to work.

Marie: I checked with the accountant and he said that the share capital will be 150,000 ordinary shares of one euro each. But once we form a limited company the liability of each member is limited to the shares bought.

Pat: Well, I've agreed to buy forty thousand shares.

John: I said I would buy twenty-five thousand shares.

Marie: And I said I would buy thirty thousand shares.

Pat: All we need to agree on now is the company name and the chairperson, and I think with Marie's expertise she should be the one.

John: That's fine by me.

Marie: Thank you, I'm honoured and I won't let you down.

John: So will we call ourselves a technology or a consultancy company?

Pat: We know more about consultancy than technology.

Marie: I agree with Pat, we should stick with what we know best.

John: Consultancy sounds good to me. So do any of you consultants know what I should do with these three pieces of stationery?

3. Complete this memorandum of association for Riverview from the information contained in the previous question.

Memorandum of Association

The name of the company is ....

The objectives for which the company is established are:

....

....

....

....

The liability of the members is ....

The share capital of the company is ....
divided into ....

....

....

....

We the several persons whose names, addresses and descriptions are subscribed wish to be formed into a Company in pursuance of the Memorandum of Association and we agree to take the number of shares in the Capital of the Company set opposite our respective names.

Name and address of each subscriber   *Number of shares taken by each subscriber*

Dated:

LESSON 2: PRACTICE

1. On 1 February Rachel and Tony Dunne form a limited company called RTD Ltd. The company has an authorised capital of 40,000 €1 ordinary shares. Rachel and Tony each buy 20,000 shares.
  (a) The money received from the sale of the shares is lodged to the company bank account. Show the entries in the bank account and the ordinary share capital account.
  (b) On 2 February the company buys a small office for €30,000. Show the entries in the bank account and in the premises account.
  (c) Balance the bank account and extract a trial balance. They want to buy a van costing €15,000.
  (d) Has the company got enough in the bank to afford the van?
  (e) Can the company issue more shares to pay for the van?
  (f) How do you think they could finance the purchase of the van?

2. On 1 March Teresa and Debbie Keogh form a hairdressing company called Heads Ltd. The authorised capital is 60,000 €1 ordinary shares. Teresa buys 10,000 shares and Debbie buys 20,000 shares in the company.
  (a) What is the objective of this company as it might appear in the memorandum of association?
  (b) Each share has one vote. Who controls the company? Give a reason for your answer.
  (c) The money received from the sale of the shares is lodged to the company bank account. Show the entries in the bank account and the ordinary share capital account.
  (d) On 2 March the company buys the lease on a small shop for €20,000. Show the entries in the bank account and in the premises account.
  (e) Balance the bank account and extract a trial balance.
  (f) They need an extra €20,000 to equip the hair salon. How do you suggest they could finance this?

3. On 1 June Mary Maguire, Gareth Keogh and Peter Sweeney form a company called M1 Service Station Ltd. The authorised share capital is 200,000 €1 ordinary shares. Mary buys 80,000 shares, Gareth buys 30,000 shares and Peter buys 50,000 shares.
  (a) Draw up the memorandum of association for the company.
  (b) Give one reason for forming a private limited company.
  (c) The money from the sale of the shares is lodged in the bank. Show the entries in the bank account and the ordinary share capital account.
  (d) They buy a garage on 3 June for €100,000 and pay by cheque. Show the entries in the bank account and the premises account.
  (e) Balance the bank account and extract a trial balance.
  (f) Each share has one vote. Can Mary control this company? Give a reason for your answer.

STATE EXAM PRACTICE

1. This question includes elements of the formation of a company, marketing and presentation and calculation of company results/figures. Tom and Tina Boland have decided to form a private limited company called T and T Fast Foods Ltd.
   (a) Give two reasons for forming a private limited company.
   (b) Name two documents associated with the formation of a private limited company. Give a brief description of either of them.
   (c) Suggest three suitable methods that T and T Ltd could use to promote their fast food business.
   (d) State three methods that T and T Ltd can use to obtain information about the market.
   (e) T and T Fast Food Ltd project their first year's costs as follows: rent €10,000; wages €15,000; light and heat €10,000; general expenses €5,000. Illustrate this information on a pie chart using graph paper.
   (f) If gross profit was projected at €65,000, what would the net profit be?
   (JCHL, adapted)

2. This is an integrated company formation question. On 1 January Ann Smyth of 2 Top Street, Carlow and Patrick Daly of 15 Cork Road, Carlow formed a private limited company called WOOD FUN LTD. They prepared a memorandum of association and sent it and all the other necessary documents to the Companies Registration Office. A Certificate of Incorporation was then issued. The objectives of the company are to manufacture and sell wooden toys. The authorised share capital of WOOD FUN LTD is 40,000 €1 ordinary shares.

   On 11 January Ann Smyth purchased 15,000 shares and Patrick Daly purchased 16,000 shares. The money received from the issue of these shares was lodged to the company bank account. On 12 January the company purchased equipment costing €15,000 by cheque.

   You are required to do the following.
   (a) Complete the memorandum of association on the blank document supplied in the Documents Book.
   (b) Name one other document that should be sent to the Companies Registration Office when forming a company.
   (c) Record the issue of the shares of 11 January in the ordinary share capital account and the bank account of WOOD FUN LTD.
   (d) Record the transaction that took place on 12 January in the appropriate accounts.
   (e) Prepare a trial balance for WOOD FUN LTD on 13 January.
   (JCHL, adapted)

15 Preparation of a Business Plan

TERMS COVERED IN THIS CHAPTER
Cash flow, business plan, estimates, profit.

INTRODUCTION

The principal has given your Business Studies class permission to run a disco in the school for third year pupils. First, however, you must give the principal a report showing how you plan to run the disco. Put your ideas on paper and then compare them with another pupil's. Write about the following.

1. Who will be in charge (the managers)?
2. How will you advertise the disco?
3. What price will you charge?
4. How much money do you need to get started?
5. What premises and equipment do you need?

LESSON 1: THE ELEMENTS OF A BUSINESS PLAN

Before applying for a loan it may be necessary to make out a business plan showing how the business will develop over the next few years. This plan will help you to:

- focus on what is really important in order to be successful.
- sound more convincing when you apply for a bank loan.
- describe the strengths of your business and the opportunities you are planning to exploit.
- identify the weaknesses and threats facing your business.

The Four Elements of a Business Plan

Management
This should show:
- the background, qualifications and experience of the managers.
- the responsibilities of each manager.

Marketing
This section describes the market:
- size.
- type of market.
- age of consumers.
- location.
- competitors.
- projected sales.
- details about the product.
- price.
- distribution methods.
- advertising plans.

Finance
An estimate of long-term and short-term finance needed for the business must be given. This should show:
- source of funds.
- projected profit.
- cash flow.

Production
This part should include:
- product description.
- details about premises (location, size).
- equipment needs.
- labour requirements.
- suppliers of raw materials.
- quality control plans.
- costings.

LESSON 2: CASH FLOW

One important short-term source of finance is the bank overdraft. This arrangement with the bank can get a company out of a temporary shortage of cash. When a company runs short of money it is said to be cash starved. This is one of the main reasons for business failure. To plan for cash shortages and to minimise them, firms need to monitor the flow of money in and out of the business – the cash flow.

ESTIMATES

One way to forecast future cash flow is to estimate monthly how much and how often cash will be received and payments made over the next year. Planning ahead like this will help identify times when cash may be scarce. Steps can then be taken to make more cash available at those times. Consider the following situation that Peter Ryan, an electrician,

finds himself in. He has been asked if he would like the job of wiring houses on a new estate. The work will take five weeks to carry out and he will get paid €8,000 when the job is completed. He has €1,000 at the moment and he estimates he will have many expenses over the five weeks. Before you read the rest of the lesson, decide if he should take the job.

Expenses
Materials:
- sockets (€40 each week).
- wire (€90 in weeks 2, 3 and 4).
- fittings (€40 in week 5).

Wages:
- for himself (€300 each week).
- for an assistant (€100 in weeks 2, 3 and 4).
- Petrol expenses (€50 each week).
- Telephone (€10 each week).
- Postage and stationery (€10 in weeks 2, 3 and 4).

CASH FLOW FORECAST

Peter uses the estimates to prepare the following cash flow forecast on a spreadsheet at his computer.

	A	B	C	D	E	F	G
1		Week 1	Week 2	Week 3	Week 4	Week 5	TOTAL
2	**RECEIPTS**						
3	Sales	0	0	0	0	5,000	5,000
4	**A›TOTAL RECEIPTS**	0	0	0	0	5,000	5,000
5	**PAYMENTS**						
6	Sockets	40	40	40	40	40	200
7	Wire		90	90	90		270
8	Fittings					40	
9	Wages for himself	300	300	300	300	300	1,500
10	Wages for assistant		100	100	100		300
11	Petrol	50	50	5	50	50	250
12	Telephone	10	10	10	10	10	50
13	Postage and stationery		10	10	10		30
14	**B›TOTAL PAYMENTS**	400	600	600	600	440	2,640
15	C›Net cash (A–B)	(400)	(600)	(600)	(600)	4,560	2,360
16	D›Opening balance	1,000	600	0	(600)	(1,200)	1,000
17	E›Closing balance (C+D)	600	0	(600)	(1,200)	3,360	3,360

PROFIT VERSUS CASH FLOW

When we summarise the receipts and payments we can see that it will be a profitable job. However, when we study the cash flow forecast we can see that Peter runs out of money in the third and fourth week. If he doesn't plan for this shortage he will go bankrupt and never get to see his profit.

Total receipts	€8,000
Total payments (400 + 600 + 600 + 600 + 450)	€2,650
Profit	€5,350

Remember: profit is not equivalent to cash.

SHOULD HE TAKE ON THE JOB?

Now that he knows where the cash problems are likely to occur, he can plan to meet them. He could:

- ask for payment in instalments.
- try to buy materials on credit from his suppliers.
- negotiate an overdraft with his bank manager.

If he solves the problem of the cash shortage in the third and fourth week, then he stands to make a sizeable profit. Otherwise, if he goes ahead with the work he will go bankrupt in the third week.

LESSON 1: PRACTICE

I. Kevin (twenty shares), Mary (twenty-five shares), Sarah (thirty shares) and Jack (twenty-five shares) are shareholders in a transition year minicompany. Here are the notes from their planning meeting. Each note refers to either management, marketing, finance, or production. Rewrite the notes in your copy using those headings to show the business plan for the minicompany.

	1.	There are 500 pupils in the school and we estimate that 200 of these would buy a doughnut at break time.
	2.	The day before the doughnut sale we will place posters around the school to remind pupils to bring in money to buy a doughnut the next day.
	3.	Sarah has experience of running the local basketball club. She has been voted in as the chief executive of the new company.
	4.	There will be 100 shares costing €1 each.
	5.	The doughnuts will be bought from a local bakery. They will be delivered on the morning of the doughnut sale along with some paper bags and wrapping paper.
	6.	The principal will let us use room A4 as a shop.
	7.	We estimate the profit will be €40.
	8.	For hygiene purposes Jack will handle all the money from the customers and Kevin, Mary or Sarah will get the customer the doughnut.
	9.	Jack will be the finance manager.
	10.	The school tuck shop is the only competition but they sell drinks and bars and they don't sell doughnuts.
	11.	Kevin is the purchasing manager.
	12.	Each doughnut will cost thirty cent but we will sell it for fifty cent.
	13.	All staff will wear plastic gloves and a baseball cap.
	14.	Mary will be the marketing manager and will also be in charge of the shop.

2.   They e-mail a local businesswoman and ask for advice on running their minicompany. Complete the e-mail they get back using words from the list.

payments	profit	flow
starved	funds	receipts

From: Shelia

To: Kevin, Mary, Sarah, Jack

Subject: Advice on running your minicompany

Greetings Kevin, Mary, Sarah and Jack,

It sounds like you have a good idea for your business. However, you must be careful not to run out of money. A company which runs short of money is said to be cash [1]_____. A cash [2]_____ is a plan of company receipts and payments and is worth preparing as it will help you control the money. Wages and other expenses should be listed as [3]_____ in the financial plan of your company. Sales are shown as [4]_____ of the business. Loans are a major source of [5]_____ for most businesses but you may not be able to get any. Finally, remember there is a big difference between [6]_____ and cash.

Best of luck with your minicompany!

Sheila O'Dwyer

LESSON 2: PRACTICE

1. Lauren (four shares), Keith (three shares) and Mike (three shares) start a school minicompany cleaning cars. Here is the cash flow forecast for the first four weeks.

	A	B	C	D	E	F
1		Week 1	Week 2	Week 3	Week 4	TOTAL
2	**RECEIPTS**					
3	Sales	50	50	50	50	200
4	**A› TOTAL RECEIPTS**	50	50	50	50	200
5						
6	**PAYMENTS**					
7	Sponges	5				5
8	Buckets	15				15
9	Hire of pressure washer	30	30	30	30	120
10	Car wax	10				10
11	Car wash concentrate	5				5
12	**B› TOTAL PAYMENTS**	65	30	30	30	155
13	C> Net cash (A–B)	(15)	30	20	20	45
14	D> Opening balance	20	52	5	45	20
15	E> Closing balance (C+D)	5	25	45	65	65

(a) What are the total sales for the company?

(b) What are the total expenses for the company?

(c) Why are the expenses so high in week one?

(d) If the €20 opening balance came from the sale of shares, how much is one share?

(e) What is their profit at the end of the four weeks?

(f) If the profit is to be divided among the shareholders, how much will each get?

(g) Which expressions in the cash flow mean the following?

    (i)   Income.

    (ii)   Expenditure.

    (iii)   Income minus expenditure.

    (iv)   Cash at the start of the month.

    (v)   Cash at the end of the month.

Use the cash flows in the Documents Book for questions 2 and 3.

2. Tom and Mary are thinking of starting an electrical shop. They will sell electrical goods and offer a repair service to their customers. Complete a cash flow for the first six months of the year given the following information.

Opening cash in hand will be €1,000.

Planned income:
- Sales of electrical goods are expected to be €3,000 per month.
- Receipts from repairs are expected to be €500 each month.

Planned expenditure:
- Repayments on van loan will cost €250 per month.
- Shop insurance premium amounts to €150 per year payable in January.
- ESB bills are expected to be €200 in February and €300 in April.
- Rent will cost €300 per month.
- The telephone bill is expected to be €130 in March and €140 in May.
- Wages are expected to be €2,000 per month.

3. Séamus is a lobster exporter. He has advance orders (sales) from European customers for the next four months as follows: May €2,000, June €3,400, July €5,700, August €7,200. This represents a huge increase in his normal business and he will require additional staff and facilities. He estimates that his expenses over the next few months will be as follows.
- Wages are expected to be €1,500 each month.
- Rent will be €250 per month.
- ESB bills are expected to be €140 in June and €110 in August.
- The telephone bill is expected to be €150 in June and €170 in August.
- Factory insurance premium is estimated at €240 per year, payable monthly.

He has opening cash in hand of €750.
(a) Make out a cash flow forecast for this business.
(b) In which weeks is there a cash shortage?
(c) Suggest how he might improve his cash flow.

STATE EXAM PRACTICE

1. (a) In the Documents Book there is a partially completed cash flow statement of NAMDOOG LTD. You are required to complete this form for the months of March, April, May and June, as well as all the total columns.

   The following information should be taken into account.
   - Monthly sales are expected to increase by thirty per cent beginning in April.
   - A European Union (EU) grant of €40,000 for equipment is expected in May.
   - The shareholders are to invest an additional €50,000 in the business in June.
   - Light and heat are expected to decrease by fifteen per cent in the months of March and May.
   - Rent and wages are expected to remain the same every month.
   - A new advertising campaign during May will cost €10,000.
   - A second motor vehicle will be purchased in April at a cost of €30,000.
   - New equipment costing €170,000 will be purchased in April.
   - Purchases will increase each month by twelve per cent beginning in March.

   (b) State two important pieces of information which NAMDOOG LTD can obtain from this cash flow statement.

   (c) NAMDOOG LTD forgot to allow for overtime payments of €5,000 for the period. State how this omission will affect the net cash position at the end of June.

2. (a) State two reasons why a business would prepare a cash flow forecast.

   (b) In the Documents Book there is a partially completed cash flow forecast of MOCELET LTD. You are required to complete this form for the months of September, October, November and December as well as the total columns.

   The following information should be taken into account.
   - Wages and advertising are expected to remain the same every month.
   - Monthly sales are expected to increase by twenty-five per cent beginning in September.
   - Monthly purchases are expected to increase by twenty per cent beginning in October.
   - Light and heat are expected to increase by twenty per cent in the months of September and November.
   - The loan repayments will cease after November.
   - The shareholders are to invest an additional €60,000 in the business in November.
   - Land is expected to be sold in September for €19,500.
   - New equipment costing €76,000 will be purchased in October.
   - A European Union (EU) grant of €50,000 for equipment is expected in December.

   (c) MOCELET LTD forgot to allow for repairs to the buildings of €8,000 during this period. State how this omission will affect the net cash position at the end of December.

   (JCHL, adapted)

3. (a) In the Document Book there is a partially completed cash flow forecast of YAM Ltd. You are required to complete this form for the months of March, April, May and June, as well as the total columns.

The following information should be taken into account.
- Monthly sales are expected to increase by twenty per cent beginning in May.
- The shareholders are expected to invest an additional €40,000 in April.
- Buildings are expected to be sold in June for €100,000.
- An EU grant of €100,000 is expected in May.
- Monthly purchases are expected to increase by thirty per cent beginning in May.
- Wages and transport costs are expected to remain the same every month.
- Light and heat expenses are expected to decrease by twenty-five per cent in the months of March and May.
- New buildings are expected to be purchased in May for €250,000.
- Shareholders are expected to be paid a dividend of €200,000 in June.

(b) YAM Ltd forgot to allow for the purchase of new machinery costing €30,000 during this period. Show the new closing cash figure for June after taking this purchase into account in the box provided.

16 Finance

TERMS COVERED IN THIS CHAPTER
Cash flow, capital, retained profit, grants, sale and leaseback, leasing.

INTRODUCTION

How far do you agree with the following statements?
1. Companies should never borrow money to buy premises.
2. Renting a van is better than borrowing money and buying a van.
3. Small companies don't need to borrow money.

LESSON I: INTERNAL AND EXTERNAL SOURCES OF FINANCE

When an entrepreneur starts a business he or she will use savings to finance some of the expenditure. This internal source of finance is rarely enough money to run the business and the entrepreneur will usually have to tap into external sources as well.

INTERNAL SOURCES

Using internal sources of finance means that there are no repayments and no interest charges. This money is used to buy premises, machinery and other long-term assets.

1. **Own funds or capital:** This is the money put into the firm by the owners. In a small firm the capital may come from the owners' savings, redundancy money or a personal loan. Larger firms get capital by issuing shares. The capital is used to buy the premises, machinery and equipment that the business needs.

2. **Retained profit:** A successful company will use its capital to make a profit. The part of the profit that is retained by the business becomes another source of money for the firm.

EXTERNAL SOURCES

External sources are used when the firm cannot supply all its own cash needs. A wide variety of finance is available but the cost of getting this outside money can be very high.

1. **Grants:** Some grants are available to small businesses from Enterprise Ireland or the County Enterprise Boards. A grant will rarely exceed thirty per cent of the total finance required by a business.

2. **Long-term loan:** Long-term loans from a bank can be expensive. However, sometimes it's the only way to get the extra money needed. Long-term loans are used to pay for premises, machinery and equipment. A company will have up to twenty years to repay the loan and they will have to give collateral (security) for the loan – usually the deeds to the property are given as security for the loan.

3. **Sale and leaseback:** This is a special type of leasing where a firm sells an asset and leases it back from the buyer. For example, a firm may be able to sell its premises and then lease the premises back from the leasing company. The firm gets a cash injection but it no longer owns its premises.

4. **Medium-term loan:** These are loans from a bank that take from one to five years to repay. The interest rate is higher than for an overdraft.

5. **Hire purchase:** This is a popular way for a business to acquire vehicles, office furniture, office fittings and computers. Under this arrangement:
    *   the firm pays regular instalments over a definite period, normally one to three years.
    *   the firm won't own the goods until the last instalment has been paid.

6. **Leasing:** Leasing is like renting, and while the firm gets the use of the asset they will never own it. With leasing:
    *   the finance company buys the goods and leases them to the business.
    *   the firm pays monthly or annual lease rent.
    *   the finance company continues to own the goods.
    *   old equipment can be replaced with newer models.

7. **Creditors:** The purchase of raw materials can be quite costly. If stock can be bought on credit, then the suppliers who give the stock are helping to finance the firm. Creditors (the suppliers) are therefore a source of short-term money. The cost to a firm of using this source of money is the discount that may be lost from the creditors.

8. **Unpaid expenses:** The money saved by not paying bills is a further source of finance for a business. For example, by not paying electricity, tax or telephone charges the company may save hundreds of euro, and this money may be used elsewhere in the firm. However, this is a most unsuitable source of funds, as the electricity or telephone company may disconnect the service to the firm. Paying bills late or not at all is a sure sign of a company in financial difficulties.

9. **Overdraft:** An overdraft is a short-term loan that permits the business to write cheques even though there is no money in the firm's current account. Interest is only paid on the amount overdrawn. The overdraft must be kept within an agreed limit and the account must be in credit, i.e. not overdrawn, for at least thirty days in the year. It should only be used to finance day-to-day expenses and lodgments should be made as soon as possible.

LESSON 2: SUITABILITY OF FINANCE

The finance a business needs falls into three areas.
- Long-term finance, which is used to pay for capital expenditure on assets with a life of more than five years.
- Medium-term finance, which is used to pay for capital expenditure on assets with a life of one to five years.
- Short-term finance, which is used to pay for revenue expenditure.

Capital expenditure is money spent on assets that the firm will use for years to come. For example, the business will need premises, equipment and vehicles. This expenditure only happens every few years but large sums of money are involved.

Revenue expenditure is quite different. It is the day-to-day spending of the business, such as the payment of wages, electricity and insurance. Buying a delivery van is capital expenditure but buying petrol for the van is revenue expenditure.

In general, a firm will use long-term money to finance long-term assets and short-term money to finance day-to-day spending.

SOURCES OF FINANCE			
Internal	**External**		
1. Own funds or capital 2. Retained profit	3. Grants 4. Long-term loan 5. Sale and leaseback	6. Medium-term loan 7. Hire purchase 8. Leasing	9. Creditors 10. Unpaid expenses 11. Overdraft
Long Term (over five years) Used to buy premises, heavy machinery and equipment		**Medium Term** (one to five years) Used to buy vehicles, computers and light equipment	**Short Term** (less than one year) Used to buy stock and pay wages, telephone, electricity and other bills

Question

Murray's Bakery got the following details about a €14,000 delivery van.

Term loan from AIB Finance: €30 per month per €1,000 borrowed for three years.

Leasing: €125 per week.

(a) What is the total cost of the term loan?

(b) How much would it cost to lease the van for three years?

(c) Which type of term loan would Murray's need?

(d) If they decide to get the term loan, how would this be recorded in their ledger accounts?

Solution

(a) Loan cost: 36 x 14 x €30 = €15,120

(b) Leasing cost: 52 x 3 x €125 = €19,500

(c) A medium-term loan.

(d) The ledger account entries in Murray's books for the term loan are as shown below. The bank account is debited with the €14,000 received. The double entry is in the credit of the AIB Finance account.

Bank Account						
Date	Particulars	Cash	Date	Particulars		Cash
Oct		€	Oct			€
7	AIB Finance	14,000				

AIB Finance Account						
			Oct			€
			7	Bank		14,000

LESSON 1: PRACTICE

1. Complete the word grid with the types of finance described below.

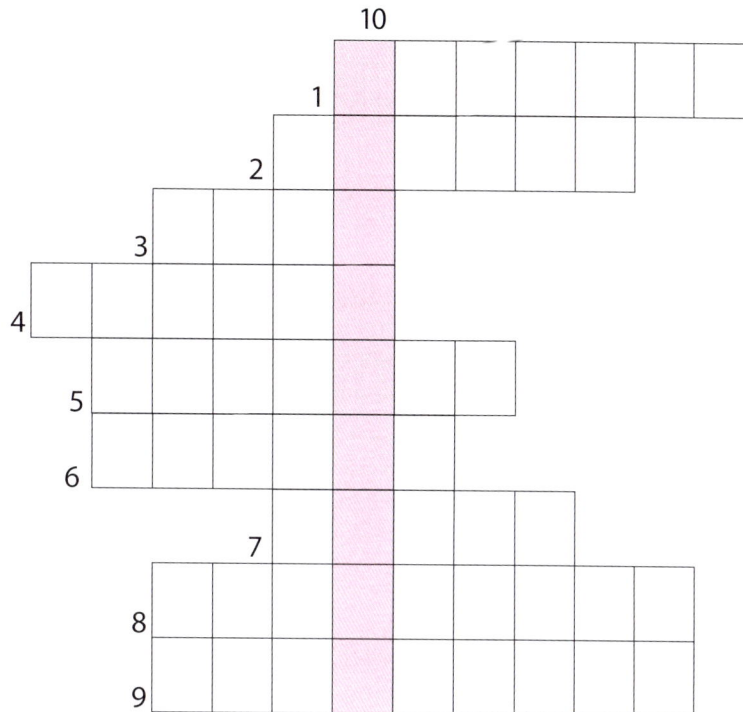

1. This is the money put into the firm by the owners.
2. In a new firm this is usually ploughed back into the business.
3. _____ purchase is a popular way for a business to acquire vehicles.
4. _____ expenses are not a good source of funds.
5. This is like renting.
6. These are available from Enterprise Ireland or the County Enterprise Boards.
7. These can be long, medium or short.
8. This is a short-term loan given to people with current accounts.
9. Sale and _____ is a good way to get a cash injection into a business.
10. These are a good short-term source of funds.

2.   Match the business needs below with an appropriate loan.

Business Needs	Loan
1. A €70,000 extension to the factory 2. Three new delivery vans 3. Extra stocks of toys for the Christmas period 4. Paying staff wages	(a) Overdraft (b) Creditors (c) Long-term loan (d) Hire purchase

3.   Complete the gaps in the table below.

> 1 ....draft
> Sale and 2 ....
> 3 ....expenses
> Hire 4 ....
> 5 ....funds
> Long 6 ....
> 7 ....profit

4.   Use words from the table above to complete this fax.

> # FAX
>
> **To:**   Robert Moore
>
> **From:** Carol Synott
>
> **RE:**   Sources of finance
>
> We nearly have all the finance ready. The 1_____ loan
> will finance the purchase of the premises and we can use our 2_____
> to pay for the equipment. Instead of renting I'm going to buy the vans
> using 3_____.
>
> Today I arranged an 4_____ at the bank to pay for any 5_____
> we might have during the year.
>
> If the business does well then we can use the 6_____
> to pay for the building of the extension you were talking about.
> We could also consider 7_____ to give us a
> cash injection.

LESSON 2: PRACTICE

1. In the case of each financial institution below, indicate whether it is a commercial bank, building society, insurance company or hire purchase company.

Financial Institution	Commercial Bank	Building Society	Insurance Company	Hire Purchase Company
Hibernian				
EBS				
National Irish				
AIB Finance & Leasing				
First National				
AXA				

2. In the case of the three companies shown below, match each item of expenditure with the appropriate source of finance.

Company A

Type of Expenditure	Source of Finance
Premises	Hire purchase
Vehicles	Bank overdraft
Wages	Long-term loan

Company B

Type of Expenditure	Source of Finance
Stock of raw materials	Capital
Heavy machinery	Leasing
Computer	Creditors

Company C

Type of Expenditure	Source of Finance
Light equipment	Long-term loan
Electricity bill	Hire purchase
Heavy equipment	Bank overdraft

3. What is (i) the cost of each of these loans and (ii) the amount of the monthly repayment on each loan?

(a) A €2,000 loan for three years if it costs €30 per month per €1,000 borrowed.

(b) A €1,500 loan for two years if it costs €50 per month per €1,000 borrowed.

(c) A €5,000 loan for six months if it costs €175 per month per €1,000 borrowed.

(d) A €3,000 loan for three years if it costs €40 per month per €1,000 borrowed.

(e) A €4,500 loan for a year and a half if it costs €70 per month per €1,000 borrowed.

4. In each of the following cases (i) calculate the hire purchase price and (ii) indicate by how much the hire purchase price is greater than the cash price.
   (a) A delivery van costs €5,200 cash or €330 per month over eighteen months.
   (b) An office computer costs €4,500 cash or €230 per month over twenty-four months.
   (c) Shop fittings cost €3,000 cash or €130 per month over thirty months.
   (d) A machine costs €15,000 cash or €570 per month over three years.
   (e) Computer programs cost €2,000 cash or €130 per month over a year and a half.

5. Calculate which is cheaper for a €4,000 loan.
   (a) A term loan if the repayments are €45 per month per €1,000 borrowed over three years.
   (b) A hire purchase arrangement for two years if the repayments are €200 per month.

6. Which of these is cheaper for a €7,000 loan?
   (a) A term loan if the repayments are €30 per month per €1,000 borrowed over four years.
   (b) A term loan for three years if the repayments are €45 per month per €1,000 borrowed.

7. Which of these is cheaper for a €5,000 loan?
   (a) A term loan if the repayments are €25 per month per €1,000 borrowed over four years.
   (b) A hire purchase arrangement for three years if the repayments are €160 per month.

8. On 1 December 2004 Xpress Delivery Co. Ltd, Dublin Road, Limerick bought a €15,000 delivery truck on hire purchase. The managing director and main shareholder, Peter McGinley, signed the HP agreement, paid a deposit of €500 and agreed to pay eighteen monthly instalments of €1,050 beginning on 1 January 2005. The hire purchase company's name is High Finance Ltd, 25 Main Street, Limerick.
   (a) What was the total cost of the delivery truck for Xpress Delivery Co. Ltd?
   (b) When would Xpress Delivery Co. Ltd become the owner of the truck?
   (c) What type of business unit is Xpress Delivery Co. Ltd? Give one reason for your answer.
   (d) Is Xpress Delivery Co. Ltd a primary, secondary or tertiary producer?

   Xpress Delivery Co. Ltd went bankrupt on 5 May 2005. On 7 May Peter McGinley wrote to the manager of the hire purchase company telling him about this. He also wrote that because of this, the company was unable to keep paying the instalments on the delivery truck. He told the manager that he wished to end the hire purchase agreement and asked him to send someone to take away the delivery truck.
   (e) Write the letter that Peter sent to the hire purchase company.

STATE EXAM PRACTICE

I. Na Fianna Sports Club, Clonkeen, Co. Kerry has 100 members. It is considering the purchase of a new grass mower, which has a retail price of €7,000. The club has got very little money to invest in it. David Donnelly, the club's treasurer, approached Money Matters Ltd, Ballyvourney, Co. Cork to investigate the sources and cost of a €7,000 loan to purchase the mower. Ciara O'Mahony, financial consultant working at Money Matters Ltd, investigated and came up with the following alternatives.

Option 1 **Bank loan**. Borrow €7,000 for three years on which interest is charged at a flat rate of eleven per cent per annum. The loan and interest would be repaid in six equal half-yearly instalments.

Option 2 **Hire purchase**. Pay a deposit of €500 plus thirty-six monthly instalments of €270 each.

Option 3 **Rental purchase**. Pay a monthly rental of €190 each month for four years plus a final payment of €99 at the end of the lease to acquire ownership of the item.

(a) Calculate the total cost of each option. Show your workings.

The consultant wrote a report to the treasurer of the club showing the total cost of each option and recommended the cheapest one. The consultant also suggested in the report that the club should organise a fundraising activity. The money raised could be used to finance future capital expenditure.

(b) Write the report that the consultant sent to the club's treasurer, using today's date.

(c) (i) Name two ways the club could raise €2,000 per annum, to be set aside for the future.

(ii) If the club managed to raise €5,000 from its fundraising activity and wished to invest it for five years, name a suitable investment for the club and give a reason for your choice.

(JCHL, adapted)

17 Commercial Banks

TERMS COVERED IN THIS CHAPTER
Night safe, specimen signature.

INTRODUCTION

Design the layout for a bank showing the counters and offices and label each part of your plan. Compare your design with another pupil's.

LESSON I: SERVICES PROVIDED BY BANKS FOR BUSINESSES

For most people, starting a small business remains little more than a dream. One of the biggest obstacles is deciding how to approach a bank for a loan. It's worth remembering, however, that banks are accustomed to dealing with the needs of businesses. They can offer basic business advice and will grant start-up loans to the right applicants. Here is a list of the main services banks provide for businesses.

1. **Deposit accounts:** Money lodged into a bank deposit account earns interest. Higher rates of interest are paid on large sums of money left for long periods of time. This interest is subject to deposit interest retention tax (DIRT).

2. **Current accounts:** No interest is paid on money lodged into current accounts. However, customers with a current account are given a cheque book and may be able to negotiate an overdraft limit. A current account is also necessary to avail of many of the money transfer facilities the banks offer.

3. **Loans:** Banks supply much of the capital required by industry. This can take the form of overdrafts, medium- to long-term loans and, in some cases, buying shares in the enterprise. By co-operating with government agencies they ensure that businesses have access to money at the best possible interest rates.

4. **Night safes:** These are used by shopkeepers and traders who wish to make lodgments outside normal banking hours. The customer deposits a special marked bag in the safe. The next day the customer goes to the bank, gets the bag and makes a lodgment in the usual way.

5. **Foreign exchange:** The banks buy and sell foreign currency.

6. **Specialist services:** Banking is so competitive that many banks have joined up with other financial institutions to offer several specialist services. This enables bank customers to:
   - take out insurance policies.
   - buy and sell shares.
   - get a mortgage.
   - get tax advice.
   - arrange a pension.

When a private limited company opens a current account it must provide the bank with the following information:

(i)   the Certificate of Incorporation.
(ii) memorandum of association.
(iii) specimen signatures of those entitled to sign cheques.

Factors that banks consider when granting a loan:
(i)   purpose of the loan.
(ii) ability to repay.
(iii) amount of the loan.
(iv) security available.

Question

Aisling and Brian Nolan run a hairdressing business in Dundalk called Short Cuts Ltd. They receive a four-year loan of €16,000 from their local bank to re-equip the salon. Their annual income is €100,000 a year and the premises have been accepted as security for the loan. Terms of the loan agreement were:

● capital repayments of €4,000 each year.
● interest twelve per cent APR.

Calculate the total interest payable over the four years.

Solution

Year 1	16,000 x 12% interest	= €1,920
Year 2	12,000 x 12% interest	= €1,440
Year 3	8,000 x 12% interest	= €960
Year 4	4,000 x 12% interest	= €480
Interest payable over the four years		= €4,800

LESSON 2: MONEY TRANSFER FACILITIES

1. **Standing order:** A standing order (SO) is an agreement between a bank and a customer to pay a stated amount of money at a specific date every month into a third party's bank account. It is used where the amount for the payment is the same each month. For example, repayment of a car loan could be paid this way.

2. **Direct debit:** When the amount of the payment is variable, a direct debit (DD) is often used. For example, payment of an electricity bill may be made using a direct debit. In this case the ESB would ask the bank concerned to pay an amount of money that will vary with each bill depending on how much electricity the consumer uses.

3. **Paypath:** Many employers pay wages and salaries directly into their employees' bank accounts. The employees can then go to a cash dispenser (ATM) and withdraw their wages. This service is known as Paypath and it is a safe and convenient way to pay wages.

4. **Bank draft:** A bank draft is a cheque written by a bank official using one of the bank's own cheques. There is a small charge for this service. Bank drafts are used when:
   - a customer has not got a current account and therefore cannot write cheques.
   - a customer is paying a firm that insists on a bank draft because the customer is not known to them, the money is to be sent through the post or guaranteed payment is required.

5. **Bank giro:** A customer who knows the bank account numbers of his or her suppliers can make payments to them using the giro system. Credit transfers (CT) like this mean that bills can be paid without the inconvenience of posting cheques because the money is transferred from one account directly to the other account.

LEDGER ACCOUNTS

The ledger account entries in Brian Nolan's books for the bank giro credit transfer to pay a local plumber is as shown below. The bank account is credited with the €12,000 paid out. The double entry is on the debit of Dundalk Bathrooms Ltd.

Bank Account								
Date	Particulars		Cash	Date	Particulars			Cash
			€	Jul				€
				27	Dundalk Bathrooms Ltd			12,000

Dundalk Bathrooms Ltd Account					
Jul			€		€
27	Balance		12,000		

MAKING A LODGMENT TO A BANK ACCOUNT

Lodgment

Please specify account: Current ☐ Savings ☐ Other ☐ ———

LODGMENT RECORD

Name(s)

Steve Burke

| 1 | 2 | 0 | 3 | 4 | 0 | 5 | 6 |

€300

Please specify account

Current ☐ Savings ☐

Other ☐ ———

Name(s) Steve Burke

Address   Dundalk

Date 26/7/2003

Paid in by   Steve Burke

Cashier's Stamp and Initials

Customer's Account Number

| 1 | 2 | 0 | 3 | 4 | 0 | 5 | 6 |

Notes   200—

Coin

Total Cash   200—

Cheques etc.   100—

Total €   300—   → The total lodged

The stub gives summary details of the lodgment

The name and address of the person lodging the money

MAKING A BANK GIRO CREDIT TRANSFER

CREDIT TRANSFER

To Bank A.I.B.

Branch   Athlone

A/C   Doris Ltd

| 7 | 8 | 0 | 9 | 0 | 1 | 2 | 0 |

€ 500—

Destination

Branch Code   90-10-28

To Bank A.I.B.   Date 27/7/2003

Branch   Athlone

Credit Account   Doris Ltd

Paid in by   Fiona

Address   Wexford

Cashier's Stamp and Initials

Customer's Account Number

| 7 | 8 | 0 | 9 | 0 | 1 | 2 | 0 |

Bank Giro

CREDIT TRANSFER

Notes   300—

Coin

Total Cash   300—

Cheques etc.   200—

Total €   500—   → The total money transferred

The stub gives summary details of the credit transfer

The name and address of the person making the transfer

APPLYING FOR A BANK DRAFT

Ulster Bank Limited

Bank Draft

27/7/2003

Pay   C.S. Supplies   Or Order

Three hundred and forty euro

€ 340—

Ulster Bank

M Griffin (mgr)

The completed bank draft

The name of the person or company that is to recieve the draft

Requisition for Demand Draft

Draft in favour of   C.S. Supplies   Date 27/7/2003

Drawn on   Linda Ryan

Account holder/Applicant   Linda Ryan

Address Sneem Road, Kenmare

Signature of applicant   Linda Ryan

Cashier's Stamp and Initials

Draft Number   2375

Amount   340—

Commission   1 50

Total €   341 50

The name and address of the person applying for the draft

The total cost to the customer

LESSON I: PRACTICE

1. Complete the loan application form for Aisling and Brian Nolan. (The details for this are in the lesson.)

AIB Loan Application

Company name:
Address:
Names of directors:
Nature of business:
Annual income:
Amount of loan required:
Purpose of loan:
Length required for:
Security available:
Signatures of directors:
Date:

2. Gavin and Liam start an electrical business in Letterkenny. They receive a two-year start-up loan of €10,000 from their local bank. Terms of the loan agreement were:
- capital repayments of €5,000 each year.
- interest ten per cent APR.

Calculate the total interest payable over the two years.

3. Janice and Nicola own a secretarial business in Cavan. They receive a three-year loan of €90,000 from their local bank to build an extension to their premises. Terms of the loan agreement were:
- capital repayments of €30,000 each year.
- interest fourteen per cent APR.

Calculate the total interest payable over the three years.

4. Conor owns a building company. He receives a two-year loan of €40,000 from the local bank. Terms of the loan agreement were:
- capital repayments of €10,000 each year.
- interest twelve per cent APR.

Calculate the total interest payable over the two years.

LESSON 2: PRACTICE

1. In this word chain the last letter of one word is the first letter of the next word. Complete the chain using the definitions below.

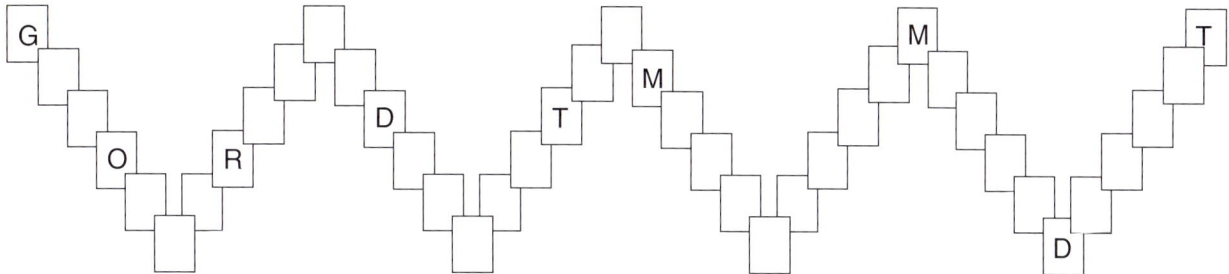

1. A bank _____ is used to transfer money directly from one bank account to another.
2. A standing _____ is used to pay bills that are the same each month.
3. A loan will usually be given to a customer who has _____ previous loans.
4. Money saved in a _____ account earns interest.
5. Banks provide long-, medium- and short-_____ loans to the right customers.
6. When a company is opening a current account, the _____ of association must be shown to a bank.
7. When making lodgments outside normal banking hours, a customer will deposit a special _____ bag in the night safe.
8. A _____ debit is used where the amount of the bill varies each month.

Use the forms in the Documents Book for questions 2 to 7.

2. Use a lodgment form to lodge the following to David Kelly's current account (number 93425169) with the Bank of Ireland, O'Connell Street, Limerick on today's date: seven €20 notes, twenty-five €10 notes, 475 €1 coins, eighty-six fifty cent coins, eight bags of coins containing €5 each and cheques for €105.70, €254.90, €76.24 and €214.50.

3. Use a credit transfer form to transfer €300 cash to Gerry Horan's current account (number 94634117) in Allied Irish Banks, Patrick Street, Cork from Pam Walton's account (number 46201345) in the Bank of Ireland, Galway. Use today's date.

4. Use a withdrawal form to withdraw €140 from Joan Kavanagh's current account (number 92011894) with the Bank of Ireland, Grattan Street, Sligo. Use today's date.

5. Use a lodgment slip to lodge the following to Olive Malone's current account (number 94132314) with Allied Irish Banks, Pearse Street, Drogheda on today's date: five €50 notes, fourteen €20 notes, nine €10 notes, 214 €1 coins, forty-two fifty cent coins, four bags of coins containing €5 each, cheques for €211.40, €152.20 and €48.40 and postal and money orders to the value of €80.

6.   Use a credit transfer form to transfer €240 to Marie Keane's current account (number 93352734) in Bank of Ireland, Dublin Road, Balbriggan from Doreen Pigott's account (number 23104587) in the Bank of Ireland, Gorey. Use today's date.

7.   Use a withdrawal form to withdraw €260 from Marion Andrew's current account (number 94255648) with the Bank of Ireland, Cabra Road, Dublin. Use today's date.

8.   Complete the following report, using words and phrases from the list.

overdraft	lodgment	deposit
Paypath	current	night safe
accounts	cash dispenser	standing order
	cheque	

CMG Ltd is a small manufacturing company. The firm has two ¹_____ in the bank. They put some money into the ²_____ account and this earns them interest. When they opened a ³_____ account they were given a ⁴_____ book and they arranged a €10,000 ⁵_____ with the bank manager. Cash received by the firm is placed in the bank's ⁶_____ each evening. The next day one of the firm's employees goes to the bank and makes a ⁷_____ in the usual way. The firm leases vehicles and has a ⁸_____ with the bank to pay the leasing company each month. The firm uses ⁹_____ to pay wages. Employees can then go to a ¹⁰_____ and withdraw part or all of their wages.

9.   Give the meaning of the following abbreviations:
(a) SO (b) CT (c) DD (d) DIRT (e) ATM (f) PIN.

10.   (a) Why is a current account not a good place to save money?
(b) Name three ways to take money out of a current account.
(c) Name three services that current account holders can avail of.
(d) Name three items that should be recorded on a cheque stub and briefly explain why it is a good idea to record this information.

11.   A Dublin firm imports raw materials from France and exports its products to Germany. The firm regularly uses many bank services.
(a) How can the bank help with paying the French supplier?
(b) What type of insurance can the firm take out against nonpayment by the German customer?

12.   A firm in Dundalk owes €725 to a supplier in Athlone. Name three methods by which the firm could pay this debt. Indicate when each may be preferable to use.

13.   Name five services banks offer business customers other than current accounts and briefly explain each one.

14. List the main sources of income for banks and the main areas where they spend money.

15. (a) What are the advantages of using Paypath for an employer?
(b) What other bank services is a business likely to use?

16. (a) List some of the problems involved in selling abroad.
(b) How can a bank help an exporter?

17. (a) Name two items a businessperson might leave in the bank's safe.
(b) Name five types of businesses that might use a bank's night safes.

18. What are the differences between a standing order and a direct debit?

19. Rachel has a current account in her local bank. She has no credit card and prefers not to carry large sums of cash. In the case of each of the following, say whether she is more likely to pay by cheque, standing order or direct debit.

	Cheque	SO	DD
(a) Annual car insurance.	○	○	○
(b) Monthly house mortgage.	○	○	○
(c) Quarterly phone bill.	○	○	○
(d) ESB bill.	○	○	○
(e) Supermarket checkout bill.	○	○	○
(f) Yearly rates charge.	○	○	○
(g) Weekly rent of flat.	○	○	○
(h) €25 worth of petrol.	○	○	○
(i) Theatre tickets.	○	○	○
(j) Driving licence.	○	○	○

STATE EXAM PRACTICE

1. (a) Name four services provided by banks for businesses.
   (b) List three pieces of information that a private limited company must provide when opening a current account in a bank.
   (c) State four factors that banks consider when granting a loan.
   (d) F & M Ltd receive a three-year loan of €15,000. Terms of the loan agreement were capital repayments of €5,000 per year and interest twelve per cent APR. Calculate the total interest payable over the three years.

18 Business Insurance

INTRODUCTION

How far do you agree with the following statements?
1. Insurance is a waste of money.
2. The only thing a company should bother insuring is its vehicles.

LESSON 1: BUSINESS RISKS

Businesses need profits to survive, hence most firms prefer to pay small sums of money for insurance and thereby avoid large losses. A businessperson must assess the risks involved in the firm and take out an insurance policy that gives protection according to the firm's needs.

There are many risks in business and there are insurance policies to cover most of them. Here is a list of some risks and the insurance cover that is available for them.

- **Fire and special perils insurance:** This covers buildings, stock, machinery and office furniture against destruction or damage.
- **Employer's liability insurance:** This insures against injury, illness or disease caused to employees in the course of their work.
- **Product liability insurance:** This covers injury, illness or disease caused to any member of the public by the product or service that the business supplies.
- **Burglary and hold-up insurance:** This covers the business against property being lost, damaged or stolen.
- **Public liability insurance:** This insures against injury, illness or disease caused to any member of the public not working for the firm, such as if a customer trips and gets injured while on the business premises.

- **Vehicle insurance:** It is compulsory for a company to insure its vehicles.
- **Glass and signs insurance:** This covers breakage of glass or business signs at the firm's premises.
- **E-commerce insurance:** This covers damage caused by computer hackers and viruses.

LESSON 2: CALCULATING THE INSURANCE PREMIUM

Question

Office Fitters Ltd wants to insure the following: buildings €100,000; machinery €50,000; two vans at €15,000 each; stock €70,000; office cash €3,500.

They got the following quotation from Coverall Insurers Ltd: insurance for buildings and machinery €4 per €1,000 insured; vehicle insurance €900 per van; stock insurance €9 per €1,000 insured; cash insurance €10 per €500 insured. As new clients they are entitled to a twenty per cent discount off the total premium.

Office Fitters Ltd agreed to take out this insurance on everything at replacement cost (as stated above) except for the buildings, which they insured for €75,000.

(a) Calculate the total amount of the premium paid by Office Fitters Ltd.

(b) In the event of damage to the buildings of €40,000, how much compensation would Office Fitters Ltd receive?

(c) Show how to record the payment of the total premium in the ledger on 2 Feb.

Solution

(a) BUILDINGS: $\dfrac{€75,000 \times €4}{€1,000}$ = €300

   MACHINERY: $\dfrac{€50,000 \times €4}{€1,000}$ = €200

   VANS: $2 \times €900$ = €1800

   STOCK: $\dfrac{€70,000 \times €9}{€1,000}$ = €630

   CASH: $\dfrac{€3,500 \times €10}{€50}$ = €70

	€3,000
less discount	€600
TOTAL PREMIUM	€2,400

(b) Average clause applies because the buildings are underinsured:

$\dfrac{\text{Sum Insured}}{\text{Actual Value}} \times \text{Claim}$

$\dfrac{€75,000}{€100,000} \times €40,000 = €30,000$

The compensation paid would be €30,000.

(c) The ledger account entry for the payment of insurance is as shown on the right. The bank account is credited with the €2,400 insurance premium for the year. The double entry is on the debit of the insurance account. On 31 December, €2,200 is transferred to the profit and loss account and €200 is carried down to next year.

RB 3

Dr				Bank Account				Cr
Date	Particulars		Cash	Date	Particulars			Cash
				Feb				€
				2	Insurance			2,400

		Insurance Account				
Feb			€	Dec			€
						2,200
2	Bank		2,400	31	P+L		200
			2,400	31	Balance	c/d	2,400
Jan 1	Balance	b/d	200			

LESSON 1: PRACTICE

1. For each of the businesses listed below, identify one appropriate risk from the list on the right.

Business	Risks
1. Supermarket	(a) Petrol going on fire
2. Chocolate manufacturer	(b) Freezer breaking down
3. Meat exporter	(c) Bricks falling on passers-by
4. Garage	(d) Trawler sunk by submarine
5. Builder	(e) Armed raid
6. Building society	(f) Damage to car
7. Farmer	(g) Sweets making a consumer ill
8. Car hire company	(h) Shop window breaking
9. Ice cream company	(i) Foreign customer not paying up
10. Fisherman	(j) Sheep killed by dogs

2. Answer true or false to each of these statements. You may need to revise Chapter 9 first.

	True	False
(a) You must tell the truth when applying for insurance.	◯	◯
(b) Any risk can be insured.	◯	◯
(c) You always get the full amount you claim.	◯	◯
(d) If your €5,000 car is stolen you can claim €6,000.	◯	◯
(e) You cannot insure your local bank against robbery.	◯	◯
(f) An employer must ensure the factory is safe for employees to work in.	◯	◯
(g) You can insure your premises with two different companies and, if an accident occurs, claim the full amount from each company.	◯	◯
(h) If a truck crashes into your car, your insurance company can look for compensation from the truck owner once they pay you compensation.	◯	◯
(i) If you are underinsured you may not get the full amount you claim.	◯	◯
(j) A food factory must pay compensation to a customer who gets ill from eating their product.	◯	◯

3. Name the type of insurance which a shop owner would take out to cover the following risks.
(a) An employee is injured at work.
(b) A customer gets sick from eating bread baked on the shop premises.
(c) The shop van crashes while on a home delivery run.
(d) The shop window is smashed by vandals.
(e) A customer slips on a wet floor after it was washed.
(f) A computer virus destroys the shopkeeper's accounts.
(g) An employee steals cash from the cash register.
(h) The shop goes on fire.

4. Annie Jones owns a boutique in Gurranabraher, Co. Cork. She stocks only designer labels such as Gucci, Dolce and Gabana, Prada and so on. She carries a large range of very expensive items. She needs insurance to cover her boutique and asks insurance broker Graham Jordan to assess her needs and give her a quotation.

burglary	fire	vehicle	liability	signs	public

Complete his report using words from the list above.

Annie Jones needs ^{1}_____ and special perils cover to insure her property, office furniture and stock against destruction or damage. As Annie employs one female assistant she also needs employer's ^{2}_____ to insure against injury, illness or disease caused to any employee in the course of their work. In addition, ^{3}_____ liability insurance is also a requirement as it covers injury, damage or illness to members of the public using Annie's shop. Because of the expensive stock, ^{4}_____ and hold-up cover is essential to cover property and stock against loss or damage in the event of a robbery. Glass and ^{5}_____ are also items that can get broken and need to be insured. Annie just has one van to transport stock and it is compulsory for her to get ^{6}_____ insurance for this van.

5. Before he wrote the above report Graham had to ask Annie about her business. Here are Annie's answers, but can you make up the questions Graham asked?

(a) _____?
    A boutique.

(b) _____?
    Designer labels like Gucci and Prada.

(c) _____?
    Yes, one assistant.

(d) _____?
    Once they smashed in the front window and stole twenty coats.

(e) _____?
    A small van for collections and deliveries.

6. Place the following sequence of events in the correct order.
(a) The insurance company sent out a cheque as compensation for the damage done.
(b) Annie's business was robbed and she filled out an insurance claim form.
(c) The insurance company sent Annie her insurance certificate.
(d) Annie talked to the insurance broker about the possible risks she should insure against.
(e) The insurance company sent out a loss adjuster to look at the damage done to Annie's business.
(f) Annie filled out an insurance proposal form and paid her insurance premium.

LESSON 2: PRACTICE

1.   In each of the following cases calculate the total premium payable.

(a) Wheels of Wexford Ltd wish to insure the following: showrooms €180,000; office equipment and computers €35,500; two delivery vans valued at €17,000 each; stock of cars €85,000; cash held in the office €1,250.

They get the following quotation for one year's insurance: insurance for showrooms €3.50 per €1,000 value; insurance for equipment and computers €3.50 per €1,000 value; van insurance €760 per van; stock insurance €12.50 per €1,000; cash insurance €10 per €500.

(b) Office Supplies Ltd wish to insure the following: warehouse €175,000; office computers €20,000; four delivery vans valued at €15,000 each; stock of office equipment €95,000; cash held in the office €1,750.

They get the following quotation for one year's insurance: insurance for warehouse €2.50 per €1,000 value; insurance for computers €2.50 per €1,000 value; van insurance €820 per van; stock insurance €10.50 per €1,000 value; cash insurance €11 per €500.

2.   You may need to revise insurance principles in Chapter 9 before attempting this question.

indemnity   utmost good faith   average   insurable interest   contribution   subrogation

In the case of each of the following, state which of the above principles of insurance applies and say what impact it will have on each situation.

(a) Margaret Doyle's factory has increased in value from €25,000 to €50,000 in the last fifteen years, yet it is still insured against fire and theft for the original sum.

(b) The insurance company has paid €7,000 as compensation for the damage caused to your motorboat. They now wish to take possession of the wreck so that they can salvage part of it.

(c) A businessman wishes to insure stock owned by another firm against theft because he believes that the other firm is easily burgled.

(d) A shopkeeper puts in a claim for €270 damage to windows although it will only cost €180 to replace the damaged glass.

(e) A shipowner insures the €40,000 cargo on his ship with two insurance companies. The cover is for loss or damage to a value of €40,000 in each case.

(f) When applying for car insurance, an electrician fails to tell her insurance company that she had a major accident last year.

(g) A container load of computer parts is stolen from your factory three days before it was due for shipment to Britain. The insurance company compensates you for the loss. Some time later the container is found with its contents intact.

(h) A firm insures a €15,000 machine for €20,000. During the August holidays, vandals set fire to the workshop and the machine is destroyed.

(i) An insurance loss adjuster inspects the damage caused to your warehouse after severe flooding. You have put in a claim for damages for €12,000. The lost adjuster believes you were underinsured.

(j) Manus O'Connor insures his business property for €50,000. He fails to disclose that the building is built on reclaimed marshy land.

Insurance Account

Date	Particulars	Cash	Date	Particulars	Cash
Jan 1	Balance	400			
Apr 25	Bank	1,100			

3. The account above appeared in the ledger of Murray's Ltd. Complete the sentences below to explain the entries in the account.

On 1 January Murray's Ltd _____.

On 25 April Murray's Ltd _____.

Insurance Account

Date	Particulars	Cash	Date	Particulars	Cash
2003			2003		
Jan 1	Balance	400	Dec 31	Balance	500
Mar 27	Bank	2,000			
		2,400			2,400
2004					
Jan 1	Balance	500			

4. The account above appeared in the ledger of O'Hara's Ltd. Complete the sentences below to explain the entries in the account.

On 1 January 2003 O'Hara's Ltd _____

On 27 March O'Hara's Ltd _____.

On 1 January 2004 O'Hara's Ltd _____.

STATE EXAM PRACTICE

1. Shopfitters Ltd have decided to change their insurers and have asked Sword Insurers Ltd to give them a quotation for insuring the following: buildings €135,000; machinery €70,000; three delivery vans valued at €18,000 each; stock of shop fittings €85,000; cash held in the office €1,250.

Sword Insurers Ltd supplied the following quotation for one year's insurance: insurance for buildings and machinery €3.50 per €1,000 value; motor van, third party fire and theft €710 per van; stock insurance €11.50 per €1,000 value; cash insurance €12 per €500.

New business introductory offer: twenty per cent discount off total premium.

Shopfitters Ltd accepted the quotation and took out insurance on everything at replacement cost (as stated above) except the machinery, which they insured for €50,000.

Shopfitters Ltd paid the premium by cheque on 1 July 2004.

Answer the following.
(a) Calculate the amount of the premium paid by Shopfitters Ltd on 1 July 2004. (Show your workings clearly.)
(b) The insurance account in Shopfitters Ltd ledger has an opening debit balance of €1,700. Record the payment to Sword Insurers Ltd on 1 July 2004. Balance the insurance account on 31 December 2004 (the end of their trading year), clearly showing the amount to be transferred to the profit and loss account.
(c) In the event of fire damage to machinery of €35,000, how much compensation would Shopfitters Ltd receive? (Show your workings.)
(d) Name two other types of insurance you think Shopfitters Ltd should have.
(JCHL, adapted)

19 Communications

INTRODUCTION

Work in pairs. List the different forms of communication you can find around a school. Think in terms of:

- written.
- visual.
- verbal.

LESSON 1: THE IMPORTANCE OF COMMUNICATION FOR A BUSINESS

Communication involves sending a message from one person to another. With good communication the message sent will be understood by the person receiving it and some response will take place.

INTERNAL AND EXTERNAL COMMUNICATION

Communication in business can be internal or external. Information exchanged within a business is known as internal communication, e.g. instructions between a manager and a subordinate or messages sent between colleagues. Communication between the business and outsiders is known as external communication, e.g. communication with suppliers, customers, shareholders, the general public or the media.

SELECTING A FORM OF COMMUNICATION

The choice of a form of communication will be influenced by:

- **speed** – how quickly must the message be delivered?
- **reliability** – is the message likely to be lost or misunderstood?
- **cost** – how expensive is the system going to be?
- **security** – must the message be kept secret?

TYPES OF COMMUNICATION

VERBAL

Verbal communication in business can occur at meetings or on the telephone. This is a quick and informal way of communicating. Meetings are essentially a verbal form of communication but visual and written communication will also occur.

- **Agenda:** This lists the items that will be discussed at the meeting. It is usually sent in advance to the people who will attend the meeting.
- **Minutes:** This is a written record of what was said and/or the actions that were agreed by those attending the meeting.
- **Reports:** These are often given by people attending a meeting to show the progress of a project.
- **Visual aids:** These are used to make a presentation more interesting. Showing slides or charts with the latest sales figures is more appealing than just reading a list of figures to the meeting.

WRITTEN

Written communication is slower than verbal communication but at least you have a record of what you said. These messages can take time to prepare and can make the sender take more care about what is being communicated. Written communication in business can take many forms.

- **Memorandums** (or memos) are short informal notes that are now often sent in the form of an e-mail.
- **Letters** are more formal. Within a business letters may take the form of a letter of appointment to a job, letter of promotion, letter of warning or a letter of dismissal. Letters, newsletters, contracts and brochures are also used in external communication with customers and suppliers.
- **Reports** are often used internally to give an update on the progress of a project. Reports have a standard format:
  - (i)   introduction
  - (ii)   findings
  - (iii) conclusion
  - (iv)   recommendations.
- **Trading documents** are another form of written communication that a business uses both internally and externally. This takes the form of quotations, invoices, delivery dockets, credit notes, statements and receipts. These provide a written record of the buying and selling transactions that have taken place.

VISUAL

Visual communication can take the form of diagrams, charts or graphs. These are often easier to understand than lists of figures. There are four main types of graphic displays: line graphs, pie charts, bar charts and pictograms.

LINE GRAPHS

Line graphs are particularly useful for comparing two or more sets of figures. A line graph is sometimes called a trend graph because trends or patterns can be spotted in this type of presentation.

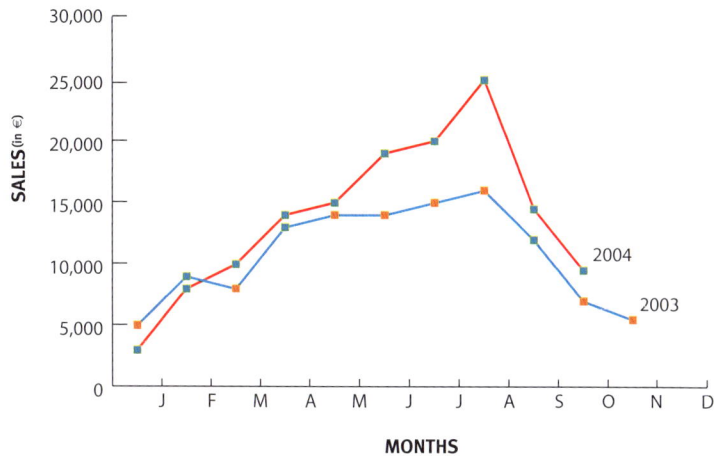

PIE CHARTS

A pie chart is a round graph like a cake with sectors drawn in different sizes to display figures or percentages proportionally.

Question

A class of thirty pupils was asked where they went on holidays last summer. Fifteen had stayed in Ireland, ten went to the Continent and five had a holiday in the United States. Show this information in a pie chart.

Solution

Ireland: $\dfrac{15}{30} \times \dfrac{360}{1} = 180$

Continent: $\dfrac{10}{30} \times \dfrac{360}{1} = 120$

United States: $\dfrac{5}{30} \times \dfrac{360}{1} = 60$

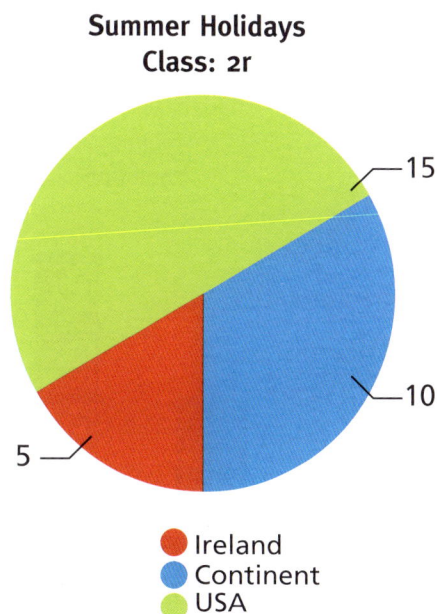

Summer Holidays
Class: 2r

BAR CHARTS

A bar chart is used to display information as a series of bars. It is particularly useful for presenting a large number of categories

Question

An ice cream company had the following sales for each month of the year.

Sales	€
January	5,000
February	8,000
March	9,000
April	11,000
May	13,000
June	24,000
July	26,000
August	27,000
September	14,000
October	8,000
November	7,000
December	6,000

Solution

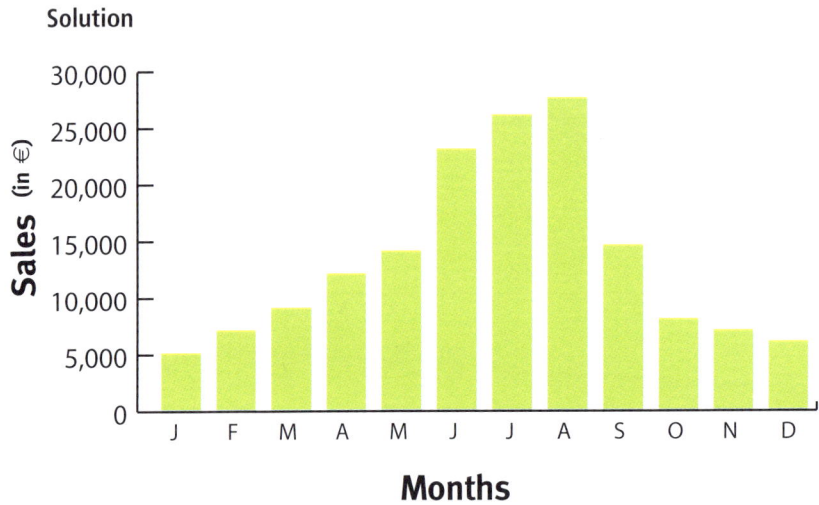

Represent this information in a bar chart.

PICTOGRAMS

Pictograms represent information using pictures instead of bars and lines.

Question

A factory had the following sales of cola for the first four months of the year.

Sales	€
January	1,000
February	2,000
March	1,500
April	2,500

Present this information in a pictogram.

Solution

LESSON 2: AGENCIES INVOLVED IN COMMUNICATION

POSTAL SERVICES

An Post operates the national and international postal service for Ireland. The main services they provide are:

- **Publicity post**: An Post will deliver leaflets directly to the customers you wish to target in a specific area. This is a useful way to advertise your product or service.
- **Post aim**: This is a 'mail-shot' where letters are sent to people whose names you know, e.g. customers, suppliers and so on. The letters may be sent for about half the price of a standard letter.
- **Business reply service**: This service allows people to post their orders or enquiries to a company without the expense and trouble of buying a stamp and posting a letter. The company is only billed for letters received. It is a cheap way of encouraging more business.
- **SwiftPost**: This gets priority over other post so it arrives more quickly than normal mail. Letters are guaranteed to arrive the next day in Ireland and within two to four days within Europe.
- **Freepost**: This service allows potential customers to write to a company free of charge. No special envelope is required. The customer simply includes the word 'Freepost' in the address on the envelope.

TELECOMMUNICATIONS SERVICES

There are now several telecommunication service providers operating in Ireland, e.g. Eircom, Vodafone and Esat BT. Between them they provide a variety of telecommunication services to individuals and businesses.

- **Telephones and mobile phones.**
- **Freefone 1-800**: This service allows a customer to ring the company and the company will pay for the call.
- **Teleconferencing and video conferencing**: Teleconferencing allows three or more people to talk to each other during the same call. A video conference is similar in that it connects people from different areas together using cameras to transmit pictures of the people.
- **Fax**: This combines the facilities of a telephone and a photocopier. It permits the electronic transfer of documents over the telephone line.
- **Internet**: This gives access to the World Wide Web and e-mail.

LESSON 1: PRACTICE

1. Paul Begley is the marketing manager for a large ice cream manufacturer. His company uses the following forms of communication internally and externally. He is preparing a report and has asked you to help him by sorting the list into written, oral or visual communication.

(a) telephone
(b) letter
(c) electronic mail
(d) report
(e) graphs and charts
(f) intercom
(g) videos

(h) meetings
(i) photographs
(j) telex
(k) fax
(l) data transmission
(m) memo
(n) videotext

(o) paging
(p) slides
(q) teleconference
(r) television
(s) diagrams
(t) notice board

2. The pie chart shows the percentage breakdown of sales for the seasons. Read the fax and decide on a suitable label for each segment, then work out the sales for each season.

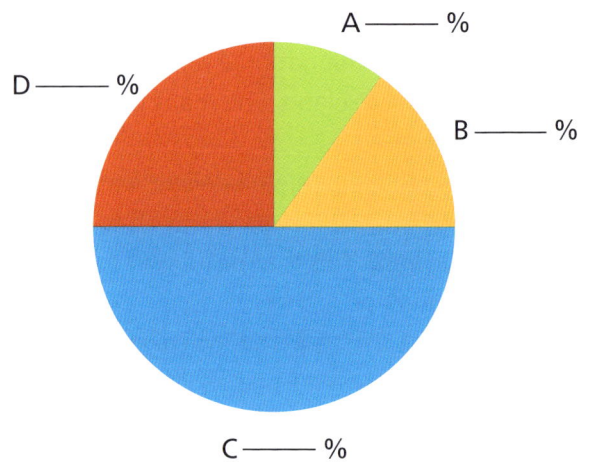

A —— %
D —— %
B —— %
C —— %

FAX

To: Hughes
From: Paul Begley
RE: Sales Report

Total sales of ice cream were €200,000 for the year. Half of these sales were during the summer months and a quarter of sales were in autumn. Sales dropped to ten per cent in winter.

Overall it was a very good year, helped by the advertising campaign launched in the spring. A full report with more charts will be available at the executive meeting next Wednesday.

Paul Begley
Marketing Manager

3. Paul has asked you to prepare the charts he needs for the meeting on Wednesday.

(a) Prepare a bar chart to show the sales in Cork for the first six months of the year.

January	10,000
February	15,000
March	20,000
April	25,000
May	20,000
June	35,000

(b) Prepare a pie chart to show the sales in Galway for the year.

First quarter	5,000
Second quarter	9,000
Third quarter	12,000
Fourth quarter	10,000

(c) Prepare a pie chart to show the expenses for the marketing department.

Light and heat	6,000
Salaries	66,000
Postage and stationery	6,000
Phone calls	12,000

(d) Draw line graphs to compare this year's sales with last year's.

	Ulster	Munster	Leinster	Connacht
Last year	20,000	60,000	50,000	30,000
This year	25,000	50,000	80,000	45,000

LESSON 2: PRACTICE

1.   Complete the gaps in the table below.

1. ....Post

tele 2. ....

3. ....fone

business 4. ....

5. ....net

publicity 6. ....

7. ....mail

free 8. ....

9. ....aim

mobile 10. ....

2.   Use the words from the previous question to list the services provided by An Post and the telecom companies.

An Post	Telecom Companies

3. Use words from the table in the previous question to complete Jim's diary.

October

2 Monday

Received an ¹_____ from Mike with an agenda for Tuesday's meeting.

3 Tuesday

²_____ with Mike, Joanne and myself to discuss location of the new factory.

4 Wednesday

Sent map showing location of factory by ³_____ to Mike and Joanne.

5 Thursday

Joanne rang me on my ⁴_____ to say she had not received the map yet.

October

Friday **6**

Checked An Post website using the ⁵_____. It showed the map was delivered today.

Saturday **7**

Received some ⁶_____ with information about weekend breaks in Ireland.

Sunday **8**

Phoned the ⁷_____ number to book a hotel for a break next weekend.

4. Jim is the finance manager with Ross Ltd, a clothing company that exports sixty per cent of the high-quality garments it makes. The company needs to improve its communication system. Jim has asked you to help him prepare a report suggesting:

(a) three internal methods it might use.

(b) three methods it might use to convey information outside the firm.

(c) an occasion when the firm might use each method suggested.

5. Up to this point Ross Ltd has communicated with its ninety customers in writing only.
   (a) Suggest three alternatives to this system.
   (b) Name three occasions when it should continue to use letters.
   (c) What are the likely costs and benefits to the firm if it decides to use the telephone more often?

STATE EXAM PRACTICE

The graph below shows the trends in employment in agriculture, industry and the service sectors from 1975 to 1989 in the EU.

(a) Which sector lost most workers over the period 1975–1989?

(b) How many people, in total, were employed in 1989 in the EU?

(c) By how much, if at all, did total employment change in the EU over the period 1975–1989?

(JCHL, adapted)

Trends In Employment

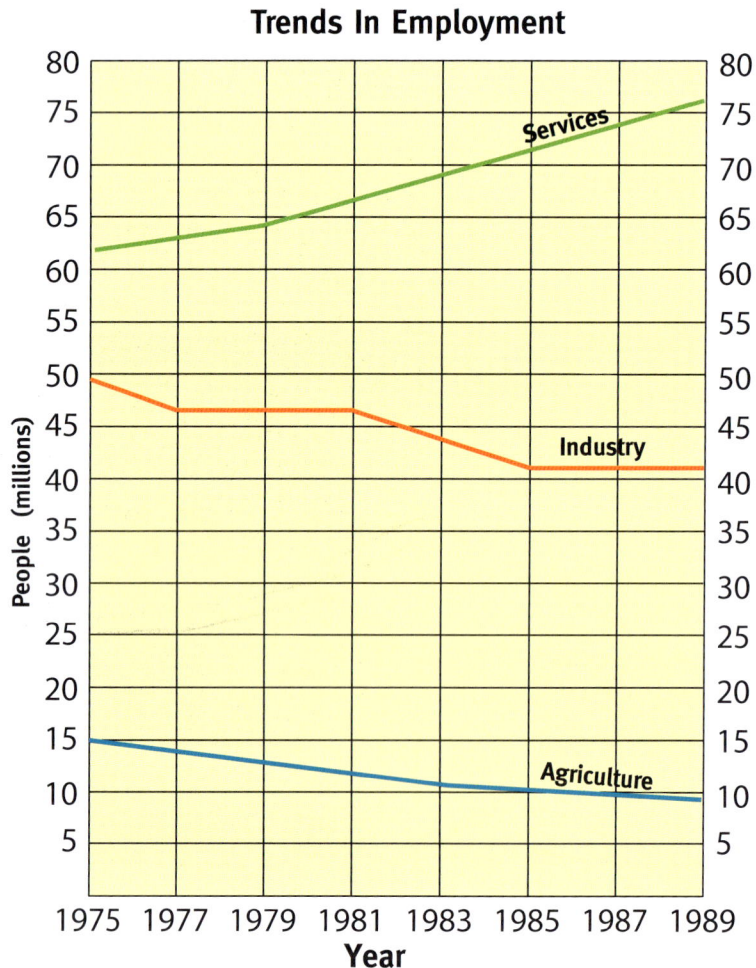

20 The Channels of Distribution

TERMS COVERED IN THIS CHAPTER
Primary, secondary, tertiary, producers, wholesalers, retailers.

INTRODUCTION

1. **Work with another pupil to carry out these tasks.**
   (a) List ten producers of a product.
   (b) List ten suppliers of a service.
   (c) List ten retailers.

2. **What do you think? Answer these questions, then discuss your answers with another pupil.**
   (a) What would it be like if there were no retailers (shops) and we had to buy everything directly from producers?
   (b) Can you list any wholesalers (firms that buy from producers and sell to retailers)?

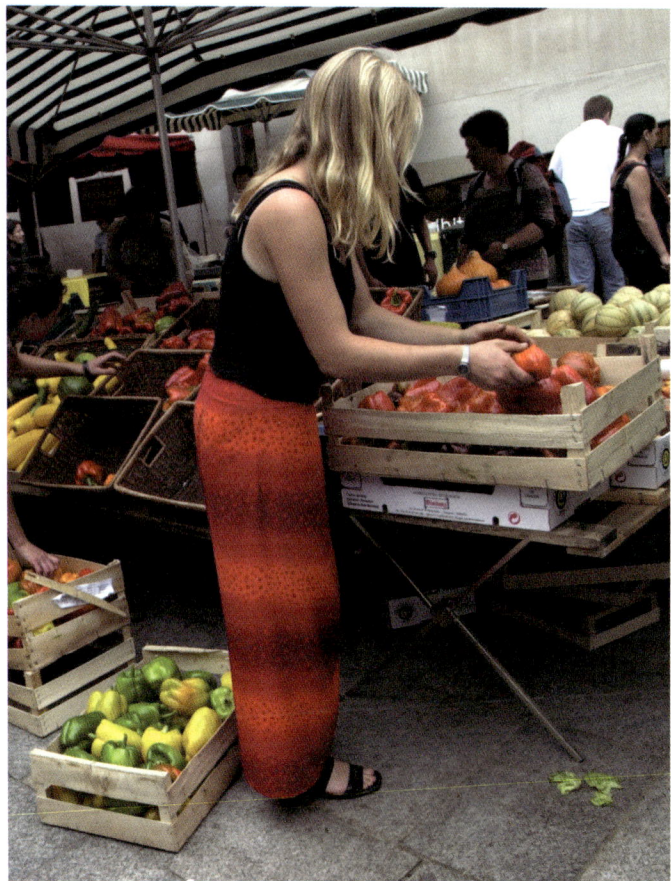

The channel of distribution is the path a product goes through from producer to wholesaler to retailer before finally reaching the consumer. Some products, such as fruits and vegetables, may go direct from the farmer (the producer) to the consumer. Tea, however, is grown (by the producer), blended and packed (by the wholesaler) and then displayed in a shop (by the retailer). We will look at each of these stages now.

LESSON I: PRODUCERS AND WHOLESALERS

There are three types of producers.

Primary Producers

Primary producers take materials from the land or sea or use the land or sea to make a product. The main industries involved in primary production are:

- agriculture.
- forestry.
- fishing.
- aquaculture (fish farming).
- mining.

Secondary Producers

These manufacture and process the raw materials supplied by the primary producers. These firms fall into the following categories.

- New technology firms that produce electrical and electronic goods, chemicals and pharmaceuticals.
- Food, drink and tobacco firms that manufacture goods based on agricultural products.
- Traditional firms that make textiles, clothing, footwear, furniture, packaging and building materials.

Tertiary Producers

These don't make any products. Instead they supply the services that businesses need to operate successfully. There are two main areas.

- Commercial services, which include banking, insurance, transport and communication firms.
- Direct services, which refers to solicitors, doctors, accountants and security firms.

WHOLESALERS

Wholesalers are often called the middleman in the channel of distribution. They act as a 'go-between', buying in large quantities from the manufacturer and selling in smaller quantities to the retailer. They offer services to both the manufacturer and the retailer. Wholesalers offer the following services to the manufacturer:

- buying in bulk.
- blending and packing the goods.
- supplying the manufacturer with market information.

Wholesalers offer the following services to the retailer:

- delivering the goods.
- giving credit.
- storing a selection of goods from different manufacturers for the retailer to choose from.

There are three types of wholesalers.

- **Traditional wholesalers:** These travel around the country to shops to get orders. They usually give credit and deliver the goods to the shopkeeper.

Easons booksellers is an example of a traditional wholesaler of books and magazines.

- **Cash-and-carry wholesalers:** In this case the shopkeepers go to the wholesaler and buy the goods they need. Cash-and-carry wholesalers don't give credit and they don't deliver to the shops. Musgrave is an example of a cash-and-carry wholesaler.

- **Wholesale and symbol groups:** These are also called voluntary stores. They consist of small local shops that have come together to complete with the larger supermarkets. They purchase in bulk for their members, deliver to them and mount advertising campaigns for the group. Centra, Spar, Mace and Londis are examples.

LESSON 2: RETAILERS

Selling to consumers is known as retailing. Shops are the most visible and main form of retailing but this is changing. The advent of the Internet has meant that consumers can now do their shopping from the comfort and safety of their own homes.

Functions of the Retailer

The retailer:

- stocks a wide variety of goods.
- can give advice to the consumer on which product or service is most suitable.
- has a location that makes it easy for the consumer to shop.
- will notice consumer buying trends and give this feedback to the producer.

TYPES OF RETAILERS IN IRELAND

- **Independent retailers:** These are usually small, family-run shops, such as grocery shops or tobacco, sweets and newsagent shops (TSNs). Sometimes they specialise in one particular product, e.g. butcher, shoe shop, public house. They offer a good personal service to their customers and rarely give credit.

- **Department stores:** These are large shops selling a wide variety of consumer products, e.g. hardware, footwear, clothing, cosmetics, food and toys. The biggest department store in Ireland is Roches Stores. It has six outlets and extensive grocery sales. The other main department stores are Clerys, Brown Thomas and Arnotts.

- **Supermarkets:** These are self-service shops that stock a wide variety of goods. They operate on a cash sales basis.

- **Multiple stores:** Any group of shops with many locations around the country can be called multiple stores. The term usually refers to supermarkets like Tesco, Superquinn and Dunnes but it can also include shops like Easons. There are also international multiple retailers with branches in Ireland, e.g. Aldi and Lidl – two German food supermarket discount stores.

- **Voluntary stores:** These are independent retailers that have come together to compete with the multiples. They have similar product ranges and similar store layouts. Centra, Spar, Mace and Londis are examples. They are also called wholesale and symbol groups.

- **Franchise:** Many well-known stores are operating under a franchise arrangement, e.g. McDonald's, Pizza Hut, The Body Shop and Benetton.

MODERN TRENDS IN RETAILING

Consumers now expect retailers to offer many different ways to purchase goods and services. Of course, retailers are usually more than willing to oblige. The following are some recent trends.

INTERNET

The Internet is growing in popularity for selling goods and services and almost all the big travel, grocery and clothing retailers now have an online shopping channel. The integration of the traditional store with Internet selling is known as 'clicks and mortar', but the possibilities for selling online are not limited to these stores. Speciality stores, which only sell one product or service, also have a huge presence on the Internet and many of them don't have a traditional shop at all. This aspect of e-commerce has benefits for both the retailer and the consumer.

Advantages for the retailer:

- The retailer is able to increase sales without the costs of purchasing, equipping and staffing a traditional bricks and mortar store.
- Employees can be given work that has a higher value for the retailer.
- The retailer can respond more easily to shifts in consumer taste.
- Orders can be filled more quickly, as less people are involved.

Advantages for the consumer:

- Consumers are more in control, as they are able to decide when and where they shop.
- The shops are always open.
- All the reputable stores will allow you to return goods and get a full refund if you aren't happy.
- Internet shopping allows the consumer to have a personal shopping experience.
- Online supermarkets are able to store shopping lists so the consumer just has to amend the list on subsequent visits.

VENDING MACHINES

This is a rapidly growing retail area that offers many benefits to both the retailer and the consumer.

Vending machines:

- Don't take vacations. They are open twenty-four hours a day, all year round.
- Offer a wide choice of products for sale, such as snack bars, hot drinks, bottled drinks, cigarettes, juices, cold foods and ice cream.
- Are an all-cash business. There are no debtors to chase for payment. Once the initial investment is made the amount of cash the retailer takes in depends on the number of vending machines he or she has and where they are located.
- Don't need advertising. The manufacturers of the products sold in the vending machines do the advertising that generates a demand for the products displayed in the vending machine.
- Even in busy locations a vending machine may only need to be serviced twice a week, which only takes about twenty minutes.

MAIL ORDER

These retailers have no shops. The goods are advertised on television and radio or in newspapers and magazines. The customer then phones a number given in the advertisement or writes a letter to order the goods. The goods are then delivered by post.

CONVENIENCE STORES

These are open long hours, providing local consumers with a small choice of basic food and household products.

LESSON I: PRACTICE

I. Complete this table to show the channels of distribution in the correct order and name the product the consumer purchases in each case. The first one is provided as an example.

	Channels of Distribution	Product
Publisher Wood Customer Paper	Wood ⇨ paper ⇨ publisher ⇨ customer	Book
Retailer Processor Customer Potatoes		
Goldsmith Gold Wholesaler Customer Jeweller		
Bakery Flour mill Customer Wheat Shop		
Refinery Oil Garage Customer Petrol company		

2.   List the following in three columns to show which are primary, secondary and tertiary producers.

footwear firms	pharmaceutical firms	accountants
insurance companies	mining	forestry
agriculture	security firms	tobacco firms
packaging firms	solicitors	clothing firms
furniture firms	transport firms	building firms
banks	textiles firms	doctors
electronics firms	drink firms	electrical firms
aquaculture	fishing	food firms
chemical firms	communications firms	

3.   Are these sentences true or false? Turn all false sentences into true sentences and copy them into your notebook.

(a)   All products must be sold to a wholesaler before going to the retailer.

(b)   Wholesalers buy in bulk and sell in smaller amounts to shops.

(c)   All wholesalers will deliver goods to the shops.

(d)   An ordinary consumer can buy goods from a wholesaler.

(e)   Cash-and-carry wholesalers give credit.

(f)   Easons is an example of a wholesaler.

(g)   Centra is an example of a voluntary store.

4.   Copy and complete these sentences in your notebook.

(a)   Spar is an example of a _____ store.

(b)   Wholesalers buy in _____ from manufacturers.

(c)   Wholesalers supply the _____ with market information.

(d)   Traditional wholesalers _____ the goods to the retailer.

(e)   Cash-and-carry wholesalers require the _____ to collect their owns goods.

(f)   The wholesaler is the middleman between the _____ and the retailer.

LESSON 2: PRACTICE

1. Based on your reading of this lesson make questions for these answers.

    (a)_____?

    They are usually small, family-run shops.

    (b)_____?

    Roches Stores.

    (c)_____?

    German food supermarkets.

    (d)_____?

    To compete with the large supermarket multiples.

    (e)_____?

    A licence to operate a particular type of business.

    (f)_____?

    The shop is always open.

2. Match each word on the left with a word (or term) on the right, using each word once only.

mail	and carry
voluntary	retailer
independent	order
cash	machine
vending	store

3. All the following answers are correct but they are in the wrong sentences. Write out each sentence fully, showing the correct answer in each sentence.

    (a) A wholesaler is *someone who sells direct to customers.*

    (b) A producer is *a 'go-between'.*

    (c) A retailer is *a method of cutting out the wholesaler.*

    (d) A franchise is *someone who makes a product.*

    (e) A primary producer is *a licence to start a certain business.*

    (f) Mail order is *someone who takes materials from the earth and sea.*

STATE EXAM PRACTICE

I. Jason mixed up the answers in his Business Studies test. He had all the correct answers but he put them in the wrong sentences.

Here is what he wrote.
1. Primary production is *where teachers, nurses and hairdressers are employed*.
2. Secondary production is *where raw materials are produced*.
3. The services industry is *where raw materials are turned into finished goods*.
4. The wholesaler is *a shop that sells airline tickets*.
5. A department store is *a slot machine where you can buy cans of orange*.
6. A shopping centre is *a retailer with branches around the country*.
7. A chain store is *a shop that sells newspapers*.
8. A vending machine is *a covered area where there are many shops*.
9. A travel agency is *a person who buys in bulk (large amounts) from the manufacturer*.
10. A newsagent is *one shop divided into many sections*.

(a)   Write out each sentence fully, showing the correct answer in each sentence.

(b)   Name two other types of retail shops that are not mentioned above and state the service that each of them provides.

(JCOL)

21 People at Work

TERMS COVERED IN THIS CHAPTER
Work, employment, unemployment, employee responsibilities, self-employment, job sharing, teleworking, labour force, organisation chart.

INTRODUCTION

1. Answer these questions, then discuss your answers with another pupil.
   (a) Do you carry out any charity work?
   (b) What part-time job would you like to have when you are sixteen?
   (c) Where would you like to work when you finish school/college?

2. What do you think? Work with another pupil on these tasks.
   (a) Make a list of ten jobs that you think pay well.
   (b) Make another list of ten jobs that you think don't pay as well.
   (c) Make a third list of ten jobs that you could be asked to do that pay nothing.
   (d) Pick a job from each list and name a skill you would need to do the job.
   (e) Why do you think people get paid for some work and not paid for other work?

LESSON 1: EMPLOYMENT AND UNEMPLOYMENT

Work is any task or duty performed in order to produce goods or a service. Working for someone else and getting paid for this work is called employment.

THE NATURE OF EMPLOYMENT

You must be at least sixteen years of age to get most jobs and most workers retire at sixty-five years of age. The average employee works forty hours a week and is paid a wage less tax. Having a paid job means you can afford some luxuries and money gives great independence.

EMPLOYEES' RESPONSIBILITIES

All employees have certain obligations and responsibilities. These are like the rules of working for the company. For example, employees must be punctual and able to follow instructions. They must also be polite and friendly with the other members of the staff. Nowadays many jobs require the worker to share duties and be part of a team. There is just no place in most companies for 'dead wood' and everyone is expected to do an honest day's work. Stealing, of course, could result in instant dismissal and workers must also respect the employer's property.

WHERE PEOPLE WORK

Over half the people employed in Ireland are working in service companies like banking, insurance and transport. This is the real growth sector for jobs and where most school leavers find employment. These are all companies that aren't making a product but instead supply a service to the other businesses in Ireland that make products. For example, many people are employed in new technology computer firms. Food, drink and tobacco firms and traditional firms like clothing and footwear also offer good employment opportunities. There are very few people now employed in agriculture and the number working here is dropping each year as people leave the land and work in cities in service and manufacturing companies.

SELF-EMPLOYMENT

Of course, not everyone likes working for an employer and they may start their own business. These self-employed people work long hours and take few holidays. They take all the risk of the business failing and they finance the business themselves from their savings and personal loans. This can be stressful but it can also be highly motivating as the self-employed person gets to keep all the profits.

The Labour Force			
	Employed	Unemployed	Labour Force
1983	1,100,000	180,800	1,280,800
2002	1,749,900	77,200	1,827,100

MODERN TRENDS IN EMPLOYMENT

- **Job sharing:** Job sharing means that two (or more) workers share one full-time position. This offers a more flexible work arrangement than the traditional job and allows the worker to have more time with his or her family and still earn a living and sustain a career.
- **Compressed work week:** Under this arrangement the employee can work fewer days by working four 10-hour days instead of five 8-hour days.
- **Teleworking:** The employee has a home office and carries out his or her work as if on the company premises. This is suitable for jobs where the employee can use the phone or the Internet to conduct work.
- **Term time:** In this case the employee only works during the school term. When the students are on their summer holidays the employee is given unpaid leave.

UNEMPLOYMENT

Unemployed people suffer the loss of their income. Most people do not choose unemployment – it is forced on them. Some people are quickly able to find another job but others find they are unemployed for a long time, which can make it difficult to get back into a job. FÁS can help by providing valuable training. Learning new skills is often the best way to find a new job.

Labour Force Status

LESSON 2: STUDENT EMPLOYMENT

A survey of pupils in Irish schools found that seventy-three per cent of the pupils have a part-time paid job and they work an average of fourteen hours per week. Of these, thirty-nine per cent work in shops or supermarkets, twenty-six per cent work in pubs, twelve per cent work in restaurants, eight per cent work in a garage and the remainder work in various other locations. Over one-fifth reported they have been injured at work, while slightly more than half said they felt tired in school the day after work.

The pupils were asked to give the reasons for having a job. Not surprisingly, they want the money but they have other reasons too.

Carmel, who has a part-time job as a shop assistant, said her job gives her a break away from daily school. When she gets home from school she changes into her work uniform and heads off to work for a few hours each evening. She usually has to stack shelves or pack bags at the checkout. Only the older staff work at the cash register. 'Sometimes I don't get to complete my homework,' she said, but she can usually organise to fit everything in.

Another pupil, Jane, works in the evenings as a waitress in a pub. Besides taking orders she has to pack the dishwasher and check on the toilets during the night. 'Working helps you to mature,' she believes. She is saving her money for her holidays but she said that besides the money, she likes meeting people and the job can be good fun.

Most of the pupils don't intend going into this line of work when they finish in school. Cathal, for instance, is working as an assistant waiter in a restaurant. When the kitchen is busy he helps to clean vegetables but otherwise he's out in the restaurant tidying off the tables. He says that, just like school, you have to arrive on time or you can get in trouble. He got the job because he likes to buy nice clothes and go out at the weekend with his friends.

Keith says the main reason he doesn't have a job is that he doesn't want his studies to suffer. 'I help out in the local community club but I don't get paid.'

LESSON 3: INTERNAL ORGANISATION OF A FIRM

Most firms can be divided into different departments where each section specialises in particular functions. The junior staff will report to their seniors, who in turn report to their managers. When the chain of responsibilities is drawn in the form of a diagram we get an organisation chart like the one below.

Shareholders

Board of Directors

Managing Director

| Production Manager | Administration Manager | Sales Manager | Personnel Manager | Finance Manager |

The board of directors is elected by the shareholders to run the company. The board:
- decides the overall company objectives.
- sets overall company policy.

The managing director:
- interprets the board's policies and objectives.
- makes the day-to-day decisions necessary to run the firm.
- appoints senior executives to assist in running the firm.

LESSON I: PRACTICE

1.   Quickly scan the lesson for information about people at work and then complete this summary.

All workers have certain obligations and ¹_____. Most people are employed in
²_____ companies and very few now work in ³_____. You must be ⁴____ years
of age to work in most firms. If you don't work for someone you could start your own business
and be ⁵_____ . If you still have no job you will be ⁶_____ .

2.   Orla read the first part of the lesson and wrote out this summary of employees' responsibilities in
her own words. Find the part of the lesson that she is referring to and write it into the following
chart. The first one has been answered for you.

Orla's Answer	Written in the Lesson
Get up early.	An employee has to be punctual.
Listen carefully and do as you're told.	1.
Smile.	2.
No DIY.	3.
Don't waste time.	4.
Don't write graffiti and don't rob.	5 .

3.   Now read the rest of the lesson and complete a summary of it in the following chart.

Employed Person	Self-Employed Person	Unemployed Person
Is between sixteen and sixty-five years of age.	1.	6.
Works forty hours a week.	2.	7.
Is paid a wage less tax.	3.	8.
Can afford some luxuries.	4.	9.
Has independence.	5.	10.

4. Rewrite each sentence using the correct word from the list (one of the words doesn't match any sentence).

| unemployment | service | skilled |
| unskilled | self-employed | luxuries |

(a) The typical employee can usually afford some _____.

(b) A taxi driver is an example of a _____ person.

(c) The _____ rate in Ireland has dropped recently.

(d) An electrician has a _____ job.

(e) Most people work in _____ industries.

5. Study the following pairs of sentences and decide who said each one. Is it an employed person, self-employed person or unemployed person?

A: I have nothing to do all day except watch TV and hang around with my friends.

B: You're lucky. I never seem to have enough hours in the day to do everything and I get very few holidays.

C: When I leave the job at five o'clock I don't think about the place until the next morning.

D: I get so worried that something will go wrong and the business will collapse that sometimes I can't sleep at night.

E: I have great independence and I can afford many nice luxuries.

F: I use my spare time to help out down at the community centre. Next week I'm starting a FÁS course where I'll learn new skills.

6. All the following answers are correct but they are in the wrong sentences. Write out each sentence fully, showing the correct answer in each sentence.

(a) An unskilled person *has no job*.

(b) A sole trader *leaves the country to look for work*.

(c) An unemployed person *keeps financial records for the company*.

(d) A finance manager *has no training*.

(e) An emigrant *takes all the risk of the business*.

LESSON 2: PRACTICE

1.   The following figures are mentioned in the lesson. What do they relate to?
      (a) 73%
      (b) 14 hours
      (c) 39%
      (d) 12%
      (e) one-fifth
      (f) more than half

2.   Read the remainder of the lesson and complete the following chart.

Name	Position/Job Title	Reason
Carmel	Shop assistant	Helps to give her a break away from daily school
Jane	1.	2.
3.	Assistant waiter	4.
5.	6.	7.

3.   Complete the following chart to show three duties and responsibilities for each of the three employees.

Carmel	Jane	Cathal
1.	4.	7.
2.	5.	8.
3.	6.	9.

LESSON 3: PRACTICE

1. Working in groups of three, role-play this conversation between Liam, Mary and Noel, who are on their coffee break.

Liam: Hi, I'm Liam. I'm the new production manager.

Mary: Hi Liam, I'm Mary, the administration manager, and this is Noel, the sales manager.

Noel: Hi Liam. So how are you settling in?

Liam: Not bad. I met Kevin, the stock controller in my department, but Tom, the storeman, is out sick so we're trying to cover for him.

Mary: Fiona, the typist in my department, is also out sick. I think there's a bug going round.

Liam: So is there no chance of getting a temporary replacement when someone is out sick?

Noel: Well, you could ask the personnel manager.

Liam: Who's that?

Noel: It's Jenny, her office is just beside yours.

Liam: I suppose I give her my tax forms as well.

Noel: No, give them to Caroline, the wages clerk in the finance department.

Liam: OK. I better go then.

Mary: Bye, see you later at the meeting with Paul.

Liam: With who?

Noel: Paul, the MD, didn't he interview you for the job?

Liam: No, it was a guy called James.

Mary: James, the finance manager?

Liam: Yes, he said Paul was on holidays!

2. Use the information in the conversation to write the names of the employees above the different positions in this organisation chart.

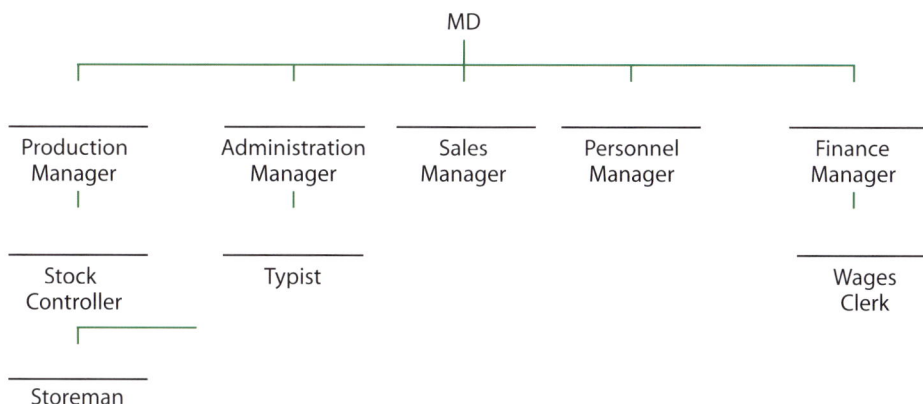

MD

Production Manager	Administration Manager	Sales Manager	Personnel Manager	Finance Manager
Stock Controller	Typist			Wages Clerk
Storeman				

STATE EXAM PRACTICE

1. (a) In business, a sole trader is one of the following.
   (i)   A person who checks the quality of new shoes.
   (ii) A person who receives dividends.
   (iii) A person who sells fish for a company.
   (iv) A business run by its owner.
   (v)   A business that is always losing money.
   Write in your copy in full the most accurate meaning of a sole trader from the above list.

   (b) From the following figures draw a bar chart showing the sales of toys in Play Ltd, a toy store, for the last six months of 2004.

JULY	AUG	SEPT	OCT	NOV	DEC
€	€	€	€	€	€
2,000	1,000	3,000	4,000	6,000	8,000

   (c) What was the total value of toys sold by the store for the whole six months?
   (d) What was the average monthly sale of toys?
   (e) Mary Moran is employed as a shop assistant at Play Ltd. She and all the other employees have certain duties and responsibilities towards their employer. In your copy, write out three of the duties or responsibilities that Mary would have.
   (JCOL, adapted)

2. 'Emigration, unemployment and inflation are problems facing the Minister for Finance when the government's annual budget is being prepared.'
   (a) Explain two of the italicised words.
   (b) Explain the difference between work and employment, giving one example of each.
   (c) Eric Hughes, who is employed as a factory worker, has a number of responsibilities towards his employer. State two of those responsibilities.
   (d) Self-employment (running your own business) has its rewards and also its risks. State two rewards and two risks of self-employment.
   (JCOL)

TEST YOURSELF AT
my-etest.com

22 Employers

TERMS COVERED IN THIS CHAPTER
CV, contract, induction, piece rate, time rate, commission, cash analysis.

INTRODUCTION

1. How far do you agree with the following statements?
   (a) Employers can do what they like because they are in charge.
   (b) An employer can hire and fire anyone.
   (c) An employer can pay the staff whatever he or she likes.
   (d) Most employers take care of their staff.

2. What do you think the following terms mean?
   (a) References.
   (b) Curriculum vitae.
   (c) Staff turnover.
   (d) Box number.
   (e) Wages negotiable.

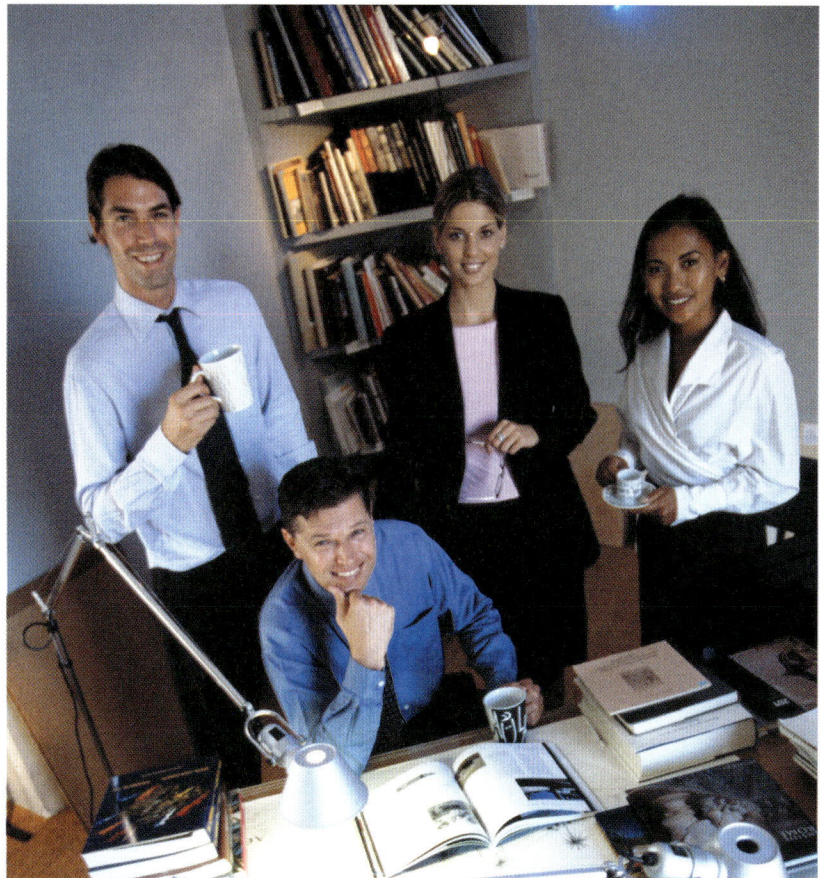

LESSON 1: HIRING STAFF

Pete Bradly is looking for a new sales representative.

Ingrid Kelly applies for the job and sends in her CV.

COVER LETTER

Mr P. Bradley
It Suits Ltd
Sligo

Rosses Point Crescent
Sligo

Dear Mr Bradley,

I wish to apply for the position of sales representative as advertised in today's *Independent*. Having worked in Dublin for the past three years in Arnotts I am keen to find a job in my hometown. I am very interested in the clothing industry and believe I would fit in well in your company. Please find enclosed a copy of my CV. I am available to meet you at any time that suits.

Yours sincerely,

Ingrid Kelly

Ingrid Kelly

CURRICULUM VITAE

NAME:	Ingrid Kelly
ADDRESS:	Rosses Point Crescent, Sligo
EDUCATION:	1980–1989 St Kevin's NS 1989–1994 Sligo Community School 1994–1997 UCG
WORK RECORD:	1993 Local Centra shop, part-time cashier 1995 Burger King, part-time counter staff 1997– Arnotts, Dublin, finance department administrator
HOBBIES:	Acting: member Sligo Drama Society Basketball: member local club

Pete interviews her and offers her the job. She signs an employee contract.

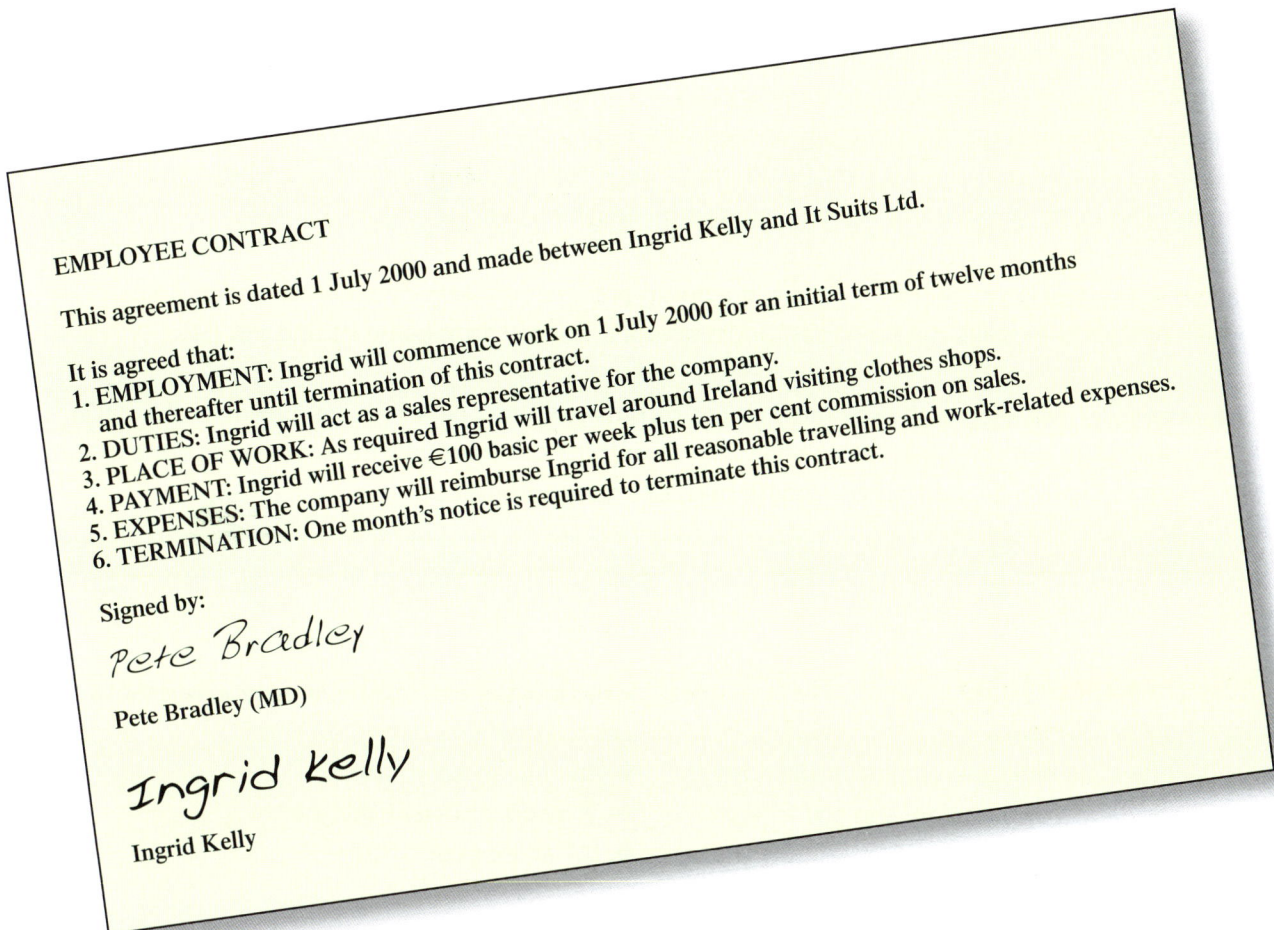

EMPLOYEE CONTRACT

This agreement is dated 1 July 2000 and made between Ingrid Kelly and It Suits Ltd.

It is agreed that:
1. EMPLOYMENT: Ingrid will commence work on 1 July 2000 for an initial term of twelve months and thereafter until termination of this contract.
2. DUTIES: Ingrid will act as a sales representative for the company.
3. PLACE OF WORK: As required Ingrid will travel around Ireland visiting clothes shops.
4. PAYMENT: Ingrid will receive €100 basic per week plus ten per cent commission on sales.
5. EXPENSES: The company will reimburse Ingrid for all reasonable travelling and work-related expenses.
6. TERMINATION: One month's notice is required to terminate this contract.

Signed by:

Pete Bradley

Pete Bradley (MD)

Ingrid Kelly

Ingrid Kelly

EMPLOYEE RECORD

NAME:	Ingrid Kelly
ADDRESS:	Rosses Point Crescent, Sligo
EDUCATION:	1980–1989 St Kevin's NS
	1989–1994 Sligo Community School
	1994–1997 UCG
WORK RECORD:	1997–2000 Arnotts, Dublin
	2000 joined It Suits Ltd
	2000–2001 Finance Department
	2002– Marketing Department

Thousands of people have jobs in Ireland, so it must be easy to get a job, right? Wrong! You may not realise it but giving someone a job is complicated and most employers are very careful about who they hire. This lesson explains why.

When an employer hires a worker he or she takes on certain responsibilities. The employer must allow the worker to join a trade union and the worker is also entitled to get time off, e.g. maternity leave or holidays. Women must get the same pay as men where they are doing the same work and the employer must look after the workers' health and safety. Therefore, equipment must be in good condition and in certain jobs the workers must be given protective clothing.

To avoid any confusion a contract is usually drawn up between the employer and the employee. This will contain things like details of pay, hours of work, holiday arrangements and sick pay.

A wise employer will keep employee records. The records will show personal and educational details about the worker, but it will also show salary details and the different jobs the worker has done in the firm. This information is useful when making decisions about promotion.

Hiring a worker is not as easy as you might think. The procedure can be complicated and takes several weeks.

JOB DESCRIPTION

First the employer makes out a job description. This describes the work the employee will have to do. It gives details of the salary and any fringe benefits the employee will have. It also lists the qualities, experience and age required (for certain jobs). Finally, it mentions how soon the firm needs this worker.

JOB ADVERTISEMENT

The details for the advertisement are taken from the job description. Most firms need to advertise in newspapers and magazines but some will fill vacancies from among existing staff or their friends. The local FÁS office may also have a list of suitable candidates.

INTERVIEW

Suppose you decide to apply for the job – what can you expect? The employer will go through the letters of application and pick out a few to interview. If you are among the lucky ones then you will usually have to supply a curriculum vitae (CV) and a few references. The employer may ring the referees and talk about you. At the interview the employer will ask you questions to get to know you better, such as:

- Tell me about yourself.
- Why do you want this job?
- What are your skills?

SELECTION

After the interviews the employer may shortlist a few candidates and interview these a second time. Only after careful consideration will a candidate be chosen.

INDUCTION

The process is not over yet, however. Picking the right person for the job doesn't mean they will stay in the job. If you don't feel welcome in the job then you will leave. High staff turnover is not good for a company and so some effort should be made to help the new worker settle into the job. If after all this you are happy and the employer is happy then you have a job that could last weeks or years, depending on how you like it. When you leave your employer has to start the whole process all over again.

LESSON 2: CALCULATING WAGES

There are three methods of payment commonly used to calculate wages.

PIECE RATE

This is a payment for each unit produced by an employee. This encourages staff to work 'flat out' to maximise their earnings. Workers in clothing and building firms are paid this way. For example, David works in the local service station. He is paid €2 for every car he cleans using the power hose. Last week he washed fifty cars and earned €100 (50 x €2).

TIME RATE

Office workers are usually paid for the hours they work. The normal working week will contain forty basic hours and any additional hours worked may be paid at overtime rates or given as time off. For example, Sarah gets an office job and is paid €8 an hour and overtime is paid at time and a half, i.e. €12 an hour. Last week she worked fifty hours and was paid €440 (40 hours x €8 plus 10 hours x €12).

COMMISSION

Commission is a payment for every unit sold, or in some cases it may be a percentage of total sales. It is normally paid to salespeople to encourage them to sell more. They often receive a basic salary in addition to the commission they may earn. For example, Orla sells carpets and is paid €200 a week plus five per cent commission on sales. Her sales last week were €6,000. Therefore, her wages were €500 (€200 plus five per cent of €6,000).

Question

Hugh worked fifty hours this week. He is paid €12 per hour for a basic forty-hour week and time and a half for any overtime worked. His tax credits are €30 per week. His rate of tax is twenty-five per cent. PRSI is five per cent of gross and his other deductions are union dues €5, VHI €15 and pension €10. Calculate his net pay and complete the pay slip.

Solution

1. Gross pay

Basic: 40 hours x €12 = €480
OT: 10 hours x €18   = €180
Total gross pay   = €660

5. Net pay

Gross pay   = €660
Less deductions = €198
Net pay   = €462

NAME	GROSS PAY			DEDUCTIONS					NET PAY
	Basic	O/Time	Total	PAYE	PRSI	Union	VHI	Pension	
David Kelly	480	180	660	135	33	5	15	10	462

2. PAYE

Gross pay   = €660
25% of gross pay = €165
Less tax credits   = €30
Tax due this week = €135

3. PRSI

Gross pay = €660
5% of 660 = €33

4. Deductions

Union dues   = €5
VHI   = €15
Pension   = €10
PAYE   = €135
PRSI   = €33
Total deductions = €198

LESSON 3: RECORDING WAGES

Doris, Hugh and Ingrid will not get to take home all the money they earn. They will have to pay tax (PAYE) and insurance (PRSI) and there may be other deductions like pension and VHI. This information is recorded in the wages and salaries book by the wages clerk.

Given the following additional information, complete the wages and salaries book shown below.
- Doris: basic pay €250; no overtime or commission; PAYE €40; PRSI €20; VHI €8.68.
- Hugh: basic pay €480; overtime (OT) €180; PAYE €135; PRSI €33; pension €10; union dues €5; VHI €15.
- Ingrid: basic pay €100; commission €600; PAYE €110; PRSI €40; VHI €12.12.
- The employer's rate of PRSI is ten per cent of gross pay.

Wages and Salaries Book

Date	Name	Basic Pay	OT/ Comm	Total Gross Pay	PAYE	PRSI	Other	Total Deductions	Net Pay	Employer's PRSI
1 Nov	Doris Burke	250	–	250	40	20	8.68	68.68	182.32	25
	Hugh Jones									
	Ingrid Kelly									
TOTALS			1.	2.	3.	4.	5.	6.	7.	8.

If the firm is paying the employees in cash then the wages clerk has to go to the bank and take out enough coins and notes to make up the pay packets for the staff, so before going to the bank the clerk will prepare a cash analysis chart. Complete the chart below.

Cash Analysis

Name	Net Pay	€50	€20	€10	€5	€2	€1	50c	20c	10c	5c	2c	1c
Doris Burke	182.32	3	1	1		1			1	1		1	
Hugh Jones													
Ingrid Kelly													
TOTALS		1.	2.	3.	4.	5.	6.	7.	8.	9.	10.	11.	12.

This information is also recorded in the company's ledger accounts. The bank account is credited as money is going out of the firm, and the double entry is on the debit of the wages account. Write these accounts into your copy.

Bank A/C						
				Nov 1	Wages	€

Wages A/C				
Nov 1	Bank	€		

LESSON 1: PRACTICE

1. What does the start of the lesson say about the following terms?
   (a) Employers' responsibilities.
   (b) Contract.
   (c) Employee records.

2. The rest of the lesson is divided into five sections, each with a separate heading. Read each section and note the main points in the relevant part of the following chart. When you have finished, compare your notes with another pupil.

JOB DESCRIPTION	
JOB ADVERTISEMENT	
INTERVIEW	
SELECTION	
INDUCTION	

3. Read the advertisements below and then answer these questions.

   (a) Refer to the advertisement for a car sales assistant.
      (i)   What fringe benefits are being offered?
      (ii) Why is a box number used in this case?

   (b) Refer to the advertisement for an engineer.
      (i)   What is a CV?
      (ii) What is meant by 'wages negotiable'?
      (iii) Why does this firm want the applicant to supply references?
      (iv) What qualities is the firm looking for in the applicants?

   (c) Refer to the advertisements.
      (i)   Name the company that is looking for an office clerk.
      (ii) What sort of work would this involve?
      (iii) What qualities is the firm looking for in the applicants?

   (d) Refer to the advertisement for a wages clerk.
      (i)   Why is no experience necessary for this position?
      (ii) Write an application letter for this position.

CAR SALES ASSISTANT wanted for busy garage in southwest Donegal. Top wages, five weeks' holiday and annual bonus. Apply to Box PC 1234.

WAGES CLERK required for textile factory. No experience necessary as training will be given. Applications in writing to Pete Bradley, It Suits Ltd, Sligo.

ENGINEER experienced in installing and maintaining alarm systems required by small expanding firm, main areas south Dublin and Wicklow. Wages negotiable. Apply with references and CV to Red Alert Alarms, Stand Road, Wicklow.

OFFICE CLERK required. Must be prepared to work hard. Duties may include any of the following: debtors, creditors, bank reconciliation, wages and typing. Please send CV giving phone number to Susan Kennedy, personnel mgr, Kennedy Meat Processors, Carlow, or e-mail skennedy@kmp.com for more information.

LESSON 2: PRACTICE

1.   Calculate the net pay for each of these workers.
  (a) Deirdre Kelly has a basic rate of €4 per hour. She works forty hours at basic rate and eight hours overtime at time and a half. Her deductions are PAYE €42, PRSI €19 and VHI €6.
  (b) Valerie Poole is paid €1.50 for every dress she makes and 75c for every blouse. In one week she completes fifty dresses and twenty-four blouses. Her deductions are pension €4, PAYE €35 and PRSI €16.
  (c) Cathal McCarthy is paid a basic salary of €200 a month and commission of 9c on every box of chocolate and 3c on every carton of biscuits sold. In one month he sells 5,000 boxes of chocolate and 3,500 cartons of biscuits. His deductions are pension €12, PAYE €62 and PRSI €27.

2.   In these questions you have to work out the PAYE and PRSI before you find the net pay and complete a payslip. (Use the payslips in the Documents Book.)
  (a) Shane Tierney got a part-time job as a garage forecourt assistant. He is paid €5 per hour and last week he worked twenty-one hours. His tax credits are €45 per week. His rate of tax is twenty-five per cent, PRSI is five per cent of gross and his other weekly deduction is VHI €3.
  (b) Janice Buckley works as a shop assistant in a chemist. She is paid €170 for a basic thirty-nine-hour week and €7 per hour overtime. Last week she worked forty-seven hours. Her tax credits are €30 per week. Her rate of tax is twenty-five per cent, PRSI is five per cent of gross and her other weekly deductions are pension €4 and VHI €5.
  (c) Peter Lloyd is a trainee barman. He is paid €180 for a basic forty-hour week and €6 per hour overtime. Last week he worked forty-nine hours. His tax credits are €40 per week. His rate of tax is twenty-five per cent, PRSI is five per cent of gross and his other weekly deductions are union dues €2 and VHI €4.

3.   Complete this chart by placing a tick in the appropriate box to show how you would pay the wages of these workers.

Methods of Payment

Job	Piece Rate	Time Rate	Commission
1. A bricklayer is paid for every brick he cements down.			
2. A supermarket shop assistant is paid for the hours worked.			
3. A car salesperson gets ten per cent of the price of the car sold.			
4. A barman is paid for the hours worked during the evening.			
5. A motorbike courier is paid for every delivery made.			

4. Before you read the article, answer the following questions. Then discuss your answers in small groups.

(a) Besides money, can you think of other reasons for getting a job?

(b) If you were an employer, how could you use money to get workers to work harder?

Surviving payday

Are workers ever happy with their wages? Not according to Pete Bradley, owner of It Suits Ltd and employer of fifty workers at his factory in Sligo.

'I look after my workers,' Pete maintains. 'I pay them well but still they complain.' Over the years he has tried different ways to pay wages. His main aim is to reward employees who are prepared to work hard and increase the company profits. His company makes suits that are sold all over Ireland.

The machinists are paid for the trousers and jackets they make. The **piece rate** is €20 for every pair of trousers they make and €30 for every jacket. This encourages them to work 'flat out' to maximise their earnings. Doris,

the best machinist, can usually make eight pairs of trousers and three jackets in a week.

The office staff cannot be paid like this as they don't make anything. They look after the phones, filing and writing letters for the whole factory. They are paid for the amount of hours they work. The **time rate** is €6 per hour and most office staff work forty hours a week. If they have to work more than this they are paid an overtime rate of time and a half, that is, €9 per hour. Last week Hugh, a payroll clerk, worked forty hours plus seven hours overtime.

It Suits also has four sales reps travelling the country selling suits to shops. These reps don't make anything and so cannot be paid a piece rate. They work very long

hours travelling and meeting people so a time rate is not suitable either. Instead, they are paid **commission** on every suit they sell. They get ten per cent of the sales for the month and this encourages them to sell as many suits as possible. They also receive a basic salary in addition to their commission. Last month Ingrid, one of the sales reps, had a basic salary of €100 per month plus commission on sales of €6,000.

5. Complete this table and calculate the wages for Doris, Hugh and Ingrid from the information given in the article.

	Method of Payment	Rate of Pay	Wages
Doris	1.	2.	3.
Hugh	4.	5.	6.
Ingrid	7.	8.	9.

LESSON 3: PRACTICE

1. You work in the accounts department of Kelly Ltd and are given the following information about three of the employees. (Use the documents in the Documents Book.)

- Linda: basic pay €193; overtime €20; PAYE €45; PRSI €23.42; union dues €2.
- Claire: basic pay €217; overtime €16; PAYE €52.64; VHI €4.
- Eoin: basic pay €181; overtime €63; PAYE €62; pension €5.27.

(a) Complete wages slips for each employee.

(b) Prepare the wages and salaries book from the above data.

(c) Prepare a cash analysis for the net pay.

(d) Show the entries in the bank and wages ledger accounts to record the payment of wages.

2. All the following answers are correct but they are in the wrong sentences. Write out each sentence fully, showing the correct answer in each sentence.

(a) A contract is *a selection of likely candidates for a job.*

(b) An interview is *an agreement between people.*

(c) A CV is *a payment made to salespeople.*

(d) A shortlist is *the way of introducing a new employee into a firm.*

(e) Commission is *a document that lists a person's qualifications and personal details.*

(f) Induction is *a talk between an employer and a possible employee.*

3. **Case Study**

Joan owns a fast food restaurant and requires a sales assistant for the take-away counter. She pays €7 per hour and the sales assistant will have to work six evenings a week from 7:00 pm to 1:00 am. The chef has worked for Joan for years but there is a high turnover among the rest of the staff. They usually leave and move to a better job. Joan wants to hire someone neat and tidy to work at the food counter. The new employee must be friendly and trustworthy with money. She has decided to advertise the position in the local newspaper.

Discussion

Working in pairs or small groups, discuss the following questions.

(a) How many hours will the sales assistant work in a week?

(b) How much will the sales assistant earn in a week?

(c) What could Joan do to reduce staff turnover?

(d) Besides the newspaper, how could Joan advertise this position?

Writing

(a) Write out a job description for this vacancy.

(b) Write the advertisement for the newspaper.

(c) Write the questions Joan should ask at an interview.

Role-play: Interview

In pairs, role-play the interview for the job, taking it in turns to play the employer (Joan) and the person looking for the job as a sales assistant.

STATE EXAM PRACTICE

1. The following advertisement appeared in a recent newspaper.

SWIFT ELECTRONICS

Required: Electronic Technician to join our maintenance team.
Qualifications: Electronic engineering qualification. Two years' work experience.
Candidate: He/she should be hard working, self-motivating with good communication skills.

Apply to: Human Resource Manager,
Swift Electronics,
Fermoy, Co. Cork

Closing Date: 1 June 2004

SWIFT ELECTRONICS **is an equal opportunities employer**

John Murray is twenty-five years of age and lives at 6 Laurel Drive, Tramore, Co. Waterford. He studied electronics at the Waterford Institute of Technology from 1997 to 2000 and graduated with an Honours Diploma in Electronic Engineering. For the past four years he has worked at Instomtec Ltd, Carlow as a technician.

(a) (i) As John Murray, write a letter dated 22 May 2004 applying for the position, giving all relevant personal details and stating that you are available for interview.

(ii) Name two sources of information on job vacancies other than the newspaper.

(iii) Name two people whom John Murray could give as suitable referees if required.

(iv) Name two requirements for the job.

(b) John's application for the job was successful and he will earn €28,000 gross per annum. The tax rate is twenty cent in the euro. His tax credits are €2,480.

(i) Calculate his tax bill for the year.

23 Industrial Relations

TERMS COVERED IN THIS CHAPTER
Trade union, shop steward, collective bargaining, trade disputes, conciliator, arbitrator.

INTRODUCTION

1. There are three teachers' unions in Ireland. Can you guess what the letters stand for?
    (a) INTO
    (b) ASTI
    (c) TUI

2. What do you think? Answer these questions and then discuss your answers with another pupil.
    (a) When you get a job will you join a trade union?
    (b) How could the union help you?
    (c) If you were an employer, would you like your employees to join a union?

LESSON 1: TRADE UNIONS

A trade union is a group of workers who come together to protect and advance the interests of the members. By joining together the members are in a better position to negotiate with employers. Everyone has the right to join a trade union, except those people employed in the Gardai or army. For example, if you get a job in a bank you will be invited to join the IBOA (Irish Bank Officials Association) and if you get a job as a national schoolteacher you will be able to join the INTO (Irish National Teachers' Organisation).

Gardai and army personnel aren't allowed to join a trade union. However, each group has a representative body.

The Garda Representative Association (GRA) represents the 9,000 Gardai in Ireland in discussions on pay and conditions. The association is not a trade union and the members cannot go on strike.

The Permanent Defence Force Other Ranks Representative Association (PDFORRA) represents the army, naval service and air corps in matters of pay and conditions. Like the GRA it is not a trade union and the members are not entitled to strike.

FUNCTIONS OF A TRADE UNION

The main functions of a trade union are to:

- negotiate better pay and working conditions with the employers.
- provide legal advice to the members so they are protected against unfair dismissal or redundancy.
- act as a pressure group in discussions with businesses and the government.
- monitor the workplace to ensure the members are getting the legal rights they are entitled to, e.g. maternity leave and sick pay.

Other benefits of joining a trade union are:

- financial advice and services such as group insurance schemes and credit unions.
- training and education courses.
- sports and social events.
- discounts on some goods and services.
- medical benefits.

Trade Union	Membership
IBOA	18,000
ASTI	17,000
SIPTU	220,000
NUJ	3,900
CPSU	13,000
POA	3,500

TYPES OF TRADE UNIONS

There are over 100 registered unions in Ireland. They come in different sizes and represent workers in all types of jobs. They can be grouped into the following four areas.

- **Craft unions:** These are the oldest form of trade union. The members complete a long apprenticeship to become highly skilled in a specific trade, e.g. actors join the Irish Actors Equity Group and butchers join the Irish Master Butchers Federation.
- **Industrial unions:** The members in these all work in the same industry. For example, the IBOA is a finance union representing bank officials, while prison officers join the Prison Officers Association (POA).
- **General unions:** These unions cater for all different types of workers, e.g. cleaners, electricians, clothing workers and nurses. The main general unions are Services, Industrial, Professional and Technical Union (SIPTU) and the Amalgamated Transport and General Workers Union (ATGWU).
- **White-collar unions:** These represent professional workers, e.g. teachers join the Association of Secondary Teachers in Ireland (ASTI), the Teachers' Union of Ireland (TUI) or the INTO. Civil servants join the Civil and Public Service Union (CPSU).

THE ROLE OF THE SHOP STEWARD (UNION REPRESENTATIVE)

The shop steward is the union representative at local level. He or she is elected by co-workers every twelve months and carries out the following union duties:

- provides members with information from head office.
- recruits new members to the union.
- solves problems before a dispute arises.
- negotiates agreements and checks to make sure agreements are kept.

LESSON 2: TRADE DISPUTES

On the one hand we have the unions and on the other we have the employers. The unions want good conditions and fair wages for their members, and the employers want to remain competitive and keep costs down. To avoid conflicts both parties usually try to agree in advance on an acceptable wage level. This is called collective bargaining.

COLLECTIVE BARGAINING

Discussions between employers' organisations, trade unions and the government in relation to the level of wages is known as collective bargaining. The actions that are decided are called National Wage Agreements. These agreements give rise to good industrial relations and in recent years they have been responsible for fewer strikes and less conflict between managers and staff. However, each year there are always a few disagreements that lead to trade disputes.

Irish Congress of Trade Unions (ICTU)
There are sixty-four trade unions affiliated to the ICTU and consequently it represents 750,000 workers and their families. One of the main functions of the Congress is to represent its members in the collective bargaining process.

Employers' Organisations
In the same way as employees have trade unions to protect their rights, employers also group together to negotiate with trade unions. Here are some examples of the types of organisations employers form.
- Irish Business and Employers Confederation (IBEC)
- Irish Small and Medium Enterprises Association (ISME)
- Construction Industry Federation (CIF)
- Small Firms Association (SFA)

TRADE DISPUTES

A trade dispute is a disagreement between workers and employers. Disputes may be about:
- discrimination.
- unsafe working conditions.
- unfair dismissal.
- membership of a union.
- operation of trade union officials.

The shop steward and the management will resolve most disputes without any outside help. Some disputes, however, may be so complex that the shop steward has to call in the help of a full-time official from the union head office. This official will meet the management and discuss the disagreement. If the dispute is still not resolved, then there may be a strike or a third party will be consulted.

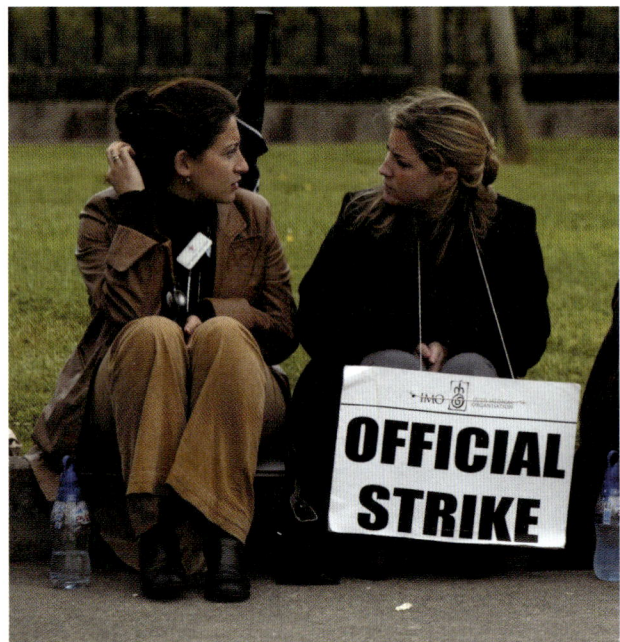

STRIKES

A strike is a withdrawal of labour and is the union's ultimate weapon. An official strike is one that the union head office supports. An unofficial strike is one that doesn't have this approval. Workers suffer the loss of their income when they go on strike and therefore prefer to solve the dispute by negotiation.

ALTERNATIVES TO STRIKES

Before going on strike there are a number of alternatives that employees may consider.

- A go-slow is where the workers stay at their employment but slow down production.
- A work-to-rule is where the workers only follow the work as described in the job description.
- A sit-in is where the employees occupy the premises where they work; unions are rarely officially involved in a sit-in.

Steps in Resolving a Trade Dispute

1. The worker discusses the problem with his or her immediate superior. If this doesn't solve the problem, then…

2. …the worker reports the matter to the shop steward. The shop steward meets the management and tries to resolve the problem. If this doesn't work, then…

3. …the shop steward reports the problem to the union head office. Head office may now send out a union official to discuss the issue with the management. If this doesn't work the union and the management may agree to take the problem before a conciliator.

4. If there is still no agreement, both parties in the dispute may agree to let an arbitrator look at the problem. They agree in advance to accept the findings of the arbitrator.

THIRD PARTIES TO A DISPUTE

In an effort to get both sides talking again, unions and employers often call in the help of a third party.

- **The Labour Court:** This was established in 1946 and can intervene directly in an industrial dispute. It is made up of representatives of employers and workers and is able to solve most of the disputes that are referred to it.
- **Conciliator:** The conciliator works by listening to both sides of the story and encouraging the two parties to enter into further negotiations. The conciliator doesn't give his or her opinion on the merits of either case and has no power to impose a settlement.
- **Arbitrator:** An arbitrator looks at the issues of the dispute and makes a decision to settle the matter. It is normal for both sides to accept the findings of the arbitrator.
- **Rights commissioner:** A rights commissioner is an arbitrator who will investigate disputes about unfair dismissal.
- **Equality officers:** These are arbitrators that investigate claims concerning discrimination in pay or employment.

LESSON 1: PRACTICE

1.   The following trade unions are mentioned in the lesson. What do the initials stand for?

IBOA	
ASTI	
SIPTU	
NUJ	
CPSU	
POA	
GRA	
PDFORRA	

2.   Based on your reading of the lesson, place a tick opposite each statement to indicate whether it is true or false.

	True	False
(a) SIPTU is the name of a trade union.	◯	◯
(b) AIB is the name of a trade union.	◯	◯
(c) IDA is the name of a trade union.	◯	◯
(d) INTO is the name of a trade union.	◯	◯
(e) All employees are obliged to join a trade union.	◯	◯
(f) A Garda can join a trade union.	◯	◯
(g) There is no army trade union.	◯	◯
(h) If you get a job in a prison you can join the ASTI trade union.	◯	◯
(i) The IBOA is a finance union representing bank officials.	◯	◯
(j) Actors Equity is an example of a craft union.	◯	◯

3.   Stephen, Peter, Ann, Georgina and Michael meet at their past pupils' school reunion.

Peter: So how come you managed to get on TV, Ann?

Ann: Oh, I was elected shop steward for my union and I was asked to go to the annual conference in Donegal. We have 220,000 members so it was a great honour.

Georgina: I remember that conference, Ann, I was there covering it for my paper. I never saw you – the hotel was so full of delegates. My union only has 3,900 members and our conference is tiny in comparison with yours.

Peter: How many members does your union have, Michael?

Michael: It's against the law for me to join a union. We have a representative association which looks after our pay and conditions. I think we have about 9,000 members.

Peter: You're in a big trade union Stephen, aren't you?

Stephen: Yes, we have 18,000 members in our association. When I was sick last year they were very helpful with information on sick benefits.

Georgina: My union gave me terrific information about maternity leave last year when I was having the baby.

Michael: But what about you, Peter, you're asking all the questions. How many members does your union have?

Peter: Our association has 13,000 members, which is slightly smaller than John's union, which has 17,000.

Ann: Speaking of John, didn't he do a great job organising this? He's working here, you know, he never left the place.

Study the conversation and answer these questions.

(a) Why was Ann in Donegal?

(b) How did the union help Stephen?

(c) How did the union help Georgina?

(d) Why isn't Michael a member of a trade union?

(e) What type of trade union is Peter in?

3. Complete this table, showing the name of the union each friend is a member of.

	Union
Stephen	
Peter	
Ann	
Georgina	
Michael	
John	

LESSON 2: PRACTICE

1.   The following organisations are mentioned in the lesson. What do the initials stand for?

ISME	
SFA	
CIF	
IBEC	
ICTU	

2.   Place a tick opposite each statement to indicate whether it is true or false.   **True**   **False**

(a) ICTU is the name of an employers' organisation.

(b) IBEC is the name of an employers' organisation.

(c) SIPTU is the name of an employers' organisation.

(d) CIF is the name of an employers' organisation.

(e) A work-to-rule is an alternative to a strike.

(f) A conciliator will try to get both sides of a dispute talking to each other.

(g) A conciliator will not make any recommendations.

(h) An arbitrator will not make any recommendations.

(i) A rights commissioner is a type of conciliator.

(j) An equality officer is a type of arbitrator.

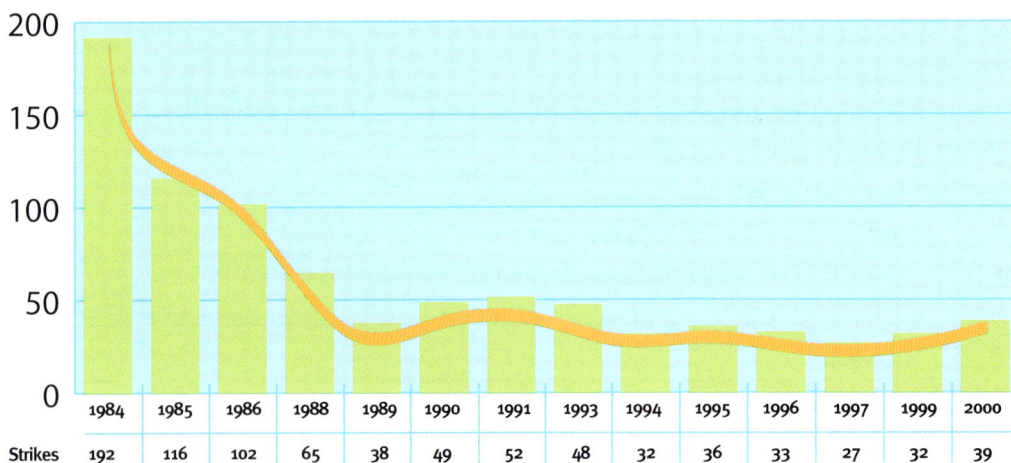

	1984	1985	1986	1988	1989	1990	1991	1993	1994	1995	1996	1997	1999	2000
Strikes	192	116	102	65	38	49	52	48	32	36	33	27	32	39

Source: Labour Relations Commission

3.   Study the chart above and answer these questions.

(a) Which year had the highest number of strikes?

(b) Which year had the lowest number of strikes?

(c) How many strikes were there in 1993?

(d) Which year had 102 strikes?

(e) Which year in the 1990s had more than fifty strikes?

(f) In general, what does this chart tell us about strikes in Ireland?

(g) Who compiled this information?

4. Compu-Parts Ltd makes circuit boards for microcomputers. Three months ago they won an *export* order for €2 million worth of their products. There is only one month left before the order must be *dispatched*. The management are getting worried that it won't be ready in time.

The management have decided to ask the employees to work overtime and they are prepared to pay them time and a quarter. They maintain that if the employees had worked harder over the last few months this problem would not have arisen.

The union claims that if their members worked any faster, the quality of the product would suffer. They feel that the firm should pay *double time* for overtime. Alternatively, they would like Compu-Parts to hire additional staff to cope with the extra work.

They agree to call in an *arbitrator.*
(a) Explain the italicised words.
(b) What would be the effect of hiring extra staff:
    (i)   on the firm?
    (ii) on the existing employees?
    (iii) on the union?
(c) In groups of three role-play the negotiation between the management, union and arbitrator.
(d) Write out a report to your supervisor explaining your point of view, the views of the others in the dispute and the conclusion reached by the arbitrator.

5. The *shop steward* in Valley Textiles Ltd, a clothing company, has asked her union head office to investigate a dispute. The problem concerns Catherine, who maintains that she was overlooked for *promotion*. Catherine's colleagues agree that she should have got the position. They have started a *work-to-rule*, with a view to an *all-out strike.*

The management are concerned that *production* for the Christmas market will be interfered with and want a speedy end to the dispute. They insist, however, that the person they promoted – Richard – is the best one for the job.
(a) Explain the italicised words.
(b) What steps have been taken so far to resolve this dispute?
(c) How would a conciliator help in resolving this dispute?

6. (a) What is the role of management in industrial relations?
(b) What is the role of trade unions in industrial relations?

7. (a) What is a shop steward?
(b) List three duties of a shop steward.

8. (a) State five reasons for trade disputes.
(b) Distinguish between a work-to-rule and a sit-in.

9. (a) What steps should be followed to resolve a trade dispute?

   (b) What is the role of a conciliator in a trade dispute?

10. (a) How does an arbitrator settle a dispute?

    (b) What type of disputes do arbitrators deal with?

STATE EXAM PRACTICE

1. (a) What is the role of a trade union?

   (b) Give three reasons why strikes take place.

   (c) Set out three steps in the resolution of an industrial relations dispute.

   (d) Study the following newspaper report and answer the questions that follow.

   (i) What was the dispute about?

   (ii) Name the parties in dispute.

   (iii) Identify two parties other than in (ii) above who were affected by the dispute.

   (iv) Name two forms of industrial action taken.

Patients first casualty of strike

Nurses in accident and emergency departments will stage a two-hour countrywide strike today.

Doctors last night warned they may be left struggling to cope with emergency patients when nurses take to the picket lines between 12:00 pm and 2:00 pm in protest at intolerable overcrowding and working conditions.

People have been urged not to turn up at casualty units in Dublin's main hospitals if possible.

All other services, including administration of waiting list patients, will go ahead as normal. From today nurses in casualty departments will operate a work-to-rule, refusing to carry out duties such as inserting intravenous drips.

2. (a) Workers sometimes receive additional rewards of a noncash form from their employment.

   (i) What are these rewards known as?

   (ii) Name two methods for calculating workers' wages.

   (iii) Name two voluntary deductions from workers' wages.

   (b) Fintan Lawlor is the shop steward at Machinery Engineering Ltd. He and all the other workers are members of the SIPTU trade union. At a recent meeting they discussed the stance/position they should take regarding future National Wage Agreements/Collective Agreements.

   (i) List two duties of a shop steward.

   (ii) List two problems that a worker might bring to the attention of his/her union.

   (iii) State one course of industrial action, other than a strike, which a union could follow in pursuit of a claim and in resolving a problem.

   (iv) What is meant by the term 'National Wage Agreement'?

   (c) It is considered that National Wage Agreements give rise to good industrial relations.

   (i) Explain what is meant by the term 'good industrial relations'.

   (ii) Fintan is also involved each weekend as a volunteer with St Vincent de Paul repairing and painting houses for old people. Is this work or employment? Give a reason for your answer.

3. (a) The following table shows the number of strikes in Ireland for the period 1990–1994.

YEAR	1990	1991	1992	1993	1994
NUMBER OF STRIKES	49	54	38	48	32

    (i) Illustrate the above information on a suitable chart or graph.

    (ii) Calculate the average number of strikes for the period 1990–1994.

    (iii) In what years were the numbers of strikes below the average for the period?

(b) Give three reasons why strikes take place.

Agriculture staff vote for action

Members of the Civil and Public Service Union in the offices of the Department of Agriculture have voted by four to one to implement industrial action because of what it calls the department's breach of an agreement on the employment of temporary staff.

The action includes a ban on overtime, refusal to perform duties appropriate to higher grades and a ban on telephone and public office queries.

(c) Study the newspaper report above and answer the questions that follow.

    (i) What was the dispute about?

    (ii) Name the two parties in the dispute.

    (iii) What forms of action did the union vote to take?

    (iv) How might the dispute be settled?

(JCHL)

24 Marketing

TERMS COVERED IN THIS CHAPTER

Target market, marketing mix, field research, sample, desk research, product differentiation, informative advertising, persuasive advertising, competitive advertising, the media, collective advertising, national press, tokens, loss leader, branding.

INTRODUCTION

1. Can you match these famous brands with their producers?

Product	Brand
501	Sony
Big Mac	Kellogg's
Yorkie	Levi's
Walkman	Nestlé
Cornflakes	McDonald's

2. Answer these questions, then discuss your answers with another pupil.
   (a) Did you buy a pair of sports shoes recently?
   (b) Did the brand name influence your choice of sports shoe?
   (c) Can you list different brands of sports shoes?
   (d) How are sports shoes marketed?

Marketing looks at what people want and tries to make products to satisfy these demands. Therefore, marketing begins by studying the market and not the product.

LESSON 1: THE MARKET

The market is the place where buying and selling occurs, e.g. the fish market, the fruit and vegetable market, the supermarket or the Internet (e-commerce). In each of these the sellers are looking for potential customers. These customers are the target market for the product or service. As a young person you are in the target market for chocolate manufacturers, drinks companies and teenage magazines. These are all trying to get you to buy their products.

TYPES OF MARKETS

- **Consumer market:** This is the most important of the markets where consumer goods and services are bought and sold, e.g. food, sweets and magazines (single-use goods); televisions and CD players (consumer durables); and cinema and dentist (services).
- **Financial markets:** These provide banking and financial services, e.g. deposit and withdrawal of money and the provision of loans and insurance.
- **The marketing mix:** The marketing mix is the way a company combines what is called the 'four Ps' in order to reach the objectives for the business. The four Ps are product, price, promotion and place. A fifth P – packaging – is also often referred to.
  - ➤ The product to produce.
  - ➤ The price to charge.
  - ➤ The promotion and advertising methods to use.
  - ➤ The place to sell.
  - ➤ The packaging to use.

MARKET RESEARCH

Market research helps a firm find out about existing and potential markets. This information will then influence the marketing mix.

- **Primary/field research:** This involves going out to collect original information in the 'field'. This provides a company with useful and relevant data but there is a big cost in collecting and analysing the data. Researchers use questionnaires to help them interview as many people as possible and since they can't get around to everyone they normally take a sample of their target market. A sample is a random collection of people who are then interviewed for their opinions and preferences.
- **Secondary/desk research:** In this case the researcher will study published and other available material. This is an inexpensive way of finding out about the market, even though it may involve extensive use of the telephone and Internet. The main sources of published information are government statistics, EU publications, trade and technical magazines and websites.

LESSON 2: PRODUCT DIFFERENTIATION

Companies need to make their products different from each other so that the consumer can distinguish one product from another. They do this by advertising, using various selling techniques and by branding.

ADVERTISING

There are four types of advertising.

- **Informative advertising:** This type of advertisement gives the public basic information about the qualities of the product, e.g. sizes available, colours, how long it should last and which shops are selling it.
- **Persuasive advertising:** These advertisements try to convince the consumer that he or she really needs the product, e.g. that you will not be clean unless you use NutriCream soap.
- **Competitive advertising:** These criticise the competitors and highlight the qualities of your own product. This in turn leads your competitors to criticise your products. It is doubtful if the consumer benefits from this form of advertising.
- **Collective advertising:** Many small firms pool their resources and advertise together. They can then mount a more effective advertising campaign on a larger budget.

Over €600 million is spent on advertising in Ireland each year. Where do advertisers spend all this money? The advertising media are the places the advertisements will be shown.

- **National press:** The newspapers are the most popular medium of advertising. They offer large and small spaces in which to advertise and reach a wide audience.
- **Television:** Consumers like this form of advertisement because they can see the product working. Advertisers like this medium because they can target their potential customers by choosing the time to show the advertisement, e.g. advertisements targeting children appear in the late afternoon. Advertisements on television is the second-most popular type of advertising and is used extensively by detergent companies.
- **Radio:** This is the third-most popular medium. As with television, the advertiser can choose when to broadcast the advertisement and can select either a long or short version of the advertisement. Newspapers advertise extensively on the radio.
- **Outdoor:** The fourth-most popular medium for advertisements is outdoor posters and hoardings. This medium is widely used by drinks companies.
- **Other media:** Other media comprise 'free' local newspapers, magazines, leaflets, carrier bags, shop windows and in-store promotions.

SELLING TECHNIQUES AND SALES PROMOTIONS

- **Special offers:** This reduces the price of the product or gives some added value to make it more attractive to the consumer, e.g. 'Buy a burger, get a drink free'.
- **Free samples:** These are given out to promote new products. In this way the consumer can 'try before you buy'.
- **Tokens:** In this case the consumer gets tokens or points and is rewarded for the amount purchased. This is used extensively by supermarkets to encourage loyalty. The tokens can be redeemed later for gifts.
- **Loss leaders:** Many retailers reduce the price of some products to attract customers to their shops. The customer will normally buy more than these loss leaders and so the shop stays profitable.
- **Sponsorship:** Many sports and cultural events are sponsored by firms to promote their products. In return for a fee paid to the organisers, the company is given advertisement space at the venue.

BRANDING

The brand is the name of the product, e.g. Nike, Adidas. It identifies the product and people will call it by that name. Advertisements emphasise the brand name, e.g. 'Enjoy the taste of Coca-Cola'. Trademarks and company logos are also forms of branding by which a product can be identified, e.g. McDonald's distinctive 'M'. A logo is the company or product name written in a distinctive style.

Coca-Cola is the number-one-selling grocery brand in Ireland with sales of €116 million and holding thirty-two per cent of the carbonated drinks market.

TOP TEN GROCERY BRANDS

		€m
1.	Coca-Cola	116
2.	Avonmore Fresh Milk	94
3.	Premier Milk	60
4.	Tayto Crisps	59
5.	Lucozade Energy	56
6.	7-Up	52
7.	Lyons Tea	50
8.	Pampers	50
9.	Denny Prepacked	49
10.	Goodfellas	45

Source: *Checkout Ireland*, 2003

PUBLIC RELATIONS (PR)

Public relations (PR) helps to improve the communications between a business and the various groups that make up the general public. This helps them maintain and increase sales. PR can affect a company's image by influencing:

- letter headings.
- telephone and e-mail manner.
- appearance of sales representatives.
- product packaging.
- advertisements.
- newspaper reports.

Trade Unions

Shareholders

The Company

Customers

Local Community

Employees

LESSON 1: PRACTICE

1.   Match these products and services with a suitable customer (target market).

Product/Service	Customers (Target Market)
1. Holidays for the over-55s	(a) Athlete
2. *RTÉ Guide* magazine	(b) Drivers
3. Baby-care products	(c) Retired people
4. Sports shoes	(d) Parents
5. Cheaper car insurance	(e) TV viewers

2.   Sort these consumer goods into (a) single-use goods (b) consumer durables and (c) services.

1.	television	9.	mobile phone
2.	cinema ticket	10.	magazine
3.	food	11.	electric guitar
4.	sweets	12.	maths grind
5.	computer	13.	orange drink
6.	CD player	14.	guitar lesson
7.	visit to the dentist	15.	scooter
8.	train ticket	16.	phone credit

3.   A businessperson is answering questions about a new product that is about to be launched. Make up the questions being asked.

(a) _____?

Chocolate cubes.

(b) _____?

60 cent.

(c) _____?

On the radio and television.

(d) _____?

In supermarkets and local shops.

(e) _____?

Small cardboard boxes.

4. ABC Advertising Ltd conducted a survey among drivers for a garage. Here is the questionnaire completed by one of the people interviewed.

Are you:
❏ male?   ☑ female?

What is your age?
❏ under 20   ☑ 21–30   ❏ 31–40

❏ 41–50   ❏ 51–65   ❏ over 65

Do you drive a:
❏ motorcycle?   ☑ car?

Does your vehicle use:
☑ petrol?   ❏ diesel?   ❏ gas?

Do you prefer:
❏ self-service?   ☑ petrol attendant?

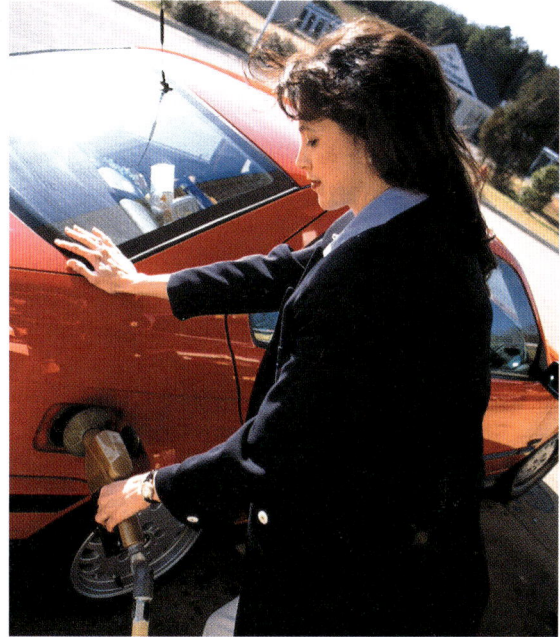

(a) Write a note about the person who completed this questionnaire.
(b) What can the garage learn from a survey like this?
(c) Write the question the survey form would use to find out how often the interviewee used the garage.

5. (a) What is marketing?
(b) List four types of markets and give examples of the types of goods or services sold in each market.

6. (a) What is market research?
(b) Describe any two market research techniques.
(c) Write a note about the marketing mix.

LESSON 2: PRACTICE

1.   Place a tick opposite each statement to indicate whether it is true or false.

	True	False
(a) Over €600 million is spent on advertising in Ireland each year.	◯	◯
(b) TV is the most popular advertising medium.	◯	◯
(c) An antismoking advertisement is an example of competitive advertising.	◯	◯
(d) Coca-Cola is the number-one-selling grocery brand in Ireland.	◯	◯
(e) Desk research involves interviewing people face to face.	◯	◯

2.   Complete the following sentences using words from the list below.

advertise	advertising
media	persuasive
slogan	brand
advertisers	advertisements
target	sample

Researchers usually survey a ^{1}_____ of their target market.

^{2}_____ advertising tries to convince consumers that they need the product.

The main advertising ^{3}_____ are newspapers, TV and radio.

People often complain about the content of certain ^{4}_____.

The ^{5}_____ name identifies the product.

A ^{6}_____ is a catchy phrase used in an advertisement.

The government has threatened to introduce legislation if ^{7}_____ do not act more responsibly.

Some magazines allow you to ^{8}_____ for free.

Good ^{9}_____ can be entertaining.

The ^{10}_____ market for petrol is car drivers.

3.   (a) Name a product that has recently been launched.

(b) In which ways is the product being advertised?

(c) What is the product's brand name?

(d) What logo and trademarks does the product have?

(e) What is the slogan that is used with the product?

4. (a) What is advertising and why is it used?
    (b) What are the differences between informative and persuasive advertisements?
    (c) Explain the following terms used in advertising: (i) hoarding (ii) in-store promotion (iii) sponsorship.

5. (a) What is PR?
    (b) What effect does it have on a firm?

6. In each of the following situations (i) name an appropriate way to advertise or promote the ventures using the specified amount of money and giving reasons for your choices, and (ii) list the motives the advertisements should appeal to.
    (a) Peter Cody and Marie O'Sullivan are opening a hairdressing salon in the local shopping centre next month. They have decided to spend €500 on advertising.
    (b) A health care company is adding a new toothpaste to its existing range of products. It has a budget of €3,000 for the advertising campaign.
    (c) A group of redundant workers has decided to set up a company manufacturing children's garden toys such as swings and slides. They have a budget of €700.
    (d) 'Mugs' is a small craft shop that wants to increase its sales. It specialises in handmade pottery mugs but also has other products it could make if the demand was there. It has a budget of €200.
    (e) Two friends plan on starting a security firm guarding 200 houses in an urban housing estate. They can only go ahead with the project if at least half the residents apply. The cost is €100 per household for twenty-four-hour protection throughout the year. They have a budget of €300 for promoting the project.
    (f) A publisher is launching a new book, a thriller that explores the drugs underworld of the 1980s in Ireland. They have a budget of €1,500 for advertising.

STATE EXAM PRACTICE

1. Peter Sports Ltd sells footballs throughout Munster. In one year the number of footballs sold in each county was as follows.

Clare	Cork	Kerry	Limerick	Tipperary	Waterford
2,000	4,000	4,500	1,500	2,500	1,000

(a) Using graph paper, draw a bar chart or a pie chart showing the above information.

(b) At €20 a football, what were the total sales for the year? (Show your workings.)

Peter Sports Ltd is also producing a new range of football boots that they hope to sell all over Munster.

(c) Write out two reasons why companies advertise their goods or services.

(d) State three methods that Peter Sports Ltd might use to advertise the football boots. Give one reason in favour of each method you mention.

(JCOL, adapted)

2. William mixed up the answers in his Business Studies test. He had all the correct answers but he put them in the wrong sentences. Here is what he wrote.

1. A market is *a reduced price offer to a customer.*
2. A questionnaire is *giving the public information about a product.*
3. Market research is *all the potential customers for a product or service.*
4. Money off is *collecting information about a market.*
5. Informative advertising is *where a firm gives money to a sports club to organise a competition.*
6. A special offer is *given to a particular good or range of goods so that it will become well known among the public.*
7. A brand name is *given to consumers for every €10 they spend in certain shops. Also called tokens, a certain number of them may be exchanged for a free gift.*
8. A target market is *giving extra value for money, such as three for the price of two.*
9. A coupon is *a list of questions consumers are asked.*
10. Sponsorship is *a place where goods are bought and sold.*

(a) Write out each sentence fully, showing the correct answer in each sentence.

(b) The logos of three well-known companies are shown below. State the product for which each of the companies is famous.

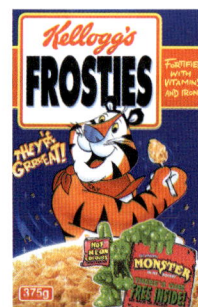

(c) Many people listen to their local radio station every day. State two products or services that would be suitable for advertising on local radio.

(JCOL, adapted)

3. Oakfield Second-Level School, situated three kilometres from the nearest town, has 500 students. The school is considering providing students with hot meals at lunchtime, at a price of €1.50 per meal. The school's board of management has asked P & M Marketing Ltd, Naas, County Kildare to carry out a survey to see if the idea will be successful. The survey findings were as follows.

Total number of students willing to buy meals	350
Types of hot food preferred by students willing to purchase the meals:	
Burger and chips	210
Chicken curry and rice	91
Lasagne and salad	49
Cost of meals:	
Food	€0.95
Other costs	€0.30

Assume you are Patricia Moore, marketing consultant, P & M Marketing Ltd. Prepare a report on today's date for the board of management of Oakfield Second-Level School. Your report should include:

(i) the percentage of students in the school willing to purchase hot meals.

(ii) the percentage of students requiring the different types of meals.

(iii) the daily profit to be made by the school if 350 meals are sold.

(iv) three suitable methods of promoting the hot meals in the school.

(v) recommendation, with reason(s), on whether or not to go ahead with the provision of hot meals.

25 Delivery Systems

TERMS COVERED IN THIS CHAPTER
Fixed costs, variable costs, container traffic, toll.

INTRODUCTION

1. Which of these opinions do you agree with? Give reasons for your choice.
   (a) Companies should buy their own delivery vans. They can then decorate them with their company name and create a mobile advertisement.
   (b) Companies should rent delivery vans when they need them. Buying vans is too expensive and the money can be better used elsewhere in the company.

LESSON 1: TRANSPORT IN IRELAND

ROADS

Road transport is the most common means of delivering goods in Ireland. Ease of access to all our ports and the fact that we are a small country makes road transport reasonably cheap and easy to use. Motorways offer a direct route from one city to another, bypassing smaller towns and villages. This takes heavy goods vehicles away from towns and speeds up delivery. Many firms prefer to buy their own fleet of delivery vans. There are several advantages to this.

- They can advertise their products or services on the vans.
- They have greater security.
- They have more control over their delivery schedules.
- There will be less damage to the products caused by handling.

The costs involved in road transport can be put into two groups.

- **Fixed costs:** The fixed costs are the annual costs of running the vehicles, e.g. motor tax, insurance and annual repairs. These costs do not change with the amount of driving.

- **Variable costs:** These are the daily costs of running a vehicle, e.g. petrol and toll charges. The more the vehicle is used, the greater the variable costs.

RAIL

This may be quicker than road delivery over long distances. However, goods can only be delivered from station to station on fixed routes. Railways operate to a regular timetable and are ideal for bulky loads such as cement.

Iarnród Éireann Freight provides many types of freight services, from the delivery of a single letter to a full trainload of cargo. It has a wide network of freight depots located all around the country and it uses both road and rail to ensure quick and safe delivery of cars, containers and kegs of beer. It also has the Fastrack service, which provides a same-day delivery of parcels and letters.

AIR

This is the fastest form of transport. Over three million people use Irish airports each year, while another three million travel by sea. Because air transport is expensive, the goods transported usually have a high value, e.g. jewellery and parcels for next-day delivery. Air transport is also used to deliver urgently needed products, e.g. spare parts and perishable goods such as fresh fruit.

In recent years there has been an increase in the use of air transport. There are a number of reasons for this.

- It is less expensive now due to increased competition.
- More airports have been opened.
- Modern planes can carry greater loads.

SEA

Around ten ships leave Irish ports every day for Britain and the Continent. Sea transport is ideal for bulky loads over long distances. Both 'roll-on, roll-off' trailers (RO-RO) and 'lift-on, lift-off' containers (LO-LO) travel this way. Many trailers use the 'land bridge' to the Continent, i.e. they get a ferry to Britain, drive to a southern British port and get another ferry or use the Channel Tunnel to the Continent.

Rosslare Port is Ireland's busiest ferry port. It is operated by Iarnród Éireann and is the closest point from the southern part of Ireland to the UK and European mainland.

Dublin Port is another busy port but it is situated right in the centre of Dublin. The new Port Tunnel will make access to the port easier.

INLAND WATERWAYS

Although Ireland has an extensive canal and river network it is not used for transporting goods. They are a big tourist attraction, however, generating much revenue from the hire of boats for cruising and fishing.

PIPELINES

We make extensive use of pipelines to transport gas, oil and water. Gas is piped from the natural gas fields off the south coast of Ireland as far north as Dundalk. Pipelines are also used to deliver airport fuel from Dublin Port to Dublin Airport. These pipelines are expensive to set up but cheap to operate. However, they are only suitable for certain types of products.

LESSON 2: CHOOSING THE RIGHT METHOD

COST

Anything that increases costs will reduce a product's competitiveness. Therefore, it is important to select a method of transport that does not greatly add to costs.

- Air transport is vastly more expensive than sea transport and is therefore only suitable for products with a high value. Bulky products will be transported by sea, e.g. coal and anything in containers.
- Over short distances (less than 300 km) road transport is cheaper than rail transport.
- Having a return load greatly reduces costs.

DISTANCE

Exporting a long distance is expensive: the goods are loaded onto a ship or plane and unloaded at the port or airport. Then they may be loaded onto a truck or train and unloaded again at the new destination. To save money goods may be placed into containers, as these are easy to transfer between the different methods of transport.

SPEED

Producers usually operate within strict deadlines, so they need fast systems that will permit them to meet delivery dates.

- Air transport is fast but only suitable for certain goods.
- Transport by sea is slow and subject to weather conditions.
- Rail transport is fast but only operates station to station and is tied to a timetable.
- Road transport is fast but is subject to poor roads and congestion.

RELIABILITY

It would be unwise to select a method of transport that breaks down frequently, since this might result in a firm missing its deadlines and losing orders.

CALCULATING THE COST OF ROAD DELIVERY

Question

(a) Calculate the cost of the round trip from Cavan to Cork, given the following information.

    (i)   The annual motor tax is €480.

    (ii)   The annual van insurance is €750.

    (iii)   The annual maintenance costs are €270.

    (iv)   It is 300 km from Cavan to Cork.

    (v)   The driver is paid €50 per day.

    (vi)   The van covers 12 km per litre of diesel.

    (vii) Diesel costs 48 cent a litre.

    (viii) The company is open 250 days a year.

(b) Express the total cost of the return journey as a percentage of the invoice value of the goods, given as €1,600. Give one reason why it is important to know this percentage.

Solution

(a) **Fixed costs:**

	€
Motor tax:	480
Insurance:	750
Maintenance:	270
Total fixed costs:	1,500
Amount for day:	€1,500 ÷ 250 = €6

Variable costs:

Distance:	300 km x 2 = 600 km
Diesel used:	600 km ÷ 12 = 50 litres
Fuel costs:	50 litres x 48 cent = €24
Labour costs:	€50
Total variable costs:	€74
Fixed costs for day:	€6
Cost of journey:	€80

(b)

$$\frac{\text{Cost of journey}}{\text{Invoice value of goods}} = \frac{80}{1,600} \times \frac{100}{1} = 5\%$$

It costs five per cent of the value of the goods to deliver the goods. Therefore, the firm should ensure that its profit on sales is greater than the five per cent cost.

LESSON 1: PRACTICE

1. Select an appropriate delivery system for each of the following situations.

	Road	Rail	Air	Sea	Pipes
(a) Delivering newspapers from a city to the provinces.	○	○	○	○	○
(b) Delivering two Aran sweaters to a customer in Boston.	○	○	○	○	○
(c) A consignment of cattle for a Mediterranean country.	○	○	○	○	○
(d) Chocolate for the British market.	○	○	○	○	○
(e) Butter for the German market.	○	○	○	○	○
(f) Fresh lobsters for the Japanese market.	○	○	○	○	○
(g) Delivery of woven fabric from Donegal to Kilkenny.	○	○	○	○	○
(h) Gas from Kinsale to Wexford.	○	○	○	○	○
(i) Powdered milk for a famine-stricken part of Africa.	○	○	○	○	○
(j) Whiskey for the Italian market.	○	○	○	○	○

2.

Clifden

300	Dublin								
148	230	Ennis							
79	216	70	Galway						
251	120	150	170	Kilkenny					
410	192	375	340	320	Larne				
222	80	160	143	120	210	Mullingar			
352	163	246	274	100	360	200	Rosslare		
170	217	195	140	240	241	135	327	Sligo	
330	142	227	253	80	346	180	20	307	Wexford

Refer to the distance chart to calculate the following.

(a) The distance between each of the towns listed below.

(b) The time it would take to travel that distance at an average speed of 60 km/hr.

   (i)   Sligo to Kilkenny

   (ii)   Galway to Sligo

   (iii)   Dublin to Clifden

   (iv)   Kilkenny to Dublin

   (v)   Mullingar to Wexford

LESSON 2: PRACTICE

Modern Developments

1. A sugar manufacturer is considering different forms of transport. The firm wishes to deliver large quantities of sugar to wholesalers and multiples throughout the country.
   (a) Which forms of transport are most widely used within Ireland for the delivery of goods?
   (b) Which is the cheapest method for the delivery of large loads of sugar within a 150 km distance?
   (c) Which is the cheapest method for deliveries of more than 300 km distance?
   (d) What factors are likely to affect the firm's choice of a delivery system?

2. A butter manufacturer intends to export to Britain and Continental Europe.
   (a) Which forms of transport are most widely used to export goods from Ireland?
   (b) Which of these is the firm likely to select to deliver to Britain?
   (c) Which method is it likely to choose for delivering goods to Continental Europe?
   (d) What is the 'land bridge'?
   (e) What factors are likely to affect the firm's choice of a delivery system?

3. (a) List the factors that influence a firm's choice of a delivery system.
   (b) Explain the following terms:
       (i)   cargo liner.
       (ii) trailer.
       (iii) refrigerated transport.

4. (a) Give three reasons why there has been an increase in the use of air transport in recent years.
   (b) Why will other forms of transport continue to carry a larger quantity of goods than air transport?
   (c) List five occasions when a firm would choose air transport. Give a reason for each example.

5. Fast Forward Ltd is a courier service that guarantees overnight delivery anywhere in Ireland. Due to an increase in their business they need to buy an additional van. They have two choices:
       (i) pay €12,000 by cheque.
       (ii) hire purchase: pay a deposit of €2,000 plus thirty-six monthly repayments of €350.
   (a) What is the total cost of buying the van by hire purchase?
   (b) Give two reasons why Fast Forward should buy their own vans.
   (c) Name two fixed costs and two variable costs involved in road transport.
   (d) Fast Forward decided to pay by cheque. Record this in the relevant ledger accounts.

Calculating the Cost of Road Delivery

1. Calculate the cost of the round trip from Larne to Portlaoise, given the following information.
   (i)   The annual motor tax for the van is €370.
   (ii)   The annual van insurance is €640.
   (iii) The annual maintenance cost is €240.
   (iv)   The distance from Larne to Portlaoise is 288 km.
   (v)   The driver is paid €60 per day.
   (vi)   The van covers 12 km per litre of diesel.
   (vii) Diesel costs 50 cent a litre.
   (viii) The company operates 250 days of the year.

2. Calculate the total cost of a journey from just outside Wexford to Clifden and back again to Wexford, given the following information.
   (i)   The annual motor tax for the truck is €360.
   (ii)   The annual truck insurance is €920.
   (iii) The annual repairs are €520.
   (iv)   The distance from Wexford to Clifden is 330 km.
   (v)   The driver is paid €70 per day.
   (vi)   The truck covers 11 km per litre of diesel.
   (vii) Diesel costs 45 cent a litre.
   (viii) The company operates 300 days of the year.

3. Calculate the cost of delivering goods (one way) from Mullingar to Carlow, given the following information.
   (i)   The annual motor tax for the van is €490.
   (ii)   The annual van insurance is €850.
   (iii) The annual maintenance cost is €130.
   (iv)   The distance from Mullingar to Carlow is 96 km.
   (v)   The driver's average speed is 48 km/hr.
   (vi)   The driver is paid €11 for each hour of driving, plus a €30 overnight allowance.
   (vii) The van covers 8 km per litre of diesel.
   (viii) Diesel costs 50 cent a litre.
   (ix)   The company operates 294 days of the year.

STATE EXAM PRACTICE

1.   (a) (i)   What is meant by the term 'channels of distribution'?

(ii)   Describe (illustrate) three channels of distribution and give an example of a good distributed by each channel.

(b) Transport is very important in the distribution of goods. Explain three factors that should be taken into account when deciding on the type of delivery system to be used by a business.

(c) What is the name given to the cost of delivering goods in the accounts of a business?

(d) Champ Ltd, Sligo asks you to calculate the total cost of a journey (round trip) from Sligo to Dublin and back again to Sligo on 29 May 2004 from the following data.

(i)   The distance from Sligo to Dublin is 217 km.

(ii)   The diesel van can do 14 km per litre of diesel.

(iii)   The cost of diesel is 50 cent per litre.

(iv)   The van driver's wages are €75 per day.

(v)   The annual motor tax is €450.

(vi)   The annual motor insurance is €1,200.

(vii)   The annual repairs are €600.

(viii)   Champ Ltd operates 300 working days of the year.

(JCHL, adapted)

2.   (a) State three factors a company would consider when choosing a delivery system.

(b) Answer each of the questions that follow using this Iarnród Éireann timetable.

(i)   What time does the first train for Galway leave Dublin Heuston station?

(ii)   What time does the 11:00 train from Dublin Heuston station arrive in Athlone?

(iii)   If you were in Clara at 1:00 pm, when could you get the next train to Galway?

(iv)   If you travelled on the 14:25 train from Dublin Heuston, how long would it take you to get to Ballinasloe?

(JCOL, adapted)

DUBLIN-GALWAY

WEEKDAYS

		▲	▲	▲ SO (S)	▲		▲ FO	▲	▲	▲	▲ FX	▲ FO
DUBLIN Heuston. Dep	07:30	08:05	11:00	11:25	12:55	14:40	16:25	16:50	18:00	18:05	19:00	19:00
Sallins . . . . Dep	06:30									18:26		
Newbridge. . . . . . Dep	06:38	08:30	10:20					17:03		18:35		
Kildare . . . . Dep	06:44		10:32		13:24		17:00	17:19		18:41		
Monasterevan. . . . Dep	06:52											
Portarlington . . . . Dep	08:08		11:44		13:36	15:21	17:13	17:31		18:56		19:44
Tullamore . . . . Dep	08:27	09:02	12:05	12:27	13:55	15:40		17:50		19:15	20:06	20:08
Clara . . . . Dep	08:38		12:16		14:06			18:01		19:26		
Athlone . . . . Arr	09:02	09:43	12:35	13:01	14:24	16:10	17:55	18:23	19:21	19:59	20:39	20:38
Athlone . . . . Dep	09:08	09:45	12:36	13:02	14:25	16:11	17:57	18:24	19:22	. . . .	20:41	20:39
Ballinasloe . . . . . . Dep	09:24		12:52	13:18		16:28		18:41		. . . .	20:57	20:55
Woodlawn. . . . . . . Dep	09:35		13:06	13:32		16:39				. . . .	21:10	21:09
Attymon . . . . Dep	09:42									. . . .	21:18	21:18
Athenry . . . . Dep	09:52		13:20	13:50		16:54		19:09		. . . .	21:28	21:26
GALWAY . . . . Arr	10:12	TO WESTPORT	13:41	14:09	TO WESTPORT	17:15	TO BALLINA	19:28	TO WESTPORT	. . . .	21:49	21:46

3. (a) State three factors a business would consider when choosing a delivery system.

(b) Answer each of the questions that follow this Iarnród Éireann timetable.

Dublin Heuston	0525	0710	0830	1050	1320	1520	1710	1835	1915
Newbridge	–	–	–	–	–	–	–	–	1941
Kildare	–	–	0900	–	–	–	–	–	1950
Portarlington	–	–	–	–	1402	–	–	–	2007
Portlaoise	0616	0800	0925	–	1414	–	–	–	2019
Ballybrophy	–	–	0941	–	–	–	–	–	2035
Templemore	–	–	0955	–	1440	–	–	–	2048
Thurles	0651	0836	1009	1211	1454	1644	–	1956	2103
Limerick Junction	0713	0858	1031	1233	1516	1706	1849		2125
Charleville	0733		1053	1253	1537			2035	2146
Mallow (arrival)	0748	0931	1108	1309	1552	1738	1921	2050	2202
Mallow (departure)	0750	0933	1121	1311	1554	1739	1923	2100	2203
Cork	0819	1001	1149	1339	1622	1807	1951	2130	2231

    (i) What time does the first train for Cork leave Dublin Heuston station?

    (ii) What time does the 8:30 am train from Dublin Heuston arrive in Thurles?

    (iii) If you travelled on the 7:50 pm (19:50) train from Kildare, how long would it take you to get to Charleville?

(c) Drof Ltd, a manufacturing company, uses rail transport to deliver most of its goods around the country.

    (i) State three advantages for Drof Ltd of using rail transport.

    (ii) State three disadvantages for Drof Ltd of using rail transport to deliver its goods.

(d) In recent years there have been many improvements to the transport system. The use of containers and *roll-on/roll-off ferries* has helped to make it easier to *export* and *import* goods. New motorways are being built which will enable *couriers* and other road users to complete their journeys more quickly. *Toll roads, tachographs* and *refrigerated transport* are other recent developments.

Explain three of the italicised words, giving an example or diagram in each case.

(JCOL, adapted)

26 Stages in a Business Transaction

TERMS COVERED IN THIS CHAPTER
Enquiry, quotation, order, invoice, delivery docket, debit note, credit note, statement, receipt.

INTRODUCTION

The buying and selling of goods involves communication between two businesses. In order to keep track of the transactions, a business will issue a number of documents. These give both the buyer and the seller a written record of the transaction and the documents are usually filed for future reference. They also help to avoid any error in processing the order. Below is a list of the business documents issued in the course of a transaction. What do you notice about most of the arrows?

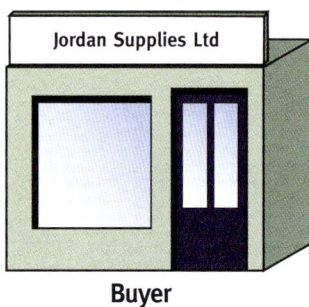

1. ENQUIRY ────────────────────────►

◄──────────────────────── 2. QUOTATION

3. ORDER ────────────────────────►

◄──────────────────── 4. CHECK CREDIT RATING

◄──────────────────────── 5. CHECK STOCK

◄──────────────────────── 6. INVOICE

◄──────────────────── 7. DELIVERY DOCKET

◄──────────────────────── 8. CREDIT NOTE

◄──────────────────────── 9. DEBIT NOTE

◄──────────────────────── 10. STATEMENT

11. PAYMENT ────────────────────────►

◄──────────────────────── 12. RECEIPT

Jordan Supplies Ltd

Cabinet Makers Ltd

Buyer   **Seller**

LESSON 1: DEALING WITH ENQUIRIES

A letter of enquiry is sent by the customer to the supplier to enquire about prices and goods available. A customer may send letters of enquiry to different suppliers. The supplier with the best conditions of sale will then be selected.

The letter below is being sent by Jordan Supplies Ltd to Cabinet Makers Ltd. Jordan Supplies Ltd wish to enquire about some furniture they believe Cabinet Makers Ltd have for sale.

LETTER OF ENQUIRY

Jordan Supplies Ltd

Main Street
Newbridge
Co. Kildare
Telephone 045 654321
Fax 045 654322
E-mail: info@jordan.ie
VAT reg. no. 765432A

Cabinet Makers Ltd

Northside Industrial Estate

Dublin

20/10/2005

Dear Sir or Madam,

Please send me details of the range of office cabinets you supply and the terms you are prepared to offer.

Yours sincerely,

G. McDonnell

G. McDonnell
Director

QUOTATION

A quotation is sent by the supplier to customers who have enquired about goods for sale. It gives details about the goods they have in stock, such as prices, delivery dates, VAT and terms of trade. Some suppliers may have price lists or catalogues they will send out instead of a quotation.

On the right is the requested quotation sent by Cabinet Makers Ltd to Jordan Supplies Ltd.

COMPARING QUOTATIONS

Compare the quotations in relation to price (including VAT), the carriage and the terms of trade before deciding on the best deal.

VAT

Value-added tax (VAT) is a tax on goods sold. It is a percentage of the price of the goods after trade discount has been allowed. It increases the charge to the customer. There are different rates of VAT and they may change each year with the budget.

Cabinet Makers Ltd

Northside Industrial Estate
Dublin
Telephone (01) 8322222 Fax (01) 8322223
E-mail: cabinetmakers@indigo.ie
VAT reg. no. 534936F

QUOTATION

Jordan Supplies Ltd
Main Street
Newbridge
Co. Kildare

Date: 27/10/2005

Model	Description	Price
		€
CSU	Corner storage unit	350
TDD	Three drawer desk	150
MDU	Mobile drawer unit	170
UDU	Under desk unit	90

+20% VAT on all models
Trade discount 10%. Carriage paid. Terms: 5% one month.

CARRIAGE

This is the transport arrangement for the delivery of the goods.

- **Carriage paid:** In this case the supplier will deliver the goods free.
- **FOR (free on rail):** The supplier will pay for the delivery of the goods by train to the station nearest the customer.
- **Ex works:** The prices quoted do not include the delivery of the goods. You must make your own arrangements to collect the goods from the factory or pay the supplier to deliver to you.
- **CWO (cash with order):** In this case the customer must pay for the goods when they are being ordered.
- **COD (cash on delivery):** This means the buyer must pay for the goods when they are delivered.

TERMS OF TRADE

The order form is sent by the customer to the supplier, indicating the goods the customer wishes to purchase. Many suppliers have standard order forms that customers complete. On the right is the order sent by Jordan Supplies Ltd to Cabinet Makers Ltd.

- **Trade discount:** This is a discount given to regular customers who are 'in the trade', i.e. when the buyer and the seller are in the same line of business. This discount is a deduction from the list price, made by the supplier in order that the retailer can make a profit when the goods are sold at the list price.
- **Cash discount:** This is a discount given to customers who pay up promptly. 'Five per cent for cash in seven days' means the customer will get a five per cent discount if he or she pays within seven days. 'Three per cent for cash in one month' means the customer is given a three per cent discount if he or she pays within a month. Notice that the amount of the discount decreases with time.

Jordan Supplies Ltd

Main Street
Newbridge
Co. Kildare
Telephone 045 654321
Fax 045 654322
E-mail: info@jordan.ie
VAT reg. no. 765432A

ORDER FORM

Cabinet Makers Ltd
Northside Industrial Estate
Dublin

Date: 16/11/2005

Qty	Model	Description	Price
			€
2	CSU	Corner storage unit	350
4	TDD	Three drawer desk	150
2	MDU	Mobile drawer unit	170
4	UDU	Under desk unit	90

CHECKING CREDIT RATING

When an order is received, the sales office must check the customer's credit rating. Regular customers who pay within a reasonable time will have no trouble getting credit. Other customers may have to pay cash on delivery or cash with order. New customers must be investigated and a decision made whether to give them credit or not. These customers may be required to give references of other suppliers they deal with. This will show whether the supplier should give them credit.

The seller could look for:
- a reference from the customer's bank (a bank reference).
- a reference from another company the customer does business with (a trade reference).

LESSON 2: SENDING THE GOODS

CHECKING STOCK

It is now necessary for the supplier to check if the goods the customer wants are in stock. Otherwise, part of the order might have to be left out. In this case, the supplier may be tempted to include items not ordered by the customer. It is up to the customer to check that the goods delivered are the goods ordered. If the supplier is out of stock, this means a loss of sale for that item as the customer may be able to go elsewhere and get the goods. Suppliers can easily lose customers by not having sufficient quantities of a product in stock. It is essential that they avoid being out of stock if possible.

STOCK CONTROL

To avoid being out of stock, a firm should operate a proper stock control system with the following policies.

- **Decide suitable stock levels**: There are a number of factors that will influence the maximum and minimum quantities that the supplier should have on hand, such as:
  (i)   storage facilities.
  (ii) stock and warehousing costs.
  (iii) experience of the amount of sales at certain times of the year.
- **Decide reorder quantities and reorder times**: If new stock can be quickly delivered to the suppliers, then they may decide to order little and often. This is the basis of the 'just in time' stock system. This policy reduces warehousing costs and the amount of money tied up in stock. However, the supplier may lose any discounts for buying in bulk.
- **Carry out stocktaking regularly**: Many firms have computerised stock control systems that give them a continuous update of their stock position. In other firms a manual count of the stock is made. Either way, the supplier must know when it is time to reorder.

INVOICE

The invoice is sent by the supplier to the customer. It gives details of the goods being dispatched. The final figure is the amount the customer owes the supplier. The invoice shows the trade discount given (if any), the VAT charged and the terms of trade.

ERRORS IN DOCUMENTS

Since errors may occur in drafting such a document, it also frequently includes the phrase E&OE ('Errors and omissions excepted'). This gives the company issuing the invoice the right to correct any errors they discover later.

On the right is the invoice sent by Cabinet Makers Ltd to Jordan Supplies Ltd.

Cabinet Makers Ltd

Northside Industrial Estate
Dublin
Telephone (01) 8322222 Fax (01) 8322223
E-mail: cabinetmakers@indigo.ie
VAT reg. no. 534936F

INVOICE NO. 209

Jordan Supplies Ltd
Main Street
Newbridge
Co. Kildare

Date: 23/11/2005   Your order no. S/345

Qty	Description	Price	Total
		€	€
2	CSU Corner storage unit	350 each	700
4	TDD Three drawer desk	150 each	600
2	MDU Mobile drawer unit	170 each	340
4	UDU Under desk unit	90 each	360
		2000	
	Less trade discount 10%		200
			1800
	VAT 20%		360
			2160

E&OE Carriage paid. Terms 5% one month.

CHECKING THE INVOICE

When Jordan Supplies Ltd get this invoice they should:

- check the accuracy of the figures.
- check that they got the agreed discount.
- compare the invoice with the order form to make sure they are getting what they ordered.
- file it for future reference.
- when the goods are delivered they can compare the invoice with the delivery note to make sure they have received what they are being charged for.

DELIVERY DOCKET

The delivery docket or delivery note is signed by the customer on receipt of the goods. The customer keeps a copy and a duplicate copy is returned by the delivery person to the supplier. It proves that the goods have reached their destination. It is only used when the supplier delivers the goods to the customer. The customer should compare the delivery docket with the original order and check for damage to the goods.

Here is the delivery docket brought by the Cabinet Makers Ltd driver to Jordan Supplies Ltd.

Cabinet Makers Ltd

Northside Industrial Estate
Dublin
Telephone (01) 8322222 Fax (01) 8322223
E-mail: cabinetmakers@indigo.ie
VAT reg. no. 534936F

DELIVERY DOCKET NO. 113

Jordan Supplies Ltd
Main Street
Newbridge
Co. Kildare

Date: 24/11/2005

Qty	Description	Total
		€
2	CSU Corner storage unit	700
4	TDD Three drawer desk	600
2	MDU Mobile drawer unit	340
4	UDU Under desk unit	360
		2000
	Less trade discount 10%	200
		1800
	VAT 20%	360
		2160

E&OE

Customer signature: ....

LESSON 3: DEALING WITH PROBLEMS

Many transactions do not go smoothly and this is where a company will use either a credit note or a debit note.

CREDIT NOTE

This is given by the supplier to the customer. There are two occasions when it is used:

(i)   when a customer returns goods.

(ii) when a customer has been overcharged.

On the right is a credit note sent by Cabinet Makers Ltd to Jordan Supplies Ltd.

Cabinet Makers Ltd

Northside Industrial Estate
Dublin
Telephone (01) 8322222 Fax (01) 8322223
E-mail: cabinetmakers@indigo.ie
VAT reg. no. 534936F

CREDIT NOTE NO. 78

Jordan Supplies Ltd
Main Street
Newbridge
Co. Kildare

Date: 27/11/2005
Your order no. S/345

Qty	Description	Price	Total
		€	€
1	MDU Mobile drawer unit (faulty castors, inv. no. 209)	170 each	170.00
	Less trade discount 10%		17.00
			153.00
	VAT 20%		30.00
			183.00

E&OE

DEBIT NOTE

This is sent by the supplier to the customer:

(i)   when the customer has been undercharged.

(ii) when some item has been omitted from the invoice.

Here is a debit note sent by Cabinet Makers Ltd to Jordan Supplies Ltd.

Cabinet Makers Ltd

Northside Industrial Estate
Dublin
Telephone (01) 8322222 Fax (01) 8322223
E-mail: cabinetmakers@indigo.ie
VAT reg. no. 534936F

DEBIT NOTE NO. 53

Jordan Supplies Ltd
Main Street
Newbridge
Co. Kildare

Date: 27/11/2005
Your order no. S/345

Qty	Description	Price	Total
		€	€
1	TDD Three drawer desk Undercharge (inv. no. 209)		10.00
	Less trade discount 10%		1.00
			9.00
	VAT 20%		1.80
			10.80

E&OE

LESSON 4: GETTING PAID

Cabinet Makers Ltd

Northside Industrial Estate
Dublin
Telephone (01) 8322222 Fax (01) 8322223
E-mail: cabinetmakers@indigo.ie
VAT reg. no. 534936F

STATEMENT OF ACCOUNT NO. 1020

Jordan Supplies Ltd
Main Street
Newbridge
Co. Kildare

Date: 20/1/2005
Terms: 5% one month

Date	Description	Debit	Credit	Balance
		€	€	€
12/10/04	Balance forward			120.00
23/11/04	Invoice no. 209	2,160.00		2,280.00
27/11/04	Credit note no. 78		183.00	2,097.00
27/11/04	Debit note no. 53	10.80		2,107.80
15/01/05	Cheque no. 110		500.00	1,607.80

STATEMENT OF ACCOUNT

The statement is sent by the supplier and gives a summary of the transactions that have occurred with a particular customer over the previous month. A 'balance forward' figure is the amount the customer owed previously. The final figure shows the amount the customer now owes the supplier. On the left is the statement sent by Cabinet Makers Ltd to Jordan Supplies Ltd.

CHECKING THE STATEMENT

Jordan Supplies Ltd should now:
- check that the calculations are correct.
- check that all transactions have been invoiced.
- check that the terms are correct.
- file it for future reference.

PAYMENT

The customer will usually pay by cheque. Most will pay promptly to avail of discounts.

The company may now issue a receipt. This concludes the transaction.

Cabinet Makers Ltd

Northside Industrial Estate
Dublin
Telephone (01) 8322222 Fax (01) 8322223
E-mail: cabinetmakers@indigo.ie
VAT reg. no. 534936F

RECEIPT

Date: 15/1/2006   No. 231
Received from   Jordan Supplies Ltd

The sum of   Five hundred euro €500

With thanks   Signed
                                   M. Moore
                                   Accounts Dept

LESSON 1: PRACTICE

Dealing with Enquiries

Billy Stafford is the purchasing manager at Alto Ltd. On 28 April 2004 he received the following quotation.

Music Wholesalers Ltd

Quotation No. 2253

Lucy Industrial Estate, Dublin 9

Telephone: 01 6655440	VAT Reg. No. IE 88774455
Fax: 01 6677889	
E-mail: info@mw.ie	

The Purchasing Manager	27 April 2004
Alto Ltd	
Mountain View Road	
Skerries	
Co. Dublin	

Model No.	Description	Price Each €	Delivery
MJ35	Malaga Junior Spanish Guitar	25.00	Ready
OA67	Orlando Acoustic Guitar	70.00	Ready
VE24	Vender Electric Guitar	80.00	Ready
EM17	Epic Mini-Amplifier	60.00	Ready

Trade discount 25% on all goods
VAT 20% on all goods
Carriage paid
For acceptance within 30 days

1. The following numbers and codes are all mentioned in the quotation. Match them with their correct meaning.

1.	25	(a)	Fax number
2.	70.00	(b)	Number of days Billy has to make up his mind
3.	30	(c)	Trade discount offered
4.	2253	(d)	The model number of the Vender Electric Guitar
5.	20	(e)	VAT registration number
6.	6677889	(f)	VAT payable on all goods
7.	VE24	(g)	Price of Orlando Acoustic Guitar
8.	88774455	(h)	Quotation number

2. Billy decides not to buy the Epic Mini-Amplifiers. Prepare the order (no. 778) he sends to Music Wholesalers Ltd for ten Malaga Junior Spanish Guitars, eight Orlando Acoustic Guitars and five Vender Electric Guitars (use the blank documents in the Documents Book).

LESSON 2: PRACTICE

Sending the Goods

Office Furnishers Ltd

Airways Industrial Estate, Dublin
Telephone (01) 462819 Fax (01) 460378
E-mail: officefurnishers@indigo.ie
VAT reg. no. 4599369F

INVOICE NO. 225

O'Connor Ltd
Corrib Road
Galway

Date: 15/1/2005
Your order no. H/284

Qty	Description	Price	Total
		€	€
4	TCS Standard typist chair	70 each	280
4	TCA Typist chair fitted with arms	100 each	400
3	TCG Typist chair, gas height-adjustable	80 each	240
3	TCAG Typist chair, gas height-adj. with arms	120 each	360
			1,280
	Less trade discount 15%		192
			1,088
	VAT 25%		272
			1,360

E&OE Carriage paid. Terms 5% one month.

1. (a) Name the buyer in this transaction.
   (b) Name the seller in this transaction.
   (c) When was this document sent?
   (d) Name three methods of communication that Office Furnishers Ltd use.
   (e) What do the letters 'VAT' stand for?
   (f) Who will pay for the transport of these goods?
   (g) How much does the buyer owe for these goods?
   (h) Make out the cheque received if the buyer pays on 20 January 2005.
   (i) Name three other business documents.

2. On 3 February O'Donoghues Book Supplies Ltd, Abbey Industrial Estate, Sligo sent an invoice, no. 136, to Cronin's Bookshop, Douglas Road, Cork for the following: twenty copies of *Tipperary Folk Songs* at €3.50 each, sixty copies of *Country Stories* at €4.70 each and ten copies of *Irish Hills and Valleys* at €15 each. The terms were trade discount, twenty per cent; cash discount, ten per cent for cash in thirty days; carriage by Iarnród Éireann.
   (a) Draft invoice no. 136, sent on 3 February (use the invoice in the Documents Book).
   (b) Draft the cheque sent by Cronin's Bookshop on 10 February (use the cheque in the Documents Book).

LESSON 3: PRACTICE

Dealing with Problems

Office Furnishers Ltd
Airways Industrial Estate, Dublin
Telephone (01) 462819 Fax (01) 460378
E-mail: officefurnishers@indigo.ie
VAT reg. no. 4599369F

CREDIT NOTE NO. 153

Suir Supplies Ltd
Waterford Road
Clonmel
Co. Tipperary

Date: 21/3/2005

Qty	Description	Price	Total
		€	€
4	TCS Standard typist chair (damaged upholstery, inv. no. 211)	70 each	280
2	TCA Typist chair fitted with arms (faulty castors, inv. no. 211)	100 each	200
			480
	Less trade discount 15%		72
			408
	VAT 25%		102
			510

E&OE Carriage paid. Terms 5% one month.

I. (a) Who sent this credit note?

(b) Why was it sent?

(c) What is 'trade discount'?

(d) Is Suir Supplies Ltd a customer or a supplier of Office Furnishers Ltd?

(e) What do the letters 'E&EO' mean?

2. On 11 June Murphy's Ltd, Furniture Suppliers, Limerick received an order no. 5 from C. Bradley Ltd, 3 Dublin Road, Nenagh for the following goods.
    ● 12 tables @ €300 each excluding VAT
    ● 18 cabinets @ €100 each excluding VAT
    ● 40 chairs @ €9 each excluding VAT
    ● 50 lockers @ €10 each excluding VAT
    Murphy's Ltd sent an invoice no. 78 on 13/6/05 to C. Bradley Ltd. This invoice stated that the trade discount would be twenty-five per cent of the retail price and the goods would be delivered by Murphy's Ltd on 16/6/05. The furniture is subject to VAT at twenty-one per cent.

    On delivery, C. Bradley Ltd examined the furniture and found that one of the cabinets was damaged and ten of the lockers had faulty doors. These were returned in the supplier's lorry and Murphy's Ltd issued a credit note no. 47 on 18/6/05. At the end of June, Murphy's Ltd sent an appropriate document to C. Bradley Ltd.
    (a) Complete the invoice of 13/6/05 and the credit note of 18/6/05 using the blank documents supplied in the Documents Book.
    (b) Outline the procedure for dealing with incoming invoices.

LESSON 4: PRACTICE

Getting Paid

Office Furnishers Ltd
Airways Industrial Estate, Dublin
Telephone (01) 462819 Fax (01) 460378
E-mail: officefurnishers@indigo.ie
VAT reg. no. 4599369F

STATEMENT NO. 273

Golden Supplies Ltd
Cashel Road
Tipperary

Date: 27/2/2005

Date	Description	Debit €	Credit €	Balance €
03/01/05	Balance forward			160
10/01/05	Invoice no. 226	1,600		1,760
14/01/05	Credit note no. 125		140	1,620
23/01/05	Debit note no. 48	20		1,640
25/01/05	Cheque no. 129		1,000	640
26/01/05	Invoice no. 231	1,200		1,840

E&OE Carriage paid. Terms 5% one month.

		True	False
1.	(a) Golden Supplies Ltd sent this statement to Office Furnishers Ltd.	○	○
	(b) On 10/01/05 Office Furnishers Ltd bought goods for €1,600 from Golden Supplies Ltd.	○	○
	(c) On 14/01/05 Golden Supplies Ltd returned goods to Office Furnishers Ltd.	○	○
	(d) On 25/01/05 Golden Supplies Ltd bought goods from Office Furnishers Ltd.	○	○
	(e) On 26/01/05 Golden Supplies Ltd owed Office Furnishers Ltd €1,840.	○	○

2. Seller: Kissane Ltd, Edward Street, Tralee. Buyer: O'Grady Ltd, Bridge Street, Westport. On 1 March the buyer owed the seller €2,100. The following transactions took place during March.

3 March: Sales to O'Grady Ltd, invoice no. 403: €1,140.

8 March: Sales to O'Grady Ltd, invoice no. 415: €1,320.

11 March: Seller sent credit note no. 147 to buyer regarding faulty goods sold on 3 March: €200.

18 March: O'Grady Ltd sent a cheque to Kissane Ltd: €3,000.

19 March: Sales to O'Grady Ltd, invoice no. 438: €2,560.

23 March: Seller sent debit note no. 53 to buyer regarding undercharge on goods sold on 19 March: €130.

(a) Draft the credit note sent on 11 March using the blank document supplied in the Documents Book.

(b) Draft the debit note sent on 23 March using the blank document supplied in the Documents Book.

(c) Draft the statement sent on 31 March using the blank document supplied in the Documents Book.

3. The following details refer to the sale of goods on credit by Foley Ltd to Delaney Ltd, 24 Boyne Road, Drogheda for the month of June.

On 1 June, there was a balance due of €500 in Delaney's account in Foley's books.

5 June: Foley sent invoice no. 7 to Delaney Ltd for €5,000.

7 June: Foley sent invoice no. 20 to Delaney Ltd for €15,000.

12 June: Foley sent credit note no. 57 to Delaney Ltd for goods returned, €500 + 20% VAT.

14 June: Foley received cheque from Delaney Ltd for €16,000.

18 June: Foley sent invoice no. 34 to Delaney Ltd for €20,000.

20 June: Foley sent credit note no. 61 to Delaney Ltd for goods returned, €800 + 20% VAT.

28 June: Foley sent invoice no. 45 to Delaney Ltd for €12,000.

On 30 June Foley Ltd sent a statement of account to Delaney Ltd.

Delaney Ltd paid the amount due on the statement by cheque.

Foley Ltd issued a receipt on 17 July, signed by Hilary Foley.

You are required to do the following.

(a) Complete the statement sent by Foley Ltd on 30 June using the blank document supplied in the Documents Book.

(b) Complete the receipt issued by Foley Ltd on 17 July using the blank document supplied in the Documents Book.

(c) List two checks that Delaney Ltd should carry out before paying the amount due on the statement.

STATE EXAM PRACTICE

1. Lisa Cronin is employed in the sales department of Denim Wholesalers Ltd, Dangan Industrial Estate, Galway. On 10 May she receives the following order.

Order No. 792

Telephone: 0905-17685 Fax: 0905-17686	VAT Reg. No. IE722241B

Smartstyles Ltd

14 Aughrim Street, Ballinasloe, Co. Galway

8 May 2005

The Manager
Denim Wholesalers Ltd
Dangan Industrial Estate
Galway

Please supply the following goods:

Quantity	Description	Price Each
		€
100	'Ringer' Jeans (style 236)	24.00
150	'Hooper' Jeans (style 464)	35.00
300	'Dinger' T-shirts (style 147)	6.50
200	'Zapper' Jackets (style 850)	42.00
	Signed: Rachel Duffy	
	Title: Purchasing Manager	

The goods ordered are in stock except for the 'Zapper' jackets. Lisa gets all the other items packed for sending out. An invoice (no. 1327) is then made out.

Lisa telephones Rachel Duffy at Smartstyles Ltd to tell her that they are out of 'Zapper' jackets at the moment but that the rest of the goods ordered would be delivered the next morning. She also informs Rachel of the total cost of the goods being delivered.

The goods arrive at Smartstyles Ltd the next day in a delivery van. The driver also hands Rachel the invoice (no. 1327).

After she checks the goods, Rachel hands a cheque (no. 015329) for the total amount, signed by herself, to the driver to bring back to Denim Wholesalers Ltd.

(a) From the above details complete invoice no. 1327 using the blank invoice in the Documents Book. VAT is charged at the rate of twenty-one per cent on all items on the invoice.

(b) Complete cheque no. 015329 using the blank cheque in the Documents Book.

(c) Using the bank account in the Documents Book, show how the cheque payment of 11 May would be recorded in Smartstyle Ltd's bank account.

(JCOL, adapted)

2. John Russell is the purchasing manager at Tenor Ltd. On 20 March 2005 he received the following quotation.

Ceol Wholesalers Ltd	Quotation No. 5322
Hamilton Industrial Estate, Dublin 9	

Telephone: 01-1657832	VAT Reg. No. IE 4886114
Fax: 01-1657966	
E-mail: ceol@comair.net	

The Purchasing Manager	19 March 2005
Tenor Ltd	
Sea Road	
Bray	
Co. Wicklow	

Model No.	Description	Price Each €	Delivery
WO53	Westlife New Compact Disc	20.00	Ready
U276	U2 Latest Compact Disc	18.00	Ready
D142	De Danann Collection Compact Disc	15.00	Ready
B317	Boyzone Greatest Compact Disc	25.00	Ready

Trade discount 25% on all goods
VAT 20% on all goods
Carriage paid
For acceptance within 30 days

John decides that the Boyzone CDs are too costly. He sends an order (no. 877) to Ceol Wholesalers Ltd for 500 Westlife New CDs, 1,000 U2 Latest CDs and 600 De Danann Collection CDs. These goods are delivered in a van to Tenor Ltd on 25 March 2005. John checks the goods when they arrive and finds everything correct. After he signs the delivery note he is handed invoice no. 3776, dated 24 March 2005, by the van driver.

(a) From the above details, complete the blank invoice no. 3776 in the Document Book.

John then writes out a cheque on behalf of Tenor Ltd in full payment for the goods and hands it to the driver to bring back to Ceol Wholesalers Ltd.

(b) Enter the payment in the bank account of Tenor Ltd using the blank bank account in the Documents Book.

A receipt for the payment arrives the next day from Ceol Wholesalers Ltd, dated 25 March 2005 and signed by Ann Hogan, Cashier.

(c) Complete the receipt (no. 314) using the blank receipt in the Documents Book.

(d) In the space provided in the Documents Book state one reason why a receipt is an important document.

27   Purchases

TERMS COVERED IN THIS CHAPTER
Invoice, credit note, day books, ledger, posting, balancing accounts, trial balance.

INTRODUCTION

1. Your school has many suppliers. Some of these insist on a cash payment, while others give your school a few weeks of credit. Suppliers show they trust your school when they have credit transactions.
   (a)   What goods and services might suppliers provide your school?
   (b)   What examples of credit transactions can you give from your own experience?
   (c)   What kind of credit transactions might happen in your school?

LESSON I: RECORDING PURCHASES

When you purchase goods you probably pay cash for them. The shopkeeper does not need to ask you your name and you do not need to know the shopkeeper's name. When you run a business it is a little different. For a start, you may not have to pay for the goods immediately. This is known as a credit transaction. It means you get a chance to sell the goods and get cash in before you have to pay your supplier. To keep track of credit transactions it is necessary to take note of certain details, which are all contained in the invoice.

THE INVOICE

This is a document that the supplier sends you when you buy goods. It contains five important items of information that you record in the purchases day book:
- the seller's name (Clooney Ltd).
- the invoice number (280).
- the date (1/8/2004).
- the net amount before VAT (€3,500).
- the total amount plus VAT (€4,200).

THE CREDIT NOTE

When you return damaged or faulty goods to the supplier, the supplier will send you a credit note. Once again this document contains five important items of information that you record in the purchases returns day book:
- the seller's name (Clooney Ltd).
- the credit note number (80).
- the date (4/8/2004).
- the net amount before VAT (€1,500).
- the total amount plus VAT (€1,800).

INVOICE			
No. 280	Clooney Ltd		
Ryan Ltd	Killester		1/8/2004
Stillorgan			
QTY	DESCRIPTION	PRICE	TOTAL
		€	€
2	Desktop Computers	1,500 each	3,000
2	Fax Machines	250 each	500
			3,500
		VAT 20%	700
			4,200
E&OE			

CREDIT NOTE			
No. 80	Clooney Ltd		
Ryan Ltd	Killester		4/8/2004
Stillorgan			
QTY	DESCRIPTION	PRICF	TOTAL
		€	€
1	Desktop Computer	1,500 each	1,500
		VAT 20%	300
			1,800
			120
E&OE			

					RB 2
Purchases Day Book					
Date	Particulars	F	Net	VAT	Total
Aug			€	€	€
1	Clooney Ltd (no. 280)	PL5	3,500	700	4,200
Purchases Returns Day Book					
Aug			€	€	€
4	Clooney Ltd (no. 80)	PL5	1,500	300	1,800

POSTING TO THE LEDGER

We have already seen that a ledger account has two sides: the debit (left) and the credit (right). You will also remember that in double-entry bookkeeping the total debits must equal the total credits, so when we record the purchase we must ensure that €4,200 in total is entered on the debit and €4,200 in total is entered on the credit.

								RB 3
Dr				**General Ledger**				**Cr**
Date	Particulars	F	Total	Date	Particular	F	Total	
Purchases (page 10)								
Aug			€					
1	Clooney Ltd	PB	3,500					
Purchases Returns (page 11)								
				Aug			€	
				4	Abbott Ltd	PRB	1,500	
VAT (page 12)								
Aug			€	Aug			€	
1	Clooney Ltd	PB	700	4	Abbott Ltd	PRB	300	
				31	Balance	c/d	400	
			700				700	
Sep								
1	Balance	b/d	400					

To record the purchase from your supplier you use the purchases account and show the net amount (€3,500) on the debit side of the purchases account. The VAT amount (€700) is also recorded on the debit side of the VAT account. This means that €4,200 has now been entered on the debit of the ledger. The double entry is the total amount of the purchase (€4,200), which is recorded on the credit side of Clooney's account.

Purchases return is the opposite of a purchase and so it will be recorded in the accounts on the opposite sides. Enter the net amount (€1,500) on the credit side of the purchases returns account. Enter the VAT amount (€300) on the credit side of the VAT account. Enter the total amount (€1,800) on the debit side of Clooney's account.

								RB 3
Dr				**Purchases Ledger**				**Cr**
Date	Particulars	F	Total	Date	Particulars	F	Total	
Clooney Ltd (page 5)								
Aug			€	Aug			€	
4	Returns	PRB	1,800	1	Purchases	PB	4,200	
31	Balance	c/d	2,400					
			4,200				4,200	
				Sep				
				1	Balance	b/d	2,400	

BALANCING THE ACCOUNTS

The VAT account now has two entries in it: one on the debit and one on the credit. The difference between the two figures (€400) is the balance in the account. Clooney's account also has two entries in it, and in this case the balance is €2,400.

			Debit	Credit
Trial Balance as at 31 August 2004				RB 2
	F		Debit	Credit
			€	€
Purchases	GL10		3,500	
Purchases returns	GL11			1,500
VAT	GL12		400	
Clooney Ltd	PL5			2,400
			3,900	3,900

THE TRIAL BALANCE

Once the accounts have been balanced you can prepare the trial balance. To do this you take the balance from each account and list it in the debit or credit column. For example, the purchases account has €3,500 on the debit side, so this is listed in the debit column of the trial balance. Clooney's account has €2,400 on the credit side, so this is shown in the credit column of the trial balance. The total of the two columns will be the same if your ledger account work is correct. If they are not the same, then you know you have made a mistake.

LESSON 2: SAMPLE QUESTION AND SOLUTION

Question

The following transactions took place during the month of September.

Sep

6   Purchased goods on credit from Hart Ltd, invoice no. 333, €1,200 + 20% VAT

7   Returned goods to Hart Ltd, credit note no. 50, €200 + 20% VAT

14   Purchased goods on credit from Richard Ltd, invoice no. 420, €2,500 + 20% VAT

21   Purchased goods on credit from Doyle's Ltd, invoice no. 511, €3,000 + 20% VAT

24   Returned goods to Richard Ltd, credit note no. 60, €300 + 20% VAT

You are required to:

(i)   show the entries in the day books.

(ii)   post to the ledger.

(iii)   balance the accounts on 30 September.

(iv)   extract a trial balance as on that date.

Solution

(i) The Day Books

List the three purchases in the purchases day book. Add up the net, VAT and total columns.

RB 2

Purchases Day Book

Date	Particulars	F	Net	VAT	Total
Sep			€	€	€
6	Hart Ltd (no. 333)	PL7	1,200	240	1,440
14	Richard Ltd (no. 420)	PL9	2,500	500	3,000
21	Doyle's Ltd (no. 511)	PL8	3,000	600	3,600
			6,700	1,340	8,040

Purchases Returns Day Book

Date	Particulars			
Sep		€	€	€
7	Hart Ltd (no. 50)	200	40	240
24	Richard Ltd (no. 60)	300	60	360
		500	100	600

Next list the two returns in the purchases returns day book and add up the net, VAT and total columns.

(ii) Posting to the Ledger

From the purchases day book post the totals of the net and the VAT columns to the general ledger. First debit the purchases account with €6,700 and debit the VAT with €1,340. Then credit Hart with €1,440, credit Richard with €3,000 and credit Doyle's with €3,600. In this way the debits (€6,700 + €1,340 = €8,040) will equal the credits (€1,440 + €3,000 + €3,600 = €8,040).

RB 3

Dr				General Ledger			Cr
Date	Particulars	F	Total	Date	Particulars	F	Total
		Purchases (page 20)					
Sep			€				
30	Net from DB	PB	6,700				
		Purchases Returns (page 21)					
				Sep			€
				30	Net from DB	PRB	500
		VAT (page 22)					
Sep			€	Sep			€
30	VAT from PB	PB	1,340	30	VAT from PRB	PRB	100
				30	Balance	c/d	1,240
			1,340				1,340
Oct			€				
1	Balance	b/d	1,240				

Purchases returns is the opposite to purchases, so in this case credit purchases returns with €500, credit VAT with €100, debit Hart with €240 and debit Richard with €360. Once again the total debits are equal to the total credits.

RB 3

Dr			Purchases Ledger				Cr
Date	Particulars	F	Total	Date	Particulars	F	Total
			Hart (page 7)				
Sep			€	Sep			€
7	Purchases returns	PRB	240	6	Purchases	PB	1,440
30	Balance	c/d	1,200				
			1,440				1,440
				Oct			€
				1	Balance	b/d	1,200
			Doyle's LTD (page 8)				
				Sep			€
				21	Purchases	PB	3,600
			Richard LTD (page 9)				
Sep			€	Sep			€
24	Purchases returns	PRB	360	14	Purchases	PB	3,000
30	Balance	c/d	2,640				
			3,000				3,000
				Oct			€
				1	Balance	b/d	2,640

(iii) Balancing the Accounts

Hart's account now has an entry on the debit (€240) and on the credit (€1,440). The credit side is bigger by €1,200 and this is the balance in the account. This balance is shown once above the total (on the smaller side) and once below the total (on the opposite side). The balance in the account is said to be €1,200 credit, i.e. the position below the total.

Similarly, the balance in Richard's account is €2,640. There is no need to balance Doyle's account as it only has one entry in it.

The VAT account (on the bottom of the opposite page) has a balance of €1,240 debit, i.e. €1,340 – €100.

(iv) The Trial Balance

The trial balance works by taking the balance from each account and listing it in the debit or credit column. For example, the purchases account has €6,700 on the debit side, so this is listed in the debit column of the trial balance; Hart Ltd has €1,200 on the credit side, so this is shown in the credit column of the trial balance. Continue until you have all balances listed. When you total both columns you should get the same amount. If you do not, then you know you have made a mistake.

RB 2

		F		Debit	Credit
	Trial Balance as at 30 September				
				€	€
	Purchases	GL20		6,700	
	Purchases returns	GL21			500
	VAT	GL22		1,240	
	Hart Ltd	PL7			1,200
	Doyle's Ltd	PL8			3,600
	Richard Ltd	PL9			2,640
				7,940	7,940

LESSON I: PRACTICE

Invoice and Credit Note Practice

1. Study the following document and answer the questions.
   (a) Name this document.
   (b) Who is the buyer?
   (c) Who is the seller?
   (d) How much does the buyer owe the seller?
   (e) Show the entries in the ledger accounts of Global Deliveries Ltd.

No. 353	**Office Supplies Ltd**		
	Oldcastle		
Global Deliveries Ltd			20/7/2004
Galway			
QTY	DESCRIPTION	PRICE	TOTAL
		€	€
5	Boxes of disks	20 each	100
2	Boxes of paper	15 each	30
			130
		VAT 20%	26
			156
E&OE			

2. Study the following document and answer the questions.
   (a) Who sent this document?
   (b) Why was it sent?
   (c) Show the entries in the ledger accounts of Ballymote Computers Ltd.

No. 43	**Computer Superstore Ltd**		
	Sligo		
Ballmote Computers Ltd			25/9/2004
Ballymote			
QTY	DESCRIPTION	PRICE	TOTAL
		€	€
2	Colour printers (faulty switch)	600 each	1,200
		VAT 20%	240
			1,440
E&OE			

Practice Recording Purchases

3. The following transactions took place during the month of January.

   Jan
   4   Purchased goods on credit from Coyle Ltd, invoice no. 128, €460 + 20% VAT
   17 Purchased goods on credit from Dunne's Ltd, invoice no. 462, €340 + 20% VAT
   28 Purchased goods on credit from Evan's Ltd, invoice no. 912, €580 + 20% VAT

   You are required to:
   (i)   show the entries in the day books.
   (ii) post to the ledger.
   (iii) extract a trial balance as on 31 January.

4.   The following transactions took place during the month of February.

Feb

2   Purchased goods on credit from Finn's Ltd, invoice no. 63, €280 + 20% VAT

17   Purchased goods on credit from Gahan's Ltd, invoice no. 142, €300 + 20% VAT

23   Purchased goods on credit from Hickey's Ltd, invoice no. 464, €420 + 20% VAT

You are required to:

(i)   show the entries in the day books.

(ii)   post to the ledger.

(iii)   extract a trial balance as on 28 February.

5.   The following transactions took place during the month of March.

Mar

4   Purchased goods on credit from Ingram's Ltd, invoice no. 114, €370 + 20% VAT

10   Purchased goods on credit from Joyce's Ltd, invoice no. 72, €540 + 20% VAT

19   Purchased goods on credit from Kennedy's Ltd, invoice no. 47, €280 + 20% VAT

25   Purchased goods on credit from Joyce's Ltd, invoice no. 80, €470 + 20% VAT

You are required to:

(i)   show the entries in the day books.

(ii)   post to the ledger.

(iii)   extract a trial balance as on 31 March.

6.   The following transactions took place during the month of April.

Apr

2   Purchased goods on credit from Lawlor's Ltd, invoice no. 52, €160 + 10% VAT

12   Purchased goods on credit from Murray's Ltd, invoice no. 68, €530 + 10% VAT

23   Purchased goods on credit from Lawlor's Ltd, invoice no. 415, €370 + 10% VAT

27   Purchased goods on credit from Nugent's Ltd, invoice no. 162, €940 + 10% VAT

You are required to:

(i)   show the entries in the day books.

(ii)   post to the ledger.

(iii)   extract a trial balance as on 30 April.

LESSON 2: PRACTICE

Practice Recording Purchases and Returns

1.   The following transactions took place during the month of March.

Mar

4   Purchased goods on credit from Curry's Ltd, invoice no. 32, €2,040 + 20% VAT

7   Purchased goods on credit from Flood's Ltd, invoice no. 40, €1,960 + 20% VAT

8   Returned goods to Curry's Ltd, €240, credit note no. 23

13   Purchased goods on credit from Davies Ltd, invoice no. 357, €4,320 + 20% VAT

25   Returned goods to Flood's Ltd, €60, credit note no. 14

You are required to:

(i)   show the entries in the day books.

(ii)   post to the ledger.

(iii)   extract a trial balance as on 31 March.

2.   The following transactions took place during the month of April.

Apr

4   Purchased goods on credit from O'Malley's Ltd, invoice no. 171, €540 + 20% VAT

6   Returned goods to O'Malley's Ltd, €50, credit note no. 25

8   Purchased goods on credit from Nally Ltd, invoice no. 240, €720 + 20% VAT

17   Purchased goods on credit from McMahon Ltd, invoice no. 351, €350 + 20% VAT

28   Returned goods to Nally Ltd, €70, credit note no. 26

You are required to:

(i)   show the entries in the day books.

(ii)   post to the ledger.

(iii)   extract a trial balance as on 30 April.

3.   The following transactions took place during the month of May.

May

14   Purchased goods on credit from O'Byrne's Ltd, invoice no. 125, €1,380 + 10% VAT

18   Purchased goods on credit from Tierney Ltd, invoice no. 461, €2,650 + 10% VAT

21   Returned goods to Tierney Ltd, €50, credit note no. 73.

26   Purchased goods on credit from Clancy Ltd, invoice no. 521, €1,740 + 10% VAT

27   Returned goods to Clancy Ltd, €70, credit note no. 338

You are required to:

(i)   show the entries in the day books.

(ii)   post to the ledger.

(iii)   extract a trial balance as on 31 May.

4. The following transactions took place during the month of June.

Jun

9   Purchased goods on credit from Kavanagh Ltd, invoice no. 451, €1,930 + 20% VAT

18   Returned goods to Kavanagh Ltd, €90, credit note no. 67

23   Purchased goods on credit from Feeney Ltd, invoice no. 311, €1,500 + 20% VAT

25   Purchased goods on credit from Kavanagh Ltd, invoice no. 360, €1,450 + 20% VAT

27   Returned goods to Feeney Ltd, €150, credit note no. 68

You are required to:

(i)   show the entries in the day books.

(ii)   post to the ledger.

(iii)   extract a trial balance as on 30 June.

5. The following transactions took place during the month of July.

Jul

13   Purchased goods on credit from O'Halloran Ltd, invoice no. 132, €2,500 + 20% VAT

24   Returned goods to O'Halloran Ltd, €150, credit note no. 21

25   Purchased goods on credit from McGuinness Ltd, invoice no. 321, €2,000 + 20% VAT

26   Purchased goods on credit from Thomas Ltd, invoice no. 638, €1,250 + 20% VAT

27   Returned goods to Thomas Ltd, €200, credit note no. 79

You are required to:

(i)   show the entries in the day books.

(ii)   post to the ledger.

(iii)   extract a trial balance as on 31 July.

6. The following transactions took place during the month of August.

Aug

11   Purchased goods on credit from Masterson Ltd, invoice no. 215, €1,700 + 10% VAT

18   Returned goods to Masterson Ltd, €60, credit note no. 33

22   Purchased goods on credit from Kinsella Ltd, invoice no. 291, €3,500 + 10% VAT

27   Purchased goods on credit from Masterson Ltd, invoice no. 220, €1,600 + 10% VAT

29   Returned goods to Masterson Ltd, €200, credit note no. 62

You are required to:

(i)   show the entries in the day books.

(ii)   post to the ledger.

(iii)   extract a trial balance as on 31 August.

28 Sales

INTRODUCTION

1. Which of the following famous companies sell on credit to the public?
   (a) Easons
   (b) Dunnes Stores
   (c) ESB
   (d) McDonald's
   (e) Vodafone

LESSON I: RECORDING SALES AND RETURNS

When you sell goods on credit it will be impossible to remember the names of everyone who owes you money, so it is a good idea to write down the details of each transaction. This information can be found in the invoice.

THE INVOICE

The invoice contains five important items of information that you record in the sales day book:

- the buyer's name (Healy's Ltd).
- the invoice number (374).
- the date (12/10/04).
- the net amount before VAT (€1,700).
- the total amount plus VAT (€2,040).

THE CREDIT NOTE

When goods are returned you will send a credit note to the customer. Once again this document contains five important items of information that you record in the sales returns day book:

- the buyer's name (Healy's Ltd).
- the credit note number (83).
- the date (15/10/04).
- the net amount before VAT (€100).
- the total amount plus VAT (€120).

	INVOICE		
No. 374	Burke Ltd		
Healy's Ltd	Westmeath		12/10/04
Drumlish			

QTY	DESCRIPTION	PRICE	TOTAL
		€	€
3	Fridge Freezers	500 each	1,500
2	Microwave Cookers	100 each	200
			1,700
		VAT 20%	340
			2,040
E&EO			

	CREDIT NOTE		
No. 83	Burke Ltd		
Healy's Ltd	Westmeath		15/10/04
Drumlish			

QTY	DESCRIPTION	PRICE	TOTAL
		€	€
1	Microwave Cooker	100 each	100
		VAT 20%	20
			120
E&EO			

RB 2

Sales Day Book

Date	Particulars	F	Net	VAT	Total
Oct			€	€	€
12	Healy's Ltd	SL4	1,700	340	2,040

Sales Return Day Book

Date	Particulars	F	Net	VAT	Total
Oct			€	€	€
15	Healy Ltd	SL4	100	20	120

POSTING TO THE LEDGER

The information from the day books is now posted to the ledger. You may remember that in the last chapter purchases were entered on the debit of the purchases account. Sales is the opposite to a purchase and you can probably guess that it will be recorded on the credit of the sales account. Here's how it's done.

To record the sale you use the sales account and show the net amount (€1,700) on the credit side of the sales account. The VAT amount (€340) is also recorded on the credit side of the VAT account. The total amount of the sale (€2,040) is recorded on the debit side of Healy's account. This means that we have entered €2,040 in total on the credit of the ledger and €2,040 in total on the debit of the ledger.

Dr				General Ledger				Cr
Date	Particulars	F	Total	Date	Particulars	F	Total	
				Sales (page 30)				
				Oct				€
				12	Healy's Ltd	SB	1,700	
				Sales Returns (page 31)				
Oct			€					
15	Healy's Ltd	SRB	100					
				VAT (page 32)				
Oct			€	Oct				€
18	Healy's Ltd	SRB	20	12	Healy's Ltd	SB	340	
31	Balance	c/d	320					
			340				340	
				Nov				€
				1	Balance	b/d	320	

Dr				Sales Ledger				Cr
Date	Particulars	F	Total	Date	Particulars	F	Total	
				Healy's Ltd (page 4)				
Oct			€	Oct				€
12	Sales	SB	2,040	18	Sales returns	SRB	120	
				31	Balance	c/d	1,920	
			2,040				2,040	
Nov			€					
1	Balance	b/d	1,920					

Sales return is the opposite to a sale and you can probably guess it will be recorded on the debit side of the account. Enter the net amount (€100) on the debit side of the sales returns account. Enter the VAT amount (€20) on the debit side of the VAT account. Enter the total amount (€120) on the credit side of Healy's account. In this case we have entered €120 in total on the credit of the ledger and €120 in total on the debit of the ledger.

BALANCING THE ACCOUNTS

The VAT account now has two entries in it: one on the debit and one on the credit. The difference between the two figures (€320) is the balance in the account. Healy's account also has two entries in it, and in this case the balance is €1,920.

	Trial Balance as at 31 October 2004				
		F		Debit	Credit
				€	€
Sales		GL30			1,700
Sales returns		GL31		100	
VAT		GL32			320
Healy's Ltd		SL4		1,920	
				2,020	2,020

THE TRIAL BALANCE

Once the accounts have been balanced you can prepare the trial balance. To do this you take the balance from each account and list it in the debit or credit column. For example, the sales account has €1,700 on the credit side, so this is listed in the credit column of the trial balance. Healy's account has €1,920 on the debit, so this is shown in the debit column of the trial balance. The trial balance is your way of checking that you are correct. If the two totals are not the same, then you know you have made a mistake.

LESSON 2: SAMPLE QUESTION AND SOLUTION

Question

The following transactions took place during the month of November.

Nov

10	Sold goods on credit to O'Neill Ltd, invoice no. 456, €1,200 + 20% VAT
14	Sold goods on credit to Jackson Ltd, invoice no. 516, €800 + 20% VAT
16	O'Neill Ltd returned goods, credit note no. 26, €80
26	Sold goods on credit to Jones Ltd, invoice no. 781, €1,000 + 20% VAT
28	Jones Ltd returned goods, credit note no. 43, €120 + 20% VAT

You are required to:

(i)   show the entries in the day books.

(ii)   post to the ledger.

(iii) balance the accounts on 30 November.

(iv) extract a trial balance as on 30 November.

Solution

(i) The Day Books

First prepare the sales day book to show the invoices sent to O'Neill, Jackson and Jones. Add up the net, VAT and total columns.

Next prepare the sales returns day book and, once again, add up the net, VAT and total columns.

RB 2

Sales Day Book

Date	Particulars	F	Net	VAT	Total
Nov			€	€	€
10	O'Neill Ltd (no. 456)	SL5	1,200	240	1,440
14	Jackson Ltd (no. 516)	SL6	800	160	960
26	Jones Ltd (no. 781)	SL7	1,000	200	1,200
			3,000	600	3,600

Sales Returns Day Book

Date	Particulars	F	Net	VAT	Total
Nov			€	€	€
16	O'Neill Ltd (no. 26)	SL5	80	16	96
28	Jones Ltd (no. 43)	SL7	120	24	144
			200	40	240

(ii) Posting to the Ledger

The ledger is now prepared using the figures from the day books. Credit sales with €3,000, credit VAT with €600, debit O'Neill with €1,440, debit Jackson with €960 and debit Jones with €1,200. In this way you will have credits of €3,600 (€3,000 + €600) and debits of €3,600 (€1,440 + €960 + €1,200).

Debit sales returns with €200, debit the VAT with €40, credit O'Neill with €96 and credit Jones with €144. This gives debits of €240 (€200 + €40) and credits of €240 (€96 + €144).

RB 3

Dr				General Ledger			Cr
Date	Particulars	F	Total	Date	Particulars	F	Total
			Sales (page 50)				
				Nov			€
				30	Net from DB	SB	3,000
			Sales Returns (page 51)				
Nov			€				
30	Net from DB	SRB	200				
			VAT (page 52)				
Nov			€	Nov			€
30	VAT from SR	SRB	40	30	VAT from SB	SB	600
30	Balance	c/d	560				
			600				600
				Dec			€
				1	Balance	b/d	560

(iii) Balancing the Accounts

O'Neill's account now has an entry on the debit (€1,440) and on the credit (€96). The debit side is bigger by €1,344, which is the balance in the account. This balance is shown once above the total (on the smaller side) and once below the total (on the opposite side). The balance in the account is said to be €1,344 debit, i.e. the position below the total. Similarly, the balance in Jones's account is €1,056 debit. There is no need to balance Jackson's account as it only has one entry in it. The VAT account (on the bottom of the opposite page) has a balance of €560 credit, i.e. €600 − €40.

RB 3

Dr					Sales Ledger				Cr
Date	Particulars	F	Total		Date	Particulars	F		Total
			O'Neill Ltd (page 5)						
Nov		€			Nov				€
8	Sales	SB	1,440		12	Sales returns	SRB		96
					30	Balance	c/d		1,344
			1,440						1,440
Dec		€							
1	Balance	b/d	1,344						
			Jackson Ltd (page 6)						
Nov		€							
10	Sales	SB	960						
			Jones Ltd (page 7)						
Nov		€			Nov				€
20	Sales	SB	1,200		24	Sales returns	SRB		144
					30	Balance	c/d		1,056
			1,200						1,200
Dec		€							
1	Balance	b/d	1,056						

(iv) The Trial Balance

There are six ledger accounts in this question: sales, sales returns, VAT, O'Neill, Jackson and Jones. These six accounts are listed in the trial balance together with the balance from each account. The balances from the accounts are shown either in the debit or the credit column. The two columns are then totalled.

RB 3

Trial Balance as at 30 November		F		Debit	Credit
				€	€
	Sales	GL50			3,000
	Sales returns	GL51		200	
	VAT	GL52			560
	O'Neill Ltd	SL5		1,344	
	Jackson Ltd	SL6		960	
	Jones Ltd	SL7		1,056	
				3,560	3,560

LESSON 3: CALCULATING MARK-UP AND MARGIN

In order to make a profit goods are sold at a higher price than they were bought at:

cost price + profit = selling price

Most businesses would like to know how much of a profit they are making. Two measures of this are mark-up and margin. Mark-up relates the profit to the cost of the goods. Margin relates the profit to the selling price.

Mark-up = $\dfrac{\text{Profit}}{\text{Cost price}}$ x   100

Margin = $\dfrac{\text{Profit}}{\text{Selling price}}$ x   100

Question
A firm sells goods for €500. The cost of these goods was €400. Calculate:
(a) the profit.
(b) the mark-up.
(c) the margin.

Solution
(a) Profit = selling price – cost price
€500 – €400 = €100

(b) Mark-up = $\dfrac{\text{Profit}}{\text{Cost price}}$ x 100

$\dfrac{100}{400}$ x 100 = 25%

(c) Margin = $\dfrac{\text{Profit}}{\text{Selling price}}$ x 100

$\dfrac{100}{500}$ x 100 = 20%

LESSON I: PRACTICE

Recording Sales

1. Study the following document and answer the questions.
   (a) On what date was this document issued?
   (b) Who issued it?
   (c) How much does the purchaser have to pay for the vans?
   (d) Why is it necessary for the seller to record this information?
   (e) Show the entries in the ledger accounts of The Van Centre Ltd.

INVOICE

No. 396   The Van Centre Ltd

G. North   Westward Business Park   10/2/05

Wexford   Enniscorthy

QTY	DESCRIPTION	PRICE	TOTAL
		€	€
2	Vans (petrol type)	15,000 each	30,000
2	Vans (diesel type)	16,000 each	32,000
			62,000
		VAT 20%	12,400
			74,400

E&EO

CREDIT NOTE

Bricks 'N' Blocks

Builders' Providers Ltd

No. 24   Palmerstown

D & R Construction   11/6/05

Rathmines

QTY	DESCRIPTION	PRICE	TOTAL
		€	€
5	Interior doors (damaged)	50 each	250
		VAT 20%	50
			300

E&EO

2. Study the following document and answer the questions.
   (a) On what date was this document issued?
   (b) Who issued it?
   (c) Why was it issued?
   (d) Show the entries in the ledger accounts of Bricks 'N' Blocks Builders' Providers Ltd.

3.   The following transactions took place during the month of March.

Mar

4   Sold goods on credit to Tobin Ltd, invoice no. 413, €4,050 + 20% VAT

7   Sold goods on credit to Rooney Ltd, invoice no. 414, €3,540 + 20% VAT

25   Sold goods on credit to Treanor Ltd, invoice no. 415, €8,400 + 20% VAT

You are required to:

(i)   show the entries in the day books.

(ii)   post to the ledger.

(iii)   extract a trial balance as on 31 March.

4.   The following transactions took place during the month of April.

Apr

4   Sold goods on credit to Carroll Ltd, invoice no. 515, €8,250 + 20% VAT

8   Sold goods on credit to Egan Ltd, invoice no. 516, €3,800 + 20% VAT

22   Sold goods on credit to Elliott Ltd, invoice no. 517, €2,600 + 20% VAT

You are required to:

(i)   show the entries in the day books.

(ii)   post to the ledger.

(iii)   extract a trial balance as on 30 April.

5.   The following transactions took place during the month of May.

May

6   Sold goods on credit to Mooney Ltd, invoice no. 200, €800 + 20% VAT

9   Sold goods on credit to Dixon Ltd, invoice no. 201, €940 + 20% VAT

17   Sold goods on credit to Lawlor Ltd, invoice no. 202, €1,000 + 20% VAT

24   Sold goods on credit to O'Sullivan Ltd, invoice no. 203, €1,200 + 20% VAT

You are required to:

(i)   show the entries in the day books.

(ii)   post to the ledger.

(iii)   extract a trial balance as on 31 May.

6.   The following transactions took place during the month of June.

Jun

7   Sold goods on credit to Tuite Ltd, invoice no. 113, €1,240 + 20% VAT

10   Sold goods on credit to Barry Ltd, invoice no. 114, €680 + 20% VAT

16   Sold goods on credit to Cleary Ltd, invoice no. 115, €1,680 + 20% VAT

27   Sold goods on credit to Barry Ltd, invoice no. 116, €1,540 + 20% VAT

You are required to:

(i)   show the entries in the day books.

(ii)   post to the ledger.

(iii)   extract a trial balance as on 30 June.

LESSON 2: PRACTICE

Recording Sales and Returns

1. The following transactions took place during the month of January.

   Jan

   5   Sold goods on credit to Hanley Ltd, invoice no. 410, €800 + 20% VAT

   6   Sold goods on credit to Reddy Ltd, invoice no. 411, €650 + 20% VAT

   9   Hanley Ltd returned goods, credit note no. 40, €200

   24   Sold goods on credit to Browney Ltd, invoice no. 412, €1,200 + 20% VAT

   25   Reddy Ltd returned goods, credit note no. 66, €120

   You are required to:
   (i)   show the entries in the day books.
   (ii) post to the ledger.
   (iii) balance the accounts on 31 January.
   (iv) extract a trial balance as on 31 January.

2. The following transactions took place during the month of February.

   Feb

   1   Sold goods on credit to Weir Ltd, invoice no. 231, €1,500 + 20% VAT

   6   Weir Ltd returned goods, credit note no. 60, €500

   14   Sold goods on credit to Grant Ltd, invoice no. 232, €1,200 + 20% VAT

   15   Sold goods on credit to Casey Ltd, invoice no. 233, €960 + 20% VAT

   16   Grant Ltd returned goods, credit note no. 61, €100

   You are required to:
   (i)   show the entries in the day books.
   (ii) post to the ledger.
   (iii) balance the accounts on 28 February.
   (iv) extract a trial balance as on 28 February.

3. The following transactions took place during the month of March.

   Mar

   5   Sold goods on credit to Hoey Ltd, invoice no. 414, €800 + 20% VAT

   10   Sold goods on credit to Lennon Ltd, invoice no. 415, €1,450 + 20% VAT

   16   Lennon Ltd returned goods, credit note no. 40, €150

   21   Sold goods on credit to Cully Ltd, invoice no. 416, €1,820 + 20% VAT

   24   Cully Ltd returned goods, credit note no. 46, €400

   You are required to:
   (i)   show the entries in the day books.
   (ii) post to the ledger.
   (iii) balance the accounts on 31 March.
   (iv) extract a trial balance as on 31 March.

4. The following transactions took place during the month of April.

Apr

9   Sold goods on credit to Proctor Ltd, invoice no. 221, €1,400 + 20% VAT

13   Purchased goods on credit from Quinn Ltd, invoice no. 213, €1,600 + 20% VAT

15   Returned goods to Quinn Ltd, credit note no. 21, €300

21   Sold goods on credit to McGovern Ltd, invoice no. 222, €1,020 + 20% VAT

25   McGovern Ltd returned goods, credit note no. 48, €120

You are required to:

(i)   show the entries in the day books.

(ii)   post to the ledger.

(iii) balance the accounts and extract a trial balance as on 30 April.

5. The following transactions took place during the month of May.

May

9   Purchased goods on credit from Monaghan Ltd, invoice no. 414, €2,400 + 20% VAT

16   Returned goods to Monaghan Ltd, credit note no. 24, €400

21   Sold goods on credit to Deegan Ltd, invoice no. 220, €750 + 20% VAT

22   Sold goods on credit to Corrigan Ltd, invoice no. 221, €850 + 20% VAT

26   Corrigan Ltd returned goods, credit note no. 31, €50

You are required to:

(i)   show the entries in the day books.

(ii)   post to the ledger.

(iii) balance the accounts and extract a trial balance as on 31 May.

6. The following transactions took place during the month of June.

Jun

5   Sold goods on credit to Flynn Ltd, invoice no. 691, €3,000 + 20% VAT

8   Flynn Ltd returned goods, credit note no. 69, €150

12   Purchased goods on credit from Kennedy Ltd, invoice no. 121, €4,000 + 20% VAT

21   Returned goods to Kennedy Ltd, credit note no. 70, €800

28   Sold goods on credit to Richmond Ltd, invoice no. 692, €750 + 20% VAT

You are required to:

(i)   show the entries in the day books.

(ii)   post to the ledger.

(iii) balance the accounts and extract a trial balance as on 30 June.

LESSON 3: PRACTICE

Mark-up and Margin

1. Calculate the mark-up on goods that cost €800 and were sold for €850.

2. Calculate the mark-up on goods that cost €500 and were sold for €620.

3. Calculate the mark-up on goods that cost €900 and were sold for €1,050.

4. Calculate the margin on goods that cost €1,000 and were sold for €1,240.

5. Calculate the margin on goods that cost €200 and were sold for €520.

6. Calculate the mark-up and the margin on goods that cost €5,250 and were sold for €6,250.

7. Calculate the mark-up and the margin on goods that cost €4,250 and were sold for €6,000.

8. Calculate the mark-up and the margin on goods that cost €8,200 and were sold for €10,200.

9. Calculate the mark-up and the margin on goods that cost €9,000 and were sold for €9,500.

10. Calculate the mark-up and the margin on goods that cost €20,500 and were sold for €22,750.

29 Analysed Cash Book

TERMS COVERED IN THIS CHAPTER
Folio column.

INTRODUCTION

1. **What do you think?**

   Schools cannot exist without cash. They get cash from the Department of Education and fundraising.

   (a) Can you think of some other ways your school gets cash?

   (b) What does your school spend this cash on?

   (c) How does vandalism of school property and graffiti waste this cash?

LESSON 1: UNDERSTANDING THE ANALYSED CASH BOOK

The cash book is used to record money coming into and being paid out of a business. This money will either be cash or cheques. Any cash received or paid is shown in the cash column, while cheques are shown in the bank column.

MONEY IN

Money received (incoming) is shown on the debit side. In our example the firm received cash from sales (€4,320).

MONEY OUT

Money going out (payments) is shown on the credit side.

RB 3

Dr							Cash Book	(page 2)								Cr
Date	Particulars	F	Debtors	Sales	VAT	Bank		Date	Particulars	F	Wages	Cred.	Purch.	VAT	Bank	
Feb			€	€	€	€		Feb				€	€	€	€	
1	Balance	b/d				6,500		2	Purchases	85			1,400	280	1,680	
6	Sales	GL15		3,600	720	4,320		4	Wages	86	4,000				4,000	
7	Cullen	SL41	600			600		6	Jordan	87		1,300			1,300	
								7	Balance	c/d					4,440	
			600	3,600	720	11,420					4,000	1,300	1,400	280	11,420	
			SL41	GL15	GL18						GL19	PL46	GL17	GL18		
8	Balance	b/d				4,440										

OVERHEADS

Overheads are the expenses of running a business. When they are paid, money goes out of the business. Therefore, they are recorded on the credit side of the cash book. Examples of overheads are:

- light and heat (electricity).
- rent and rates.
- insurance.
- interest on loans.
- advertising.
- telephone.

\

LESSON 2: SAMPLE QUESTION AND SOLUTION

Question

The following trial balance was extracted from the books of Harte Ltd on 1 February.

	€	€
Cash at bank	6,500	
Debtor: Cullen	800	
Creditor: Jordan		1,300
Ordinary share capital		6,000
	7,300	7,300

The following bank transactions took place during the first week of February.

Feb

2	Purchased goods by cheque (no. 85), €1,400 + 20% VAT
4	Paid wages by cheque (no. 86), €4,000
6	Cash sales lodged, €3,600 + 20% VAT
6	Paid Hamill by cheque (no. 87), €1,300
7	Received cheque from Cullen, €600, and lodged it

You are required to do the following.

(a) Enter the trial balance figures into relevant accounts.

(b) Record the transactions for the first week of February in the cash book, using the following column headings:

Debit side: Debtors, Sales, VAT, Bank

(c) (i) Post the relevant figures to the ledger.

(ii) Balance the accounts on 7 February.

(iii) Extract a trial balance as on that date.

Solution

RB 3

Dr						Cash Book		(page 2)							Cr
Date	Particulars	F	Debtors	Sales	VAT	Bank		Date	Particulars	F	Wages	Cred.	Purch.	VAT	Bank
Feb			€	€	€	€		Feb				€	€	€	€
1	Balance	b/d				6,500		2	Purchases	85			1,400	280	1,680
6	Sales	GL15		3,600	720	4,320		4	Wages	86	4,000				4,000
7	Cullen	SL41	600			600		6	Jordan	87		1,300			1,300
								7	Balance	c/d					4,440
			600	3,600	720	11,420					4,000	1,300	1,400	280	11,420
			SL41	GL15	GL18						GL19	PL46	GL17	GL18	
8	Balance	b/d				4,440									

RB 3

Dr	General Ledger			Cr			
Date	Particulars	F	Total	Date	Particulars	F	Total
Ordinary Share Capital (page 1)							
Feb				Feb			€
				1	Balance	b/d	6,000
Sales (page 15)							
Feb				Feb			€
				7	Bank	CB2	3,600
Purchases (page 17)							
Feb			€				€
7	Bank	CB2	1,400				
VAT (page 18)							
Feb			€	Feb			€
7	Bank (purchases)	CB2	280	7	Bank (sales)	CB2	720
7	Balance	c/d	440				
			720				720
				8	Balance	b/d	440
Wages (page 19)							
Feb			€				
7	Bank	CB2	4,000				
Sales Ledger							
Cullen (page 41)							
Feb			€	Feb			€
1	Balance	b/d	800	7	Bank	CB2	600
				7	Balance	c/d	200
			800				800
8	Balance	b/d	200				
Purchases Ledger							
Jordan (page 66)							
Feb			€	Feb			€
6	Bank	CB2	1,300	1	Balance	b/d	1,300
			1,300				1,300

RB 2

Trial Balance as at 7 February			Debit	Credit
	F		€	€
Ordinary share capital				6,000
Sales				3,600
Purchases			1,400	
VAT				440
Wages			4,000	
Cullen			200	
Bank			4,400	
			10,040	10,040

1. Refer to the trial balance. The cash at bank (€6,500) is entered on the debit of the cash book. Open ledger accounts for the other trial balance figures. If it is debit in the trial balance, then it is debit in the ledger. If it is credit in the trial balance, then it is also credit in the ledger. Write 'balance' in the particular column of each account.

2. Prepare the cash book. Cheques paid will be credit. Sales and cheques received will be debit. Balance the cash book.

3. Post the cash book. Credit entries are posted to the debit in the ledger and debit entries are posted to the credit.

4. Balance VAT, Cullen and Jordan. The other accounts only have one entry in them and do not need balancing.

5. Prepare the trial balance. Write out the account names from the ledger in the trial balance. Omit Jordan as this account is closed. Now for the figures: if it is debit in the ledger, then it is debit in the trial balance. If it is credit in the ledger, then it is credit in the trial balance. Remember to include the bank balance from the bank book.

6. Total the trial balance. If you have made no mistakes, then the debit and credit totals will be the same.

LESSON 1: PRACTICE

																RB 3

Dr   Cash Book   (page 2)   **Cr**

Date	Particulars	F	Debtors	Sales	VAT	Bank			Date	Particulars	F	Wages	Cred.	Purch.	VAT	Rent	Bank
Mar			€	€	€	€			Mar				€	€	€	€	
2	Balance	b/d				400			2	Rent	23					170	170
5	Sales			1,000	210	1,210			3	Brennan	24		290				290
9	Kennedy		300			300			6	Purchases	25			200	42		242
									7	Wages	26	540					540
									9	Balance	c/d						668
			300	1,000	210	1,910						540	290	200	42	170	1,910
Mar																	
10	Balance	b/d				668											

1. Jessica Keogh starts a dress design company. She prepares the above cash book for the first week of March. Indicate whether these statements are true or false.

	True	False
(a) She received €290 from Brennan.	○	○
(b) She received €300 from Kennedy.	○	○
(c) She sold goods on 6 March.	○	○
(d) On 7 March she paid wages of €26.	○	○
(e) The purchases cost her a total of €242.	○	○
(f) She had €400 in the bank at the start of the week.	○	○
(g) She had €1,910 in the bank at the end of the week.	○	○
(h) During the week she paid out a total of €1,910.	○	○
(i) The VAT on her sales was €1,000.	○	○
(j) The next cheque she writes will be cheque number 27.	○	○

2. Jessica then sends an e-mail to her friend telling her about her first week in business. Fill in the missing figures in the e-mail using the appropriate number from the cash book in the previous question.

From: Jessica

To: Ashley

Subject: Business has started

Hi Ashley,

I can't believe I survived my first week. The rent on the premises is only [1]_____ each week but wages are costing me [2]_____ each week.

Anyway, the cash position is not too bad. I had [3]_____ at the start of the week and I took in another [4]_____ during the week, so I had a total of [5]_____ available for spending. I only spent a total of [6]_____. This means I have [7]_____ left to spend next week.

Not bad for my first few days in business.

See you later to celebrate!

Jess

LESSON 2: PRACTICE

Practice Preparing Cash Book, Ledger and Trial Balance

1. The following trial balance was extracted from the books of Brennan Ltd on 1 August.

	€	€
Cash at bank	5,200	
Debtor: O'Flaherty	600	
Creditor: McDonagh		700
Ordinary share capital		5,100
	5,800	5,800

The following bank transactions took place during the week.

Aug

2   Cash sales lodged, €650 + 20% VAT

3   Paid McDonagh €700 by cheque (no. 76)

4   Received cheque from O'Flaherty, €600, and lodged it

5   Cash sales lodged, €540 + 20% VAT

6   Purchased goods by cheque no. 77, €300 + 20% VAT

You are required to do the following.

(a) Enter the above trial balance figures into relevant accounts.

(b) Record the transactions in the cash book using the following column headings.

   Debit side: Debtors, Sales, VAT, Bank

   Credit side: Creditors, Purchases, VAT, Bank

(c) Post the relevant figures to the ledger, balance the accounts on 7 August and extract a trial balance as on that date.

2. The following trial balance was extracted from the books of Moore Ltd on 1 September.

	€	€
Cash at bank	3,020	
Debtor: Pearse	700	
Creditor: Farrell		400
Ordinary share capital		3,320
	3,720	3,720

The following bank transactions took place during the week.

Sep

2   Cash sales lodged, €1,500 + 20% VAT

3   Paid Farrell by cheque no. 64, €400

4   Received cheque for €665 from Quinn and lodged it

5   Purchased goods for cheque no. 65, €880 + 20% VAT

6   Cash sales lodged, €3,500 + 30% VAT

You are required to do the following.
(a) Enter the above trial balance figures into relevant accounts.
(b) Record the transactions in the cash book using the following column headings.
   Debit side: Debtors, Sales, VAT, Bank
   Credit side: Creditors, Purchases, VAT, Bank
(c) Post the relevant figures to the ledger, balance the accounts on 7 September and extract a trial balance as on that date.

3. The following trial balance was extracted from the books of Daly Ltd on 1 October.

	€	€
Cash at bank	4,300	
Debtor: Crowley	500	
Creditor: O'Connor		200
Ordinary share capital		4,600
	4,800	4,800

The following bank transactions took place.
Oct
1   Cash sales lodged, €350 + 20% VAT
2   Received cheque from Crowley, €300, and lodged it
2   Paid O'Connor by cheque no. 77, €200
3   Paid wages by cheque no. 78, €300
4   Purchased goods by cheque no. 79, €120 + 20% VAT
5   Cash sales lodged, €290 + 20% VAT
6   Paid wages by cheque no. 80, €300

You are required to do the following.
(a) Enter the above trial balance figures into relevant accounts.
(b) Record the transactions in the cash book using the following column headings.
   Debit side: Debtors, Sales, VAT, Bank
   Credit side: Wages, Purchases, VAT, Bank
(c) Post the relevant figures to the ledger, balance the accounts on 7 October and extract a trial balance as on that date.

4. The following trial balance was extracted from the books of Lawlor Ltd on 1 November.

	€	€
Cash at bank	2,540	
Debtor: Mulligan	300	
Creditor: Blackwell		600
Ordinary share capital		2,240
	2,840	2,840

The following bank transactions took place.

Nov

1	Paid petrol by cheque no. 86, €30
2	Paid Blackwell by cheque no. 87, €600
3	Cash sales lodged, €640 + 20% VAT
3	Paid wages by cheque no. 88, €730
4	Received cheque from Mulligan, €300, and lodged it
5	Cash sales lodged, €700 + 20% VAT
6	Purchased goods by cheque no. 89, €100 + 20% VAT

You are required to do the following.

(a) Enter the above trial balance figures into relevant accounts.

(b) Record the transactions in the cash book using the following column headings.

Debit side: Debtors, Sales, VAT, Bank

Credit side: Others, Creditors, VAT, Bank

(c) Post the relevant figures to the ledger, balance the accounts on 7 November and extract a trial balance as on that date.

5. The following trial balance was extracted from the books of Taylor Ltd on 1 December.

	€	€
Cash at bank	1,000	
Debtor: King	6,000	
Creditor: Jackson		3,000
Ordinary share capital		4,000
	7,000	7,000

The following bank transactions took place.

Dec

10	Paid wages by cheque no. 56, €500
11	Cash sales lodged, €2,000 + 20% VAT
12	Purchased goods by cheque no. 57, €1,400 + 20% VAT
14	Received cheque from King, €2,500, and lodged it
16	Paid wages by cheque no. 58, €500
18	Cash sales lodged, €4,200 + 20% VAT
22	Paid Jackson by cheque no. 59, €3,000

You are required to do the following.

(a) Enter the above trial balance figures into relevant accounts.

(b) Record the transactions in the cash book using the following column headings.

Debit side: Debtors, Sales, VAT, Bank

Credit side: Wages, Creditors, VAT, Bank

(c) Post the relevant figures to the ledger, balance the accounts on 31 December and extract a trial balance as on that date.

6. The following trial balance was extracted from the books of Bradley Ltd on 1 June.

	€	€
Bank	5,000	
Creditor: Ring		15,000
Fixed assets: machinery	50,000	
Ordinary share capital		40,000
	55,000	55,000

The following bank transactions took place.

Jun

1   Cash sales lodged, €40,000 + 20% VAT

2   Purchases for resale by cheque no. 60, €20,000 + 20% VAT

3   Paid wages by cheque no. 61, €3,000

4   Cash sales lodged, €30,000 + 20% VAT

5   Paid Lynch by cheque no. 62, €10,000

6   Purchased machinery by cheque no. 63, €15,000

You are required to do the following.

(a) Enter the above trial balance figures into relevant accounts.

(b) Write up the bank transactions using the following column headings.

Debit side: Sales, VAT, Bank

Credit side: Others, Creditors, Purchases, VAT, Bank

(c) Post the relevant figures to the ledger, balance the accounts on 7 June and extract a trial balance as on that date.

30 Petty Cash Book

TERMS COVERED IN THIS CHAPTER
Voucher, imprest.

INTRODUCTION

Look at the petty cash book in Lesson 2 and discuss the following questions.
1. How can you explain the need for so many columns?
2. Which do you think you could leave out?
3. How do the columns make it easy to summarise the information?
4. What do you think is the purpose of the 'voucher number'?

LESSON I: UNDERSTANDING THE PETTY CASH PROCESS

There are many small expenses for a business in the normal course of a week's work. For example, an employee may be asked to drive into town to collect a parcel. The employee is entitled to claim petrol expenses for this journey. Similarly, an employee who is asked to post a letter for the business can claim the cost of the stamp. In addition, the office must be cleaned and paper must be bought for the printer and photocopier.

The petty cash book is used to record these expenses. It is similar to a cash book but has extra columns to give an analysis of the payments. Expenses that are similar are shown in the same column, e.g. petrol, oil and puncture repairs are all shown in the motor expenses column.

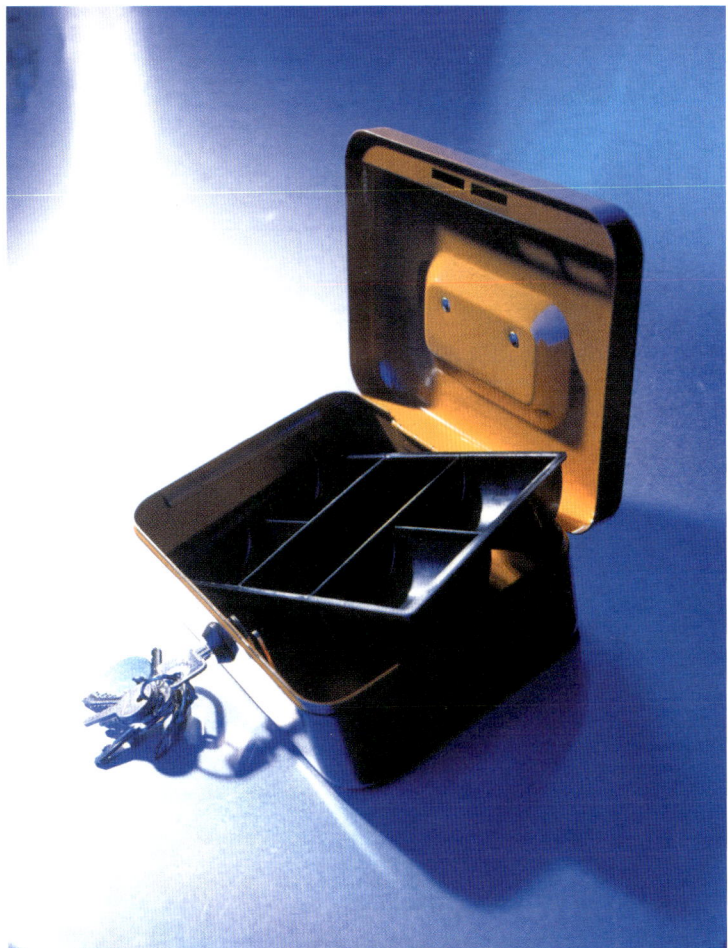

THE IMPREST

The petty cashier is the person who is appointed to pay the petty cash expenses. He or she is given cash, known as the imprest, which is given out to employees who make a claim for expenses. At the end of the month the petty cashier receives more money to restore the imprest back to its original amount. Therefore, the money received each month is equal to the amount spent.

PETTY CASH VOUCHER

An employee who wishes to make a claim for expenses must complete a petty cash voucher. This contains:

- the date.
- the reason for the claim.
- the amount claimed.
- the signature of the person making the claim.
- the signature of another person, usually a superior, who authorises the claim.

PETTY CASH BOX

The imprest is usually kept in a petty cash box and money should not be taken out of this without a voucher for the same value being placed in the box. At the end of the month the petty cashier prepares the petty cash book using the vouchers in the box. The total value of the vouchers should equal the amount needed to restore the imprest.

ADVANTAGES

The advantages of this system are:

- the company has a record of the small payments (the vouchers).
- the company can monitor and control small payments.
- the financial manager is not disturbed by claims for many small sums of money.

Petty Cash Voucher

Ref. no. 27

Date: 8/1/05

Details	Amount	
Computer paper	15	00
Paper clips & folders	12	00
	27	00

Signature: John Devine

Passed by: Eileen Clancy

LESSON 2: SAMPLE QUESTION AND SOLUTION

Question

Prepare a petty cash book from the following information to show analysis columns for motor, postage, stationery and sundry expenses. The imprest is €200 and the cashier restores the imprest on 31 January.

Jan

1	Petty cash on hand (float), €200
3	Paper, €8 (no. 11)
4	Stamps, €15 (no. 12)
4	Paper, €10 (no. 13)
6	Envelopes, €8.40 (no. 14)
7	Petrol, €30 (no. 15)
11	Stamps, €9 (no. 16)
14	Taxi, €35 (no. 17)
16	Motor oil, €15.60 (no. 18)
20	Stamps, €10.50 (no. 19)
25	Petrol, €25 (no. 20)

Solution

RB 1

Dr Petty Cash Book (page 2) **Cr**

Date	Particulars	F	Cash receiv					Date	Particulars	F	Cash paid	Motor	Post.	Stat.	Sundry
Jan			€					Jan			€	€	€	€	€
1	Balance	c/d	200					3	Paper	11	8			8	
								4	Stamps	12	15		15		
								4	Paper	13	10			10	
								6	Envelopes	14	8.40			8.40	
								7	Petrol	15	30	30			
								11	Stamps	16	9		9		
								14	Taxi	17	35				35
								16	Motor Oil	18	15.60	15.60			
								20	Stamps	19	10.50		10.50		
								25	Petrol	20	25	25			
									Total		166.50	70.60	34.50	26.40	35 33.50
			200					31	Balance	c/d	200	GL14	GL32	GL33	GL41
Feb															
1	Balance	b/d	33.50												
1	Bank	CB1	166.50												

RB 3

Dr							Cr
Date	Particulars	F	Total	Date	Particulars	F	Total
Motor Expenses (Page 14)							
2005 Jan 31	Petty Cash		€ 70.60				
Postage Expenses (Page 32)							
2005 Jan 31	Petty Cash		€ 34.50				
Stationery Expenses (Page 14)							
2005 Jan 31	Petty Cash		€ 26.40				
Sundry Expenses (Page 14)							
2005 Jan 31	Petty Cash		€ 35.00				

POSTING TO THE LEDGER

At the end of the month, each expense column is totalled and the total is then posted to the ledger. In this way, for example, one figure for motor expenses is posted rather than many small amounts.

LESSON 1: PRACTICE

Understanding the Petty Cash Process

1. Martha is the petty cashier in her company. Help her classify these expenses by placing the cost in the appropriate column, then total each column.

	Cost €	Motor Expenses	Postage and Stationery Expenses	Travelling Expenses	Cleaning Expenses
Stamps	15				
Petrol	42				
Plastic folders	6				
Taxi	17				
Envelopes	5				
Cleaner's wages	60				
Puncture repairs	26				
Train fare	4				
Furniture polish	3				
Bus fares	2				
TOTALS					

2. Complete the e-mail that Martha sends to the finance manager.

From: Martha

To: Rachel

Subject: Petty cash expenses

Hi Rachel,

The petty cash expenses are very high this week. The ¹_____ wages is our biggest expense but we also had a claim of ²_____ for petrol. The total claims for the week amounted to ³_____. A total of €23 was spent on ⁴_____ expenses. We also spent ⁵_____ on postage and stationery and ⁶_____ expenses came to €63. The system is working very well but not everyone making a claim filled out a petty cash ⁷_____.

See you at the finance meeting on Monday morning.

Best wishes,
Martha

LESSON 2: PRACTICE

1.   Prepare a petty cash book from the following information to show analysis columns for motor, postage, stationery and travelling expenses. The imprest is €250 and the cashier restores the imprest on 31 July.

Jul

1	Petty cash on hand (imprest), €250
3	Stamps (no. 20), €23.50
3	Oil (no. 21), €18
5	Taxi (no. 22), €20
7	Stamps (no. 23), €11.75
8	Paper (no. 24), €7
9	Petrol (no. 25), €30
9	Stamps (no. 26), €1.88
10	Bus fares (no. 27), €10
21	Petrol (no. 28), €25
28	Envelopes (no. 29), €3.87

2.   Prepare a petty cash book from the following information to show analysis columns for motor, postage, stationery and travelling expenses. The imprest is €300 and the cashier restores the imprest on 31 August.

Aug

1	Petty cash on hand (imprest), €300
5	Stamps (no. 70), €6
8	Paper (no. 71), €12.50
9	Train fares (no. 72), €19
10	Stamps (no. 73), €32
11	Taxi (no. 74), €20
15	Petrol (no. 75), €30
15	Stamps (no. 76), €10
17	Petrol (no. 77), €25
18	Envelopes (no. 78), €14
19	Puncture repair (no. 79), €2.50
24	Taxi (no. 80), €15
24	Stamps (no. 81), €12
28	Paper (no. 82), €16.50
30	Petrol (no. 83), €12

3. Prepare a petty cash book from the following information to show analysis columns for motor, postage, stationery and cleaning expenses. The imprest is €200 and the cashier restores the imprest on 30 September.

Sep

1   Petty cash on hand (imprest), €200

5   Envelopes (no. 10), €4.70

5   Cleaning liquids (no. 11), €10

6   Puncture repair (no. 12), €6.30

8   Stamps (no. 13), €4.70

11 Petrol (no. 14), €20

12 Cleaning cloths (no. 15), €10

15 Paper (no. 16), €15

22 Stamps (no. 17), €9.40

28 Petrol (no. 18), €20

29 Cleaner's pay (no. 19), €60.60

STATE EXAM PRACTICE

1. Henry Taylor is the office manager in a limited company. He uses a petty cash book to keep an account of small office expenses. He begins each month with an imprest of €150. Here is what happened in May.

May

1	Balance (imprest) on hand, €150
2	He paid €6 for postage (petty cash voucher no. 101)
4	He bought envelopes for €4 (petty cash voucher no. 102)
6	He paid €10 out of petty cash to a local charity for a raffle ticket (petty cash voucher no. 103)
7	He bought writing paper (stationery) for €12 (petty cash voucher no. 104)
8	He paid taxi fare €17 for sales representative (petty cash voucher no. 105)
9	He paid the office cleaner €21 (petty cash voucher no. 106)
11	He paid €8 for postage (petty cash voucher no. 107)
14	He paid €20 for repairs to a swivel chair (petty cash voucher no. 108)
17	He posted a parcel – the stamp cost €7 (petty cash voucher no. 109)
19	He paid €9 train fare for a sales manager (petty cash voucher no. 110)
23	He paid the office cleaner €15 (petty cash voucher no. 111)
28	He purchased computer paper (stationery) for €11 (petty cash voucher no. 112)

(a) State what is meant by the imprest system of petty cash.

(b) Write up the petty cash book for the month of May using the following analysis columns: Postage, Stationery, Cleaning, Travel, Sundries. Total each analysis column and balance the petty cash book at the end of May.

(c) How much money will Henry receive from the chief cashier to enable him to start next month with an imprest of €150?

(JCOL, adapted)

2. Helen Cruise is the office manager in a limited company. She uses a petty cash book to keep an account of small office expenses. She begins each month with an imprest of €300. Here is what happened in May 2004.

May

1   Balance (imprest) on hand, €300

2   She bought writing paper (stationery) for €28 (petty cash voucher no. 501)

3   She bought envelopes for €19 (petty cash voucher no. 502)

6   She paid €14 for postage (petty cash voucher no. 503)

8   She paid €29 for cleaning materials for the office (petty cash voucher no. 504)

9   She paid €8 bus fare for a visit to an office demonstration (petty cash voucher no. 505)

14   She paid train fare €35 for sales manager (petty cash voucher no. 506)

17   She paid the office cleaner €40 for cleaning materials (petty cash voucher no. 507)

20   She paid €30 for repairs to a printer (petty cash voucher no. 508)

22   She paid €15 to a courier to deliver a parcel (petty cash voucher no. 509)

24   She purchased computer paper (stationery) for €33 (petty cash voucher no. 510)

28   She paid €25 from petty cash to a local charity for a raffle (petty cash voucher no. 511)

30   She paid €16 for postage (petty cash voucher no. 512)

(a) State what is meant by the imprest system of petty cash.

(b) Write up the petty cash book for the month of May using the following analysis columns: Postage, Stationery, Travel, Cleaning, Sundries. Total each analysis column and balance the petty cash book at the end of May.

(c) How much money will Helen receive from the chief cashier to enable her to start next month with an imprest of €300?

31 The General Journal

TERMS COVERED IN THIS CHAPTER
Narration.

LESSON 1: UNDERSTANDING THE NEED FOR A GENERAL JOURNAL

Computers Direct Ltd is a shop that sells computers. They purchase a variety of goods during the normal course of their business. For example:

4 Sep   Purchased computers on credit from The Computer Warehouse Ltd, €50,000
8 Sep   Purchased heating oil for €400 and paid by cheque
9 Sep   Purchased van on credit from Brookfield Motors, €14,000

Each of these transactions must be recorded in Computer Direct Ltd's books. But before we continue take a few moments to answer these questions.

● What do you think they will do with the computers they purchased on 4 September?
● What do you think they will use the heating oil to heat?
● What do you think they will use the van for?
● One of the above is recorded in the purchases day book. Can you guess which one?
● One of the above is recorded in the cash book. Can you guess which one?

Where will they record the purchase of the computers on credit? As you can probably guess they intend to resell the computers, so the purchase of the computers is recorded in the purchases day book.

Where will they record the purchase of the heating oil? The heating oil will be used by the business to heat the shop. As it was paid for by cheque the purchase of the heating oil is recorded in the cash book.

Where will they record the purchase of the van on credit? Do you think they intend to resell it (like the computers) or do you think they intend to use it in the firm (like the heating oil)? The answer is they intend to use the van in the firm, perhaps for deliveries and collections. This purchase cannot be recorded in the purchases day book, as the van is not for resale in the shop. Nor can it be recorded in the cash book, as Computers Direct Ltd bought the van on credit from Brookfield Motors Ltd. Instead it is recorded in a book called the general journal.

RECORDING IN THE GENERAL JOURNAL

The general journal shows how the ledger accounts will record the transaction. It summarises the ledger entries and includes a short narration (in brackets) to explain what is happening.

RECORDING IN THE LEDGER

Most students find it easier to figure out where the entries in the ledger will occur and then go back and prepare the general journal. In this case the entry in the van account (an asset) will be debit as it is being increased in value. The Brookfield Motors Ltd account, on the other hand, is credit because they are owed €14,000.

RB 2

		F		Debit	Credit
	General Journal				
				€	€
Jan 1	Van			14,000	
	Brookfield Motors				14,000
	(purchased van on credit)				

RB 3

Dr								Cr
Date	Particulars	F	Total	Date	Particulars	F	Total	
			Van					
			€					
Jan 1	Van		14,000					
			Brookfield Motors					
							€	
				Jan 1	Van		14,000	

LESSON 2: SAMPLE QUESTION AND SOLUTION

Question

Truckmotors Ltd is a garage that sells and repairs trucks. They have the following transactions during February, which you are asked to record in the general journal.

1 Feb   Purchased computer on credit from Data Ltd, €15,000

3 Feb   Purchased heating oil on credit form Emu Oil Ltd, €500

7 Feb   Purchased equipment on credit from Road Supplies Ltd, €9,000 + 10% VAT

8 Feb   Sold old machinery on credit to Roche Ltd, €10,000

9 Feb   A debtor, A. Lindsey who owes €3,000, has been declared bankrupt and is only able to pay €500. The remaining €2,500 is to be written off as a bad debt.

Solution

Remember! Decide first where the entries will appear in the ledger, then write up the general journal.

Notes

- The general journal is the book of first entry for the purchase of assets, e.g. the computer bought on 1 February and the equipment bought on 7 February.
- It also records the sale of assets, e.g. the machinery sold on 8 February.
- Heating oil is a nontrading stock and it, too, is recorded in the general journal. Another nontrading stock for most firms is stationery.
- Each of these is a credit transaction. If cash or cheques are involved, then the transaction is recorded in the cash book.
- The general journal is also used to record bad debts, e.g. the €3,000 owed by A. Lindsey.
- Sometimes you will have to include VAT in the transaction, as in the entry on 7 February.

RB 2

	General Journal		Debit	Credit
			€	€
Feb				
1	Computer		15,000	
	Data Ltd			15,000
	(purchased computer on credit)			
3	Heating oil		500	
	Emu Oil Ltd			500
	(purchased heating oil on credit)			
7	Equipment		9,000	
	VAT		900	
	Road Supplies Ltd			9,900
	(purchased equipment on credit)			
8	Roche Ltd		10,000	
	Machinery			10,000
	(sold old machinery on credit)			
9	Cash		500	
	Bad Debts		2,500	
	A. Lindsey			
	(writing off a bad debt)			3,000

Notes

1 Feb The computer is an asset and as it is being bought, the value of the asset will have to be increased, i.e. the entry in the computer account must be debit. Therefore, the double entry in the Data Ltd account must be credit.

RB 3

Dr							Cr
Date	Particulars	F	Total	Date	Particulars	F	Total
			Computer				
			€				€
Feb 1	Data Ltd				15,000		
			Data Ltd				
			€				€
				Feb 1	Computer		15,000

3 Feb The heating oil is a nontrading stock (an asset). Once again we must debit the heating oil account and credit Emu Oil Ltd.

			Heating Oil				
Feb 3	Emu Oil		500				
			Emu Oil Ltd				
				Feb 3	Heating oil		500

7 Feb The VAT in this transaction makes it different from the earlier examples. The equipment account is debited with the €9,000 equipment and the VAT account with the €900 VAT. The double entry is on the credit of Road Supplies Ltd.

			Equipment				
Feb 7	Road Supplies Ltd		9,000				
			VAT				
Feb 7	Road Supplies Ltd		900				
			Road Supplies Ltd				
				Feb 7	Equipment and VAT		9,900

8 Feb The next transaction requires you to sell machinery. Selling machinery (an asset) is recorded by crediting the machinery account. The double entry is on the debit of Roche's account.

			Roche Ltd				
Feb 8	Machinery		10,000				
			Machinery				
				Feb 8	Roche Ltd		10,000

9 Feb A. Lindsey (a debtor) who owes €3,000 has been declared bankrupt. She is able to pay €500 so this is shown on the debit of the cash account. Bad debts is debited with the €2,500 and the double entry is on the credit of A. Lindsey's account.

			Cash				
Feb 9	A. Lindsey		500				
			Bad Debts				
Feb 9	A. Lindsey		2,500				
			A. Lindsey				
				Feb 9	Cash		500
				Feb 9	Bad debts		2,500

LESSON 3: RECORDING OPENING BALANCES

Question

Regan Ltd had the following balances in its general journal on 1 January.

RB 2

General Journal					Debit	Credit
					€	€
Motor vehicles					40,000	
Equipment					25,000	
Bank					8,000	
Debtor: Dolan Ltd					2,000	
Creditor: Fahy Ltd						25,000
Ordinary share capital						50,000
					75,000	75,000

(a) Post the balances on 1 January given in the general journal to the relevant accounts.

(b) Regan Ltd has the following transactions during January, which you are asked to record in the general journal.

12 Jan   Purchased equipment on credit from Fahy Ltd, €5,000

21 Jan   Dolan Ltd is declared bankrupt and is only able to pay 50 cent in the €

The remaining balance is to be written off as a bad debt.

Solution

Notes

1. The equipment account (an asset) is debited, as €5,000 worth of equipment is being bought. Fahy Ltd are credited because they are owed €5,000.

2. In the second transaction Dolan has been declared bankrupt and is only able to pay 50 cent in the €. This means Dolan can only pay €1,000 and the remaining €1,000 is a bad debt.

RB 2

		General Journal			Debit	Credit
					€	€
Jan 12	Equipment				5,000	
	Fahy Ltd					5,000
	(purchased equipment on credit)					
21	Bank				1,000	
	Bad Debts				1,000	
	Dolan Ltd					
	(writing off a bad debt)					2,000

Notes

1. The six entries on 1 January in the general journal appear as six accounts in the ledger. Each of the accounts is shown with a balance b/d on 1 January.

2. If the money is debit in the general journal, then the balance is debit in the ledger account. If it is credit in the general journal, then it is credit in the ledger account.

3. The other entries in the accounts are from the transactions that took place on 12 and 21 January.

				RB 3				
Dr								**Cr**
Date	Particulars	F	Total	Date	Particulars		F	Total
				Motor Vehicles				
			€					€
Jan 1	Balance	b/d	40,000					
				Equipment				
			€					€
Jan 1	Balance	b/d	25,000					
12	Maguire Ltd		5,000	Jan 31	Balance		c/d	30,000
			30,000					30,000
Feb 1	Balance	b/d	30,000					
				Bank				
			€					€
Jan 1	Balance	b/d	8,000					
21	Brady Ltd		1,000	Jan 31	Balance		c/d	9,000
			9,000					9,000
Feb 1	Balance	b/d	9,000					
				Brady Ltd				
			€					€
Jan 1	Balance	b/d	2,000	Jan 21	Bank			1,000
				21	Bad debts			1,000
			2,000					2,000
				Maguire Ltd				
			€					€
				Jan 1	Balance		b/d	25,000
Jan 31	Balance	c/d	30,000	12	Equipment			5,000
			30,000					30,000
				Feb 1	Balance		b/d	30,000
				Ordinary Share Capital				
			€					€
				Jan 1	Balance		b/d	50,000
				Bad Debts				
			€					€
Jan 21	Brady Ltd		1,000					

LESSON 1: PRACTICE

1. Loughnane Garage Ltd sells petrol, diesel and other car products. They also sell new and used cars. Tick the appropriate book of first entry in which Loughnane Garage Ltd should record each of the following transactions.

	Purchases Day Book	Sales Day Book	Cash Book	General Journal
(a) Purchased cash register on credit from O'Brien's Ltd, €10,000.	○	○	○	○
(b) Purchased petrol for resale on credit from Emu Oil Ltd, €8,000.	○	○	○	○
(c) Sold car on credit to P. Fagan, €12,500.	○	○	○	○
(d) Bought equipment and paid by cheque, €6,000.	○	○	○	○
(e) Bought equipment on credit from Car Wash Supplies Ltd, €6,000.	○	○	○	○
(f) Sold old equipment on credit to Maguire's Ltd, €3,000.	○	○	○	○

2. In these questions remember that assets and expenses (AE) are debited when they are increased in value. Liabilities and gains (LG) are credited when they are increased in value – say it as AELG. The two to the left (debit) are AE and the two to the right (credit) are LG.

Now look at the transactions below and complete the table to show the amount entered in each account. The first one is completed for you as an example.

		Debit	Credit
1	You buy a van on credit for €14,000 from ValuTrux Ltd. Van account (increasing an asset) ValuTrux account (increasing a liability)	14,000	14,000
2	You buy equipment on credit for €30,000 from Henderson Ltd. Equipment account Henderson account		
3	You buy a photocopier on credit for €800 from Jones Ltd. Office equipment account Jones account		
4	You sell old machinery on credit for €700 to Jennings Ltd. Jennings account Machinery account		
5	You sell an old computer on credit for €400 to Carrick Ltd. Carrick Ltd account Computer account		

LESSON 2: PRACTICE

1. Star-Tri Ltd is a stationery shop. Record the following transactions in their general journal and post to the ledger.
    1 Mar   Purchased shop fittings on credit from Quick Fit Ltd, €10,000
    6 Mar   Purchased burglar alarm on credit from Nobel Ltd, €3,000
    8 Mar   Sold old office equipment on credit to Office Supplies Ltd, €6,000

2. Kiddie Clothes Ltd is a baby boutique. Record the following transactions in their general journal and post to the ledger.
    1 Apr   Purchased buggies on credit from Dooley's Ltd, €18,000
    4 Apr   Sold old computer on credit to J. Andrews, €12,500
    9 Apr   Purchased computer on credit from Classic Computers Ltd, €4,000

3. Curtain Call Ltd is a curtain-making service. Record the following transactions in their general journal and post to the ledger.
    2 May   Purchased sewing machines on credit from F. Adams, €75,000
    5 May   Purchased equipment on credit from Burke's Ltd, €40,000
    8 May   Sold old computer to G. Burke, €1,000

4. TeaTotal Ltd is a company that imports and distributes pottery products. Record the following transactions in their general journal and post to the ledger.
    1 Jun   Purchased warehouse on credit from Johnston Ltd, €150,000
    3 Jun   Sold old van on credit to T. Carey, €10,000
    9 Jun   Carr's Tearooms, who owe €4,000, have been declared bankrupt. It has been decided to write off the full amount as a bad debt.

5. Duggan & Duggan Ltd is a door supply company. Record the following transactions in their general journal and post to the ledger.
    2 Jul   Purchased machinery on credit from Door to Door Ltd, €12,500
    4 Jul   Kelly Ltd, who owe €5,000, have been declared bankrupt. They are able to pay €1,500. The balance is to be written off as a bad debt.
    8 Jul   Sold used equipment on credit to Power Ltd, €8,750

LESSON 3: PRACTICE

1.   Norris Ltd had the following balances in its general journal on 1 February.

General Journal		Debit	Credit
		€	€
Premises		240,000	
Furniture		100,000	
Bank		50,000	
Debtor: ABR Ltd		30,000	
Creditor: McKinney			120,000
Ordinary share capital			300,000
		420,000	420,000

(a) Post the balances on 1 February given in the general journal to the relevant accounts.

(b) They have the following transactions during February, which you are asked to record in the general journal.

   17 Feb   Purchased furniture on credit from McKinney Ltd, €12,000

   26 Feb   Sold old furniture on credit to ABR Ltd, €10,000

2.   O'Brien's Ltd had the following balances in its general journal on 1 March.

General Journal		Debit	Credit
		€	€
Bank		95,000	
Premises		100,000	
Vehicles		80,000	
Debtor: ABR Ltd		25,000	
Ordinary share capital			300,000
		300,000	300,000

(a) Post the balances on 1 March given in the general journal to the relevant accounts.

(b) They have the following transactions during March, which you are asked to record in the general journal.

   14 Mar   Purchased premises on credit from Travers Ltd, €30,000

   28 Mar   ABR Ltd is declared bankrupt and is only able to pay 50 cent in the €.
             The remaining balance is to be written off as a bad debt.

TEST YOURSELF AT

my-etest.com

32 Worked Example

Question

Trial balance of Duffy's Ltd:

	€	€
Bank	4,000	
Creditor: Weston's Ltd		2,000
Debtor: Grogan's Ltd	1,000	
Fixed asset: machinery	7,000	
Ordinary share capital		10,000
	12,000	12,000

CREDIT TRANSACTIONS:

3/3/04   Purchased goods on credit from Weston's Ltd, invoice no. 76, €5,000 + 20% VAT

9/3/04   Returned goods to Weston's Ltd, credit note no. 43, €300 + 20% VAT

16/3/04   Sold goods on credit to Grogan's Ltd, invoice no. 59, €2,000 + 20% VAT

BANK TRANSACTIONS:

7/3/04   Paid telephone by cheque no. 47, €600

14/3/04   Purchased goods by cheque no. 48, €1,000 + 20% VAT

17/3/04   Cash sales lodged, €6,000 + 20% VAT

21/3/04   Grogan Ltd settled their account in full by cheque and it was lodged

27/3/04   Paid Weston's Ltd by cheque no. 49, €5,000

You are required to do the following.

(a) Enter the above trial balance figures into the relevant accounts.

(b) Record the transactions in the appropriate books of first entry and post to the ledger.

(c) Balance the accounts on 31 March 2004 and extract a trial balance as on that date.

Solution

(i) The Day Books

The day books record the credit transactions of Duffy's Ltd. There is only one purchase, one sale and one return to write up.

RB 3

Purchases Day Book

Date	Particulars	F	Net	VAT	Total
Mar			€	€	€
3	Weston's Ltd (no. 76)		5,000	1,000	6,000
			5,000	1,000	6,000

Sales Day Book

			€	€	€
Mar					
16	Grogan's Ltd (no. 59)		2,000	400	2,400
			2,000	400	2,400

Purchase Returns Day Book

			€	€	€
Mar					
9	Weston's Ltd (no. 43)		300	60	360
			300	60	360

RB 3

Dr							Cash Book		(page 2)						Cr
Date	Particulars	F	Debtors	Sales	VAT	Bank		Date	Particulars	F	Other	Cred.	Purch.	VAT	Bank
Mar			€	€	€	€		Mar			€	€	€	€	
1	Balance	b/d				4,000		7	Telephone	47	600				600
17	Sales	GL2		6,000	1,200	7,200		14	Purchases	48			1,000	200	1,200
21	Grogan's Ltd	SL1	3,400			3,400		27	Weston's Ltd	49		5,000			5,000
								31	Balance	c/d					7,800
			3,400	6,000	1,200	14,600					600	5,000	1,000	200	14,600
			SL1	GL2	GL5						GL7	PL1	GL3	GL5	
Apr 1	Balance	b/d				7,800									

(ii) The Cash Book

The cash book records the five bank transactions from the question. Only the bank column is balanced. The other columns are totalled.

(iii) Posting to the Ledger

The figures given in the trial balance in the question are recorded as the balance b/d in the accounts. The €4,000 bank balance is shown as debit in the cash book. The other figures are shown as balances b/d in Weston's, Grogan's, machinery and ordinary share capital.

Post the net and VAT figures from the day books to the purchases, sales and VAT accounts. Post the totals from the day books to Weston's and Grogan's accounts. Post the credit figures in the cash book to the debit of telephone, purchases and Weston's accounts. Post the debit figures to the credit of sales and Grogan's.

(iv) Balancing the Accounts

Any account with two or more entries must be balanced: sales, purchases, VAT, Weston's. Grogan's account is closed because the debit entries (€1,000 + €2,400) are equal to the credit entry of €3,400.

(v) The Trial Balance

The open accounts are listed in the trial balance. The figures are entered in the debit or credit column as appropriate. Total both columns.

RB 3

Dr				Ordinary Share Capital (page 1)			Cr
Date	Particulars	F	Total	Date	Particulars	F	Total
				Mar 1	Balance	b/d	10,000

Sales (page 2)

				Mar 16	Grogan's Ltd	SB	2,000
Mar 31	Balance	c/d	8,000	17	Bank	CB3	6,000
			8,000				8,000
				Apr 1	Balance	b/d	8,000

Purchases (page 3)

Mar 3	Weston's Ltd	PB	5,000				
Mar 14	Bank	CBS	1,000	Mar 31	Balance	c/d	6,000
			6,000				6,000
Apr 1	Balance	b/d	6,000				

Purchases Returns (page 4)

				Mar 9	Weston's Ltd	PRB	300

VAT (page 5)

Mar 3	Weston's Ltd	PB	1,000	Mar 9	Weston's Ltd	PRB	60
14	Bank (Purchases VAT)	CB3	200	16	Grogan's Ltd	SB	400
31	Balance	c/d	460	17	Bank (Sales VAT)	CB3	1,200
			1,660				1,660
				Apr 1	Balance	b/d	460

Machinery (page 6)

Mar 1	Balance	b/d	7,000				

Telephone (page 7)

Mar 7	Balance	CB3	600				

Weston's Ltd (page 1)

Mar 9	Purchases Returns	PRB	360	Mar 1	Balance	b/d	2,000
27	Bank	CB3	5,000	3	Purchases	PB	6,000
31	Balance	c/d	2,640				
			8,000				8,000
				Apr 1	Balance	b/d	2,640

Grogan's Ltd (page 1)

Mar 1	Balance	b/d	1,000	Mar 21	Bank	CB3	3,400
16	Sales	SB	2,400				
			3,400				3,400

RB 2

Trial Balance as at 31 March 2004			Debit	Credit
	F		€	€
Ordinary share capital				10,000
Sales				8,000
Purchases			6,000	
Purchases returns				300
VAT				460
Machinery			7,000	
Telephone			600	
Weston's Ltd				2,640
Bank			7,800	
			21,400	21,400

PRACTICE: DAY BOOKS AND CASH BOOK TO LEDGER AND TRIAL BALANCE

1. The following trial balance was extracted from the books of Hopkin's Ltd.

	€	€
Bank	6,000	
Debtor: Kealy's Ltd	2,000	
Creditor: Rooney's Ltd		5,000
Fixed asset: vehicles	9,000	
Ordinary share capital		12,000
	17,000	17,000

The following transactions took place.

CREDIT TRANSACTIONS:

5/5   Purchased goods on credit from Rooney's Ltd, invoice no. 146, €3,000 + 20% VAT

12/5   Sold goods on credit to Kealy's Ltd, invoice no. 79, €4,000 + 20% VAT

15/5   Returned goods to Rooney's Ltd, credit note no. 52, €200 + 20% VAT

BANK TRANSACTIONS:

4/5   Paid electricity by cheque no. 86, €400

11/5   Cash sales lodged, €9,000 + 20% VAT

13/5   Purchased goods by cheque no. 87, €3,000 + 20% VAT

22/5   Paid Rooney's Ltd by cheque no. 88, €4,000

24/5   Kealy's Ltd settled their account in full by cheque and it was lodged

You are required to do the following.

(a) Enter the above trial balance figures into the relevant accounts.

(b) Record the transactions for the month of May in the appropriate books of first entry and post relevant figures to the ledger.

(c) Analyse the bank transactions using the following column headings.
    Debit (receipts) side: Bank, VAT, Debtors
    Credit (payments) side: Bank, Purchases, VAT, Creditors, Other

(d) Balance the accounts on 31 May and extract a trial balance as on that date.

2.   The following trial balance was extracted from the books of Russell's Ltd.

	€	€
Creditor: Dempsey's Ltd		8,000
Debtor: Hogan's Ltd	7,000	
Bank	9,000	
Motor vehicles	18,000	
Premises	50,000	
Ordinary share capital		76,000
	84,400	84,400

The following transactions took place.

CREDIT TRANSACTIONS:

3/6   Purchased goods on credit from Dempsey's Ltd, invoice no. 312, €5,000 + 20% VAT

11/6   Sold goods on credit to Hogan's Ltd, invoice no. 126, €7,000 + 20% VAT

18/6   Hogan's Ltd returned goods, credit note no. 43, €600 + 20% VAT

BANK TRANSACTIONS:

6/6   Cash sales lodged, €6,000 + 20% VAT

9/6   Paid wages by cheque no. 74, €5,000

11/6   Purchased goods by cheque no. 75, €2,500 + 20% VAT

18/6   Paid Dempsey's Ltd by cheque no. 76, €2,000

26/6   Hogan's Ltd settled their account in full by cheque and it was lodged

You are required to do the following.

(a) Enter the above trial balance figures into the relevant accounts.

(b) Record the transactions for the month of June in the appropriate books of first entry and post relevant figures to the ledger.

(c) Analyse the bank transactions using the following column headings.
    Debit (receipts) side: Bank, Sales, VAT, Debtors
    Credit (payments) side: Bank, Purchases, VAT, Creditors, Other

(d) Balance the accounts on 30 June and extract a trial balance as on that date.

3. The following trial balance was extracted from the books of Timmons Ltd on 31 July.

	€	€
Bank	7,000	
Debtor: J. Dillon	20,000	
Fixed assets: fixtures	70,000	
Ordinary share capital		97,000
	97,000	97,000

Credit transactions for the week ended 7 August were recorded as follows.

Sales Day Book

Date	Details	Inv.	Net	VAT	Total
			€	€	€
1/8	J. Dillon	412	30,000	3,000	33,000
4/8	J. Dillon	413	20,000	2,000	22,000
			50,000	5,000	55,000

Sales Returns Day Book

Date	Details	Note No.	Net	VAT	Total
			€	€	€
5/8	J. Dillon	131	5,000	500	5,500
			5,000	500	5,500

The following bank transactions took place during the week ending 7 August.

1/8	Cash sales lodged, €50,000 + 10% VAT
2/8	Purchases for resale by cheque no. 80, €30,000 + 10% VAT
3/8	Paid electricity bill by cheque no. 81, €2,000
4/8	Paid wages by cheque no. 82, €3,000
5/8	Received cheque from J. Dillon and lodged it, €25,000
6/8	Purchased fixtures by cheque no. 83, €10,000

You are required to do the following.

(a) Enter the above trial balance figures into the relevant accounts.

(b) Post the relevant figures from the sales and sales returns day books to the ledger.

(c) Write up the bank transactions using the following column headings.

Debit side: Debtors, Sales, VAT, Bank

Credit side: Other, Purchases, VAT, Bank

(d) Balance the accounts and extract a trial balance as on 7 August.

4. The following trial balance was extracted from the books of Watkin's Ltd on 31 January.

	€	€
Bank		5,000
Creditor: M. Fagan		35,000
Vehicles	8,000	
Reserves		4,000
Premises	80,000	
Ordinary share capital		44,000
	88,000	88,000

Credit transactions for the week ended 7 February were recorded as follows.

1/2   Purchases from M. Fagan, invoice no. 521, €20,000 + 20% VAT

4/2   Purchases from M. Fagan, invoice no. 545, €15,000 + 20% VAT

5/2   Returns to M. Fagan, credit note no. 243, €3,000

Bank transactions for the week were recorded as follows.

Cash Book

Date	Particulars	Sales	VAT	Bank	Date	Particulars	Purchases	VAT	Bank
		€	€	€			€	€	€
1/2	Sales	50,000	10,000	60,000	1/2	Balance b/d			5,000
4/2	Sales	60,000	12,000	72,000	2/2	Purchases	40,000	8,000	48,000
					3/2	Telephone bill			2,000
					5/2	M. Fagan			25,000
					6/2	Premises			11,000
					7/2	Balance c/d			41,000
		110,000	22,000	132,000			40,000	8,000	132,000
8/2	Balance b/d			41,000					

You are required to do the following.

(a) Enter the above trial balance figures into the relevant accounts.

(b) Write up the purchases and purchases returns day books and post the relevant figures to the ledger.

(c) Post the relevant figures from the cash book to the ledger.

(d) Balance the accounts and extract a trial balance as on 7 February.

5. The following trial balance was extracted from the books of Coffey's Ltd at 31 October.

	€	€
Bank	6,000	
Creditor: F. Lalor		25,000
Stock 31/10/05	5,000	
Reserves		11,000
Fixed assets	75,000	
Ordinary share capital		50,000
	86,000	86,000

Credit transactions for the week ended 7 November were recorded as follows.

Purchases Day Book					
Date	Details	No.	Net	VAT	Total
			€	€	€
1/11/05	F. Lalor	312	20,000	5,000	25,000
4/11/05	F. Lalor	313	16,000	4,000	20,000
			36,000	9,000	45,000
Purchases Returns Day Book					
5/11/05	F. Lalor	131	4,000	1,000	5,000
			4,000	1,000	5,000

The following bank transactions took place during the week ending 7 November.

1/11   Cash sales lodged, €60,000 + 20% VAT

2/11   Purchases for resale by cheque no. 70, €40,000 + 20% VAT

3/11   Paid telephone bill by cheque no. 71, €1,000

4/11   Cash sales lodged, €80,000 + 20% VAT

5/11   Paid F. Lalor by cheque no. 72, €30,000

6/11   Purchased machinery by cheque no. 73, €10,000

You are required to do the following.

(a) Enter the above trial balance figures into the relevant accounts.

(b) Post the relevant figures from the purchases and purchases returns day books to the ledger.

(c) Write up the bank transactions using the following column headings.
     Debit side: Sales, VAT, Bank
     Credit side: Other, Creditors, Purchases, VAT, Bank

(d) Post the relevant figures to the ledger, balance the accounts on 7 November and extract a trial balance as on that date.

PRACTICE: BOOK OF FIRST ENTRY AND LEDGER QUESTION

Sunshine Paints Ltd had the following balances in its general journal on 1 May.

RB 2

Date	Details	F	Dr	Cr
May 1	Premises	GL1	70,000	
	Motor vans	GL2	30,000	
	Bank		5,000	
	Debtor: J.J. Builders Ltd	DL1	3,000	
	Creditor: Throne Paints Ltd	CL1		48,000
	Ordinary share capital	GL3		60,000
			108,000	108,000

General Journal

The following transactions took place during the month of May.

CREDIT TRANSACTIONS:

4/5   Purchased paint for resale on credit from Throne Paints Ltd, invoice no. 361, €40,000 + 20% VAT

10/5   Sold paint on credit to Brushwell Ltd, invoice no. 120, €5,000 + 20% VAT

17/5   Sold paint on credit to J.J. Builders Ltd, invoice no. 121, €25,000 + 20% VAT

BANK TRANSACTIONS:

6/5   Cash sales lodged, €9,000 (this includes €1,500 VAT)

8/5   Paid wages, cheque no. 75, €1,050

15/5   Purchased paint, cheque no. 76, €1,200 + 20% VAT

22/5   J.J. Builders Ltd settled their account in full by cheque and it was lodged

28/5   Paid Throne Paints Ltd, cheque no. 77, €35,000

You are required to do the following.

(a) Post the balances on 1 May given in the general journal to the relevant accounts.

(b) Record the transactions for the month of May in the appropriate books of first entry and post relevant figures to the ledger.

(c) Analyse the bank transactions using the following column headings.
   Debit side: Bank, Sales, VAT, Debtors
   Credit side: Bank, Purchases, VAT, Creditors, Wages

(d) Balance the accounts on 31 May and extract a trial balance as on that date.

(JCHL, adapted)

33 Presentation of Ledger Accounts

INTRODUCTION

Look at the ledger accounts at the bottom of this page.

1. Do they look the same?
2. Do they contain similar words and figures?
3. Do they have the same opening and closing balances?
4. Which one do you think is easier to understand?

LESSON 1: SAMPLE QUESTION AND SOLUTION

There are two ways to present ledger accounts: T account and continuous presentation. The **T account** uses debit and credit sides to show double-entry bookkeeping, while the **continuous presentation** uses debit and credit columns and a running balance column.

Question

Jan

1   Balance in Bill Cronin account is €1,500 DR

5   Sold goods on credit to Bill Cronin, €2,000

6   Bill Cronin returned goods to the value of €70

7   Sold goods on credit to Bill Cronin, €1,050

10 Bill Cronin sent us a cheque for €1,000

(a) Represent this information in Bill Cronin's T account and balance the account.

(b) Show the same information in a continuous presentation.

(b) In each case the amount outstanding is €3,480. In the T account this is shown as a 'balance b/d', whereas in the continuous presentation it is the final figure in the balance column.

RB 2

Dr		Bill Cronin			Cr
			Debit	Credit	Balance
Jan 1	Balance b/d				1,500
5	Sales		2,000		3,500
6	Sales returns			70	3,430
7	Sales		1,050		4,480
10	Bank			1,000	3,480

Solution

(a)

RB 3

Dr				Bill Cronin				Cr
Date	Particulars	F	Total	Date	Particulars	F	Total	
2005			€	2005			€	
Jan 1	Balance	b/d	1,500	Jan 6	Sales return		70	
Jan 5	Sales		2,000	Jan 6	Sales return		1,000	
Jan 7	Sales		1,050	Jan 10	Bank		3,480	
			4,550				4,550	
Feb 1	Balance	b/d	3,480					

PRACTICE PREPARING T ACCOUNTS AND CONTINUOUS PRESENTATION

In each of the following questions:

(a) represent the information in a T account and balance the account.

(b) show the same information in a continuous presentation.

1.   The following transactions took place in January.

Jan

1   Balance in Daly's account is €240 DR

4   Sold goods on credit to Daly, €500

5   Daly sent us a cheque for €1,000

10   Sold goods on credit to Daly, €1,200

15   Daly returned goods to the value of €300

2.   The following transactions took place in February.

Feb

1   There was a €1,200 CR balance in Peter King Ltd's account

5   Bought goods on credit from Peter King Ltd, €1,480

10   Bought goods on credit from Peter King Ltd, €2,880

14   Returned goods to Peter King Ltd to the value of €520

20   Sent a cheque for €4,000 to Peter King Ltd

3.   The following transactions took place in March.

Mar

1   Balance in Melanie O'Neill's account is €300 DR

8   Sold goods on credit to Melanie O'Neill, €850

10   Sold goods on credit to Melanie O'Neill, €1,600

12   Melanie O'Neill returned goods to the value of €200

14   Melanie O'Neill sent us a cheque for €2,000

4.   The following transactions took place in April.

Apr

1   €1,260 CR balance in the account of Henderson's Ltd

7   Bought goods on credit from Henderson's Ltd, €1,500

11   Bought goods on credit from Henderson's Ltd, €700

15   Sent a cheque for €2,700 to Henderson's Ltd

21   Returned goods to Henderson's Ltd to the value of €250

5.   The following transactions took place in May.

May

1   Balance in Larry Lloyd's account is €360 DR, balance in Pat Russell Ltd is €960 CR

5   Sold goods on credit to Larry Lloyd, €1,760

7   Larry Lloyd sent us a cheque for €1,000

9   Bought goods on credit from Pat Russell, €2,400

10   Larry Lloyd returned goods to the value of €120

13   Bought goods on credit from Pat Russell Ltd, €1,000

18   Sold goods on credit to Larry Lloyd, €1,440

21   Sent a cheque for €2,800 to Pat Russell Ltd

27   Returned goods to Pat Russell Ltd to the value of €160

PRACTICE CONVERTING ACCOUNTS

Study the following accounts.

1.

RB 3

Dr				John Egan			Cr
Date	Particulars	F	Total	Date	Particulars	F	Total
			€				€
Jul 1	Balance	b/d	540	Jul 9	Sales returns		85
7	Sales		13,400	21	Bank		1,200

(a) What is the closing balance in the above account?

(b) Convert the above account to continuous presentation.

2.

RB 3

Dr				Paul Connolly			Cr
Date	Particulars	F	Total	Date	Particulars	F	Total
			€				€
Aug 7	Purchases returns		120	Aug 1	Balance	b/d	390
10	Purchases returns		105	5	Purchases		12,275
28	Bank		900	8	Purchases		12,000

(a) What is the closing balance in the above account?

(b) Convert the above account to continuous presentation.

3.

RB 2

Dr			Vera Hayden		Cr
			Debit	Credit	Balance
Sep 1	Balance	b/d			600
7	Sales		15,200		15,800
9	Sales returns			340	15,460
18	Sales		350		15,810
20	Bank		1,275		14,535

(a) Is Vera Hayden a debtor or a creditor?

(b) Convert the above to a T account.

4.

			Noelle Jordan		
			Debit	Credit	Balance
Oct 1	Balance	b/d			750CR
3	Purchases			1,550	2,300
6	Purchases returns		525		1,775
11	Purchases			900	2,675
15	Bank		1,285		1,390

(a) Is Noelle Jordan a debtor or a creditor?

(b) Convert the above to a T account.

34 Control Accounts

TERMS COVERED IN THIS CHAPTER
Debtors control, creditors control.

INTRODUCTION

Classrooms are not the only places where control is needed. Businesses also need to stay in control. Bookkeeping can help by controlling the ledger (trial balance) and the money in the bank (bank reconciliation). Bookkeeping can also check on debtors and creditors.

1. What do you think would happen if your bicycle got out of control as you cycled to school?
2. Can you guess what would happen if your debtors got out of control in your business?
3. What do you think would happen if your creditors got out of control?

LESSON 1: UNDERSTANDING CONTROL ACCOUNTINGS

Control accounts are used to check the accuracy of credit transactions. They summarise entries and make early detection of mistakes possible.

RB 3

Dr				Debtors Control Account			Cr
Date	Particulars	F	Total	Date	Particulars	F	Total
			€				€
Dec 1	Balance	b/d	7,000	Dec 31	Sales returns		925
31	Sales		26,750	31	Bank		19,050
				31	Balance	c/d	13,775
			33,750				33,750
Jan 1	Balance	b/d	13,775				

DEBTORS CONTROL ACCOUNT

The **debtors control account** checks the sales ledger. It is also called the **sales ledger control account**.

● **Balance b/d:** This is the amount for debtors outstanding at the beginning of the month, i.e. debtors owe €7,000 on 1 December.

● **Sales:** This is the total of credit sales during December, taken from the sales day book.

● **Sales returns:** These are the goods that were returned, perhaps because they were faulty.

● **Bank:** This is the amount of money received from debtors (customers).

● **Balance:** The final balance of €13,775 is the amount of debt outstanding at the end of the month. This becomes the opening balance for January.

CREDITORS CONTROL ACCOUNT

The **creditors control account** checks the purchases ledger. It is also called the **purchases ledger control account**.

RB 3

Dr				Creditors Control Account			Cr
Date	Particulars	F	Total	Date	Particulars	F	Total
			€				€
Dec 31	Purchases returns		700	Dec 1	Balance	b/d	4,400
31	Bank		11,000	31	Purchases		10,500
				31	Balance	c/d	3,200
			14,900				14,900
Jan 1	Balance	b/d	3,200				

- **Balance b/d:** This is the amount of credit outstanding at the beginning of the month, i.e. we owe €4,400 to our creditors.
- **Purchases:** This is the total of the credit purchases from the purchases day book for December.
- **Returns:** €700 is the total value of goods we returned.
- **Balance:** The final balance of €3,200 is the amount we still owe our creditors.

PRACTICE: GIVEN CONTROL ACCOUNTS

I.   Study the following control account.

RB 3

Dr			Control Account				Cr
Date	Particulars	F	Total	Date	Particulars	F	Total
			€				€
Jan 1	Balance	b/d	7,000	Jan 31	Sales returns		1,500
31	Sales		21,000	31	Bank		15,000

(a) Which type of control account is this?

(b) Explain the entry on 1 January.

(c) Explain the entry on 31 January, 'Sales €21,000'.

(d) What do the letters 'b/d' mean?

(e) What is the balancing figure on 31 January?

2.   Study the following control account.

Dr			Control Account				Cr
Date	Particulars	F	Total	Date	Particulars	F	Total
			€				€
Mar 31	Purchases returns		850	Mar 1	Balance	b/d	1,000
31	Bank		15,900	31	Purchases		12,800

(a) Which type of control account is this?

(b) Explain the entry on 1 March.

(c) Explain the entry on 31 March, 'Bank €15,900'.

(d) What is the balancing figure on 31 March?

PRACTICE: PREPARING CONTROL ACCOUNTS

Prepare control accounts from the following information.

1. May 1 Balance c/d €4,500 DR
  31 Sales, €23,000
  31 Sales returns, €750
  31 Bank, €16,200

2. Jun 1 Balance c/d €600 CR
  30 Bank, €10,100
  30 Purchases, €21,300
  30 Purchases returns, €540

3. Jul 1 Balance c/d €6,300 DR
  31 Sales returns, €2,400
  31 Sale, €38,250
  31 Bank, €28,200

4. Aug 1 Balance c/d €300 CR
  31 Bank, €5,100
  31 Purchases, €6,300
  31 Purchases returns, €150

5. Sep 1 Sales ledger balances, €5,100
  30 Sales day book, €16,540
  30 Returns in, €480
  30 Cheques received from debtors, €5,100

6. Oct 1 Purchases ledger balances, €360
  31 Purchases day book, €7,960
  31 Returns out, €520
  31 Cheques paid to creditors, €4,300

7. Prepare a sales ledger control account for November using only the relevant information from the following.
  Nov 1 Sales ledger balances, €7,400
  30 Sales day book, €26,300
  30 Purchases day book, €5,670
  30 Returns in, €380
  30 Returns out, €470
  30 Cheques received from debtors, €12,600

8. Prepare a purchase ledger control account for December using only the relevant information from the following.

    Dec 1 Sales ledger balances, €5,200
         1 Purchases ledger balances, €260
        30 Sales day book, €17,930
        30 Purchases day book, €14,680
        30 Returns in, €270
        30 Returns out, €430
        31 Cheques paid to creditors, €8,300

9. Prepare a sales ledger control account for January using only the relevant information from the following.

    Jan 1 Sales ledger balances, €6,300
        31 Sales day book, €14,600
        31 Returns in, €240
        31 Returns out, €760
        31 Cheques received from debtors, €6,800
        31 Cheques paid to creditors, €3,400

10. Prepare a sales ledger control account and a purchases ledger control account for February from the following information.

    Feb 1 Sales ledger balances, €5,400
         1 Purchases ledger balances, €3,200
        28 Sales day book, €16,500
        28 Purchases day book, €8,640
        28 Returns in, €170
        28 Returns out, €350
        28 Cheques paid to creditors, €5,680
        28 Cheques received from debtors, €12,620

35 The Trading Account

TERMS COVERED IN THIS CHAPTER
Gross profit, gross loss, returns, carriage in, cost of goods available for sale, cost of sales, trading period, opening stock, closing stock.

INTRODUCTION

What do you think?

1. What happens to businesses that make a loss every year?
2. Most businesses have to pay tax every year. What do you think determines the amount of tax they must pay?
3. Suppose you own a newspaper shop and you want to sell it. How will you decide what price to ask?

LESSON I: MODERN VERTICAL PRESENTATION OF THE TRADING ACCOUNT

Question

Prepare a trading account for the year ended 31 December 2005 from the following information.

	€
Sales	5,400
Sales returns	100
Purchases	3,200
Purchases returns	150
Carriage in	200
Opening stock	250
Closing stock	400

Solution 1: Modern Vertical Presentation

RB 2

Trading Account for the Year Ended 31 December 2005			
	€	€	€
Sales			5,400
less sales returns			100
			5,300
Less cost of sales:			
opening stock		250	
purchases	3,200		
less purchases returns	150		
	3,050		
add carriage in	200	3,250	
Cost of goods available for sale		3,500	
less closing stock		400	
Cost of sales			3,100
Gross profit			**2,200**

LESSON 2: USING LEDGER ACCOUNTS TO PREPARE THE TRADING ACCOUNT

Solution 2: Using the Ledger

Notes

- The accounts on the right show the balances brought down for the year and the double entry to post these balances to the trading account. For example, sales has a credit balance brought down of €5,400. This is posted to the trading account by debiting the sales account and crediting the trading account.

- **Returns: Purchases returns** are goods that we send back to our suppliers. They are going out of our firm, so they are also known as **returns out**. They reduce the amount of our purchases.

- **Sales returns** are goods that are sent back to us by our customers. Since these are coming back into our firm, they are known as **returns in**. They reduce the amount of our sales. Net sales may also be called the **turnover** of the firm.

- **Opening stock:** The closing stock in December 2004 will become the opening stock in January 2005. At the end of the year it is transferred to the trading account by crediting the stock account and debiting the trading account.

- **Carriage in:** This is the cost of transporting the goods and is added to the purchases.

RB 3

Dr								Cr
General Ledger								
Date	Particulars	F	Total	Date	Particulars	F	Total	
Sales								
2005			€	2005			€	
Dec 31	Trading		5,400	Dec 31	Balance	b/d	5,400	
Sales Returns								
2005			€	2005			€	
Dec 31	Balance	b/d	100	Dec 31	Trading (deduct)		100	
Purchases								
2005			€	2005			€	
Dec 31	Balance	b/d	3,200	Dec 31	Trading		3,200	
Purchases Returns								
2005			€	2005			€	
Dec 31	Trading (deduct)		150	Dec 31	Balance		150	
Carriage In								
2005			€	2005			€	
Dec 31	Balance	b/d	200	Dec 31	Trading		200	
Stock								
2005			€	2005			€	
Jan 1	Balance	b/d	250	Dec 31	Trading		250	
Dec 31	Trading (deduct)		400					

Trading Account for the Year Ended 31 December 2005

			€				€
Opening stock			250	Sales			5,400
Purchases	3,200			less returns			100
less returns	150						5,300
	3,050						
add carriage in	200	3,250					
		3,250					
less closing stock		400					
Cost of goods sold		3,100					
Gross profit c/d		2,200					
		5,300					5,300
				Gross profit		b/d	**2,200**

LESSON 1 AND 2: PRACTICE PREPARING TRADING ACCOUNTS

1. From the following information prepare a trading account for the year ended 31 December 2005.

	€
Sales	5,700
Sales returns	120
Purchases	2,900
Purchases returns	100
Opening stock	400
Closing stock	450

2. From the following information prepare a trading account for the year ended 31 March 2005.

	€
Sales	6,500
Sales returns	110
Purchases	3,100
Purchases returns	200
Opening stock	500
Closing stock	570

3. From the following information prepare a trading account for the year ended 31 December 2005.

	€
Sales	7,000
Sales returns	200
Purchases	3,000
Purchases returns	100
Carriage in	300
Opening stock	500
Closing stock	700

4. From the following information prepare a trading account for the year ended 30 September 2005.

	€
Opening stock	1,500
Purchases	12,000
Sales	26,000
Sales returns	800
Purchases returns	600
Carriage in	170
Closing stock	1,600

5. From the following information prepare a trading account for the year ended 31 December 2005.

	€
Returns in	400
Opening stock	3,200
Purchases	18,400
Sales	27,600
Returns out	300
Carriage in	400
Closing stock	2,900

6. From the following information prepare a trading account for the year ended 31 December 2005.

	€
Sales	90,000
Sales returns	3,000
Purchases	37,000
Purchases returns	4,000
Opening stock	9,000
Closing stock	10,000
Carriage in	2,100

7. From the following information prepare a trading account for the year ended 31 December 2005.

	€
Sales	76,000
Purchases	31,000
Sales returns	12,000
Purchases returns	2,000
Opening stock	11,000
Closing stock	13,000
Carriage in	4,000

8. From the following information prepare a trading account for the year ended 31 December 2005.

	€
Sales	100,000
Purchases	42,000
Sales returns	12,000
Purchases returns	4,000
Opening stock	16,000
Closing stock	20,000
Customs duty	2,000

9. Study the following trading account.

RB 2

Trading Account for the Year Ended 31 December 2005	€	€	€
Sales			8,000
less returns			100
			7,900
Opening stock		200	
Purchases	3,900		
less returns	100	3,800	
		4,000	
less closing stock		300	
Cost of goods sold			3,700
Gross profit c/d			4,200

(a) What trading period does this account refer to?

(b) What are the returns out for the year?

(c) How much stock was there at the beginning of the year?

(d) What is the turnover?

36 The Profit and Loss Account

INTRODUCTION

What do you think? Answer these questions and then discuss your answers with another pupil.

1. It must be quite expensive to run a school. Can you list these expenses?

2. Look at the solution to the question in Lesson 2. List the expenses for this company.

3. List some other expenses this company might have.

LESSON 1: UNDERSTANDING THE PROFIT AND LOSS ACCOUNT

The profit and loss account continues on from where the trading account left off. The starting point, therefore, is the gross profit (or loss) arrived at in the trading account. To this profit are added any gains made by the firm. From the profit are taken any expenses incurred during the year by the firm. The difference is the **net profit** or **net loss** of the business.

RB 2

Trading, Profit and Loss Account of Suredata Ltd for the Year Ended 31 December 2005			
	€	€	€
Sales			34,000
less returns			4,000
			30,000
Opening stock		2,300	
Purchases	15,000		
less returns	200		
	14,800		
add carriage in	150	14,950	
		17,250	
less closing stock		2,250	
Cost of goods sold			15,000
Gross profit			**15,000**
Discount received			1,850
			16,850
Rent		890	
Electricity		720	
Salaries		8,500	
Carriage out		340	
Discount allowed		400	10,850
Net profit			**6,000**

CARRIAGE

Carriage is the transport of the goods to and from the business. Transporting the goods into the firm is carriage in and transporting them out of the business is carriage out. While both of these are expenses of the firm, they are shown in different parts of the accounts.

Carriage in is shown as an expense added to the purchases in the trading account. This is because carriage in increases the cost of the purchases.

Carriage out is shown as an expense in the profit and loss account. It is an expense related to selling the product.

REVENUE EXPENDITURE

Expenditure on items that are used within the year is **revenue expenditure**, e.g. diesel, electricity, telephone and insurance. These revenue expenses are recorded in the profit and loss account.

DISCOUNT

The discount we give to our customers is called **discount allowed**. It is shown as an expense of the firm in the profit and loss account. The discount we get from our suppliers is called **discount received**. This is a gain for the business and is added to the gross profit in the profit and loss account. A firm may also have other gains, such as **interest received** and **commission received**.

GP% AND NP%

The gross profit percentage (GP%) and the net profit percentage (NP%) are ratios that are used to show how profitable a firm is. The GP% shows the gross profit earned by each €100 of sales. The NP% shows the net profit earned on each €100 of sales. The GP% and the NP% are calculated as follows.

GP%   = $\dfrac{\text{gross profit}}{\text{sales}}$ x   100

NP%   = $\dfrac{\text{net profit}}{\text{sales}}$ x   100

In the question above, the GP% is:

$\dfrac{40{,}000}{80{,}000}$ x 100 = 50%

The NP% is:

$\dfrac{20{,}000}{80{,}000}$ x 100 = 20%

LESSON 2: SAMPLE QUESTION AND SOLUTION

Question

Prepare a trading, profit and loss account for Skynet Ltd for the year ended 31 December 2005 from the following information.

	€	
Purchases	40,500	T
Sales	85,000	T
Purchases returns	400	T
Sales returns	5,000	T
Rent	1,200	E
Electricity	2,400	E
Salaries	16,200	E
Carriage in	900	T
Carriage out	1,400	E
Discount allowed	1,800	E
Discount received	3,000	G
Opening stock	5,000	T
Closing stock	6,000	T

Solution

Rough Work:

Before you begin to work on a trading, profit and loss account, decide whether items listed are trading (T), gains (G) or expenses (E).

RB 2

Trading, Profit and Loss Account of Skynet Ltd for the Year Ended 31 December 2005

	€	€	€
Sales			85,000
less returns			5,000
			80,000
Opening stock		5,000	
Purchases	40,500		
less returns	400		
	40,100		
add carriage in	900	41,000	
		46,000	
less closing stock		6,000	
Cost of goods sold			40,000
Gross profit			**40,000**
Discount received			3,000
			43,000
Rent		1,200	
Electricity		2,400	
Salaries		16,200	
Carriage out		1,400	
Discount allowed		1,800	23,000
Net profit			**20,000**

LESSON 1: PRACTICE

Capital and Revenue Expenditure

Place a tick in the appropriate box to indicate whether each of the following is an example of capital expenditure or revenue expenditure.

		Capital Expenditure	Revenue Expenditure
(a)	Purchase of delivery van.	○	○
(b)	Purchase of petrol for delivery van.	○	○
(c)	Wages for van driver.	○	○
(d)	Payment of annual insurance premium for delivery van.	○	○
(e)	Payment for extension to existing premises.	○	○
(f)	Purchase of heating oil.	○	○
(g)	Payment of rent for warehouse used to store raw materials.	○	○
(h)	Purchase of computer.	○	○
(i)	Wages of secretary.	○	○
(j)	Payment for repairs to computer.	○	○
(k)	Purchase of printer.	○	○
(l)	Purchase paper for printer.	○	○
(m)	Payment of advertising expenses.	○	○
(n)	Payment of commission to sales representatives.	○	○
(o)	Conversion of old storeroom to staff canteen.	○	○

Calculating GP% and NP%

1. Calculate the net profit percentage for a firm with sales of €50,000 and net profit of €10,000.
2. A firm has sales of €8,000 and cost of sales is €6,000. Calculate the gross profit percentage for the firm.
3. Calculate the net profit percentage for a firm with sales of €40,000 and net profit of €8,000.
4. A firm has sales of €20,000 and cost of sales is €16,000. Calculate the gross profit percentage for the firm.
5. Calculate the net profit percentage for a firm with sales of €3,000 and a net profit of €300.
6. A firm has sales of €25,000 and cost of sales of €5,000. Calculate the gross profit percentage for the firm.
7. Calculate the net profit percentage for a firm with sales of €36,000 and expenses of €24,000.
8. Calculate the net profit percentage for a firm with sales of €39,000 and net profit of €26,000.
9. Calculate the gross profit percentage and the net profit percentage for a firm with sales of €100,000, cost of sales €40,000 and expenses €20,000.
10. Calculate the net profit percentage for a firm with sales of €40,000, cost of sales €14,000 and expenses €18,000.
11. Calculate the net profit percentage for a firm with sales of €27,000, cost of sales €9,000 and expenses €3,000.

12. Calculate the net profit percentage for a firm with sales of €30,000, cost of sales €10,000 and expenses €5,000.

13. Calculate the net profit percentage for a firm with sales of €70,000, cost of sales €10,000 and expenses €20,000.

14. A firm has sales of €60,000, purchases of €20,000, closing stock of €2,000 and expenses of €78,000. Calculate the gross profit percentage and the net profit percentage.

15. A firm has sales of €80,000, cost of sales of €40,000 and expenses of €10,000. Calculate the gross profit percentage and the net profit percentage.

LESSON 2: PRACTICE

Preparing Profit and Loss Accounts

1. Prepare a trading, profit and loss account for the year ended 31 December 2005 from the following information.

	€	
Purchases	7,000	T
Sales	20,000	T
Motor expenses	1,000	E
Electricity	500	E
Opening stock	400	T
Closing stock	600	T

2. Prepare a trading, profit and loss account for the year ended 31 December 2005 from the following information.

	€	
Sales	18,000	T
Purchases	7,100	T
Insurance	1,200	E
Opening stock	700	T
Interest on loan	400	E
Closing stock	600	T

3. Prepare a trading, profit and loss account for the year ended 31 December 2005 from the following information.

	€
Sales	20,000
Opening stock	1,500
Advertising	2,000
Purchases	7,000
Telephone	600
Closing stock	1,500

4. Prepare a trading, profit and loss account for the year ended 31 December 2005 from the following information.

	€
Purchases	16,000
Sales	40,000
Rent	2,000
Motor expenses	4,000
Electricity	3,000
Salaries	8,000
Opening stock	1,000
Closing stock	1,200

5. Prepare a trading, profit and loss account for the year ended 31 December 2005 from the following information.

	€	
Purchases returns	600	T
Sales returns	400	T
Opening stock	2,000	T
Sales	50,000	T
Stationery	700	E
Purchases	20,000	T
Motor expenses	4,000	E
Light and heat	700	E
Salaries	16,000	E
Discount allowed	300	E
Closing stock	1,500	T

6. Prepare a trading, profit and loss account for the year ended 31 December 2005 from the following information.

	€
Purchases returns	500
Sales returns	800
Purchases	6,000
Sales	22,000
Carriage in	300
Motor expenses	600
Electricity	200
Discount allowed	100
Interest received	4,000
Opening stock	500
Closing stock	800

7. Prepare a trading, profit and loss account for the year ended 31 December 2005 from the following information.

	€
Sales returns	300
Purchases returns	400
Sales	14,000
Purchases	5,000
Carriage in	300
Insurance	900
Carriage out	200
Opening stock	700
Interest paid on loan	400
Commission received	2,500
Closing stock	900

8. Prepare a trading, profit and loss account for the year ended 31 December 2005 from the following information.

	€
Sales	18,000
Opening stock	900
Carriage out	300
Sales returns	400
Advertising	600
Discount allowed	200
Purchases	8,100
Purchases returns	350
Closing stock	1,250

9. Prepare a trading, profit and loss account for the year ended 31 December 2005 from the following information.

	€
Purchases	31,000
Discount allowed	400
Sales	67,500
Sales returns	3,200
Purchases returns	1,700
Rent	800
Carriage in	200
Motor expenses	3,000
Discount received	600
Salaries	20,000
Opening stock	1,200
Closing stock	1,300

10. Prepare a trading, profit and loss account for the year ended 31 December 2005 from the following information.

	€
Opening stock	3,100
Sales	54,000
Stationery	1,350
Discount received	700
Purchases	18,500
Motor expenses	2,700
Sales returns	3,200
Purchases returns	4,100
Carriage in	200
Carriage out	630
Light and heat	850
Discount allowed	480
Salaries	23,600
Closing stock	3,400

TEST YOURSELF AT
my-etest.com

37 The Profit and Loss Appropriation Account

TERMS COVERED IN THIS CHAPTER
Dividend, reserve, retained earnings, share capital, authorised share capital, issued share capital.

INTRODUCTION

Do you agree with the following statements?

1. I think all the profit a business makes should be given to the shareholders.
2. If a business makes a big profit I think they should give money back to their customers.
3. A business can never make a big enough profit.

LESSON I: UNDERSTANDING THE NEED FOR AN APPROPRIATION ACCOUNT

The appropriation account shows how the profit earned by the firm is used. Most firms will give some of the profit out to the shareholders in the form of a **dividend**. The rest is reinvested in the business. This reinvestment often takes the form of a **reserve**, which the business will use to buy new assets or to expand the firm. Money not given out remains the property of the shareholders and is called **retained earnings**.

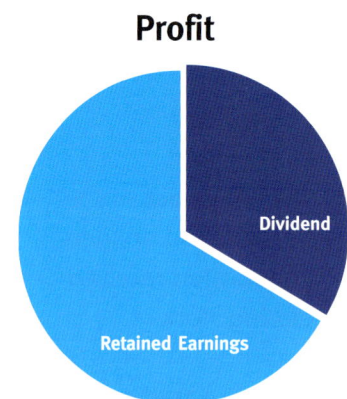
Profit (pie chart showing Dividend and Retained Earnings)

Memorandum of Association

1. Company Name:	All Weather Ltd
2. Company Address:	Beachview Avenue, Dublin
3. The liability of the members is limited.	
4. Company Objectives:	To manufacture sports equipment
5. Authorised Share Capital:	100,000 €1 Ordinary Shares

Shareholder's name and address	Number of shares taken
Ciaran Lillis Beachview Avenue, Dublin	40,000
Hilda Lillis Beachview Avenue, Dublin	40,000
Total	80,000

Date: 1 October 2004
Signed: Ciaran Lillis   Hilda Lillis
Witness: P. O'Byrne, Earl Street, Dublin

SHARE CAPITAL

The memorandum of association gives details about the authorised and the issued share capital. As you can see in the example, All Weather Ltd has an authorised share capital of 100,000 €1 ordinary shares. This is the maximum amount of shares they are permitted to issue. They have, in fact, only issued 80,000 of these shares: 40,000 to Ciaran Lillis and 40,000 to Hilda Lillis.

LESSON 2: SAMPLE QUESTION AND SOLUTION

CALCULATING ORDINARY SHARE DIVIDENDS

The ordinary share dividend is expressed as a percentage of the ordinary share capital issued. The directors decide the percentage dividend that will be issued.

Question

All Weather Ltd has 80,000 ordinary shares issued. Draft the appropriation account for the year ended 31 December 2005 given the following information.

● Net profit is €30,000.
● Last year's reserve (profit and loss balance) was €14,000.
● The directors proposed a twenty per cent ordinary share dividend.

Solution

Proposed dividend = 20% of €80,000 = €16,000

			€	€
Profit and Loss Appropriation Account of All Weather Ltd for the Year Ended 31 December 2005				RB 2
Net Profit				30,000
+ reserves (profit and loss balance)				14,000
				44,000
– dividends				16,000
New reserve balance				28,000

LAST YEAR'S BALANCE

The balance in last year's appropriation account must be shown in this year's appropriation account. There are two possibilities.

(i)   Last year's balance was **credit**. This is added to this year's net profit, as it represents a profit brought forward from last year.

(ii) Last year's balance was **debit**. This is a loss brought forward from last year. It is subtracted from this year's net profit.

LESSON 1: PRACTICE CALCULATING DIVIDENDS

Dividends

1. A company has 50,000 ordinary shares of €1 each issued. Calculate the dividend if the directors propose a five per cent ordinary share dividend.

2. A company has 30,000 ordinary shares of €1 each issued. Calculate the dividend if the directors propose a ten per cent ordinary share dividend.

3. A company has 40,000 ordinary shares of €1 each issued. Calculate the dividend if the directors propose a fifteen per cent ordinary share dividend.

4. A company has 25,000 ordinary shares of €1 each issued. Calculate the dividend if the directors propose a twenty per cent ordinary share dividend.

5. A company has 60,000 ordinary shares of €1 each issued. Calculate the dividend if the directors propose an eight per cent ordinary share dividend.

LESSON 2: PRACTICE PREPARING THE APPROPRIATION ACCOUNT

Appropriation Accounts

1. Atkins Ltd has 100,000 €1 ordinary shares issued. Draft the appropriation account for the year ended 31 January 2005 given the following information.
    *   Net profit is €25,000.
    *   The directors proposed a ten per cent ordinary share dividend.

2. Brennan Ltd has 80,000 €1 ordinary shares issued. Draft the appropriation account for the year ended 28 February 2005 given the following information.
    *   Net profit is €26,000.
    *   The directors proposed a fifteen per cent ordinary share dividend.

3. Cogen Ltd has 200,000 €1 ordinary shares issued. Draft the appropriation account for the year ended 31 March 2005 given the following information.
    *   Net profit is €22,000.
    *   The directors proposed a five per cent ordinary share dividend.

4. Duggan Ltd has 70,000 €1 ordinary shares issued. Draft the appropriation account for the year ended 30 April 2005 given the following information.
    *   Net profit is €12,000.
    *   The directors proposed a seven per cent ordinary share dividend.

5. Egan Ltd has 40,000 €1 ordinary shares issued. Draft the appropriation account for the year ended 31 May 2005 given the following information.
- Net profit is €17,000.
- The directors proposed a twenty per cent ordinary share dividend.

6. Fahy Ltd has 80,000 €1 ordinary shares issued. Draft the appropriation account for the year ended 30 June 2005 given the following information.
- Net profit is €15,000.
- Last year's reserve (profit and loss balance) was €2,500 CR.
- The directors proposed a ten per cent ordinary share dividend.

7. Gahan Ltd has 70,000 €1 ordinary shares issued. Draft the appropriation account for the year ended 31 July 2005 given the following information.
- Net profit is €21,000.
- Last year's reserve (profit and loss balance) was €3,000 CR.
- The directors proposed a fifteen per cent ordinary share dividend.

8. Hayes Ltd has 60,000 €1 ordinary shares issued. Draft the appropriation account for the year ended 31 August 2005 given the following information.
- Net profit is €11,000.
- Last year's reserve (profit and loss balance) was €4,000 CR.
- The directors proposed a five per cent ordinary share dividend.

9. Irwin Ltd has 50,000 €1 ordinary shares issued. Draft the appropriation account for the year ended 30 September 2005 given the following information.
- Net profit is €16,000.
- Last year's reserve (profit and loss balance) was €5,000 CR.
- The directors proposed a fifteen per cent ordinary share dividend.

10. Jarvis Ltd has 200,000 €1 ordinary shares issued. Draft the appropriation account for the year ended 31 October 2005 given the following information.
- Net profit is €90,000.
- Last year's reserve (profit and loss balance) was €8,000 CR.
- The directors proposed a twenty per cent ordinary share dividend.

38 The Balance Sheet

TERMS COVERED IN THIS CHAPTER
Assets, liabilities, fixed, current, capital employed, working capital.

INTRODUCTION

What do you think? Work with another pupil on these tasks.

1. Think of a local business, e.g. a shop, factory or bank.
2. List all the assets you think this business owns. Be as specific as possible, e.g. premises, counter, cash register, oven, fridge and so on.
3. Swap your list with another pair of pupils. Can you guess the business they were thinking of?

LESSON 1: UNDERSTANDING THE PARTS OF A BALANCE SHEET

The balance sheet is the last stage in the preparation of the final accounts of a business. At first glance a balance sheet looks very complicated. However, you should think of it simply as a statement about a business. It lists what the firm owns and what it owes. It is like a picture of the company on one day of the year.

ASSETS

The things the firm owns are called **assets**. **Assets** that will be in the firm more than a year are considered long-term or **fixed assets**, e.g. machinery, fixtures, premises and vehicles. Other assets frequently change in value. These are called **current assets**, e.g. stock, debtors, cash at bank and cash on hand.

RB 2

Balance Sheet of Comtec Ltd as at 31 December 2005			
	€	€	€
Fixed Assets			
Premises			50,000
Vehicles			17,000
			67,000
Current Assets			
Stock	5,000		
Debtors	18,000		
Cash on hand	2,000	25,000	
Current liabilities			
Creditors	5,000	12,000	
Bank overdraft	7,000		
Working capital			13,000
			80,000
Financed by:			
Ordinary share capital			70,000
Reserves:			
Profit and loss			10,000
			80,000

WORKING CAPITAL

The working capital is the difference between the current assets and the current liabilities. In a healthy company the current assets will be greater than the current liabilities. In this balance sheet the working capital is €13,000.

Working capital = current assets – current liabilities

LIABILITIES

Liabilities are amounts of money that the firm owes. Some of these are owed in the short term and are called **current liabilities**, e.g. bank overdraft and creditors. Other liabilities are more permanent and will not be repaid for many years, e.g. bank loans and capital.

CAPITAL EMPLOYED

Capital employed is the money that is being used in the company. It is arrived at by adding the fixed assets to the working capital. In this balance sheet the capital employed is €80,000.

Capital employed = fixed assets + working capital

LESSON 2: SAMPLE QUESTION AND SOLUTION

Question

The following trial balance was extracted from the books of Comtec Ltd on 31 December 2005. From this information prepare a trading, profit and loss and appropriation account for the year ended 31 December 2005 and a balance sheet as at that date.

	Dr	Cr
	€	€
Stock 1 January 2005	6,000	
Purchase returns		2,000
Sales returns	3,000	
Purchases	31,400	
Sales		61,000
Interest on overdraft	900	
Electricity	1,100	
Salaries	10,000	
Carriage in	600	
Carriage out	1,000	
Premises	50,000	
Vehicles	17,000	
Debtors	18,000	
Creditors		5,000
Ordinary share dividend	4,000	
Bank overdraft		7,000
Cash on hand	2,000	
Ordinary share capital		70,000
	145,000	145,000

Stock at 31 December 2005 was €5,000.

Solution

RB 2

Trading, Profit and Loss Account of Comtec Ltd for the Year Ended 31 December 2005

	€	€	€
Sales			61,000
less returns			3,000
			58,000
Opening stock		6,000	
Purchases	31,400		
less returns	2,000	29,400	
Carriage in		600	
		36,000	
less closing stock		5,000	
Cost of goods sold			31,000
Gross profit			27,000
Interest on overdraft		900	
Electricity		1,100	
Salaries		10,000	
Carriage out		1,000	13,000
Net profit			14,000

RB 2

Appropriation Account of Comtec Ltd for the Year Ended 31 December 2005

	€	€
Net profit		14,000
– ordinary share dividend		4,000
Balance		10,000

THE TRIAL BALANCE

Information for the preparation of a company's final accounts is usually presented in the form of a **trial balance**. Debit entries in the trial balance will either be assets or expenses. The only exceptions are stock, purchases and sales returns. Credit entries in the trial balance will either be liabilities or gains. In this case, the exceptions are sales and purchases returns.

The closing stock for the period concerned is written below the trial balance.

RB 2

Balance Sheet of Comtec Ltd as at 31 December 2005

	€	€	€
Fixed assets:			
Premises			50,000
Vehicles			17,000
			67,000
Current assets:			
Stock	5,000		
Debtors	18,000		
Cash on hand	2,000	25,000	
Current liabilities:			
Creditors	5,000		
Bank overdraft	7,000	12,000	
Working capital			13,000
			80,000
Financed by:			
Ordinary share capital			70,000
Reserves:			
Profit and loss			10,000
			80,000

LESSON I: PRACTICE USING THE BALANCE SHEET

I.   Study the following balance sheet.

(a) What trading period does this balance sheet refer to?

(b) Name two fixed and two current assets of Caltec.

(c) What is this firm's working capital?

(d) What is this firm's capital employed?

(e) What is the amount of retained earnings for this year?

Balance Sheet of Caltec Ltd as at 31 December 2005

	€	€	€
Fixed assets:			
Premises			160,000
Vehicles			40,000
			200,000
Current assets:			
Stock	7,000		
Debtors	23,000		
Cash at bank	12,000	42,000	
Current liabilities:			
Creditors	20,000	20,000	
			22,000
			222,000
Financed by:			
Ordinary share capital			180,000
Reserves:			
Profit and loss			42,000
			222,000

2. Study the following balance sheets, then tick the correct box

Balance Sheets of Bailey Ltd						
	31 December 2004			**31 December 2005**		
	€	€	€	€	€	€
Fixed assets:						
Premises			200,000			200,000
Vehicles			20,000			15,000
Equipment						15,000
			220,000			230,000
Current assets:						
Stock	40,000			26,000		
Debtors	90,000			110,000		
Cash at bank	15,000			20,000		
Cash on hand	5,000	150,000		4,000	160,000	
Current liabilities:						
Creditors	50,000	50,000		40,000	40,000	
			100,000			120,000
			320,000			350,000
Financed by:						
Ordinary share capital			270,000			320,000
Reserves:						
Profit and loss			50,000			30,000
			320,000			350,000

	True	False
(a) Vehicles of €4,000 were sold during 2005.	○	○
(b) Bailey bought fixtures during 2005.	○	○
(c) Customers owed more on 31 December 2004 than on 31 December 2005.	○	○
(d) Bailey had more stock left on hand on 31 December 2004 than on 31 December 2005.	○	○
(e) Bailey issued more shares during the year.	○	○
(f) The working capital of this firm on 31 December 2005 was €85,000.	○	○
(g) The capital employed on 31 December 2005 was €80,000.	○	○

LESSON 2: PRACTICE PREPARING THE TRADING, PROFIT AND LOSS AND BALANCE SHEET

1. The following trial balance was extracted from the books of Kealy Ltd on 31 December 2005. From this information prepare a trading and profit and loss account for the year ended 31 December 2005 and a balance sheet as on that date.

	Dr	Cr
	€	€
Stock 1 January 2005	2,600	
Purchases	12,700	
Sales		36,800
Advertising	800	
Insurance	600	
Salaries	12,000	
Vehicles	18,660	
Premises	26,100	
Equipment	10,000	
Debtors	6,000	
Creditors		3,500
Cash at bank	840	
Ordinary share capital		50,000
	90,300	90,300

Stock at 31 December 2005 was €5,000.

2. The following trial balance was extracted from the books of Larkin Ltd on 31 December 2005. From this information prepare a trading and profit and loss account for the year ended 31 December 2005 and a balance sheet as on that date.

	Dr	Cr
	€	€
Stock 1 January 2005	2,000	
Purchases returns		600
Sales returns	300	
Purchases	32,000	
Sales		80,000
Debtors	16,000	
Creditors	11,000	
Cash at bank	5,000	
Advertising	1,200	
Insurance	2,500	
Salaries	35,600	
Premises	140,000	
Vehicles	27,000	
Ordinary share capital		170,000
	261,600	261,600

Stock at 31 December 2005 was €3,000.

3. The following trial balance was extracted from the books of Miller Ltd on 31 December 2005. From this information prepare a trading and profit and loss account for the year ended 31 December 2005 and a balance sheet as on that date.

	Dr €	Cr €
Stock 1 January 2005	6,000	
Advertising	6,500	
Salaries	24,000	
Insurance	4,000	
Electricity	14,000	
Purchases returns		2,000
Sales returns	3,500	
Purchases	40,000	
Sales		99,000
Debtors	33,000	
Creditors		16,000
Premises	200,000	
Equipment	20,000	
Cash at bank	6,000	
Ordinary share capital		240,000
	357,000	357,000

Stock at 31 December 2005 was €7,000.

4. The following trial balance was extracted from the books of Nolans Ltd on 31 December 2005. From this information prepare a trading and profit and loss account for the year ended 31 December 2005 and a balance sheet as on that date.

	Dr €	Cr €
Stock 1 January 2005	4,000	
Purchases returns		1,500
Sales returns	3,600	
Purchases	23,000	
Sales		80,000
Debtors	54,000	
Creditors		23,000
Bank overdraft		17,000
Premises	160,000	
Vehicles	24,000	
Equipment	16,000	
Interest on overdraft	1,200	
Salaries	28,000	
Carriage in	2,500	
Insurance	1,200	
Advertising	4,000	
Ordinary share capital		200,000
	321,500	321,500

Stock at 31 December 2005 was €6,000.

5. The following trial balance was extracted from the books of O'Reilly's Ltd on 31 December 2005. From this information prepare a trading and profit and loss account for the year ended 31 December 2005 and a balance sheet as on that date.

	Dr	Cr
	€	€
Stock 1 January 2005	5,000	
Interest on overdraft	1,500	
Advertising	7,500	
Insurance	3,600	
Salaries	45,000	
Debtors	52,000	
Purchases returns		2,000
Sales returns	3,000	
Purchases	290,000	
Sales		100,000
Premises	190,100	
Vehicles	26,000	
Equipment	18,000	
Creditors		21,000
Bank overdraft		7,600
Ordinary share capital		250,000
	380,600	380,600

Stock at 31 December 2005 was €2,600.

6. The following trial balance was extracted from the books of Pender's Ltd on 31 December 2005. From this information prepare a trading and profit and loss and appropriation account for the year ended 31 December 2005 and a balance sheet as on that date.

	Dr	Cr
	€	€
Stock 1 January 2005	4,000	
Purchases returns		6,000
Sales returns	5,000	
Purchases	80,000	
Sales		180,000
Interest on overdraft	2,000	
Advertising	3,500	
Insurance	2,700	
Telephone charges	2,400	
Electricity	2,100	
Salaries	46,000	
Carriage in	1,100	
Carriage out	1,200	
Premises	190,000	
Vehicles	38,000	
Machinery	10,000	
Debtors	63,000	
Creditors		34,000
Dividend paid	12,000	
Bank overdraft		23,000
Ordinary share capital		220,000
	463,000	463,000

Stock at 31 December 2005 was €6,000.

7. The following trial balance was extracted from the books of Quinn's Ltd on 31 December 2005. From this information prepare a trading and profit and loss and appropriation account for the year ended 31 December 2005 and a balance sheet as on that date.

	Dr	Cr
	€	€
Stock 1 January 2005	14,000	
Purchases	45,000	
Purchases returns		3,000
Sales		160,000
Sales returns	2,000	
Advertising	1,200	
Insurance	6,000	
Salaries	46,000	
Carriage in	2,000	
Carriage out	4,000	
Premises	170,000	
Vehicles	30,000	
Fixtures	40,000	
Debtors	45,000	
Creditors		26,000
Dividend paid	24,000	
Cash at bank	9,000	
Ordinary share capital		260,000
	449,300	449,300

Stock at 31 December 2005 was €12,000.

8. The following trial balance was extracted from the books of Reid's Ltd on 31 December 2005. From this information prepare a trading and profit and loss and appropriation account for the year ended 31 December 2005 and a balance sheet as on that date.

	Dr	Cr
	€	€
Stock 1 January 2005	21,000	
Sales returns	4,000	
Purchases returns		6,000
Interest on overdraft	3,000	
Insurance	12,000	
Electricity	6,000	
Premises	260,000	
Vehicles	34,000	
Salaries	72,000	
Carriage in	4,000	
Purchases	46,000	
Sales		190,000
Machinery	58,000	
Debtors	43,000	
Creditors		21,000
Dividend paid	20,000	
Bank overdraft		16,000
Ordinary share capital		350,000
	583,000	583,000

Stock at 31 December 2005 was €12,000.

9. The following trial balance was extracted from the books of Shaw's Ltd on 31 December 2005. From this information prepare a trading and profit and loss and appropriation account for the year ended 31 December 2005 and a balance sheet as on that date.

	Dr	Cr
	€	€
Stock 1 January 2005	18,000	
Purchases	42,000	
Sales		140,000
Advertising	4,000	
Insurance	6,000	
Carriage out	2,000	
Debtors	65,000	
Salaries	44,000	
Purchases returns		5,000
Sales returns	6,000	
Carriage in	4,000	
Equipment	50,000	
Creditors		43,000
Dividend paid	15,000	
Premises	160,000	
Bank overdraft		12,000
Ordinary share capital		240,000
	428,000	428,000

Stock at 31 December 2005 was €6,000.

10. The following trial balance was extracted from the books of Treacy's Ltd on 31 December 2005. From this information, prepare a trading and profit and loss and appropriation account for the year ended 31 December 2005 and a balance sheet as on that date.

	Dr	Cr
	€	€
Stock 1 January 2005	22,000	
Purchases returns		2,000
Sales returns	4,000	
Purchases	27,000	
Sales		130,000
Interest on overdraft	2,000	
Insurance	7,000	
Salaries	48,000	
Carriage in	1,000	
Electricity	6,000	
Premises	130,000	
Machinery	170,000	
Debtors	34,000	
Creditors		16,000
Dividend paid	15,000	
Bank overdraft		23,000
Ordinary share capital		142,000
	313,000	313,000

Stock at 31 December 2005 was €8,000.

STATE EXAM PRACTICE

1. Chapters Ltd is a company with an authorised capital of 250,000 ordinary shares at €1 each. The following trial balance has been taken from its books on 31 December 2005, the end of its financial year.

(a) From the figures, prepare a trading and a profit and loss and appropriation account for the year ended 31 December 2005 and a balance sheet as at that date.

(b) What percentage of sales is the net profit?

(c) State one reason why a limited company prepares a trading account each year.

(JCOL, adapted)

Trial Balance as at 31 December 2005	Dr €	Cr €
Issued share capital in €1 shares		210,000
Cash sales		275,000
Cash purchases for resale	215,000	
Opening stock at 01/01/05	62,500	
Carriage inwards	2,500	
Dividend paid	24,000	
Light and heat	9,750	
Insurance	4,250	
Interest on overdraft	2,650	
Wages	42,500	
Telephone	2,100	
Bank overdraft		31,900
Cash in hand	650	
Premises	112,000	
Furniture and fittings	39,000	
	516,900	516,900

Closing stock at 31 December 2005 was €93,750.

2. Limestone Ltd is a company with an authorised capital of 250,000 ordinary shares at €1 each. The following trial balance was taken from its books on 31 December 2004, the end of its financial year.

(a) From the figures, prepare a trading and profit and loss and appropriation account for the year ended 31 December 2004 and a balance sheet as at that date.

(b) State one reason why all limited companies should keep accounts.

(c) What percentage of the cash sales is the gross profit? Show your workings.

Trial Balance as at 31 December 2004	Dr €	Cr €
Cash sales		237,600
Carriage inwards	1,450	
Cash purchases for resale	181,350	
Opening stock at 1 January 2004	37,400	
Advertising	5,800	
Telephone	1,650	
Wages	24,600	
Interest on overdraft	1,550	
Heating and lighting	3,700	
Dividend paid	12,000	
Bank overdraft		17,000
Cash on hand	2,650	
Issued share capital in €1 shares		180,000
Buildings	98,500	
Machinery	63,950	
	434,600	434,600

Closing stock at 31 December 2004 was €42,000.

39 Adjustments

TERMS COVERED IN THIS CHAPTER
Prepayments, rent receivable, accruals, bad debts, straight-line depreciation, scrap value, nontrading stocks.

LESSON 1: PREPAYMENTS

The final accounts are prepared from the trial balance. However, some of the information in the trial balance may not be up to date. It is therefore necessary to adjust certain trial balance figures. The next few lessons look at how you would do this.

Many expenses are paid in advance. For example, you pay insurance for the year ahead or you pay rent for the month or week ahead. Where the payment goes beyond the accounting period it is said to be a **prepayment**.

Prepayments affect the final accounts in two ways.
- They reduce the expense in the profit and loss account.
- They are listed as current assets in the balance sheet.

Question

The annual premium of €3,000 for insurance was paid on 1 March. Record this in the ledger account to show the amount transferred to the profit and loss account on 31 December and the amount carried down to next year.

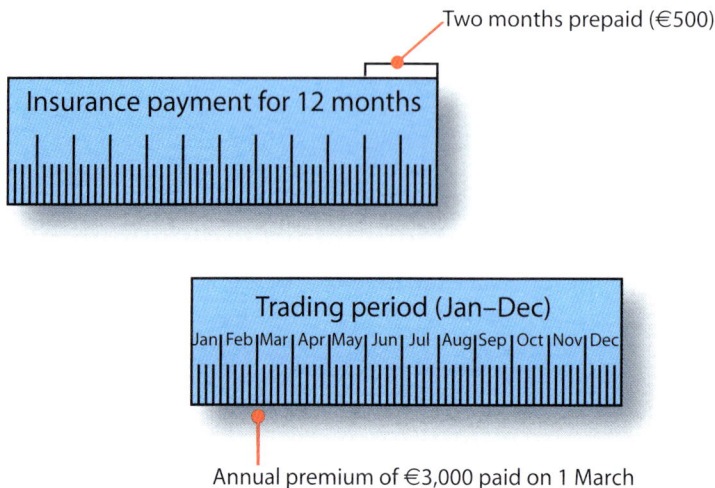

Two months prepaid (€500)

Insurance payment for 12 months

Trading period (Jan–Dec)

Jan Feb Mar Apr May Jun Jul Aug Sep Oct Nov Dec

Annual premium of €3,000 paid on 1 March

Solution

The €3,000 covers insurance for the twelve months March to February. The last two months are in the next year and are considered a prepayment. Two months are one-sixth of the year. Therefore, one-sixth of €3,000, or €500, is prepaid.

RB 3

Dr				Insurance			Cr
Date	Particulars	F	Total	Date	Particulars	F	Total
			€				€
Mar 1	Bank		3,000	Dec 31	Profit and loss		2,500
				31	Balance	c/d	500
			3,000				3,000
Jan 1	Balance	b/d	500				

The insurance account shows the payment of insurance on 1 March. The prepayment is recorded as a credit balance carried down to next year of €500.

RB 2

Profit and Loss Account for Year Ended 31 December 2005 (extract)			
Expenses		€	
Insurance (€3,000 – €500)		2,500	

The double entry for the €2,500 is shown as an expense in the profit and loss account.

RB 1

Balance Sheet as at 31 December 2005 (extract)			
Currents assets:		€	
Insurance prepaid		500	

The balance b/d of €500 is debt in the ledger and hence a current asset in the balance sheet.

RENT RECEIVABLE PREPAID

In the case of rent receivable we are getting money in rather than paying money out. This can occur when we sublet a garage or office space that we are not using. For example, we might have a garage at the back of our factory and we could rent this to someone. The rent the client pays is called **rent receivable** and is a gain for our business.

Rent receivable prepaid affects the final accounts in two ways.

● It reduces the gain in the profit and loss account.
● The amount of the prepayment is shown as a current liability in the balance sheet.

Question

Quinn's Ltd rent a room they are not using to Marie Hannifin. Marie paid an annual rent of €800 on 30 June 2005 to Quinn's Ltd. Show the entries in the rent receivable account of Quinn's Ltd on 31 December 2005. Also show the entries in the profit and loss account and in the balance sheet.

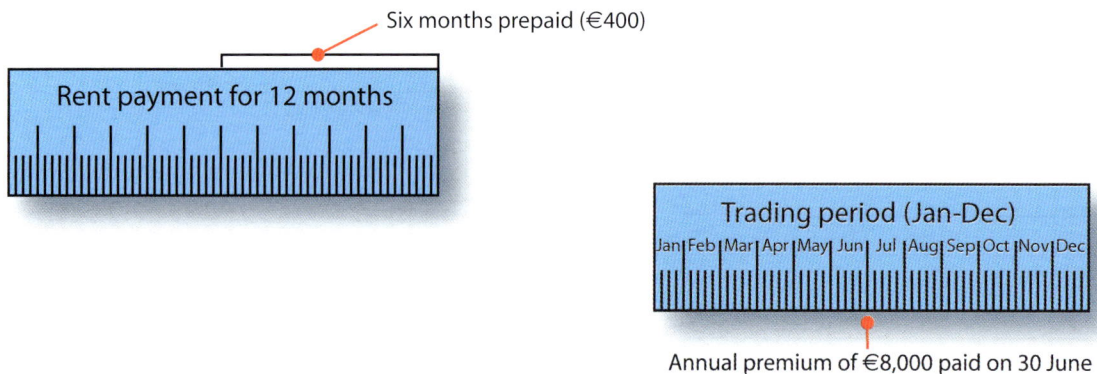

Six months prepaid (€400)

Rent payment for 12 months

Trading period (Jan-Dec)

Jan Feb Mar Apr May Jun Jul Aug Sep Oct Nov Dec

Annual premium of €8,000 paid on 30 June

Solution

The rent receivable account shows the €800 received on the credit. Only €400 of this refers to this year; the other €400 relates to next year. This is why €400 is shown as a balance in the account.

Dr				Rent Receivable				Cr	RB 3
Date	Particulars	F	Total	Date	Particulars	F	Total		
			€				€		
Dec 31	Profit and loss		400	Jun 30	Bank		800		
31	Balance	c/d	400						
			800				800		
				Jan 1	Balance	b/d	400		

The €400 that refers to this trading year is added to the gross profit in the profit and loss account.

Profit and Loss Account for Year Ended 31 December 2005 (extract)				RB 2
Gains			€	
Insurance (€800 – €400)			400	

The €400 prepaid to next year is shown as a liability of the firm on the balance sheet.

Balance Sheet as at 31 December 2005 (extract)				RB 2
Current liabilities:			€	
Rent receivable prepaid			400	

LESSON 2: ACCRUALS

Most expenses will be paid after the use of the product or service, e.g. you use electricity and pay for it two months later, or an employee does a day's work and is paid at the end of the week. These are said to be **accruals**, i.e. the expense **accrues** until it is paid.

Accruals affect the final accounts in two ways.
- They increase the expense in the profit and loss account.
- They are shown as current liabilities in the balance sheet.

Question

During the year the following electricity payments are made: 10 Feb, €300; 3 April, €500; 7 June, €300; 20 August, €400; 5 October, €500. Electricity accrued on 31 December is €240. Record this in the appropriate ledger account.

Solution

Electricity paid is shown on the debit side. The amount accrued is entered as a debit balance c/d of €240, therefore the charge to the profit and loss account must be €2,240.

RB 3

Dr				Electricity			Cr
Date	Particulars	F	Total	Date	Particulars	F	Total
			€				€
Feb 10	Bank		300	Dec 31	Profit and loss		2,240
Apr 3	Bank		500				
Jun 7	Bank		300				
Aug 20	Bank		400				
Oct 5	Bank		500				
Dec 31	Balance	c/d	240				
			2,240				2,240
				Jan 1	Balance	b/d	240

The €2,240 is entered as an expense in the profit and loss account.

RB 2

Profit and Loss Account for Year Ended 31 December 2005 (extract)				
Expenses			€	
Electricity (€2,000 + €240)			2,240	

The €240 accrued appears as a credit balance b/d in the ledger and is therefore listed as a current liability in the balance sheet.

RB 2

Balance Sheet as at 31 December 2005 (extract)				
Current liabilities:			€	
Electricity accrued			240	

LESSON 3: BAD DEBTS

BAD DEBTS

Debtors are customers who owe us money. Sometimes they fail to pay the amount due and the firm may decide to write it off as a **bad debt**.

Bad debts yet to be written off affect the final accounts in two ways.
- They are entered as an expense in the profit and loss account.
- They reduce the 'debtors' figure in the current assets of the balance sheet.

BAD DEBTS WRITTEN OFF

The adjustment described above must not be confused with a bad debts figure that may appear in the trial balance. In such a case the debtors have already been reduced by the amount of the bad debt and it is only necessary to show the amount as an expense in the profit and loss account.

Question

Debtors are €20,000. Bad debts of €2,000 are to be written off. Show the entries in the debtors, bad debts and profit and loss accounts. Also show the entry in the balance sheet.

Solution

The bad debts figure of €2,000 is shown on the credit of the debtors (to reduce the debtors) and on the debit of the bad debts.

RB 3

Dr					Debtors				Cr
Date	Particulars	F	Total		Date	Particulars	F	Total
			€					€
	Balance		20,000			Bad debts		2,000
						Balance	c/d	18,000
			20,000					20,000
	Balance	b/d	18,000					

RB 3

Dr					Bad Debts				Cr
Date	Particulars	F	Total		Date	Particulars	F	Total
			€					€
	Debtors		2,000			Profit and loss		2,000

The €2,000 is shown in the profit and loss account as an expense.

RB 2

Profit and Loss Account for Year Ended 31 December 2005 (extract)				
Expenses			€	
Bad debts			2,000	

In the balance sheet the debtors figure will be entered as €18,000 (€20,000 − €2,000).

RB 2

Balance Sheet as at 31 December 2005 (extract)				
Currents assets:			€	
Debtors (€20,000 − €2,000)			18,000	

LESSON 4: STRAIGHT-LINE DEPRECIATION

Depreciation is the reduction in value of an asset due to wear and tear or to age. Straight-line depreciation reduces the value of the asset by an equal amount each year.

Depreciation affects the final accounts in two ways.
- It is entered as an expense in the profit and loss account.
- It reduces the value of the asset in the fixed assets of the balance sheet.

SCRAP VALUE

When an asset is bought, the company estimates the number of years they will use the asset for. They also estimate how much they will receive when it is sold after this time. This is its **scrap value**.

Question

Furniture that cost €5,000 on 1 January 2005 has an estimated life of five years and its scrap value is expected to be €500. Calculate the amount of depreciation in each year using the straight-line method.

Solution

Depreciation each year will be: (€5,000 – €500) ÷ 5 = €900.

Question

Furniture that cost €3,000 was bought on 1 January 2003. It is to be depreciated by twenty per cent of cost each year.
(a) Show the furniture account in the ledger for 2003, 2004 and 2005.
(b) Show the relevant extract from the balance sheet as on 31 December each year.

Solution

RB 3

Dr							
Dr			**Furniture**				**Cr**
Date	Particulars	F	Total	Date	Particulars	F	Total
2003			€				€
Jan 1	Bank		3,000	Dec 31	Depreciation		600
				31	Balance	c/d	2,400
			3,000				3,000
2004							
Jan 1	Balance	b/d	2,400	Dec 31	Depreciation		600
				31	Balance	c/d	1,800
			2,400				2,400
2005							
Jan 1	Balance	b/d	1,800	Dec 31	Depreciation		600
				31	Balance	c/d	1,200
			1,800				1,800
2006							
Jan 1	Balance	b/d	1,200				

RB 2

Balance Sheet as at 31 December 2003 (extract)		Cost	Depr	Net
Fixed assets:		€	€	€
Furniture		3,000	600	2,400

RB 2

Balance Sheet as at 31 December 2004 (extract)		Cost	Depr	Net
Fixed assets:		€	€	€
Furniture		3,000	1,200	1,800

RB 2

Balance Sheet as at December 2005 (extract)		Cost	Depr	Net
Fixed assets:		€	€	€
Furniture		3,000	1,800	1,200

LESSON 5: NONTRADING STOCKS

Firms that use heating fuel or stationery may have stocks of these left over at the end of the year. Since the item was not all used, it would be incorrect to charge the full amount as an expense in the profit and loss account.

Stocks affect the final accounts in two ways.
- They reduce the expense in the profit and loss account.
- They are listed as current assets in the balance sheet.

Question
€2,500 worth of heating oil was bought during the year. At the end of the year €300 worth of the oil was unused. Show the entry in the heating oil and profit and loss accounts. Show the balance sheet extract.

Solution

RB 3

Dr				Heating Oil				Cr
Date	Particulars	F	Total	Date	Particulars	F	Total
			€				€
	Bank		2,500	Dec 31	Profit and loss		2,200
					Balance	c/d	300
			2,500				2,500
	Balance	b/d	300				

RB 2

Profit and Loss Account for Year Ended 31 December 2005 (extract)						
Expenses				€		
Heating oil (€2,500 – €300)				2,200		

In the profit and loss account, €2,200 (€2,500 – €300) is shown as an expense.

RB 2

Balance Sheet as at 31 December 2005 (extract)					
Currents assets:			€		
Stock of heating oil			300		

The €300 is listed as a current asset in the balance sheet.

LESSON I: PRACTICE DEALING WITH PREPAYMENTS

1. Insurance paid during the year is €2,400. €400 of this is prepaid for next year. Show the ledger account to record this.

2. Advertising paid during the year is €5,000. €700 of this is prepaid for next year. Show the ledger account to record this.

3. Rent paid during the year is €6,000. €1,000 of this is prepaid for next year. Show the rent account in the ledger and the relevant extract from the profit and loss account.

4. The annual premium of €1,200 for insurance was paid on 1 July. Record this in the ledger account to show the amount transferred to the profit and loss account on 31 December and the amount carried down to next year.

5. The year's advertising of €2,000 was paid on 1 April. Record this in the ledger account to show the amount transferred to the profit and loss account on 31 December and the amount carried down to next year.

6. Brendan Kelly moved into new offices on 1 June 2004. He paid the following rent over the next few months.
  - 30 June 2004: €800 for the two months ended 31 July 2004.
  - 15 August 2004: €1,200 for the three months ended 31 October 2004.
  - 11 November 2004: €2,400 for the six months ended 30 April 2005.
  (a) Record this in the ledger account to show the amount transferred to the profit and loss account on 31 December and the amount carried down to next year.
  (b) Show the extract from the profit and loss account on 31 December 2004.
  (c) Show the extract from the balance sheet as on 31 December 2004.

LESSON 2: PRACTICE DEALING WITH ACCRUALS

1. Rent paid during the year is €3,300. On 31 December €300 rent is due. Show the ledger account to record this.

2. Petrol expenses paid during the year are €2,900. €1,300 is still owed on 31 December. Show the ledger account to record this.

3. Telephone bills paid during the year are €3,700 and telephone charges accrued are €400 on 31 December. Show the telephone account in the ledger and the relevant extract from the profit and loss account.

4. Advertising expenses amounted to a total of €5,400 during the year and advertising accrued is €2,000 on 31 December. Record this in the ledger account to show the amount transferred to the profit and loss account on 31 December and the amount carried down to next year.

5. During the year the following telephone payments are made: 4 April, €800; 6 June, €700; 10 August, €900. Telephone charges due on 31 December are €2,300.
   (a) Record this in the ledger account to show the amount transferred to the profit and loss account on 31 December and the amount carried down to next year.
   (b) Show the extract from the profit and loss account on 31 December 2005.
   (c) Show the extract from the balance sheet as on 31 December 2005.

LESSON 3: PRACTICE DEALING WITH BAD DEBTS

1. Debtors are €24,000. Write off €2,000 as bad debts. Show the entries in the debtors, bad debts and profit and loss accounts. Also show the balance sheet entry.

2. Debtors are €8,000. Write off €600 as bad debts. Show the entries in the debtors, bad debts and profit and loss accounts. Also show the balance sheet entry.

3. Debtors are €17,000. Write off €1,000 as bad debts. Show the entries in the debtors, bad debts and profit and loss accounts. Also show the balance sheet entry.

4. Debtors are €27,000. Write off €2,000 as bad debts. Show the entries in the debtors, bad debts and profit and loss accounts. Also show the balance sheet entry.

5. Debtors are €32,000. Write off €4,000 as bad debts. Show the entries in the debtors, bad debts and profit and loss accounts. Also show the balance sheet entry.

LESSON 4: PRACTICE DEALING WITH DEPRECIATION

1. Machinery that cost €9,000 on 1 January 2004 has an estimated life of four years and its scrap value is expected to be €1,000. Calculate the amount of depreciation each year using the straight-line method.

2. Equipment that cost €3,700 on 1 January 2005 has an estimated life of five years and its scrap value is expected to be €700. Calculate the amount of depreciation each year using the straight-line method.

3. A van costing €15,000 on 1 January 2003 is expected to last five years and to have a scrap value of €3,000. It is to be depreciated using the straight-line method.
(a) Show the van account in the ledger for 2003, 2004 and 2005.
(b) Show the relevant extract from the balance sheet as on 31 December each year.

4. Machinery costing €16,000 was bought on 1 January 2004. It is to be depreciated by twenty-five per cent of cost each year.
(a) Show the machinery account in the ledger for 2004 and 2005.
(b) Show the relevant extract from the balance sheet as on 31 December each year.

5. A van costing €24,000 was bought on 1 January 2004. It is to be depreciated by twenty per cent of cost each year.
(a) Show the van account in the ledger for 2004 and 2005.
(b) Show the relevant extract from the balance sheet as on 31 December each year.

LESSON 5: PRACTICE DEALING WITH STOCKS

1. €2,000 worth of heating oil was bought during the year. At the end of the year, €300 worth of the oil was unused. Show the heating oil and profit and loss accounts and the relevant extract from the balance sheet.

2. €500 worth of stationery was bought during the year. At the end of the year €100 worth was unused. Show the stationery and profit and loss accounts and the relevant extract from the balance sheet.

3. The following packing material was bought during the year: March, €510; June, €620; October, €430; November, €580. At the end of the year €240 worth was unused. Show the packing materials and profit and loss accounts and the relevant extract from the balance sheet.

4. The following heating oil was bought during the year: January, €1,200; February, €900; April, €600; June, €200; October, €600; December, €800. At the end of the year €700 worth was unused. Show the heating oil and profit and loss accounts and the relevant extract from the balance sheet.

TEST YOURSELF AT

my-etest.com

40 Worked Example

INTRODUCTION

This chapter combines final accounts with adjustments. The questions can be quite long, but each has three parts.

(i)   An opening paragraph that gives you the trading period and information about the authorised share capital of the company (see bottom of next page).

(ii) Next comes the trial balance itself. The debit items listed here will be either assets or expenses with the exception of opening stock, purchases and sales returns. The credit items will be either liabilities or gains with the exception of purchases returns and sales.

(iii) The final part of the question shows the adjustments. Adjustments appear twice in your solution: once in the balance sheet and once in either the trading account or the profit and loss account. In our example, salaries due of €300 are shown as a current liability in the balance sheet and are added to salaries in the profit and loss account.

It is best to start your attempt at this type of question by deciding where the adjustments will be included in your solution, then deal with the trial balance entries. Always learn from your mistakes or you are bound to repeat them in the next question.

Question

The following trial balance was extracted from the books of Toomey Ltd on 31 December 2005. You are required to prepare the firm's trading, profit and loss and appropriation account for the year ended 31 December 2005 and a balance sheet as on 31 December 2005. The authorised share capital is 200,000 €1 ordinary shares.

You are given the following information as on 31 December 2005.

(a) Stock on 31 December 2005 €18,000
(b) Salaries due €600
(c) Light and heat due €1,600
(d) Advertising prepaid €2,000
(e) Rent receivable prepaid €500
(f) Depreciation of vehicles twenty per cent of cost
(g) Depreciation of equipment twenty per cent of cost
(h) Dividends declared ten per cent

Trial Balance on 31 December 2005	Dr	Cr
	€	€
Stock 1 January	15,000	
Sales returns and purchases returns	2,000	3,000
Purchases and sales	80,000	300,000
Rent receivable		2,500
Carriage in	6,000	
Carriage out	5,000	
Light and heat	7,000	
Salaries	47,000	
Bad debts	4,000	
Advertising	8,000	
Discount allowed	3,100	
Discount received		1,600
Reserves (profit and loss balance)		8,400
Premises	160,000	
Vehicles at cost	42,000	
Equipment at cost	24,000	
Machinery at cost	16,000	
Debtors and creditors	23,000	14,500
Long-term loan		40,000
Cash at bank	27,900	
Issued share capital		100,000
	470,000	470,000

Solution

Trading, Profit and Loss	€	€	€
Sales			300,000
less returns			2,000
			298,000
Opening stock		15,000	
Purchases	80,000		
less returns	3,000	77,000	
		92,000	
plus carriage in		6,000	
		98,000	
less closing stock		18,000	80,000
GROSS PROFIT			218,000
Add gains:			
Rent receivable		2,500	
less rent receivable prepaid		500	2,000
Discount received			1,600
			221,600
Less expenses:			
Advertising		6,000	
Light and heat		8,600	
Bad debts		4,000	
Salaries		47,600	
Depreciation:			
Vehicles	8,400		
Equipment	4,800		
		13,200	
Carriage out		5,000	
Discount allowed		3,100	87,500
NET PROFIT			134,100
add reserve			8,400
			142,500
less dividend			10,000
P and L BALANCE			132,500

Balance Sheet	€	€	€
Fixed assets			
Premises	160,000	0	160,000
Vehicles	42,000	8,400	33,600
Equipment	24,000	4,800	19,200
Machinery	16,000	0	16,000
	242,000	13,200	228,800
Current assets			
Stock	18,000		
Debtors	23,000		
Advertising prepaid	2,000		
Cash at bank	27,900	70,900	
Current liabilities			
Creditors	14,500		
Salaries due	600		
Light and heat due	1,600		
Commission receivable prepaid	0		
Rent receivable prepaid	500		
Ordinary dividend due	10,000	27,200	43,700
			272,500
Financed by			
Ordinary share capital			100,000
Reserves			132,500
Long-term loan			40,000
			272,500

AUTHORISED SHARE CAPITAL

The authorised share capital is the maximum amount of capital a company may issue (sell) to the shareholders. The amount actually sold is called the **issued share capital**.

In the example above the authorised share capital is 100,000 €1 shares. This means the company may issue a maximum of 100,000 €1 shares. They have, in fact, only issued 60,0000 €1 shares.

PRACTICE

1. The following trial balance was extracted from the books of Stewart Ltd on 31 December 2005. You are required to prepare the firm's trading and profit and loss account for the year ended 31 December 2005 and a balance sheet as at 31 December 2005.

You are given the following information as at 31 December 2005.
(a) Stock on 31 December 2005 €18,000
(b) Salaries due €800
(c) Light and heat due €2,000
(d) Rent receivable prepaid €300
(e) Depreciation of vehicles twenty per cent of cost
(f) Depreciation of equipment twenty per cent of cost
(g) Dividends declared ten per cent

Trial Balance on 31 December 2005	Dr	Cr
	€	€
Stock 1 January	8,000	
Sales returns and purchases returns	500	600
Purchases and sales	60,000	157,000
Rent receivable		2,300
Carriage in	4,000	
Carriage out	3,000	
Light and heat	5,000	
Insurance	6,400	
Salaries	32,000	
Discount allowed	2,100	
Discount received		600
Reserves (profit and loss balance)		4,500
Premises	116,000	
Vehicles at cost	160,000	
Equipment at cost	10,000	
Debtors and creditors	16,000	5,000
Cash at bank	21,000	
Issued share capital		130,000
	300,000	300,000

2. The following trial balance was extracted from the books of Crawford Ltd on 31 December 2005. You are required to prepare the firm's trading and profit and loss account for the year ended 31 December 2005 and a balance sheet as at 31 December 2005.

You are given the following information as at 31 December 2005.
(a) Stock on 31 December 2005 €16,000
(b) Salaries due €1,200
(c) Insurance prepaid €600
(d) Light and heat due €75
(e) Commission receivable prepaid €500
(f) Depreciation of equipment twenty per cent of cost
(g) Depreciation of machinery twenty per cent of cost
(h) Dividends declared ten per cent

Trial Balance on 31 December 2005	Dr	Cr
	€	€
Stock 1 January	22,000	
Sales returns and purchases returns	6,000	8,000
Purchases and sales	95,000	340,000
Commission receivable		3,000
Import duty	2,400	
Light and heat	6,500	
Insurance	3,400	
Rent	2,400	
Salaries	64,000	
Discount allowed	5,900	
Discount received		3,600
Reserves (profit and loss balance)		9,000
Premises	180,000	
Equipment at cost	35,000	
Machinery at cost	42,000	
Debtors and creditors	34,000	26,000
Long-term loan		25,000
Cash at bank	16,000	
Issued share capital		100,000
	514,600	514,600

3. The following trial balance was extracted from the books of Maguire Ltd on 31 December 2005. You are required to prepare the firm's trading and profit and loss account for the year ended 31 December 2005 and a balance sheet as at 31 December 2005.

You are given the following information as at 31 December 2005.
(a) Stock on 31 December 2005 €20,000
(b) Salaries due €400
(c) Light and heat due €300
(d) Advertising prepaid €200
(e) Commission receivable prepaid €100
(f) Depreciation of premises twenty per cent of cost
(g) Depreciation of vehicles twenty per cent of cost
(h) Depreciation of equipment ten per cent of cost
(i) Dividends declared fifteen per cent

Trial Balance on 31 December 2005	Dr €	Cr €
Stock 1 January	21,000	
Sales returns	6,000	
Purchases and sales	90,000	260,000
Commission receivable		2,000
Import duty	500	
Carriage out	1,500	
Interest on overdraft	600	
Light and heat	4,000	
Salaries	64,000	
Bad debts	700	
Advertising	6,000	
Discount allowed	2,400	
Discount received		600
Reserves (profit and loss balance)		4,600
Premises	200,000	
Vehicles at cost	15,000	
Equipment at cost	6,000	
Debtors and creditors	27,500	8,000
Long-term loan		14,000
Bank overdraft		6,000
Issued share capital		150,000
	445,200	445,200

4. The following trial balance was extracted from the books of Byrne Ltd on 31 December 2005. You are required to prepare the firm's trading and profit and loss account for the year ended 31 December 2005 and a balance sheet as at 31 December 2005.

You are given the following information as at 31 December 2005.
(a) Stock on 31 December 2005 €5,000
(b) Salaries due €800
(c) Insurance prepaid €200
(d) Commission receivable prepaid €200
(e) Depreciation of vehicles twenty per cent of cost
(f) Depreciation of equipment twenty per cent of cost
(g) Dividends declared ten per cent

Trial Balance on 31 December 2005	Dr €	Cr €
Stock 1 January	6,000	
Sales returns	1,500	
Purchases and sales	46,000	120,000
Commission receivable		500
Carriage in	400	
Carriage out	700	
Interest on overdraft	450	
Light and heat	3,500	
Insurance	1,200	
Rent	600	
Salaries	37,000	
Discount allowed	1,450	
Discount received		600
Reserves (profit and loss balance)		7,000
Premises	140,000	
Vehicles at cost	26,000	
Equipment at cost	9,000	
Debtors and creditors	26,000	8,000
Long-term loan		12,000
Bank overdraft		1,700
Issued share capital		150,000
	299,800	299,800

5. The following trial balance was extracted from the books of Sloan Ltd on 31 December 2005. You are required to prepare the firm's trading and profit and loss account for the year ended 31 December 2005 and a balance sheet as at 31 December 2005.

You are given the following information as at 31 December 2005.
- (a) Stock on 31 December 2005 €16,000
- (b) Salaries due €600
- (c) Insurance prepaid €400
- (d) Light and heat due €650
- (e) Commission receivable prepaid €300
- (f) Depreciation of premises twenty per cent of cost
- (g) Depreciation of equipment twenty per cent of cost
- (h) Depreciation of machinery ten per cent of cost
- (i) Dividends declared ten per cent

Trial Balance on 31 December 2005	Dr €	Cr €
Stock 1 January	18,000	
Sales returns and purchases returns	5,000	4,000
Purchases and sales	94,000	276,000
Commission receivable		2,600
Interest on overdraft	310	
Light and heat	4,600	
Insurance	2,800	
Rent	300	
Salaries	67,000	
Discount allowed	1,400	
Discount received		340
Reserves (profit and loss balance)		7,600
Premises	220,000	
Equipment at cost	32,000	
Machinery at cost	16,000	
Debtors and creditors	14,730	7,000
Long-term loan		24,000
Bank overdraft		4,600
Issued share capital		150,000
	476,140	476,140

6. The following trial balance was extracted from the books of Tara Ltd on 31 December 2005. You are required to prepare the firm's trading and profit and loss account for the year ended 31 December 2005 and a balance sheet as at 31 December 2005. The authorised share capital is 100,000 €1 ordinary shares.

You are given the following information as at 31 December 2005.
- (a) Stock on 31 December 2005 €8,500
- (b) Insurance prepaid €460
- (c) Light and heat due €380
- (d) Rent receivable prepaid €400
- (e) Depreciation of premises twenty per cent of cost
- (f) Depreciation of vehicles twenty per cent of cost
- (g) Depreciation of equipment ten per cent of cost
- (h) Dividends declared ten per cent

Trial Balance on 31 December 2005	Dr €	Cr €
Stock 1 January	5,600	
Sales returns and purchases returns	3,200	2,400
Purchases and sales	76,000	230,000
Rent receivable		2,200
Import duty	1,200	
Light and heat	6,400	
Insurance	4,300	
Salaries	64,000	
Discount allowed	2,300	
Discount received		1,700
Reserves (profit and loss balance)		7,300
Premises	180,000	
Vehicles at cost	26,000	
Equipment at cost	30,000	
Debtors and creditors	14,000	6,000
Long-term loan		60,000
Bank overdraft		340,00
Issued share capital		100,000
	413,000	413,000

7. The following trial balance was extracted from the books of Coffee Ltd on 31 December 2005. You are required to prepare the firm's trading and profit and loss account for the year ended 31 December 2005 and a balance sheet as at 31 December 2005. The authorised share capital is 300,000 €1 ordinary shares.

You are given the following information as at 31 December 2005.
(a) Stock on 31 December 2005 €12,000
(b) Salaries due €3,000
(c) Commission receivable due €500
(d) Depreciation of vehicles twelve per cent of cost
(e) Depreciation of machinery ten per cent of cost
(f) Dividends declared fifteen per cent

Trial Balance on 31 December 2005	Dr	Cr
	€	€
Stock 1 January	15,000	
Sales returns and purchases returns	4,000	6,000
Purchases and sales	116,000	260,000
Commission receivable		3,000
Import duty	1,000	
Insurance	6,000	
Salaries	50,000	
Bad debts	2,000	
Reserves (profit and loss balance)		18,000
Premises	200,000	
Vehicles at cost	60,000	
Machinery at cost	80,000	
Debtors and creditors	20,000	15,000
Cash on hand	3,000	
Bank overdraft		5,000
Issued share capital		250,000
	557,000	557,000

8. The following trial balance was extracted from the books of Watkins Ltd on 31 December 2005. You are required to prepare the firm's trading and profit and loss account for the year ended 31 December 2005 and a balance sheet as at 31 December 2005. The authorised share capital is 250,000 €1 ordinary shares.

You are given the following information as at 31 December 2005.
(a) Stock on 31 December 2005 €14,000
(b) Advertising due €4,000
(c) Rent receivable prepaid €3,000
(d) Depreciation of premises two per cent of cost
(e) Depreciation of machinery fifteen per cent of cost
(f) Dividends declared eight per cent

Trial Balance on 31 December 2005	Dr	Cr
	€	€
Stock 1 January	15,000	
Sales returns and purchases returns	2,000	3,000
Purchases and sales	80,000	190,000
Commission receivable		5,000
Rent receivable		17,000
Import duty	4,000	
Wages	38,000	
Bad debts	4,300	
Advertising	12,000	
Reserves (profit and loss balance)		26,000
Premises	256,000	
Machinery at cost	70,000	
Debtors and creditors	22,500	18,800
Long-term loan		40,000
Cash at bank	16,000	
Issued share capital		220,000
	519,800	519,800

9. The following trial balance was extracted from the books of Evans Ltd on 31 December 2005. You are required to prepare the firm's trading and profit and loss account for the year ended 31 December 2005 and a balance sheet as at 31 December 2005. The authorised share capital is 200,000 €1 ordinary shares.

You are given the following information as at 31 December 2005.
(a) Stock on 31 December 2005 €30,000
(b) Insurance prepaid €3,000
(c) Carriage in due €2,000
(d) Depreciation of vehicles ten per cent of cost
(e) Depreciation of equipment twelve per cent of cost
(f) Dividends declared 12.5 per cent

Trial Balance on 31 December 2005	Dr €	Cr €
Stock 1 January	24,000	
Sales returns and purchases returns	40,000	50,000
Purchases and sales	190,000	400,000
Interest receivable		5,000
Carriage in	14,000	
Insurance	9,000	
Salaries	38,000	
Bad debts	6,000	
Reserves (profit and loss balance)		15,000
Premises	170,000	
Vehicles at cost	51,000	
Equipment at cost	55,000	
Debtors and creditors	48,000	23,000
Cash on hand	4,000	
Bank overdraft		6,000
Issued share capital		150,000
	649,000	649,000

10. The following trial balance was extracted from the books of Blakes Ltd on 31 December 2005. You are required to prepare the firm's trading and profit and loss account for the year ended 31 December 2005 and a balance sheet as at 31 December 2005. The authorised share capital is 250,000 €1 ordinary shares.

You are given the following information as at 31 December 2005.
(a) Stock on 31 December 2005 €13,000
(b) Insurance prepaid €2,400
(c) Commission receivable due €1,600
(d) Depreciation of vehicles twenty per cent of cost
(e) Depreciation of machinery twelve per cent of cost
(f) Dividends declared five per cent

Trial Balance on 31 December 2005	Dr €	Cr €
Stock 1 January	12,000	
Sales returns and purchases returns	8,000	5,000
Purchases and sales	62,000	165,000
Commission receivable		6,400
Import duty	5,400	
Insurance	16,000	
Salaries	14,000	
Advertising	8,700	
Reserves (profit and loss balance)		35,000
Premises	240,000	
Vehicles at cost	24,000	
Machinery at cost	56,000	
Debtors and creditors	51,000	32,000
Cash on hand	4,300	
Bank overdraft		8,000
Issued share capital		250,000
	501,400	501,400

STATE EXAM PRACTICE

1. The following trial balance was extracted from the books of Euro Ltd on 31 May 2005. The authorised share capital is 250,000 €1 ordinary shares.

(a) You are required to prepare the company's trading, profit and loss and appropriation accounts for the year ended 31 May 2005 and a balance sheet as at that date.

You are given the following information as at 31 May 2005.
(i)   Closing stock €14,000
(ii) Dividends declared eight per cent
(iii) Rent receivable prepaid €1,000
(iv) Advertising prepaid €2,600
(v)   Deprecation: machinery six per cent, motor vans ten per cent

(b) Euro Ltd is a sports equipment company. List two types of advertising it could use to advertise its products, and in each case give your reason.

(JCHL, adapted)

Trial Balance on 31 May 2005	Dr	Cr
	€	€
Purchases and sales	99,000	167,400
Sales returns and purchases returns	6,500	4,100
Issued share capital 195,000 €1 shares		195,000
Repairs	3,400	
Carriage inwards	1,800	
Advertising	7,000	
Machinery	190,000	
Debtors and creditors	16,000	19,000
Rent receivable		18,000
Motor vans	120,000	
Cash	800	
Bank overdraft		2,100
Opening stock 01/06/2004	17,000	
Long-term loan		60,000
Reserves (profit and loss balance)		17,400
Wages	21,500	
	483,000	483,000

2. The following trial balance was extracted from the books of Muprhy Ltd on 31 May 2005. The authorised share capital is 350,000 €1 ordinary shares.

(a) You are required to prepare the company's trading, profit and loss and appropriation accounts for the year ended 31 May 2005 and a balance sheet as at that date.

You are given the following information as at 31 May 2005.
(i)   Closing stock €32,000
(ii) Carriage inwards due €3,000
(iii) Insurance prepaid €2,000
(iv) Dividends declared 12.5 per cent
(v)   Depreciation: equipment twelve per cent, motor vans ten per cent

(b) List three types of insurance Murphy Ltd should take out.

Trial Balance on 31 May 2005	Dr	Cr
	€	€
Purchases and sales	185,000	400,000
Sales returns	50,000	
Opening stock 01/06/2004	25,000	
Wages	36,000	
Interest receivable		6,000
Insurance	8,000	
Carriage inwards	15,000	
Bad debts	5,000	
Buildings	169,000	
Equipment	60,000	
Debtors and creditors	49,000	17,000
Motor vans	35,000	
Cash	1,000	
Bank overdraft		5,000
Reserves (profit and loss balance)		10,000
Issued share capital:		
200,000 €1 ordinary shares		200,000
	638,000	638,000

TEST YOURSELF AT
my-etest.com

41 Assessing the Business

TERMS COVERED IN THIS CHAPTER
Trading performance, average stock, stock turnover, overtrading, return on capital employed, liquidity, working capital ratio, quick ratio, solvency.

INTRODUCTION

What do you think? Work with another pupil on these tasks.

1. List ten local businesses.
2. Suppose you won €200,000 and you decided to invest it in each business you have listed. Write the amount you wish to invest in each business. Note: try to invest something in each business.
3. Give one reason for each investment decision.

LESSON 1: RATIOS THAT ASSESS THE TRADING, PROFIT AND LOSS ACCOUNT

Question

Study the following account, then calculate the following ratios:

(a) Rate of stock turnover.

(b) Gross profit percentage (margin).

(c) Net profit percentage.

(d) Total expenses as a percentage of sales.

Trading, Profit and Loss Account for the Year Ended 31 December 2005	€	€
Sales		75,000
Opening stock	4,000	
Purchases	32,000	
	36,000	
less closing stock	6,000	
Cost of goods sold		30,000
Gross profit		45,000
Total expenses		20,000
Net profit		25,000

Solution

(a) Rate of stock turnover

$$= \frac{\text{cost of goods sold}}{\text{average stock}}$$

$$= \frac{30,000}{(4,000 + 6,000) \div 2}$$

$$= \quad 6 \text{ times}$$

(b) Gross profit percentage

$$= \frac{\text{gross profit}}{\text{sales}} \times 100$$

$$= \frac{45,000}{75,000} \times 100$$

$$= \quad 60\%$$

(c) Net profit percentage

$$= \frac{\text{net profit}}{\text{sales}} \times 100$$

$$= \frac{25,000}{75,000} \times 100$$

$$= \quad 33.33\%$$

(d) Total expenses as a percentage of sales

$$= \frac{\text{total expenses}}{\text{sales}} \times 100$$

$$= \frac{20,000}{75,000} \times 100$$

$$= \quad 26.67\%$$

LESSON 2: RATIOS THAT ASSESS THE BALANCE SHEET

Question

Study the following balance sheet, then calculate the following ratios:

(a) Working capital ratio.

(b) Quick ratio if stock is €6,000.

(c) Return on capital employed if the net profit was €25,000.

Balance Sheet as on 31 December 2005		
	€	€
Fixed assets		60,000
Current assets	15,000	
Current liabilities	5,000	
Working capital		10,000
		70,000
Financed by:		
Ordinary share capital		50,000
Reserves:		
Profit and loss		5,000
Long-term liabilities:		
Bank term loan		15,000
		70,000

Solution

(a) Working capital ratio

$$= \frac{\text{current assets}}{\text{current liabilities}}$$

$$= \frac{12,000}{6,000}$$

$$= 2:1$$

(b) Quick ratio

$$= \frac{\text{current assets} - \text{stock}}{\text{current liabilities}}$$

$$= \frac{12,000 - 6,000}{6,000}$$

$$= 1:1$$

(c) Return on capital

$$= \frac{\text{net profit}}{\text{capital employed}} \times 100$$

$$= \frac{25,000}{155,000} \times 100$$

$$= 16.13\%$$

LESSON 3: INTERPRETING THE RATIOS

The final accounts of a business are used to assess the firm's performance over the past year. From these it is possible to find out how much business was carried on and whether it was profitable.

TRADING PERFORMANCE

The rate of stock turnover shows the number of times the average stock has been sold in the year. It gives a good measure of how much business the firm had. Turnover is the same as sales.

$$\text{Average stock} = \frac{\text{opening + closing stock}}{2}$$

$$\text{Rate of stock turnover} = \frac{\text{cost of goods sold}}{\text{average stock}}$$

Profitable firms usually have a high turnover. However, turnover will vary between different kinds of businesses. Goods that do not last long (like newspapers) have high turnovers, whereas luxury goods (like jewellery) have low turnovers. A turnover of fifty-two means that on average goods were stocked for one week.

Examples of approximate turnovers

Vegetables –
52 times a year

Newspapers –
365 times a year

Meat –
75 times a year

Jewellery –
3 times a year

Furniture –
5 times a year

OVERTRADING

Some firms get too much credit without being able to sell the goods, i.e. creditors are much higher than debtors and stock levels rise. When this happens the firms are said to be **overtrading**.

PROFITABILITY

The whole objective of most firms is to make a profit. However, it is not just sufficient to make a profit – a firm must make enough of a profit to have a reason for staying in business next year. Profitability is measured by the **return on capital employed**. This is also called the **return on total investment**. The owners will want a return that is at least above that which they could get if they put their money into a bank.

Capital employed	= fixed assets + working capital
Return on capital employed	= $\dfrac{\text{net profit}}{\text{capital employed}} \times 100$

LIQUIDITY

Liquid assets are cash and those assets that can be easily turned into cash, e.g. current assets such as stock and debtors.

A firm is liquid if current assets are greater than current liabilities. **The working capital ratio** is a measure of a firm's liquidity. It is also called the **current ratio**. In a healthy firm there will be twice as many current assets as current liabilities, i.e. the working capital ratio will be 2:1.

Working capital ratio	= $\dfrac{\text{current assets}}{\text{current liabilities}}$

Another measure of liquidity is the **quick ratio**. This compares the quick assets with the current liabilities. The quick assets are current assets less stock. In a healthy company the quick assets will equal the current liabilities, i.e. the quick ratio will be 1:1.

Quick ratio	= $\dfrac{\text{currents assets} - \text{closing stock}}{\text{current liabilities}}$

SOLVENCY

A firm is solvent if total assets are greater than outside liabilities. Examples of **outside liabilities** are **current liabilities** (creditors, bank overdraft) and **fixed (long-term) liabilities** (mortgage, long-term bank loans).

LIMITATIONS OF FINAL ACCOUNTS

The final accounts give an incomplete picture of the firm's performance because:

- Only those items with a monetary value are included, i.e. they do not measure staff morale, motivation and expertise or the firm's competitive advantage.
- It is difficult, if not impossible, to get an accurate value for some of the firm's assets. For example, the true value of premises can only be found out when they are sold.
- The balance sheet shows the assets and liabilities on one day of the year. Firms with seasonal trade may therefore appear better – or worse – than normal, depending on when the accounts are made out.
- The accounts give no indication of how successful the firm is likely to be in the year ahead.

LESSON I: PRACTICE ASSESSING THE TRADING, PROFIT AND LOSS ACCOUNT

In questions 1–3 you are required to calculate the following ratios:

(a) Rate of stock turnover.

(b) Gross profit percentage.

(c) Net profit percentage.

(d) Total expenses as a percentage of sales.

1.

Trading, Profit and Loss Account for the Year Ended 31 December 2005	€	€
Sales		98,000
Opening stock	6,000	
Purchases	46,000	
	52,000	
less closing stock	8,000	
Cost of goods sold		44,000
Gross profit		54,000
Total expenses		24,000
Net profit		30,000

2.

Trading, Profit and Loss Account for the Year Ended 31 December 2005	€	€
Sales		24,000
Opening stock	16,000	
Purchases	95,000	
	111,000	
less closing stock	14,000	
Cost of goods sold		97,000
Gross profit		143,000
Total expenses		76,000
Net profit		67,000

3.

Trading, Profit and Loss Account for the Year Ended 31 December 2005	€	€
Sales		380,000
Opening stock	16,000	
Purchases	18,000	
	196,000	
less closing stock	18,000	
Cost of goods sold		178,000
Gross profit		202,000
Total expenses		120,000
Net profit		82,000

LESSON 2: PRACTICE ASSESSING THE BALANCE SHEET

Calculate the following ratios for questions 1–5 below:

(a) Working capital ratio.

(b) Quick ratio.

(c) Return on capital employed.

€

1.
	€
Fixed assets	260,000
Current assets	150,000
Closing stock	60,000
Current liabilities	70,000
Net profit	41,000

2.
Fixed assets	180,000
Current assets	76,000
Closing stock	16,000
Current liabilities	36,000
Net profit	23,000

3.
Fixed assets	110,000
Current assets	50,000
Closing stock	24,000
Current liabilities	18,000
Net profit	35,000

4.
Fixed assets	340,000
Current assets	97,000
Closing stock	32,000
Current liabilities	80,000
Net profit	26,000

5.
Fixed assets	160,000
Current assets	60,000
Closing stock	33,000
Current liabilities	45,000
Net profit	19,000

6. Study the following balance sheet, then answer the questions.

(a) What is the working capital of this firm?

(b) What is the capital employed in this firm?

(c) What is the amount of retained earnings in this company?

(d) Calculate the following ratios:

(i)   working capital ratio

(ii) quick ratio

(iii) return on capital employed if the net profit for 2005 was €22,000.

(e) Is this firm liquid? Give a reason for your answer.

Balance Sheet of Keely Ltd as at 31 December 2005		
	€	€
Fixed assets		160,000
Current assets:		
Stock	40,000	
Debtors and cash	60,000	
	100,000	
Current liabilities	50,000	
		50,000
		210,000
Financed by:		
Ordinary share capital		100,000
Profit and loss		50,000
Bank term loan		60,000
		210,000

LESSON 3: PRACTICE INTERPRETING THE RATIOS

I.   Study the following accounts, then answer the questions.

(a) What indications are there that McKenna Ltd is a private company?

(b) What percentage dividend was proposed by the directors?

(c) Calculate the following ratios:
   (i)   rate of stock turnover
   (ii)   gross profit percentage
   (iii) net profit percentage
   (iv)   total expenses as a percentage of sales
   (v)   working capital ratio
   (vi)   quick ratio
   (vii) return on capital employed.

(d) Give an example of a fixed asset this firm may have.

(e) Give an example of a current liability this firm may have.

(f) Is this firm liquid? Give a reason for your answer.

(g) Comment on this firm's performance.

(h) Name two things the final accounts do not show.

Trading, Profit and Loss and Appropriation Account of McKenna Ltd for the Year Ended 31 December 2005		
	€	€
Sales		140,000
Opening stock	12,000	
Purchases	64,000	
	76,000	
less closing stock	10,000	
Cost of goods sold		66,000
Gross profit		74,000
Total expenses		36,000
Net profit		38,000
Appropriations:		
Ordinary share dividend		20,000
		18,000

Balance Sheet of McKenna Ltd as at 31 December 2005		
	€	€
Fixed assets		134,000
Current assets	26,000	
Current liabilities	120,000	
Working capital		14,000
		148,000
Financed by:		
Ordinary share capital		100,000
Reserves:		
Profit and loss		18,000
Long-term liabilities:		
Bank term loan		30,000
		148,000

2.   Coogan Ltd has an authorised share capital of 350,000 €1 ordinary shares. It supplies the following information for the year ended 31/12/2005.

	€
Sales	380,000
Cost of sales	150,000
Expenses	120,000
Fixed assets	345,000
Current assets	160,000
Current liabilities	70,000
Issued share capital	300,000
Long-term loan	70,000
Dividends declared	15%

Assume you are S. Duggan, financial consultant of Manor Street, Limerick. Prepare a report (in the form of a business letter) for the shareholders of Coogan Ltd on today's date showing the following:

(a)   The gross profit percentage (margin).

(b)   The return on capital employed.

(c)   The working capital ratio.

(d)   The profit retained by Coogan Ltd at 31/12/2005.

3.   Aero Ltd has an authorised share capital of 300,000 €1 ordinary shares. It supplies the following information for the year ended 31/12/2005.

	€
Sales	240,000
Cost of sales	104,000
Expenses	46,000
Fixed assets	260,000
Current assets	90,000
Current liabilities	40,000
Issued share capital	200,000
Long-term loan	40,000
Dividends declared	10%

Assume you are Pat Healy, financial consultant of Finfax Ltd. Prepare a report (in the form of a business letter) for the shareholders of Aero Ltd on today's date showing the following:

(a)   The net profit percentage (margin).

(b)   The return on capital employed.

(c)   The working capital ratio.

(d)   The quick ratio if the closing stock is €15,000.

(e)   The profit retained by Aero Ltd at 31/12/2005.

(f)   The amount of extra capital Aero Ltd can raise from issuing shares.

STATE EXAM PRACTICE

1. (a) Explain two limitations of final accounts and balance sheets in assessing a business.

    (b) Examine the final accounts and balance sheets of Buz Ltd set out below for the years 2004 and 2005. Compare and comment on the performance of the company for the two years using the following ratios:

    (i) gross profit margin

    (ii) return on capital employed

    (iii) acid test (quick ratio)

    (iv) rate of dividend paid.

    Show your workings.

    (JCHL, adapted)

2004 Trading, Profit and Loss and Appropriation Account for the Year Ended 31/05/2004	€	2005 Trading, Profit and Loss and Appropriation Account for the Year Ended 31/05/2005	€
Sales	190,000	Sales	190,000
Gross profit	75,000	Gross profit	75,000
Net profit	43,000	Net profit	43,000
Dividends paid	14,300	Dividends paid	14,300
Reserves	28,700	Reserves	28,700

Balance Sheet as at 31/05/04	€	€
Fixed assets		180,000
Current assets		
(including closing stock €7,000)	25,700	
Less current liabilities	17,000	8,700
		188,700
Financed by		
130,000 €1 ordinary shares		130,000
Reserves		28,700
Long-term liabilities		30,000
		188,700

Balance Sheet as at 31/05/05	€	€
Fixed assets		198,000
Current assets		
(including closing stock €5,300)	36,800	
Less current liabilities	18,000	18,800
		216,800
Financed by		
130,000 €1 ordinary shares		130,000
Reserves		66,800
Long-term liabilities		20,000
		216,800

TEST YOURSELF AT
my-etest.com

42 Club Accounts

INTRODUCTION

Answer these questions, then discuss your answers with another pupil.

1. Do you belong to any clubs?
2. What do you know about the running of these clubs?
3. Describe a club meeting you have attended.

LESSON 1: CLUB MEETINGS

People who share a common interest in an activity or hobby often join together and form a club. The members will sometimes elect a committee to run the club. The committee will have a chairperson, secretary and treasurer.

CHAIRPERSON

The **chairperson** is the highest position in the club. He or she is responsible for leading the members and developing the club. At club meetings the chairperson will do the following.

- Take charge of the meeting.
- Ensure that the items on the agenda are followed.

SECRETARY

The **secretary** carries out the administrative duties of the club. This includes writing letters, sending e-mails, making phone calls and filing club documents. At club meetings the secretary will do the following.

- Set out the agenda for the meeting.
- Read the minutes of the previous meeting.
- Keep the minutes of the meeting.

TREASURER

The **treasurer** is responsible for the financial matters of the club and must do the following.

- Open a bank deposit account and current account in the name of the club and get a cheque book.
- Collect the **subscriptions** from members.
- Lodge receipts in the bank.
- Issue cheques or pay cash when necessary (normally cheques are signed by two people, usually the treasurer and either the secretary or president).
- Keep a record of the receipts and payments of the club.
- Draw up the final accounts of the club.

TREASURER'S REPORT

This is prepared by the treasurer and presented to the members at the annual general meeting (AGM) of the club. The purpose of this report is:

- to keep the members informed on financial matters
- to show the members that funds have been used correctly, i.e. that the committee has not been using the money for their own entertainment.

The treasurer's report should contain the following.

(a) The final accounts of the club:

(i) receipts and payments account

(ii) income and expenditure account

(iii) balance sheet.

These accounts should be signed by at least two people, normally the treasurer and either the president or secretary.

(b) Recommendations for an increase in the subscription if necessary.

(c) Suggestions about how money may be made available for new equipment, clubhouse and so on.

Contact details of the report writer	Main Street Swords swords@iol.ie
Title of the report	Treasurer's Report to AGM of Fingal Social Club
Name of the person or group who wanted the report	To: All club members
	31 December 2005
Introduction	Here is my report on the financial matters of the club for the past year. The receipts and payments account income and expenditure account and a balance sheet are enclosed with this report.
	Here are the main findings:
Body of report	The club had a surplus of €1,500 for the year and there is now €2,000 on deposit in the bank. There are now 100 members in the club. Some members still have to pay the subscription for the year. The concert was a great success and made a profit of €500 for the club. The raffle was also profitable.
	The club bought its first asset – a piano. As the club grows and gets more members it will be possible to buy additional assets.
	Although the pitch and putt competition made a loss I recommend that we run it again next year. With more entries and spending less on prizes I believe we can make a profit.
	Please contact me to discuss any aspect of this report.
	Signed:
Signature of the report writer	*Jonathan Connolly* Jonathan Connolly
Job title of the report writer	TREASURER

LESSON 2: CLUB FINANCING

The members finance the club by paying a weekly, monthly or annual fee called a subscription. For most clubs this is the main source of funds. In addition to this they may get donations, gifts or money from state agencies like the Lotto. The profit they get from holding concerts, pub quizzes, dinners, garden fêtes and so on is a further source of finance for a club. In addition, many clubs have a bar licence and make large profits from the sale of refreshments to members.

RECEIPTS AND PAYMENTS ACCOUNT

All the money coming into and going out of the club is recorded in the receipts and payments account. Receipts are shown on the debit side and payments on the credit side.

Some clubs use suitable analysis columns to get a clearer picture of where the money is coming from and where it is being spent.

The following information is available for the Roundwood Sports Club. Prepare a receipts and payments account for March 2005 to record the above, using the following headings.
Debit: Subscriptions, Competitions, Refreshments, Other
Credit: Wages, Competitions, Refreshments, Other

February 2005 €

		€				€
1	Cash on hand	900	10	Subscriptions		5,600
2	Sales of sweets and soft drinks	260	10	Cleaner's wages		1,200
3	Purchase of prizes	94	11	Dance expenses		2,100
4	Cleaner's wages	670	11	Dance receipts		3,700
5	Competition fees received	180	11	Sales of refreshments		1,400
6	Purchase of refreshments	960	11	Purchase of prizes		360
7	Stationery	240	16	Flag-day collection		1,700
8	Subscriptions	3,800	17	Competition fees received		210
9	Postage	430	18	Games equipment		5,400

Solution

RB 1

Dr	Analysed Receipts and Payments Account of Roundwood Sports Club for March							Cr

Date	Particulars	Total	Subs	Comp	Bar	Other		Date	Particulars	Total	Wages	Comp	Bar	Other
Mar		€	€	€	€	€		Mar		€	€	€	€	€
1	Cash on hand	900						3	Prizes	94		94		
2	Sales	260			260			4	Wages	670	670			
5	Comp fees	180		180				6	Purchases	960			960	
8	Subs	3,800	3,800					7	Stationery	240				240
10	Subs	5,600	5,600					9	Phone calls	430				430
11	Dance	3,700				3,700		10	Wages	1,200	1,200			
11	Sales	1,400			1,400			11	Dance	2,100				2,100
11	Raffle	1,700				1,700		11	Prizes	360		360		
17	Comp fees	210		210				18	Equipment	5,400				5,400
								28	Balance c/d	6,296				
		17,750	9,400	390	1,660	5,400				11,310	1,870	454	960	8,170
Apr														
1	Balance	b/d	6,296											

LESSON 3: SAMPLE QUESTION AND SOLUTION

FINAL ACCOUNTS

INCOME AND EXPENDITURE ACCOUNT

The income and expenditure account shows all expenses for the year, whether paid or not, and all income for the year, whether received or not. It is really the same as a profit and loss account with income shown on the credit side and expenditure on the debit side.

The difference between income and expenditure is either a **surplus** (income exceeds expenditure) or a **deficit** (expenditure exceeds income). A surplus is also called an **excess of income over expenditure**. A deficit is also called an **excess of expenditure over income**.

The income and expenditure account does not show purchases and sales of fixed assets. These are dealt with in the balance sheet, either by increasing or decreasing the asset, depending on whether the asset was sold or bought.

BALANCE SHEET OF A CLUB

The balance sheet shows the club's assets and liabilities in the usual way, except that the capital is referred to as the accumulated fund.

SUMMARY

1. Club accounts are different because they are maintained by nonprofit-making organisations.
2. The cash account is called the receipts and payments account.
3. The profit and loss account is called the income and expenditure account.
4. The difference in the income and expenditure account is not called a net profit, it is called a surplus or excess of income over expenditure. A net loss is called a deficit or excess of expenditure over income.
5. The capital is called the accumulated fund.

ADJUSTMENTS

Before the final accounts can be drawn up you must determine:

(i)   the profit or loss of any club activities
(ii) the bar profit or loss
(iii) the subscriptions for the year.

Club Activities

Question

Calculate the profit or loss of a competition given the following information. Cost of prizes, €640. Entrance fees to competition, €500.

Solution

Prizes	€640
Fees	€500
Loss on competition	€140

Bar Trading

Question

Calculate the profit or loss from the bar given the following information. Bar purchases, €17,000. Bar sales, €18,900. Closing stock of refreshments, €2,500.

Solution

Bar trading account

Bar sales		€18,900
Bar purchases	€17,000	
less closing stock	€2,500	€14,500
Bar profit		€4,400

Subscriptions

Question

Calculate the subscriptions for the year given the following information. Subs received during the year, €1,225. Subs due at end of year, €42. Subs paid in advance at end of year, €63.

Solution

Subs received	€1,225
Subs due	€42
	€1,267
less subs prepaid	€63
Subs for year	€1,204

Question

The following trial balance is available for Castletown Social Club.

	€	€
Competition prizes	140	
Cleaner's wages	240	
Bar sales		800
Bar purchases	590	
Postage	190	
Competition fees		120
Lawnmower	180	
Profit on raffle		310
Dance receipts		280
Repairs to equipment	360	
Dance expenses	170	
Cleaning liquids	55	
Cash on hand	495	
Subscriptions		870
Accumulated fund (01/01/2005)		40
	2,420	2,420

The following additional information at 31 December 2005 is also available.
(i) Subs due, €200
(ii) Subs prepaid, €70
(iii) Wages due, €350
(iv) Postage prepaid, €20
(v) Depreciation of lawnmower ten per cent of cost
(vi) Stock of refreshments, €60

(a) Prepare a bar trading account for the year ended 31 December 2005.
(b) Prepare an income and expenditure account for the year ended 31 December 2005.
(c) Prepare a balance sheet as at 31 December 2005.

Solution

Bar Trading Account for the Year Ended 31 December 2005

			€	€
Sales				800
Purchases			590	
less closing stock			60	530
Bar profit				270

Income & Expenditure Account for the Year Ended 31 December 2005

	€	€
Income:		
Bar profit		270
Raffle		310
Dance profit (280 – 170)		110
Subscriptions (870 + 200 – 70)		1,000
		1,690
Expenditure:		
Wages (240 + 350)	590	
Postage (190 – 20)	170	
Repairs to equipment	360	
Cleaning liquids	55	
Depreciation of lawnmower	18	1,213
Income over expenditure		477

Balance Sheet as at 31 December 2005

	Cost €	Depr €	NBV €
Fixed assets:			
Lawnmower	180	18	162
Current assets:			
Stock of refreshments	60		
Subs due	200		
Postage prepaid	20		
Cash	495	775	
Current liabilities:			
Subs prepaid	70		
Wages due	350	420	335
			517
Financed by:			
Accumulated fund, 1 January 2005			40
add excess of income over expenditure			477
			517

LESSON I: PRACTICE

I. Working in groups of three, role-play this conversation between Paul, Mark and Alison.

Mark:	Here's a copy of the agenda I prepared.
Alison:	You better have this, Paul, as you're in charge of the meeting.
Paul:	Alison, will you take the minutes for the meeting?
Alison:	No, Paul, that's not my job. Mark is supposed to do that.
Paul:	Well, can you write a cheque for €50 to pay for the rent of the hall this week?
Mark:	Alison can't do that either.
Paul:	Why not? I thought she was in charge of the money in this club.
Alison:	I am, but I don't have a cheque book yet.
Mark:	Paul, you have to remember that this is a new club and we're only just getting organised.
Alison:	I can't get a cheque book until I open a bank account.
Paul:	Well, how are we going to pay the rent?
Mark:	We could use some of the subs Alison collected.
Alison:	Yes, I can give you cash but I can't write a cheque yet.
Paul:	OK, so what's the first item on the agenda?
Mark:	Well, usually I would begin by reading the minutes from the previous meeting.
Alison:	But since this is our first meeting you can't do that.
Mark:	There's only one item on the agenda and that's to decide on the various duties we have to perform.
Paul:	But we've just done that, so I declare this meeting over.

2. Use the information in the conversation above to complete this chart.

Name	Position	Tasks
Mark	1	2
3	Secretary	4
5	6	7

LESSON 2: PRACTICE PREPARING RECEIPTS AND PAYMENTS

1. Write up and balance the receipts and payments account of the Duncarrick Tennis Club for March 2004. Use the following headings for receipts and payments and total each column.
Receipts: Total, Subscriptions, Bar, Other
Payments: Total, Wages, Bar, Other

Mar		€
1	Cash on hand	50
2	Bar sales	100
3	Cleaner's wages	50
4	Purchase of prizes	48
4	Competition fees received	105
5	Raffle	220
6	Cleaner's wages	50
7	Dance receipts	390
9	Subscriptions	185
10	Purchase of prizes	72
11	Bar sales	300
12	Cleaner's wages	50
14	Subscriptions	444
15	Bar purchases	92
17	Bar sales	200
20	Postage	250
22	Cleaning liquids	65
23	Competition fees received	35
25	Cleaner's wages	50
27	Bar purchases	368
28	Lawnmower	130
29	Repairs to equipment	480
30	Subscriptions	111
31	Dance expenses	110

2. Write up and balance the receipts and payments account of the Dennistown Golf Club for April 2004. Use the following headings for receipts and payments and total each column.
Receipts: Total, Subscriptions, Bar, Other
Payments: Total, Wages, Bar, Other

Apr		€
1	Cash on hand	70
2	Bar sales	367
3	Competition fees received	108
4	Subscriptions	300
6	Purchase of prizes	156
7	Groundkeeper's wages	250
8	Bar sales	550
9	Groundkeeper's wages	250
12	Lottery win	300
13	Dance receipts	480
14	Bar purchases	640
16	Subscriptions	180
17	Groundkeeper's wages	250
18	Purchase of prizes	104
20	Bar purchases	160
22	Cleaning liquids	40
23	Competition fees received	323
24	Games equipment	500
25	Subscriptions	720
26	Bar sales	183
27	Groundkeeper's wages	250
28	Dance expenses	200
29	Secretarial expenses	350

3. Write up and balance the receipts and payments account of the Lower Corrib Fishing Club for May 2004. Use the following headings for receipts and payments and total each column.
Receipts: Total, Subscriptions, Bar, Other
Payments: Total, Wages, Bar, Other

May		€
1	Cash on hand	300
2	Bar sales	350
3	Competition fees received	60
5	Subscriptions	200
7	Purchase of prizes	72
8	Bar sales	1,050
10	Boatman's wages	150
11	Subscriptions	480
13	Bar purchases	1,280
14	Boatman's wages	150
15	Postage	25
16	Bar sales	700
17	Boatman's wages	150
18	Purchase of prizes	108
19	Cleaning liquids	15
21	Bar purchases	320
23	Competition fees received	180
24	Boatman's wages	150
25	Subscriptions	120
26	Rent	45
27	Repairs to boat	30
29	Secretarial expenses	280

4. Write up and balance the receipts and payments account of the Clogher Bay Sailing Club for June 2004. Use the following headings for receipts and payments and total each column.
Receipts: Total, Subscriptions, Bar, Other
Payments: Total, Wages, Bar, Other

Jun		€
1	Cash on hand	40
2	Sales of refreshments	45
3	Cleaner's wages	150
4	Competition fees received	20
5	Subscriptions	150
6	Purchase of prizes	60
7	Cleaner's wages	150
9	Competition fees	60
10	Purchase of refreshments	248
12	Subscriptions	360
13	Sales of refreshments	135
14	Postage	18
15	Cleaner's wages	150
17	Cleaning liquids	12
18	Purchase of prizes	90
19	Purchase of refreshments	62
21	Flag day	300
23	Cleaner's wages	150
24	Sales of refreshments	90
26	Subscriptions	90
27	Repairs to boats	110
28	Secretarial expenses	75

STATE EXAM PRACTICE

1. All the members of the Uptown Bowling Club pay an annual subscription to the club. The club runs regular competitions and a disco every second week. It also employs a caretaker.

Here is what happened at the club during May 2000 (all dealings are in cash).
May

1	Cash on hand since last month €440
2	Received annual subscriptions €60
5	Paid competition prizes €35
6	Received competition entry fees €70
12	Disco night: received €360 at the door
12	Paid disc jockey (DJ) €75 for running the disco
14	Received annual subscriptions €80
15	Paid caretaker's wages €£250
16	Paid for posters for next disco €25
19	Bought prizes for next competition €40
20	Received competition entry fees €3 each from 50 members
26	Disco night: received €375 at the door
29	Paid caretaker's wages €250

(a) You are treasurer of the Uptown Bowling Club. Write up and balance the analysed receipts and payments account of the club for the month of May 2000. Use the following headings for receipts and payments and total each column.
Receipts: Total, Subscriptions, Competitions, Disco
Payments: Total, Wages, Competitions, Disco

(b) What profit (surplus) did the club make on competitions for the month?

(c) What profit (surplus) did the club make on discos for the month?

(d) State three of the duties of a club treasurer.

2.   The Keep Fit Club rents a local sports centre. They organise a weekly lotto and run a disco every two weeks in order to raise money for new equipment. They also collect annual subscriptions from each member.

Here is what happened in January 2003 (all dealings are in cash).
Jan

7	Club reopened after the holidays with cash on hand €460
8	Received subscriptions €65
9	Received €170 from sale of lotto tickets
11	Disco night: received €250 at the door
12	Lotto night: paid out €100 to winners
13	Received subscriptions €85
14	Paid for rent of sports centre €55
15	Paid €20 for posters for next disco
17	Received €135 from sale of lotto tickets
19	Lotto night: paid out €80 to winners
24	Received €190 from sale of lotto tickets
25	Disco night: received €300 at the door
26	Lotto night: paid out €150 to winners
27	Paid disc jockey €120 for running the discos
28	Paid for rent of sports centre €55

(a) You are treasurer of the Keep Fit Club. Write up and balance the analysed receipts and payments account of the club for the month of January 2003. Use the following headings for receipts and payments and total each column.
   Receipts: Total, Subscriptions, Disco, Lotto
   Payments: Total, Rent, Disco, Lotto

(b) What profit (surplus) did the club make on discos for the month? Show your workings.

(c) What profit (surplus) did the club make on the lotto for the month? Show your workings.

(JCOL, adapted)

LESSON 3: PRACTICE INCOME AND EXPENDITURE

1. Prepare a bar trading account and an income and expenditure account for the year ended 31 December 2005 from the following information.

Payments:

Insurance	€480
Hire of hall	€1,200
Purchase of lawnmower	€2,500
Bar purchases	€3,200

Receipts:

Subscriptions	€4,000
Raffle income	€2,600
Bar sales	€6,700

The following additional information is available at the end of the financial year.

Bar stock 1/1/2005	€300
Bar stock 31/12/2005	€500
Insurance prepaid	€40
Hire of hall prepaid	€200
Depreciation of lawnmower	15%
Subscriptions due	€400
Subscriptions prepaid	€600

2. Prepare a bar trading account and an income and expenditure account for the year ended 31 December 2005 from the following information.

Payments:

Insurance	€2,600
Purchase of minibus	€24,000
Bar purchases	€3,600
Travel expenses	€800
Telephone charges	€210

Receipts:

Subscriptions	€16,000
Raffle income	€12,000
Bar sales	€7,400

The following additional information is available at the end of the financial year.

Bar stock 1/1/2005	€160
Bar stock 31/12/2005	€400
Telephone charges due	€160
Insurance prepaid	€1,000
Travel expenses due	€120
Depreciation of minibus	15%
Subscriptions due	€2,500

3. Prepare a bar trading account and an income and expenditure account for the year ended 31 December 2005 from the following information.

Payments:

Insurance	€1,400
Purchase of equipment	€6,400
Bar purchases	€1,600
Telephone charges	€360

Receipts:

Subscriptions	€8,700
Raffle income	€2,100
Bar sales	€2,900

The following additional information is available at the end of the financial year.

Bar stock 31/12/2005	€340
Telephone charges due	€80
Insurance prepaid	€300
Depreciation of equipment	10%
Subscriptions prepaid	€1,300

4. Prepare a bar trading account and an income and expenditure account for the year ended 31 December 2005 from the following information.

Payments:

Insurance	€3,900
Hire of equipment	€600
Purchase of equipment	€18,000
Bar purchases	€4,600
Travel expenses	€200
Telephone charges	€650

Receipts:

Subscriptions	€9,800
Raffle income	€2,400
Bar sales	€11,700

The following additional information is available at the end of the financial year.

Bar stock 1/1/2005	€300
Bar stock 31/12/2005	€400
Telephone charges due	€160
Insurance prepaid	€240
Hire of equipment	€36
Travel expenses due	€180
Depreciation of equipment	15%
Subscriptions due	€560
Subscriptions prepaid	€340

STATE EXAM PRACTICE

1. The Knockbrack Mountaineering Club was formed on 1 May 2000. Officers were elected at its first meeting. The club had the following financial transactions for its first year to 30 April 2001.

The following additional information is available at the end of the financial year.

	€
Payments	
Insurance	2,714
Rent	1,275
Purchase of equipment	3,400
Canteen purchases	2,647
Travel expenses	1,688
Telephone	493
Receipts	
Subscriptions	2,418
Raffle income	3,786
Canteen sales	8,193
Flag day collection	1,959

(i)   Telephone bill due, €84

(ii)   Rent prepaid, €350

(iii)   Subscriptions prepaid, €180

(iv)   Equipment to be depreciated by fifteen per cent

(v)   Canteen stock, €575

(a)   From the information, prepare:

    (i)   a canteen trading account and

    (ii)   an income and expenditure account for the year ending 30 April 2001.

(b)   (i)   Name and state the figure for:

       (1) two of the club's assets and

       (2) two of its liabilities on 30 April 2001.

    (ii)   Name the three principal officers of a club.

(JCHL, adapted)

2. (a) (i) Name two duties of the chairperson of a club.

   (ii) Explain the following terms:
      (1) agenda
      (2) minutes.

   (iii) Name the official whose duty it is to look after the financial affairs of a club.

   (iv) Clubs are usually advised to open a bank current account. Give two advantages of having such an account.

(b) Southern Shore Sailing Club has prepared the following receipts and payments account for the year ended 31/12/2004.

Receipts and Payments Account				
1/1/04	Balance	15,176	Purchase of premises	40,000
	Subscriptions	9,300	Instructor's wages	12,500
	Raffle income	7,198	Telephone	635
	Dinner dance	6,430	Catering expenses	2,466
	Sale of equipment	17,500	Insurance	2,700
31/12/04	Balance	4,294	Light & heat	1,597
		59,898		59,898

You are required to prepare the club's income and expenditure account for the year ended 31/12/2004 taking the following into consideration.

   (i) The club is owed €860 in respect of the dinner dance.

   (ii) Subscriptions prepaid on 31/12/2004 were €800.

   (iii) Telephone bill due on 31/12/2004 is €147.

   (vi) Depreciation of premises is two per cent per annum.

(c) The club had a surplus of income for the year, yet it had a cash shortage on 31/12/2004. Give a reason for this.

(JCHL, adapted)

43 Farm Accounts

TERMS COVERED IN THIS CHAPTER
Income, expenditure, surplus.

INTRODUCTION

Complete these tasks with another pupil.
1. List some things a farmer has to purchase to run a farm.
2. What does the farmer sell?
3. List some expenses of running a farm.
4. List the assets a farmer might have.

There are many reasons why a farmer should keep accounts.
- To determine the profit or loss for the year.
- To estimate the value of the farm.
- To have a set of figures for presentation to the bank or government department on application for a loan or grant.
- To determine the extent and timing of expansion.

Question
Celine Leeson, farmer, keeps farm accounts and each year she prepares a statement of gross income and expenses. From the following information, prepare this statement for the year ended 31 December 2005.

Gross Income for the Year Ended 31 December 2005	
	€
Pigs	4,100
Fruit	2,600
Dairy produce	27,900
Crops	12,600
Sheep and wool	11,400
Poultry and eggs	1,800
Cattle	4,600
Vegetables	2,300
Government subsidy	5,000
Interest received on savings	200
Other receipts	900

Expenses for the Year Ended 31 December 2005	
	€
Lime	1,500
Rent of conacre	3,600
Animal feed	21,000
Fertiliser	8,000
Tractor repairs	400
Seeds	4,200
Livestock maintenance	600
Permanent labour	24,000
Casual labour	3,000
Telephone and electricity	6,400
Machinery operating expenses	800
Hire of machinery	700
Insurance	5,200
Bank charges	900
Veterinary charges	2,300

Solution

RB 2

Income and Expenditure Account of Celine Leeson for the Year Ended 31 December 2005			
		€	€
Income:			
Pigs		4,100	
Fruit		2,600	
Dairy produce		27,900	
Crops		12,600	
Sheep and wool		11,400	
Poultry and eggs		1,800	
Cattle		46,000	
Vegetables		2,300	
Government subsidy		5,000	
Interest received on savings		200	
Other receipts		900	114,800
Expenditure:			
Lime		1,500	
Rent of conacre		3,600	
Animal feed		21,000	
Fertiliser		8,000	
Tractor repairs		400	
Seeds		4,200	
Livestock maintenance		600	
Permanent labour		24,000	
Casual labour		3,000	
Car, telephone and electricity		6,400	
Machinery operating expenses		800	
Hire of machinery		700	
Insurance		5,200	
Bank charges		900	
Veterinary charges		2,300	82,600
Surplus of income over expenditure			**32,200**

The income from the sale of the farm produce is grouped together and totalled.

The expenditure is totalled and subtracted from the total income. If the income is bigger than the expenditure, there is a surplus. If the expenditure is greater than the income, there is a deficit.

PRACTICE: FARM ACCOUNTS

1. Tom Murphy, farmer, keeps farm accounts and each year he prepares a statement of gross income and expenses. From the following information, prepare this statement for the year ended 31 December 2003.

Gross Income for the Year Ended 31 December 2003	
	€
Crops	9,600
Sheep and wool	6,380
Poultry and eggs	800
Interest received on savings	1,000
Cattle	34,000
Dairy produce	36,400
Pigs	11,420
Other receipts	400

Expenses for the Year Ended 31 December 2003	
	€
Permanent labour	17,000
Casual labour	3,200
Car, telephone and electricity	4,170
Machinery operating expenses	4,080
Hire of machinery	3,250
Insurance	1,100
Rent of conacre	4,300
Animal feed	28,000
Fertiliser	9,400
Lime	2,700
Livestock maintenance	1,800

2. Seán Maguire, farmer, keeps farm accounts and each year he prepares a statement of gross income and expenses. From the following information, prepare this statement for the year ended 31 December 2004.

Gross Income for the Year Ended 31 December 2004	
	€
Cattle	21,400
Creamery	27,000
Crops	5,700
Fruit	6,300
Vegetables	5,400
Government subsidy	4,000
Other receipts	200

Expenses for the Year Ended 31 December 2004	
	€
Animal feed	19,300
Permanent labour	8,000
Casual labour	700
Fertiliser	7,400
Lime	1,600
Seeds	2,100
Machinery operating expenses	3,400
Insurance	900
Veterinary charges	600
Electricity	4,000

3. Fintan Kennedy, farmer, keeps farm accounts and each year he prepares a statement of gross income and expenses. From the following information, prepare this statement for the year ended 31 December 2005.

Gross Income for the Year Ended 31 December 2005	
	€
Crops	10,700
Sheep and wool	13,500
Fruit	18,300
Vegetables	14,700
Government subsidy	2,000
Other receipts	800

Expenses for the Year Ended 31 December 2005	
	€
Fertiliser	6,800
Seeds	3,900
Permanent labour	11,000
Casual labour	4,000
Machinery operating expenses	2,600
Insurance	1,200
Rates	3,200
Electricity	3,300

4. Pádraic Conneally, farmer, keeps farm accounts and each year he prepares a statement of gross income and expenses. From the following information, prepare this statement for the year ended 31 December 2006.

Gross Income for the Year Ended 31 December 2006	
	€
Cattle	42,000
Dairy produce	23,700
Poultry and eggs	12,000
Other receipts	800

Expenses for the Year Ended 31 December 2006	
	€
Permanent labour	10,000
Car, telephone and electricity	4,100
Machinery operating expenses	1,900
Animal feed	26,000
Fertiliser	7,000
Lime	2,400
Insurance	900
Veterinary charges	400
Rates	1,800

5. Deirdre O'Brien, farmer, keeps farm accounts and each year she prepares a statement of gross income and expenses. From the following information, prepare this statement for the year ended 31 December 2007.

Gross Income for the Year Ended 31 December 2007	
	€
Cattle	28,000
Dairy produce	14,000
Sheep and wool	21,000

Expenses for the Year Ended 31 December 2007	
	€
Permanent labour	8,000
Casual labour	3,000
Car, telephone and electricity	4,300
Machinery operating expenses	800
Insurance	700
Veterinary charges	600
Tractor expenses	1,200
Rent of conacre	3,000
Animal feed	16,000
Fertiliser	4,000
Lime	1,600

44 Service Firms

TERMS COVERED IN THIS CHAPTER
Operating statement, operating profit.

INTRODUCTION

Work in pairs.

Service firms sell a service instead of a product, such as travel agencies, dentists, taxi firms and so on. Can you list ten other service firms?

LESSON 1: ANALYSED RECEIPTS AND PAYMENTS BOOK

Service firms usually keep an analysed receipts and payments book and classify their income and expenditure under suitable headings. This helps the owners identify where money is being earned and spent.

Question

Mark Lawless owns a travel agency and keeps an analysed receipts and payments book to record his income and expenditure. He sells holidays in four main geographical areas and classifies his income using these groups: (i) Ireland (ii) Britain (iii) Continental Europe (iv) USA. He groups his expenditure using the following headings: (i) wages (ii) light and heat (iii) telephone, post, stationery (iv) other. Record the following transactions in his analysed receipts and payments book for the first week of March 2005.

March	€	
1 Cash on hand	600	
1 Cleaner's wages	120	(cheque no. 156)
1 Decorating showroom	800	(cheque no. 157)
1 Sales of holidays: USA	3,600	(receipt no. 42)
2 Stationery	80	(cheque no. 158)
2 Sales of holidays: Ireland	1,200	(receipt no. 43)
2 Telephone	400	(cheque no. 159)
2 Sales of holidays: Europe	2,600	(receipt no. 44)
3 Postage	40	(cheque no. 160)
3 Sales staff wages	1,650	(cheque no. 161)
3 Electricity	280	(cheque no. 162)
4 Sales of holidays: Ireland	3,100	(receipt no. 45)
4 Heating oil	700	(cheque no. 163)
4 Sales of holidays: Britain	900	(receipt no. 46)
5 Receptionist's wages	340	(cheque no. 164)
6 Sales of holidays: Europe	3,400	(receipt no. 47)

RB 1

Dr — Analysed Receipts and Payments Book of Mark Lawless for March 2005 — **Cr**

Date	Particulars	Rec	Total	Irl	Brit	EU	USA		Date	Particulars	Ch	Total	Wages	Light	Phone	Other	
Mar			€	€	€	€	€		Mar			€	€	€	€	€	
1	Cash on hand		600						1	Wages	156	120	120				
2	Sales	42	3,600				3,600		1	Decorating	157	800				800	
2	Sales	43	1,200	1,200					2	Stationery	158	80				80	
2	Sales	44	2,600			2,600			2	Telephone	159	400			400		
4	Sales	45	3,100	3,100					3	Postage	160	40				40	
4	Sales	46	900		900				3	Wages	161	1,650	1,650				
6	Sales	47	3,400			3,400			3	Electricity	162	280		280			
									4	Heating oil	163	700		700			
									5	Wages	164	340	340				
									5	Balance c/d		10,990					
			15,400	4,300	900	6,000	3,600					15,400	2,110	980	400	920	
Mar 6	Balance b/d		10,990														

LESSON 2: FINAL ACCOUNTS OF A SERVICE FIRM

Service firms do not have any trading stocks so there is no need to prepare a trading account. Instead you combine the trading and profit and loss accounts and prepare an operating statement. The other difference is that instead of having a net profit you will have an operating profit. Study the following question and solution to see how it is done.

Question

The following trial balance was extracted from the books of O'Brien Tours Ltd. From this information prepare an operating statement (profit and loss account) for the year ended 31 December 2005 and a balance sheet as at 31 December 2005.

Trial balance on 31 December 2005	Debit	Credit
	€	€
Sales of holidays to Spain		110,000
Sales of holidays to France		30,000
Sales of holidays to Italy		26,000
Sales of holidays to USA		78,000
Stationery	12,000	
Electricity charges	14,000	
Telephone bills	5,000	
Advertising	22,000	
Wages	80,000	
Fixtures	6,000	
Premises	250,000	
Equipment	40,000	
Debtors	14,000	
Creditors		6,000
Cash at bank	7,000	
Ordinary share capital		200,000
	450,000	450,000

Solution

Operating statement	€	€	€
Sales of holidays to Spain			110,000
Sales of holidays to France			30,000
Sales of holidays to Italy			26,000
Sales of holidays to USA			78,000
			244,000
Less expenses:			
Stationery		12,000	
Electricity charges		14,000	
Telephone bills		5,000	
Advertising		22,000	
Wages		80,000	133,000
Operating profit			111,000
Balance sheet			
Fixed assets			
Fixtures			6,000
Premises			250,000
Equipment			40,000
			296,000
Current assets			
Debtors	14,000		
Cash at bank	7,000	21,000	
Current liabilities			
Creditors	6,000	6,000	15,000
			311,000
Financed by:			
Ordinary share capital			200,000
Operating profit			111,000
			311,000

LESSON I: PRACTICE ANALYSED RECEIPTS AND PAYMENTS BOOK

1. Sarah O'Connor is an accountant and she keeps an analysed receipts and payments book to record her income and expenditure.

She classifies her income under two headings: (i) domestic (ii) commercial.

She groups her expenditure using these headings: (i) wages (ii) light and heat (iii) telephone, postage, stationery (iv) other.

Record the following transactions in her analysed cash account for the first week of January.

		€
1	Cash on hand	5,200
1	Cleaner's wages	270
2	Heating oil	800
2	Stationery	450
3	Client receipts – domestic	3,600
3	Telephone	380
4	Postage	130
4	Electricity	270
5	Client receipts – commercial	7,600
6	Secretary's salary	410
6	Client receipts – domestic	1,200

2. Clearview TV Sales keep an analysed receipts and payments book to record their income and expenditure.

They classify their income under two headings: (i) television (ii) video.

They group their expenditure using these headings: (i) wages (ii) light and heat (iii) telephone, postage stationery (iv) other.

Record the following transactions in their analysed cash account for the first week of February.

		€
1	Cash on hand	2,800
1	Cleaner's wages	260
1	Repairs to showroom	1,500
2	Heating oil	750
2	Stationery	90
3	Rental income – television	4,000
3	Telephone	340
4	Postage	140
4	Wages of repairmen	1,400
5	Electricity	250
5	Rental income – video	2,800
6	Office wages	600
6	Rental income – television	3,500

3. Ann Mulally is a dentist and she keeps an analysed receipts and payments book to record her income and expenditure.

She classifies her income under two headings: (i) receipts from patients (ii) other.

She groups her expenditure using these headings: (i) wages (ii) light and heat (iii) other.

Record the following transactions in her analysed cash account for the first week of March.

		€
1	Cash on hand	580
1	Receipts from patients	800
2	Rates	210
2	Receipts from patients	600
2	Telephone	320
3	Sale of toothbrushes	35
3	Heating oil	230
3	Receipts from patients	1,000
4	Electricity	170
4	Receipts from patients	400
5	Dental nurse's salary	420
5	Receipts from patients	700
5	Sale of toothbrushes	40
5	Receptionist's salary	380

4. Pat Comerford is a solicitor and he keeps an analysed receipts and payments book to record his income and expenditure.

He classifies his income under two headings: (i) wills (ii) house sale and purchase.

He groups his expenditure using these headings: (i) wages (ii) light and heat (iii) telephone, postage, stationery (iv) other.

Record the following transactions in his analysed cash account for the first week of April.

		€
1	Cash on hand	80
1	Receipts from clients – wills	400
1	Rent of office	600
2	Stationery	90
2	Telephone	240
2	Postage	40
3	Receipts from clients – house	2,300
4	Electricity	270
4	Search fees	80
5	Secretary's salary	410
5	Receipts from clients – house	2,800

STATE EXAM PRACTICE

I. Joe Ryan is a farmer who keeps an analysed receipts and payments book. All money received is lodged in his bank current account on the same day and all payments are made by cheque. He had the following transactions during May 2004.

May

1	Balance in bank	€2,300	
3	Sold cattle at the mart	€9,500	(receipt no. 101)
5	Purchased cattle feed	€450	(cheque no. 2354)
8	Paid fees to vet	€350	(cheque no. 2355)
10	Received a state grant	€2,000	(receipt no. 102)
12	Purchased cattle (calves)	€1,800	(cheque no. 2356)
15	Paid for repairs to fencing	€700	(cheque no. 2357)
17	Purchased diesel oil for tractors	€450	(cheque no. 2358)
18	Paid fees to vet	€175	(cheque no. 2359)
19	Sold cattle at the mart	€4,500	(receipt no. 103)
22	Purchased cattle feed	€1,560	(cheque no. 2360)
24	Purchased diesel oil for machinery	€150	(cheque no. 2361)
28	Purchased cattle (calves)	€4,400	(cheque no. 2362)

(a) Write up Joe Ryan's analysed receipts and payments book for the month of May 2004 using the following money column headings.
   Receipts: Total, Cattle, Grants, Other
   Payments: Total, Cattle, Feed, Diesel, Vet Fees, Other

   Total each analysis column and balance the total columns at the end of May.
(b) State three reasons why farmers should keep accounts.

LESSON 2: PRACTICE FINAL ACCOUNTS OF A SERVICE FIRM

1. The following trial balance was extracted from the books of O'Brien Tours Ltd. From this information prepare an operating statement (profit and loss account) for the year ended 31 December 2005 and a balance sheet as at 31 December 2005.

Trial Balance on 31 December 2005		
	Debit	**Credit**
	€	€
Sales of holidays to Spain		110,000
Sales of holidays to France		30,000
Sales of holidays to Italy		26,000
Sales of holidays to USA		78,000
Stationery	12,000	
Electricity charges	14,000	
Telephone bills	5,000	
Advertising	22,000	
Wages	80,000	
Fixtures	6,000	
Premises	250,000	
Equipment	40,000	
Debtors	14,000	
Creditors		6,000
Cash at bank	7,000	
Ordinary share capital		200,000
	450,000	450,000

2. The following trial balance was extracted from the books of Oncall Security Ltd. From this information prepare an operating statement (profit and loss account) for the year ended 31 December 2005 and a balance sheet as at 31 December 2005.

Trial Balance on 31 December 2005		
	Debit	**Credit**
	€	€
Income from security guard service		125,000
Income from courier service		46,000
Income from detective service		23,000
Income from key-holding service		6,000
Food for guard dogs	9,000	
Petrol for security vans	18,000	
Advertising	3,000	
Telephone bills	6,500	
Wages	74,500	
Vans	6,000	
Equipment	21,000	
Premises	200,000	
Debtors	26,000	
Creditors		4,000
Bank overdraft		10,000
Ordinary share capital		150,000
	364,000	364,000

3. The trial balance on the right was extracted from the books of Yellow Cabs Ltd. From this information prepare an operating statement (profit and loss account) for the year ended 31 December 2005 and a balance sheet as at 31 December 2005.

4. The trial balance below right was extracted from the books of Dr Hilda Fahey. From this information prepare an operating statement (profit and loss account) for the year ended 31 December 2005 and a balance sheet as at 31 December 2005.

5. The trial balance below was extracted from the books of Liam Henshaw Ltd. From this information, prepare an operating statement (profit and loss account) for the year ended 31 December 2005 and a balance sheet as at 31 December 2005.

Trial Balance on 31 December 2005	Debit €	Credit €
Income from tours		41,000
Income from weddings		26,000
Income from daytime city fares		46,000
Income from nighttime fares		75,000
Repairs to vehicles	18,000	
Advertising	8,000	
Wages	75,000	
Petrol	35,000	
Telephone bills	12,000	
Vehicles	80,000	
Premises	140,000	
Radio equipment	12,000	
Debtors	4,000	
Creditors		5,000
Cash at bank		9,000
Ordinary share capital		200,000
	393,000	393,000

Trial Balance on 31 December 2005	Debit €	Credit €
Income from private patients		95,000
Income from medical card holders		80,000
Income from house calls		4,500
Income from attending as medical officer at games		7,500
Insurance	26,000	
Light and heat	3,700	
Secretary's wages	16,700	
Telephone charges	6,400	
Cleaning and repairs	8,700	
Fixtures	9,000	
Premises	180,000	
Motor vehicle	34,000	
Debtors	8,500	
Creditors		600
Cash on hand		1,000
Bank overdraft		6,400
Ordinary share capital		100,000
	294,000	294,000

Trial Balance on 31 December 2005	Debit €	Credit €
Commission on sales from:		
Irish holidays		35,000
European holidays		87,000
American holidays		46,000
Insurance	3,000	
Wages	38,000	
Advertising	16,000	
Telephone charges	5,600	
Light and heat	2,400	
Office furniture	22,000	
Premises	160,000	
Motor vehicles	18,000	
Cash at bank		3,000
Ordinary share capital		100,000
	268,000	268,000

STATE EXAM PRACTICE

1. Kevin Sands Ltd, travel agent, prepares an operating statement (profit and loss A/C) and balance sheet at the end of each year.

   The following trial balance was taken from his books on 31 December 2005.
   (a) Prepare an opening statement for Kevin Sands Ltd for the year ended 31 December 2005 and a balance sheet as at that date.
   (b) Farmers also keep accounts. State two reasons why they do.
   (JCOL, adapted)

Trial Balance as at 31 December 2005	Debit	Credit
	€	€
Commission on sales from:		
Irish holidays		19,950
European holidays		60,570
American holidays		23,540
Insurance	2,330	
Advertising	14,255	
Wages	24,200	
Telephone	4,825	
Light and heat	1,950	
Postage and printing	5,610	
Bank overdraft		3,280
Cash on hand	3,670	
Ordinary share capital		
(40,000 €1 shares)		40,000
Premises	60,000	
Office furniture	18,500	
Motor vehicles	12,000	
	147,340	147,340

2. Dr Henry Faith Ltd is a general practitioner (GP). He prepares an operating statement (profit and loss A/C) and balance sheet at the end of each year.

   The following trial balance was taken from his books on 31 December 2004, the end of his financial year.
   (a) Prepare an opening statement for Dr Henry Faith Ltd for the year ended 31 December 2004 and a balance sheet as at that date.
   (b) Explain what is meant by a bank overdraft.
   (c) State three reasons why Dr Henry Faith Ltd should keep accounts.

Trial Balance as at 31 December 2004	Debit	Credit
	€	€
Income from private patients		85,000
Income from medical card holders		92,000
Income from house calls		3,500
Income from attending as medical officer at games		6,250
Heating and lighting	2,750	
Insurance	25,300	
Secretary's wages	14,900	
Telephone	4,680	
Light and heat	1,950	
Cleaning and repairs	7,820	
Petrol and car service	4,540	
Bank overdraft		3,920
Cash in hand	4,680	
Ordinary share capital		
(50,000 €1 shares)		50,000
Premises	75,000	
Motor vehicles (cars)	41,000	
Medical equipment	60,000	
	240,670	240,670

45 Information Technology

TERMS COVERED IN THIS CHAPTER
Hardware, pixel, hard copy, software, CPU, VDU, modem, mail merge, CAD, CAM, ISP.

INTRODUCTION

Discuss the following questions.
1. What would you use a computer for at home?
2. What would you use a computer for in an office?
3. How much would you expect to pay for a computer and printer?

LESSON 1: COMPUTER HARDWARE

A computer system is made up of many pieces of equipment known as the computer hardware. There are three parts to understand: output devices, input devices and the CPU.

OUTPUT DEVICES

Output devices are pieces of equipment that enable the computer to send you information. The main output devices are the monitor and the printer.

- **Monitor:** This is similar to a television screen. It displays the program you are working on. It is also known as a visual display unit (VDU). It works by turning on and off little lights called pixels. In this way the computer is able to generate pictures and words on the screen.
- **Printer:** This enables the computer to give you information on paper, called a printout or hard copy. There are two main types of printers in use today: the inkjet printer, which can print in colour, and the laser, which will normally only print in black and white. The quality of the laser printer is better but it is also a more expensive printer.

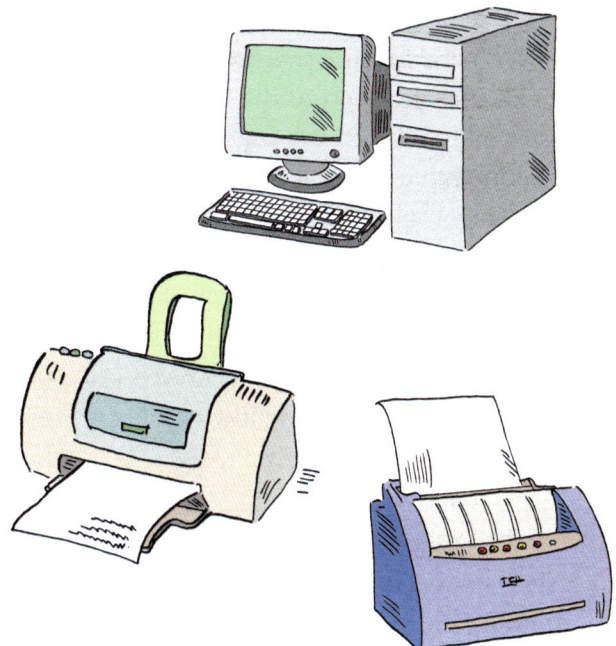

INPUT DEVICES

Input devices let you get information into the computer and give instructions to the computer. The main input devices are the keyboard and the mouse.

- **Keyboard:** The keyboard was originally developed for typewriters in 1868 by Christopher Sholes. It is called a QWERTY keyboard after the first six letters on the top left of the keyboard. In order to make it easier for salespeople to sell typewriters the keyboard was designed with all the letters of the word 'typewriter' on the top line. This meant the salesperson could quickly demonstrate how to type the word 'typewriter' and impress potential customers.
- **Mouse:** Originally invented by Douglas Engelbart in the 1960s, it was not used in a home computer until 1983 when Apple launched the Lisa computer. It enables you to launch and use programs without using the keyboard.
- Other input devices are a joystick, scanner, CD and DVD.

INPUT AND OUTPUT DEVICES

Some pieces of computer equipment are both input and output devices, such as the disk drive and the modem.

- **Disk drive:** This is the storage device used by the computer to keep a permanent copy of data. There are two types of disks: floppy disks that can be inserted and removed from the computer and a hard disk that is kept permanently in the computer. Information is stored in bytes. Each character on a page is about one byte in size, so there are thirty-one bytes in the previous sentence (each space is a byte and a full stop is a byte). The amount of information stored is measured in kilobytes (Kb), megabytes (Mb) and gigabytes (Gb). For example, a floppy disk can hold 1.4 Mb.
- **Modem:** A modem is used to connect the computer to a telephone line. The computer can then communicate with other computers, transferring data over long distances.

CENTRAL PROCESSING UNIT (CPU)

The CPU is at the heart of the computer. It consists of small microchips about the size of your little finger and has three main parts.

- **The arithmetic unit:** This carries out calculations on data.
- **The control unit:** This controls the operation of the computer.
- **The main storage or 'memory':** The computer has two types of storage: read-only memory (ROM) and random-access memory (RAM). The RAM is the computer's short-term memory and a user can put information into it. On the other hand, the ROM stores system information that the computer can read. The information in the RAM is lost when the computer is switched off, whereas that in the ROM is reread each time the machine is used.

Measurement	Number of Bytes
kilobytes (Kb)	1,000 bytes
megabytes (Mb)	1,000,000 bytes
gigabytes (Gb)	1,000,000,000 bytes

LESSON 2: COMPUTER SOFTWARE

The programs that a computer uses are called software. The main types of software used by a business are:

- word processing
- spreadsheet
- database
- desktop publishing (DTP)
- payroll
- computerised accounts
- computer-aided design (CAD)
- computer-aided manufacture (CAM).

WORD PROCESSING

Word processing is a computerised way of typing letters and other documents. Once the letter is saved it can be edited and used again. The main advantages are:

- more time is spent on new work
- multiple copies can be easily made
- work can be saved and returned to later.

SPREADSHEET

The spreadsheet is used to perform mathematical and financial calculations. Throughout this book you have seen examples of reports prepared using a spreadsheet, such as a household budget and a cash flow. You could also prepare a trading, profit and loss and balance sheet using a spreadsheet. Here are some ways businesses use a spreadsheet.

- To analyse income and expenditure.
- To create a budget or cash-flow statement.
- To make a projection of repayments on a loan.
- To estimate profit at various sales levels.
- To assess a firm's performance using financial ratios.

DATABASE

A database is a computerised filing system. It allows you to store, edit and list data in various formats. For example, if you have your customers entered into a database then you could list those in the Galway region or those who order over €2,000 a month. The type of data stored by a firm are:

- customer lists
- stock records
- wages files
- mailing lists.

MAIL MERGE

This is a way of linking names and addresses stored in a database with a letter prepared using a word processor. For example, suppose you were asked by your employer to send information about a new product to all existing customers. First you would type the letter into the word processor, then create a list of customers in your database. Finally, use a word processor's mail merge feature to link the customer list to the letter. The result is multiple copies of the same letter, but each letter has different customer details on it.

LESSON 3: BUYING A COMPUTER SYSTEM

Mark and Catherine McManus own a clothing firm called Needles Ltd. They are thinking of buying a new computer and payroll software on credit for €3,000 from PC Supplies Ltd. Before buying the computer they ask themselves a few questions.

What problems will it solve? Once they get used to it, Mark and Catherine will find that the computerised payroll system helps them to prepare the payroll more quickly. They will also be able to get summary reports, print out payslips and find the total amount of PAYE and PRSI owed to the revenue authorities.

How will the company benefit from the computer? A computerised payroll system can benefit a firm by:
- increasing productivity
- improving working conditions, as the computer takes care of the repetitive work
- improving company image.

What is the full cost of the system? Needles Ltd will have to add up all the costs involved: computer, software, paper, disks, training. Where are they going to locate the computer? Will they have to redecorate or build an extension?

Will they have to pay for training? Most computer firms give some training, but this cannot be taken for granted. Training costs from €200 to €400 a day per person and a payroll package will require about two days of training.

Will they get after-sales support? Many IT firms are only interested in selling you the hardware and software. They do not want to know about the difficulties you run into afterwards.

RECORDING THE PURCHASE

Assets purchased on credit are recorded in the general journal.

General Journal				€	€
Oct 10	Computer			3,000	
	PC Supplies Ltd				3,000
	(purchase of computer on credit)				

RB 2

In the ledger the computer account is debited, as it is an asset. The double entry is on the credit of PC Supplies Ltd.

Dr		Computer Account				Cr
Oct 10	PC Supplies Ltd	€ 3,000				

RB 3

		PC Supplies Ltd Account			
			Oct 10	Computer	€ 3,000

LESSON 4: THE INTERNET

The internet is an international network of computers that are able to communicate with each other over telephones lines. No one owns or controls the internet and every day millions of pieces of information travel over the internet. The information can take the form of e-mail, sounds and video clips.

GET THE CONNECTION!

In order to get connected to the internet you may have to make a few purchases. You need to make a shopping list with the following items. Once you get connected to the internet you can start using e-mail and visiting the World Wide Web.

	Cost
A personal computer. You are advised to get as fast a machine as you can afford.	€1,000
A modem. This connects your computer to the phone line.	€100
An internet service provider (ISP). An ISP will give you a phone number that you dial to get connected to the internet.	Free
E-mail software. This is often supplied by your ISP. It allows you to write and read messages.	Free
A web browser. This is a piece of software supplied by your ISP. It enables your computer to surf the web and view websites.	Free
Telephone calls. The biggest day-to-day cost of using the internet is the phone calls that are made to connect to the service. The charge per minute may be very low but it can quickly add up to a sizeable bill.	2c per minute
Virus-checking software. A computer virus can do major damage to your computer. Most viruses are spread by e-mail and the only way to protect your computer is to install virus-checking software. It needs to be updated regularly.	€50

E-MAIL

E-mail, or electronic mail, is a method of sending messages between computers over the internet. It is a cheap way of communicating. You should treat messages you receive from strangers with extra care. They are best deleted as they could contain a virus that might damage your computer. This is particularly the case with e-mails that contain attachments.

WORLD WIDE WEB

The World Wide Web consists of millions of pages of information with sites devoted to sports, news, politics, films, etc. It is also a great place to make new friends, some of whom you may never meet face to face. When you were young you were told to be careful of strangers and the same applies when using the internet. Great care must be taken, especially when using chat rooms.

- Never give out personal information about yourself. Don't give your full name, address, school details or anything that might be used to identify you. If a perfect stranger came up to you on the street and started asking you about where you live and what school you go to you would not tell them, so don't give this information out on the web either, even if they say they are another student like you.
- Be wary of what people say about themselves. They may not be telling the full truth. You can't see them so you can't be sure who they are.
- Never agree to meet someone on your own that you have only ever met on the internet. Get your parents to advise you if in doubt.
- Don't open an attachment unless you can trust the person sending it.

LESSON I: PRACTICE

I.   (a) Name two input devices.

(b) Name two output devices.

(c) Name the three parts of the CPU.

2.   In the case of each of the following (i) state the name of the device and (ii) whether it is an input or output device.

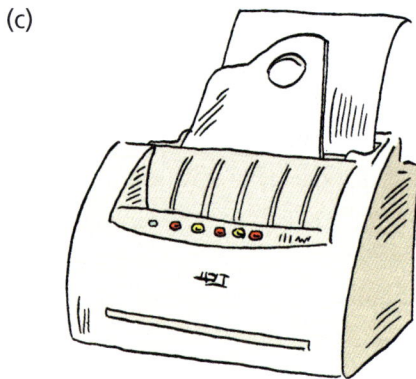

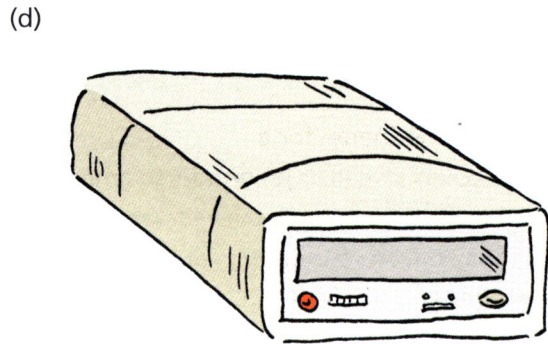

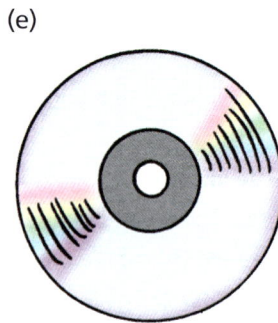

(a)

(b)

(c)

(d)

(e)

3. Different types of hardware are hidden in this grid. Find them and then use them to complete the sentences. The words can be read across, down or diagonally.

```
M  D  A  R  O  B  Y  K  I  D
D  I  S  K  P  U  C  O  S  M
M  O  D  E  M  P  T  E  C  R
O  R  I  Y  V  O  E  L  A  R
N  M  R  B  N  I  U  A  N  T
I  N  K  O  R  D  I  S  N  P
T  P  R  A  M  U  T  E  E  L
O  B  O  R  A  D  K  R  R  A
R  E  Y  D  I  S  P  L  A  Y
C  B  D  Y  R  T  A  E  O  K
```

(a) A computer uses a _____ to connect to a telephone line.

(b) The QWERTY _____ is used to type text into a computer.

(c) Another name for a _____ is a visual _____ unit.

(d) Use an _____jet printer to get a colour printout.

(e) The _____ is the computer's short-term memory.

(f) Another name for read-only memory is _____.

(g) Use a _____ to copy pictures into a computer.

(h) A _____ lets you use programs without using the keyboard.

(i) A _____ printer gives a good-quality hard copy.

(j) You can use a _____ drive as both an input and an output device.

4. Match each abbreviation on the left with its meaning on the right.

Abbreviation	Meaning
1. VDU	(a) Controls the operation of the computer.
2. RAM	(b) An input device.
3. DVD	(c) Can only be read.
4. Kb	(d) The computer's short-term memory.
5. CPU	(e) An output device.
6. ROM	(f) A way of measuring computer memory.

LESSON 2: PRACTICE

1.   Which software would you use to carry out the following operations? You want to:

(a) write a letter

(b) create a household budget

(c) store product names and quantity in stock

(d) write a book

(e) create a list of names and addresses for a mailing list

(f) estimate how much profit you will earn at various sales levels

(g) send the same letter to all your customers

(h) prepare a cash-flow forecast

(i) create a staff newsletter

(j) analyse your income and expenditure.

2.   Mistakes in a document are called 'typos'. Study the following document that Catherine has prepared using a word processor. See if you can find the ten typos she has made.

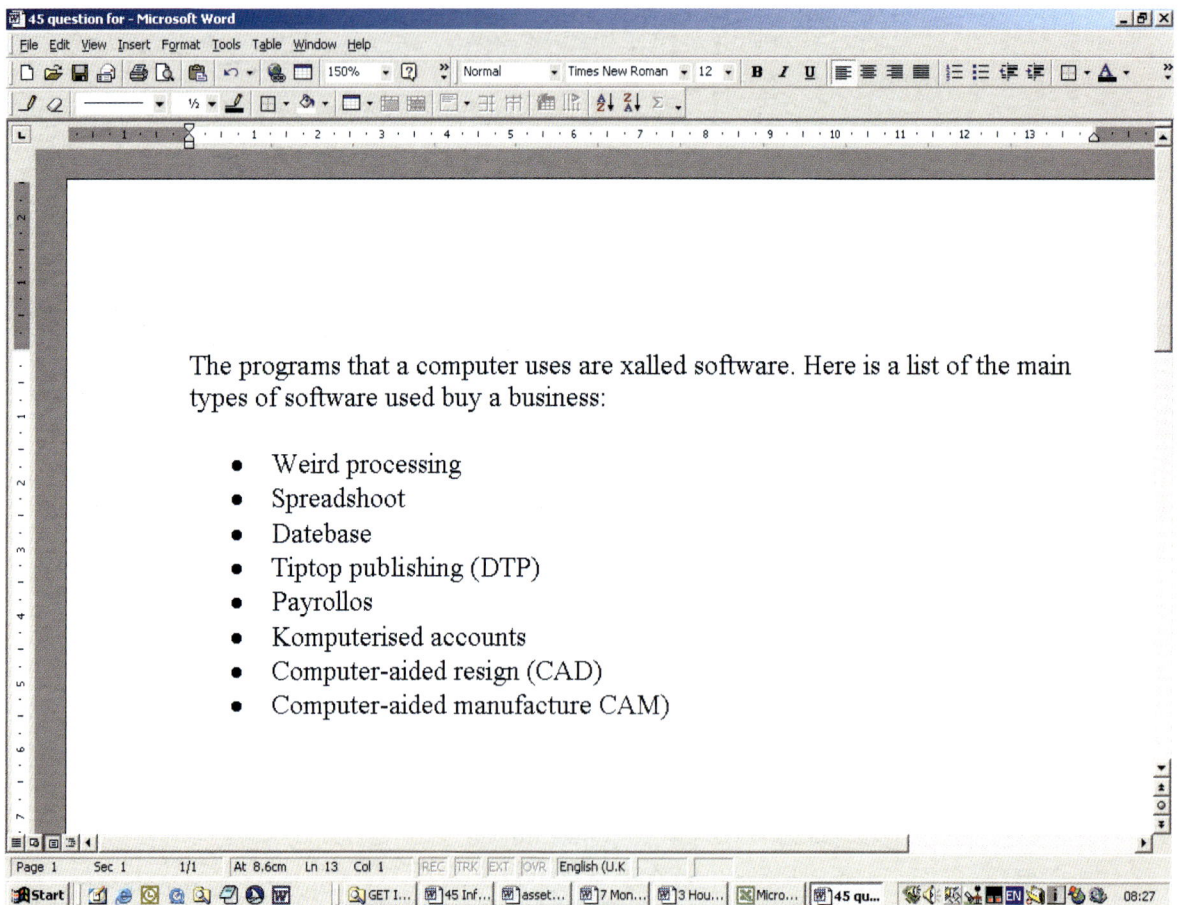

The programs that a computer uses are xalled software. Here is a list of the main types of software used buy a business:

- Weird processing
- Spreadshoot
- Datebase
- Tiptop publishing (DTP)
- Payrollos
- Komputerised accounts
- Computer-aided resign (CAD)
- Computer-aided manufacture CAM)

	A	B	C	D	E	F	G	H
1	1	Jan	Feb	Mar	Apr	May	Jun	Total
2	**2 INCOME**							
3	3 Sales in Dublin	14,000	15,400	16,940	18,634	20,497	22,547	108,019
4	4 Sales in Cork	9,000	9,900	10,890	11,979	13,177	14,495	69,440
5	5 Sales in Galway	11,000	12,100	13,310	14,641	16,105	17,716	84,872
6	**6 A>TOTAL INCOME**	**34,000**	**37,400**	**41,140**	**45,254**	**49,779**	**54,757**	**262,331**

3. A spreadsheet consists of rows and columns. The rows are numbered and the columns have letters to identify them. Study the spreadsheet above and answer the questions below.
   (a) What are the sales in Dublin for April?
   (b) What is the total income for May?
   (c) What figure is in D4?
   (d) What is written in A5?
   (e) What is written in G1?
   (f) In which cell will you find 13,310?
   (g) In which cell will you find 69,440?
   (h) In which cell will you find the word 'INCOME'?
   (i) The formula in B6 is '=B3+B4+B5'. What is the formula in F6?
   (j) What is the formula in H4?

id	email	firstName	secondName	companyName	street	city	creditLimit
213	jlawlor@comsupp.ie	Jessica	Lawlor	Comsupp Ltd	Patricks Street	Athlone	6,000
214	info@kellys.com	Derek	Kelly	Kellys Computer Shop	Main Street	Sligo	5,000
215	bmulligan@copytext.com	Breda	Mulligan	Copytext Ltd	Clare Avenue	Dublin	4,000
216	hcassidy@kernel.ie	Harry	Cassidy	Kernel Computers Ltd	Beach Street	Sligo	6,000
217	info@access.ie	Jessica	Mulligan	Access Computers Ltd	River Street	Wexford	6,000
218	tdiggins@act.com	Teresa	Diggins	Act Computers Ltd	Camden Street	Dublin	5,000
219	pmalden@alpha.ie	Patrick	Malden	Alpha Computers Ltd	Crofton Avenue	Dublin	6,000
220	sales@ard.com	Alison	Malden	Ard Computers Ltd	Eagle Road	Sligo	4,000
221	info@auto.ie	Derek	Mulligan	Auto Computers Ltd	Sea Avenue	Dublin	5,000
222	jandrews@uni.com	Jessica	Andrews	Uni Computers Ltd	Mulberry Street	Wexford	6,000

4. A database consists of columns of information. Study the above database and answer the following questions.
   (a) What is Harry's second name?
   (b) Where does Alison work?
   (c) In which city is Access Computers Ltd located?
   (d) What is the e-mail address for Kernel Computers?
   (e) Which companies have a credit limit of €4,000?
   (f) You can search a database for information. What would it find if you searched for people called 'Jessica'?
   (g) How many companies would it find if you searched for businesses in Dublin?

LESSON 3: PRACTICE

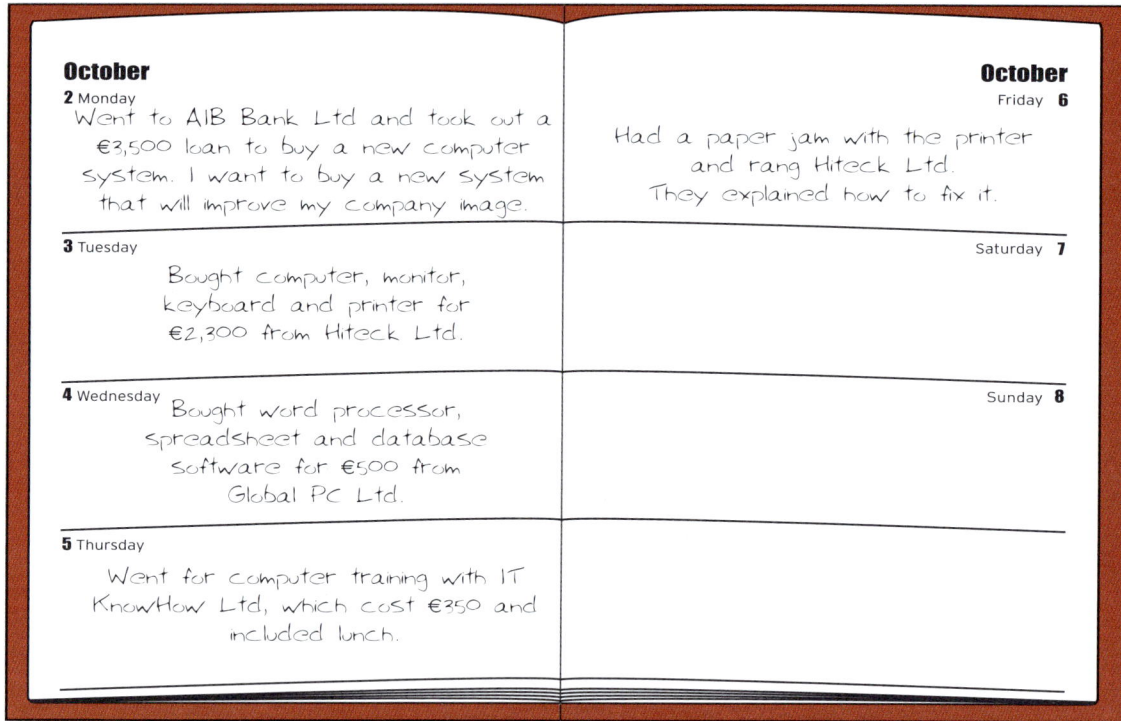

October

2 Monday
Went to AIB Bank Ltd and took out a €3,500 loan to buy a new computer system. I want to buy a new system that will improve my company image.

3 Tuesday
Bought computer, monitor, keyboard and printer for €2,300 from Hiteck Ltd.

4 Wednesday
Bought word processor, spreadsheet and database software for €500 from Global PC Ltd.

5 Thursday
Went for computer training with IT KnowHow Ltd, which cost €350 and included lunch.

October

Friday **6**
Had a paper jam with the printer and rang Hiteck Ltd. They explained how to fix it.

Saturday **7**

Sunday **8**

1.   Read Paula's diary for the week. What was the nature of her business with each of these companies mentioned in her diary?
(a) AIB Bank Ltd
(b) Hiteck Ltd
(c) Global PC Ltd
(d) IT KnowHow Ltd

2.   What was her total expenditure for the week?

3.   Why does she want to buy a new computer system?

4.   What after-sales support did Hiteck Ltd give Paula?

LESSON 4: PRACTICE

Complete the word grid using the clues in the sentences below.

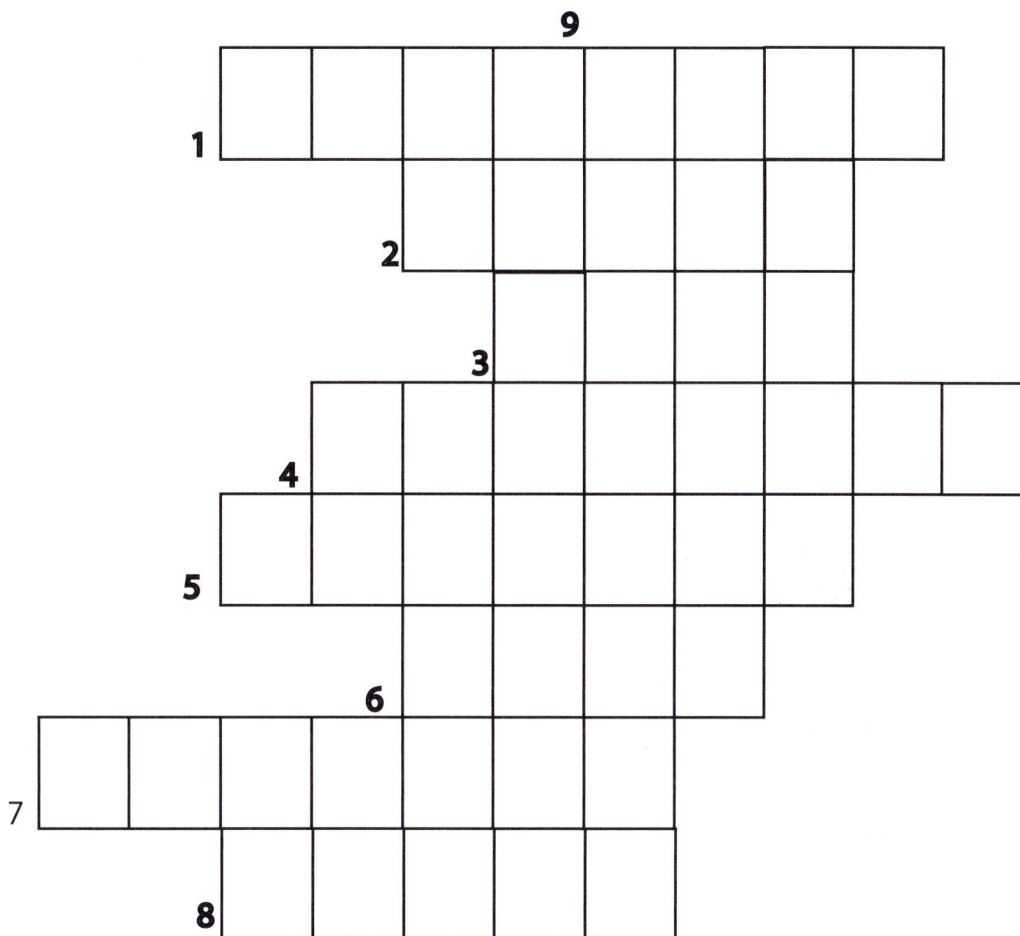

To use the web you will need a [1]_____ computer.

There are millions of pages of information on the [2]_____ Wide Web.

Don't give your [3]_____ name and address to strangers on the web.

No one owns or controls the [4]_____.

You need a web [5]_____ to view websites.

A virus is often spread as an attachment to an e-[6]_____.

The internet is an international [7]_____ of computers.

The [8]_____ connects your computer to the phone line.

Virus-checking [9]_____ will protect your computer.

STATE EXAM PRACTICE

1. Rose Barrett is hoping that her parents will buy her a personal computer for her birthday. She sees the following advertisement in her local newspaper.

> **PC FOR SALE**
> Includes CPU, keyboard and colour
> *VDU*
> 6.4 GB *hard disk*, 128 MB RAM
> 31/2 inch floppy *disk drive* and *mouse*
> Also included are
> • A word processing package
> • A database package and
> • A spreadsheet package
> and
> 12 computer games for all the family
> *GREAT VALUE AT €1,000*

(a) There are four words or terms italicised in the above advertisement. Rose's parents do not know what they mean. Explain them.

(b) State one use that could be made of a word processing package.

(c) State one use that could be made of a spreadsheet package.

(d) State whether each of the following is hardware or software: keyboard, database, computer games.

(e) State one reason that Rose might use to persuade her parents to buy the computer.

(JCOL, adapted)

2. Sharon Burke is the owner of a small business. She has little knowledge of computers but has recently done some *desk research* on them and their workings. She is confused with some of the terminology/terms used and requests your help and advice.

(a) (i) Explain what is meant by the italicised words above.

(ii) Explain the difference between computer hardware and software.

(b) What is the function of computer input devices? Give two examples of them.

(c) Name two important technical factors (excluding price) that a computer owner should take into consideration when selecting a program for a computer.

(d) What type of computer programs are required to undertake the following tasks?

(i)   Storing information.

(ii) Budgets and accounts.

(e) Sharon was offered a new computer by her local supplier of office equipment at a cash price of €3,000 or a leasing agreement at a cost of €600 per annum.

(i)   Name two advantages to Sharon of leasing rather than purchasing the computer.

(ii) If Sharon leased it, would this expense be considered a revenue or a capital expense?

(JCHL, adapted)

3. Robo Ltd of 23 High Street, Gort, County Galway is considering computerising its sports equipment manufacturing business. Robo Ltd expects to start exporting its sports equipment worldwide in 2006. It requires advice on computer systems and sources of finance.

    Assume you are Chip Micro, computer consultant, 10 Disk Road, Dublin 2. Prepare a report for the directors of Robo Ltd, on today's date, setting out the following.
    - Three factors to be considered when deciding on a computer system.
    - Three types of computer software suitable for the business.
    - Two suitable sources of finance the company could use.

    (JCHL, adapted)

4. The Walsh family runs a tourist business in Clonakilty, County Cork. Their daughter, Anne, studies business at university and hopes to travel to Germany for summer employment. She is encouraging her parents to buy a new computer and to connect to the internet, which she claims would be of immense benefit to the business. Anne's parents are not familiar with the terms used in IT.

    (a) (i)   What do the initials 'IT' stand for?
        (ii)   Explain the difference between the terms hardware and software.
        (iii) Briefly explain the function of a floppy disk.
        (iv)   What is the function of computer output devices? Give two examples.

    (b) (i)   Explain what is meant by the term 'internet'.
        (ii)   What is sending a letter by computer called?
        (iii) List two benefits to the Walsh's business of subscribing/connecting to the internet.

    (c) Anne's parents took her advice, purchased a computer and were connected to the internet. List three costs involved in operating their new system other than the price of the computer itself.

    (JCHL, adapted)

Index

Picture Credits

The author and publisher gratefully acknowledge the following for permission to reproduce photographic material:

The author and publishers have made every effort to trace all copyright holders, but if any has been inadvertently overlooked we would be pleased to make the necessary arrangements at the first opportunity.